MUSIC
A Social Experience

Steven Cornelius
Boston University

Mary Natvig
Bowling Green State University

PEARSON

Boston   Columbus   Indianapolis   New York   San Francisco   Upper Saddle River
Amsterdam   Cape Town   Dubai   London   Madrid   Milan   Munich   Paris   Montreal   Toronto
Delhi   Mexico City   São Paulo   Sydney   Hong Kong   Seoul   Singapore   Taipei   Tokyo

Editorial Director: Craig Campanella
Editor in Chief: Sarah Touborg
Executive Editor: Richard Carlin
Editorial Assistant: Lily Norton
Vice President Director of Marketing:
    Brandy Dawson
Executive Marketing Manager: Kate
    Stewart Mitchell
Managing Editor: Melissa Feimer
Project Manager: Marlene Gassler
Senior Manufacturing Manager: Mary Fischer

Senior Operations Specialist: Brian Mackey
Creative Director, Cover: Jayne Conte
Cover Designer: Suzanne Behnke
Senior Media Editor: David Alick
Media Project Manager: Richard Barnes
Full-Service Project Management:
    S4Carlisle Publishing Services
Composition: S4Carlisle Publishing
    Services
Printer/Binder: Courier/Kendallville
Cover Printer: Lehigh-Phoenix Color

Cover Photo: In this famous photograph, a group of the leading folk singers and Civil Rights Activists joined hands to sing "We Shall Overcome," in 1963. Left to right: Peter Yarrow, Mary Travers, and Noel Paul Stookey (Peter, Paul, and Mary); Joan Baez; Bob Dylan; Bernice Johnson Reagon, Cordell Hull Reagon, Charles Neblett, and Rutha Mae Harris (The Freedom Singers); and Pete Seeger. AF archive / Almay

Credits and acknowledgments borrowed from other sources and reproduced, with permission, in this textbook appear on appropriate page within text.

Library of Congress Cataloging-in-Publication Data
Cornelius, Steven
    Music : a social experience / by Steven Cornelius and Mary Natvig.
    p. cm.
ISBN-13: 978-0-13-601750-9
ISBN-10: 0-13-601750-9
    1. Music appreciation. 2. Music—Social aspects. I. Natvig, Mary   II. Title.
MT90.C69 2012
781.1'7—dc23
                                                                    2011030098

10 9 8 7 6 5 4 3 2 1

ISBN 10:   0-13-601750-9
ISBN 13:   978-0-13-601750-9
Exam Copy ISBN 10:   0-13-235728-3
Exam Copy ISBN 13:   978-0-13-235728-9

PEARSON

Dedications

To James Latimer

—Steven

To Bill Engelke

—Mary

CONTENTS

To the Students

Welcome to *Music: A Social Experience*, a new approach to learning about music. This text is based on two simple premises:

- We learn best by building on what we already know.
- Musical meaning unfolds through a web of social interactions.

Music: A Social Experience takes advantage of these simple truths by beginning with familiar pieces or concepts, then expanding outward to more distant musical traditions and cultural contexts. By focusing on the social aspects common to all music, we engage with a wide range of musical styles, cultures, and historical periods.

This approach makes for dynamic juxtapositions. In our chapter on music and politics, for example, Jimi Hendrix's Woodstock performance of "The Star Spangled Banner" opens a pathway to understanding the reception history of Ludwig van Beethoven's Symphony No. 9. The chapter on music and gender discusses songs of the 1960s then looks at issues of social empowerment in George Bizet's 1875 opera *Carmen*.

Our goals are to:

- Present ways of listening to and thinking about music from a variety of time periods and cultures.
- Promote cultural understanding through musical knowledge.
- Reveal music's relationship to the individual and to the human condition.
- Encourage self-reflection and critical thinking.

Rather than according a higher value to one type of music over another, Music: A Social Experience *demonstrates the role that all music plays in teaching us about ourselves and the world in which we live.*

Why should we study Western art music?

Art music represents Western philosophical ideals and social values. By studying art music we gain insights into Western civilization as a whole. Palestrina's *Pope Marcellus Mass,* for example, offers a glimpse at Catholicism's response to the Protestant Reformation. Borodin's orchestral tone poem *In the Steppes of Central Asia* informs us about nineteenth-century European concepts of nation and otherness; Wagner's operatic character Siegfried embodies Western heroic and masculine ideals. Like these examples, our selections are carefully chosen to demonstrate ways in which music and society interact. Thus, by engaging with Western art music on both sonic and socially meaningful levels we see how music of the past influences who we are today.

Why study the music of other cultures?

We study the music of other cultures because engaging with traditions not our own helps us to understand alternative points of view. Today's students are inheriting a world in which diverse cultures share geographic territories, even though they may not share political, philosophical, or spiritual values. Because musical practices reflect and sustain those values, they offer us important insights into how people understand their world. In *Music: A Social Experience* we look at the bards of West Africa and their influence on American music. We hear the ways in which Tibetan Buddhist chant embodies spiritual beliefs. We investigate how 1960s Chinese opera was designed to serve Communist ideology. Each example enhances our understanding of social, historical, and political perspectives that may differ from our own.

Why popular music?

Popular music is music of the moment, has wide appeal across cultures, and is based on vernacular sounds. It is perhaps also the music that most immediately reflects and gives form to our hopes, needs, and desires. We hear Aretha Franklin demanding "R-E-S-P-E-C-T" and learn about Roy Orbison and k.d. lang "Crying" for lost love. We look at the international politics that guide the annual Eurovision contest. We learn that our musical choices do more than entertain; they tell us about who we are and who we hope to become.

At course's end, students will be:

- Prepared to think ind ependently and critically about a variety of musical styles.
- Equipped with skills for listening to classical, popular, and world music.
- Able to make connections between musical experience and life experience.
- Empowered with the intellectual and creative skills necessary for lifelong musical learning.

Features of the text

- *Music: A Social Experience* encourages active learning by including "Questions for thought" and "Activities and assignments" at various points throughout the text. These features are meant to encourage students to reflect on and connect the knowledge they bring from their own life experiences with the information presented in the text. They may also be used for class or small group discussions or activities.
- Sidebars present concise summaries of people, places, things, or ideas that supplement the text's narrative. They may also serve as ideas for further research.
- Listening guides in the text provide structural road maps of featured works.
- Bolded terms can be found in the glossary.
- Web references (mysearchlab) refer to online listening guides and supplementary materials (see below).

Organization of the text

Part 1, Music Fundamentals, includes chapters 1 to 3. Chapter 1 introduces the power of music; how we perceive music in its cultural and historical context; and ways of categorizing musical styles. Chapter 2 introduces the basic vocabulary and meanings of the elements of music. Chapter 3 demonstrates how to apply the concepts learned in Chapter 2 by analyzing three short works.

Part 2, Musical Identities, includes chapters 4 to 6. These chapters focus on how music *expresses* individual and group identities and, in turn, how music *shapes* social expectations of identity. Chapter 4 investigates how musical ethnicities cross cultural, social, and geographical boundaries. Chapter 5 shows how gender is mirrored in music, in both performance roles and soundscapes. Chapter 6 explores music's connections to the sacred traditions of Buddhism, Christianity, Islam, Judaism, and the Yoruba.

Part 3, Musical Intersections, includes chapters 7 to 9. Here we explore how music crosses into the social realms of politics, conflict, and love. Chapter 7 discusses how music reflects political ideologies and national identity. Chapter 8 examines music's use in, and response to, war. Chapter 9 shows how music can express various aspects of love: young love, unattainable love, obsessive love, betrayal, and fidelity.

Part 4, Musical Narratives, includes chapters 10 to 13. These chapters focus on musical genres (theater, film, and dance) and the concert experience. We investigate the social stories they tell as well as the histories of the genres themselves. Chapter 10 focuses on three significant works of American musical theater: *Show Boat, West Side Story,* and *Sweeney Todd.*

Chapter 11 explores music's role in film, past and present, and Chapter 12 examines music's inextricable connection to dance. Chapter 13 focuses on the concert experience, with emphasis on a symphony orchestra concert, but with excursions in jazz and South Indian classical music.

Web-based materials for the student

The Web content for this course is offered on Pearson's mysearchlab (www.mysearchlab.com). Included in this material are:

- Sound examples that illustrate the elements of music (Chapter 2)
- Automated listening guides with streaming audio for most of the major works presented in the text. (For compositions or movie clips where usage rights were not available, the reader is referred to the Internet or DVD).
- Video examples
- An extended chronology of the periods of Western art music
- References to podcasts and other Web links of interest
- Supplementary materials that complement discussions in the text

For the Instructor

On-line Instructor's Manual

The Instructor's Manual includes:

- How to use this text
- Classroom activities
- Outside the classroom activities
- The first week of class
- **Notes on the chapters:** bibliographies; commentary; related repertory
- Power points
- Quizzes

PowerPoint Slides

PowerPoint slides accompanying each chapter are available for downloads.

Repertory List

Western Art Music

Medieval
Kyrie eleison (chapters 2 and 6)

Renaissance
Anonymous, "Branle des Lavandiers" (Chapter 12)
Antoine Busnoys, "Je ne puis vivre ainsy toujours" (Chapter 9)
Clement Janequin, "La guerre" (Chapter 8)
Giovanni Pierluigi da Palestrina, Kyrie from *Pope Marcellus Mass* (Chapter 2 and 6)

Baroque
J. S. Bach, Bourrée from Suite in e minor, BWV 996 (Chapter 3)
J. S. Bach, excerpt from *St. Matthew Passion* (Chapter 6)
Antonio Vivaldi, "La Primavera" ("Spring") from Concerto in E Major, op. 8 (Chapter 13)

Classical
Franz Haydn, last movement from String Quartet in E-flat Major, opus 33, no. 2, "The Joke" (Chapter 13)
W. A. Mozart, "Non so piu cosa son" from *The Marriage of Figaro* (Chapter 5)
W. A. Mozart, first movement from Symphony No. 40 in g minor (Chapter 13)

Romantic

Ludwig van Beethoven, fourth movement from Symphony No. 9 (Chapter 7)
Georges Bizet, "Habanera" from *Carmen* (Chapter 5)
Alexander Borodin, *In the Steppes of Central Asia* (Chapter 7)
John Newton (text), "Amazing Grace" performed by (1) Bernice Johnson Reagon (2)
   The Robert Shaw Festival Singers, and (3) the Old Harp Singers of Eastern Tennessee
   (Chapter 6)
Niccolò Paganini, Caprice in a minor, op. 1, number 24 (Chapter 13)
Giacomo Puccini, "Un bel dì, vedremo," from *Madama Butterfly* (Chapter 9)
Franz Schubert, "Gretchen am Spinnrade," (Chapter 9)
Richard Wagner, Act II/Scene 2, from *Siegfried* (Chapter 5)

Twentieth Century to Present

Béla Bartók, "Allegro Barbaro" (Chapter 4)
Benjamin Britten, Agnus Dei from *War Requiem* (Chapter 8)
Aaron Copland, "Hoe-Down" from *Rodeo* (Chapter 13)
George Gershwin, "Summertime" from *Porgy and Bess* (Chapter 2)
Olivier Messiaen, "Liturgie de cristal," from *Quartet for the End of Time* (Chapter 8)
Krzysztof Pendericki, *Threnody for the Victims of Hiroshima* (Chapter 8)
Astor Piazzolla, "Libertango" (Chapter 12)
Maurice Ravel, "Habanera" from *Rapsodie Espagnole* (Chapter 4)
Arnold Schoenberg, excerpt from "Kol Nidre" (Chapter 6)
William Grant Still, first movement from "Afro-American Symphony" (Chapter 4)
Igor Stravinsky, "The Augers of Spring" from *The Rite of Spring* (Chapter 12)

Film and Musical Theater

Leonard Bernstein, Quintet, finale to Act I from *West Side Story* (Chapter 10)
Bernard Herrmann, *The Day the Earth Stood Still*, opening sequence (Chapter 11)
Gottfried Huppertz, *Metropolis*, opening (Chapter 11)
Jerome Kern, *Show Boat*, opening scene (Chapter 10)
Masaru Sato, *The Hidden Fortress*, fire festival scene (Chapter 11)
Stephen Sondheim, "No Place Like London" from *Sweeney Todd* (Chapter 10)
Max Steiner, *King Kong*, fog scene (Chapter 11)
John Williams, *E.T.: The Extra-Terrestrial*, flying scene (Chapter 11)

Popular Song and Jazz

Harold Arlen, "Over the Rainbow" sung by (1) Judy Garland and (2) performed
   by Art Tatum (Chapter 3)
Bert Berns, "Hang on Sloopy" (Chapter 2)
Louise Gugliemi (music) and Édith Piaf (lyrics), "La Vie en Rose" (Chapter 9)
Miles Davis, "So What" (Chapter 13)
John Hewett, "All Quiet Along the Potomac Tonight" (Chapter 8)
B. B. King, "Sweet Little Angel" (Chapter 4)
Robin Moore and Staff Sgt. Barry Sadler, "Ballad of the Green Berets" (Chapter 8)
Otis Redding, "Respect" (Chapter 5)
Juan Tizol, "Caravan," (Chapter 4)
Hank Williams, "Cold, Cold Heart" (Chapter 9)

World Music

Tyagaraja, *Manasu Visaya* (South Indian) (chapters 2 and 13)
"His First Hunt," (Inuit) (Chapter 2)
"Nezasa Shirabe," performed by Tadashi Tajima (Shakuhachi, Japan) (Chapter 3)
"Perets-Tants" (Klezmer) (Chapter 4)
"Kelefaba" and "Kuruntu Kelafa" (West Africa) (Chapter 4)
Mekar Sari (Women's Gamelan, Bali) (Chapter 5)
Mǎ Guariță (Romanian lament) (Chapter 5)
Yamantaka (Tibetan chant) (Chapter 6)

Eleggua (Cuba) (Chapter 6)
Naat-i Sherif (excerpt) (Sufi) (Chapter 6)
"My Heart Is Bursting with Anger," Scene 9, from *Hong deng ji* (China) (Chapter 7)
"Dilmano, Dilbero" by Philip Koutev (Bulgaria) (Chapter 7)
"El himno Zapatista" (Mexican Corrido) (Chapter 7)
"Father Have Pity on Me" and "Light from Sun Is Flowing" (Arapaho and Comanche
    Ghost dance songs) (Chapter 8)
Rikle Glezer (text), "Es iz geven a zumer-tog" ("It Was a Summer's Day")
    (Holocaust song) (Chapter 8)
"Ceurik Rahwana" (Sunda) (Chapter 9)
Baamaya (Dagbamba dance style, Ghana) (Chapter 12)

Acknowledgments

We are grateful to the staff at Pearson-Prentice Hall and especially our editor, Richard
Carlin, for helping us bring this new approach to teaching music to fruition. Special
thanks go to Eleanor Olin for preparing the power points and to Norine Strang, Senior
Project Editor at S4Carlisle Publishing Services. Thanks also to our students for their
input, patience, and inspiration. Finally, as is evident from the list below, the authors are
indebted to numerous colleagues for their help and encouragement in preparing this text.

Vasile Beluska, *Bowling Green State University*
Vincent Corrigan, *Bowling Green State University*
Robert Fallon, *Carnegie Mellon University*
Heather Fischer, *Wayne State University*
David Harnish, *University of San Diego*
Ellen Koskoff, *The Eastman School of Music*
Panayotis League, *Boston University*
Sharan Leventhal, *Boston Conservatory*
Solungga Fang-Tzu Liu, *Bowling Green State University*
Jeannie Ludlow, *Eastern Illinois University*
Michael Marcuzzi, *York University*
Megan McCarty, Boston University
Kathy Meizel, *Bowling Green State University*
Elinor Olin, *National-Louis University*
Jamie K. Oxendine, *Lumbee/Creek*
Michael Pisani, *Vassar College*
Mihai Popean, *Bowling Green State University*
Mehmet Sanlikol, *Brown University*
Marilyn Shrude, *Bowling Green State University*
Andrew Smith, *Bowling Green State University*
Timothy Stulman, *Full Sail University*
Ying-Wei Sung, *Bowling Green State University*
Sean Williams, *The Evergreen State College*

Steven Cornelius specializes in music of the African diaspora, the Americas, and the music industry. He is currently a Visiting Professor of Music at Boston University, where he also serves as an associated faculty member in African Studies. Previous teaching positions include Bowling Green State University (1991–2010), Bruckner-Konservatorium Linz (adjunct faculty, 1992–1997), Pine Manor College (1989–1991), New England Conservatory (1988), and University of Wisconsin-Madison (1982, 1984–86). He also served from 1996 to 2006 as music and dance critic for *The Blade*, Toledo, Ohio's daily newspaper. Books include *Music of the Civil War Era* (Greenwood Press 2004) and *The Music of Santería: Traditional Rhythms of the Batá Drums* (co-authored with John Amira) (White Cliffs Media, 1991), as well as chapters and essays in books published by Vervuert Verlag, Garland, Routledge, and University Press of America. Articles have appeared in *Latin American Music Review, College Music Symposium,* and other journals, as well as *The Garland Encyclopedia of World Music.* Performance credits as a percussionist include work with Metropolitan Opera, New York City Opera, Radio City Music Hall, Oklahoma Symphony, and Taipei Symphony, among others. B.M.Ed., University of Wisconsin-Madison; M.M., Manhattan School of Music; Ph.D., University of California, Los Angeles.

Mary Natvig's areas of research are: the music of fifteenth-century Burgundy, women in music, and music history pedagogy. She is currently Professor of Music and Assistant Dean at Bowling Green State University's College of Musical Arts (since 1990). She taught part-time at the Eastman School of Music from 1987–1990 and was a Visiting Assistant Professor of Violin at Hope College from 1982–1984. Publications include an edited collection titled, *Teaching Music History* (Ashgate, 2001), as well chapters and essays in books published by Oxford University Press, The Alamire Foundation, and the University of California Press. Articles have appeared in *College Music Symposium, Women in Music, the New Grove Dictionary of Music and Musicians,* the *New Catholic Encyclopedia, Women of Note,* and the *American String Teacher.* Performance experience includes the BGSU Early Music Ensemble (director and performer), the Grand Rapids (MI) Symphony Orchestra (part-time), and freelance work on Baroque and modern violin. She has also been a Suzuki violin instructor through BGSU's Creative Arts Program. Eastman School of Music B.M. M.A. Ph.D.

QUESTIONS FOR THOUGHT

- What is music?
- How many kinds of music can you name? How do you generally listen to music? What do you think about when you listen?
- How does music function in your life? Do you ever make music? In what context? What types of music do you enjoy? Why?

"Music produces a kind of pleasure which human nature cannot do without."

—Confucius
(ca. 551 BCE to 479 BCE)

Introduction

Ninety-three-year-old Veva Campbell slumps wordlessly in her wheelchair. A victim of Alzheimer's disease, she has not spoken, walked, fed herself, or recognized friends and family for over two years. This afternoon, her grand-daughter, an out-of-town musician, comes to visit. There is nothing to say or do, so she pulls out her violin and begins to play. Miraculously, Mrs. Campbell sits up and begins singing along to the traditional hymns and old-time songs she recognizes from her youth. When the music stops, Mrs. Campbell retreats back into silence.

Our story is not apocryphal. Mrs. Campbell was the coauthor's grandmother. And this demonstration of music's power, remarkable as it may be, is not an isolated example. All over the world music unites and heals, transforms and inspires. This appears to have been the case since the beginning of civilization.

Music and the Brain

The foundation of musical experience resides deep within the mind. Medical science is just beginning to document these complexities. We know, for example, that severe stutterers, even those unable to get out single spoken words, can sometimes perfectly sing entire sentences. We know that by setting instructions to song, suf-ferers of autism can learn to execute sequential tasks otherwise far beyond their reach. And we know that when medication fails, those with the neuropsychiatric disorder Tourette syndrome can successfully use drum circles to calm their tics.

There is much to learn. Scientists cannot explain the case of Tony Cicoria, a middle-aged physician who, after being struck by lightning, suddenly developed a passion and gift for playing the piano and composing. Nor can they explain the case of Clive Wearing, a British amnesia victim who, despite being able to remember just a few seconds into the past, can still play the piano, read music, and even direct choral rehearsals.

The human brain seems to be programmed for song. So fundamental is the human capacity for music that it may have evolved even before speech. Physiologists have shown that a mother's lullaby does double duty by lowering a child's arousal levels while simultaneously increasing the child's ability to focus attention. Music therapists have found that listening to music induces the release of pleasure-producing endorphins that both lower blood pressure and ease the sensation of physical pain. Social scien-tists believe that music, by bringing people to-gether to perform and listen, may have provided an early model for social cooperation, cohesion, and even reproductive success. If this is correct, then music would seem to be a fundamental building block in the development of culture.

Attentive listening is good for the brain. It helps us organize our thinking, give shape to our consciousness, and focus our ideas. These phe-nomena seem to happen for a variety of reasons and in a number of ways. Our involuntary ner-vous system—including heart rate, brain waves, and other basic bodily functions—automatically entrains to the sounds we hear. We also respond to music's emotional qualities. Lovely melodies softly played relax us, whereas beating drums and searing trumpets excite us. A favorite song recalls times gone by, whereas the sounds of a national anthem invite us to reflect upon our identity.

Music helps structure the analytical mind. Psychological studies suggest that musical training improves one's organizational skills and can even

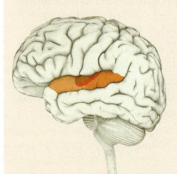

The auditory cortex, which grows with musical training, can be up to 130 percent larger in musicians than in nonmusicians. Brains grow when challenged with physical tasks as well. The part of the brain that governs a violinist's left-hand fingers will be larger than the part that governs the right-hand fingers. Presumably, Jimi Hendrix, who played the guitar "backwards," would have shown more brain growth for the right-hand fingers.

The human brain, highlighting the auditory cortex.

have a positive effect on IQ. Indeed, scientists hypothesize that while performing, musicians are actually engaged in high-powered brain calisthenics. These skills transfer to other areas of life.

Clearly, active musical experience affects consciousness in profound ways. But what does this mean for you? What if you do not play music, sing, or dance? Research shows that one need not perform to reap music's benefits. Simply engaging in *active* listening is enough to set the brain in high gear. And the best part of all this is that the effects of listening skills are cumulative. The better you learn to listen today, the more listening techniques you will have available tomorrow.

Music and Culture

Societies, both ancient and modern, have recognized music's transformative agency. Indeed, Greek mythology tells us that music had power over death itself. When Orpheus's beloved wife Eurydice died and passed into the underworld, he followed. Empowered by the irresistible strains of his lyre, Orpheus swayed the will of the gods; Eurydice was thus allowed to return to the land of the living. The idea of music's regenerative power remains relevant today. As was witnessed worldwide in the remarkable concerts following the tragedy of 9/11, music making often signifies a return to life.

Cultures around the world have stories about the power of music. For the Temiar people of Malaysia in Southeast Asia, shamans heal with songs received from spirit guides. In the American Southwest, Hopi mythology tells of the primordial beings Tawa and Spider Woman, who sat

Orpheus depicted on a Roman mosaic, playing his lyre to tame wild animals.

together and sang humanity into existence. The rhythmic dance of the Hindu deity Shiva is said to animate the universe. **mysearchlab 1.1**

The preceding paragraph opened with the word "cultures," as if its meaning were obvious. In fact, "culture" is a difficult concept to pin down. Anthropologists and sociologists have developed hundreds of definitions. Still useful today is one from British anthropologist Edward Tylor who in 1874 defined culture as a "complex whole" that includes a people's acquired knowledge and beliefs, arts and morals, laws and customs. All people everywhere have culture, said Tylor, but cultures differ significantly from each other.

Tylor saw culture as relatively static. Today, however, we understand that culture is fluid and adaptable. Culture involves material, social, and intellectual aspects of life. It is a people's way of living in the world.

- Material aspects include the things we use and how we use them.
- Social aspects include the way people interact with one another and go about organizing their communities.
- Intellectual aspects include the self-generated webs of meaning within which individuals and groups of people live their lives.

Drawing cultural boundaries is often a matter of perspective. It is easy to think of the previously mentioned Malaysian Temiar as culturally separate from the North American Hopi and separate from the Hindus of India. But what about the differences in worldview between a child raised in New York City and another raised on a Montana cattle ranch? Or what about differences in worldview between American Catholics and American Protestant evangelicals? Might these examples constitute different cultures? Perhaps yes, if their religious ideologies sufficiently impact fundamental understandings of the world.

There are micro cultures as well. Consider, for example, a large corporation such as Sony BMG Music Entertainment. Top executives live in a very different world from the company's general desk-bound workforce and from the company's contracted musicians, such as Alicia Keys or the band AC/DC.

What might constitute a musical culture? Perhaps it is a group of people who share particular values that are reflected in the way they make, hear, and use music. In North America, for example, the music industry divides itself for marketing purposes into specific **genres**—Top Forty, bluegrass, jazz, world music, classical, blues, zydeco, country and western, hip-hop, and many more. These designations offer commercial boundaries. Do they also represent distinct musical cultures?

Cultural identities are flexible and constantly negotiated. In today's society, people often move from one cultural circle to another as they pass through adolescence, go to college, learn new languages, enter the workforce, travel, or get married. Some people will use music to reinforce their identities or to form stronger links to their cultural heritage. Teenagers, however, often use music to break free of cultural expectations. For teens, listening habits often represent an expression of individuality and independence.

As you progress through this text, think about the ideas presented here. Which musical compositions are used to wield power? To persuade? To soothe? How do these works fit into the artists' cultural milieux? And finally, how might considering music from the composers' or performers' social perspectives enhance your understanding of the world and your own listening choices?

DID YOU KNOW?

MUSIC AND THE MIND

Some cultures fear music's power; others dress it in mysticism. There's good reason for this. Music activates the same chemical reactions in the brain as food, sex, and addictive drugs. Listeners really do "get high" from music. Thousands of scientific studies have been undertaken in an attempt to understand music's remarkable impact on human consciousness. **mysearchlab 1.2**

Classifying Music

There are endless ways to classify music, from very broad categories to very specific ones. For example, you and a friend might have many of the same tunes on your MP3 players but organize them under very different systems. The following text presents one common categorization system. Look carefully at the three sections. Do they make sense to you? Can you see any problem areas?

World Music

World music usually refers to local or regional music traditions that are (1) transmitted orally/aurally and (2) noncommercial in their everyday usage. World music is generally categorized by both geographic region (such as Africa, Asia, India, Eastern Europe) and ethnic origin (Tejano, Celtic, Afro-Cuban). American "folk" music, for example, might be considered one type of "world" music in that the term generally refers to noncommercial orally transmitted music of British Isles heritage.

Popular Music

Popular music is distinguished by the fact that it (1) is closely associated with the music industry, (2) is distributed through the mass media, and (3) generally appeals to a wide audience (though its attraction can be short-lived).

Western Art Music

Western art music (often called "classical music") refers to a specific body of works composed mostly by Europeans and peoples of the European diaspora from the Medieval Period to the present. Because of its long history, the music is stylistically diverse; in general, however, we can say the music's distinguishing feature is that it is composed by individuals and notated. Scholars divide Western art music into the following six historical periods. **mysearchlab 1.3**

The Medieval Period (ca. 400–1430)

The Medieval Period refers to European history from the fifth-century collapse of the Roman Empire to the beginning of the Renaissance (ca. 1430). The Catholic church dominated the social order during this time; Latin was the language of the learned.

This period saw the development of Western musical notation, which was used in music composed for the church and the nobility. Early church music was called plainchant, a single free-flowing melodic line. Between the ninth and thirteenth centuries, church musicians began to add newly composed lines above and below the original chant. This experimentation led to the development of new genres, both sacred and secular, in two, three, and four parts. Music of the nobility consisted of secular songs in local dialects, such as the chansons of the French troubadours and trouvères. Like plainchant, these love songs consisted of a single melodic line, but they had clear melodic and textural repetitions not found in chant.

The Renaissance Period (ca. 1430–1600)

The "Renaissance" was characterized by a renewed interest in the writings, philosophies, and art of ancient Greece and Rome. Renaissance music was characterized by complex intertwining melodies. Most of the music that survives is choral; instrumental music was often improvised. Although chant remained the most commonly performed church music, lavish multivoiced settings of the Catholic Mass were written for specific occasions.

During the fifteenth century, the dominant secular genre was the French chanson, now usually for three voices. A variety of national secular styles later developed, such as the madrigal in Italy and England.

German music thrived during the Protestant Reformation, in part because Martin Luther (1483–1546) believed that music was essential to worship. Many of the tunes (called chorales) written during the Reformation form the basis for modern-day hymns.

The Baroque Period (ca. 1600–1750)

The term "Baroque" refers to the highly ornamented complexity of the period's art and architecture. A feature that unifies Baroque music is the use of a continuous bass line, called *basso continuo*.

At the end of the sixteenth century, Italian humanists became interested in reviving the emotive power of ancient Greek drama, which led to the invention of opera, one of the era's most important developments.

Though incredibly popular, operas were banned during the season of Lent. Entertainment-hungry Baroque audiences found solace in oratorio, a sacred dramatic (though unstaged) genre. Today, the most well-known Baroque oratorio is G. F. Handel's *Messiah* (1741).

Many new instrumental genres arose in the Baroque period, including the suite (a collection of pieces based on courtly dances), the sonata (a work for either an unaccompanied soloist or for a solo instrument with basso continuo), and the concerto (a composition for soloist(s) and orchestra).

The Classical Period (ca. 1750–1820)

Classical period music emphasized clarity, symmetry, and formal balance—features reminiscent of the architectural ideals of Classical Greece, from which the period gets its name. Composers relied on contrasting melodies and tonal areas to delineate formal sections.

New instrumental genres—the symphony and string quartet—became concert staples. Performance gradually moved from private to public spheres as a growing middle class made its economic power felt. There were many gifted composers in the Classical Period, but history has canonized three in particular: Franz Joseph Haydn (1732–1809), Wolfgang

Amadeus Mozart (1756–1791), and Ludwig van Beethoven (1770–1827). Because these composers have enjoyed continuous popularity since their own lifetimes, all Western art music became known as "classical," though in its strictest sense the term applies only to this period of music history.

The Romantic Period (ca. 1820–1900)

The Romantic Period coincided with the nineteenth-century rise of industrialization and the West's world colonization. Spurred by rising interest in individual experience, music was infused with emotional intensity; virtuoso performers dazzled audiences with their technical abilities and bravura.

To meet these expressive demands, composers explored new sounds, textures, and harmonies. Orchestras grew in size. The symphony remained a concert staple, but new genres also developed, including the symphonic poem, which characterized musical themes from visual art and literature. Folk melodies and rhythms were often incorporated as composers colored their music with national or ethnic identities.

The Twentieth-Century Period (1900 to the Present)

The twentieth century saw remarkable changes in technology, medicine, and lifestyle—from our first electrical grids, to a man on the moon, to the World Wide Web. Unlike earlier periods, twentieth-century art music comprised a number of disparate, even conflicting, aesthetic movements. Perhaps the strongest unifying force throughout this period was the quick response to social change, whether coming from war, new technologies, or shifting values and beliefs.

Approaching the cusp of 1900, French painters and musicians developed an artistic style called Impressionism, which focused on atmosphere and mood. Shimmering colors characterized the style's painting; composers achieved similar effects with innovative tonalities and instrumental textures.

In the century's first decades, Austrian composer Arnold Schoenberg (1874–1951) and his students developed a new style of composition that reflected the aesthetics of Expressionism, a movement that sought to explore the reaches of the unconscious mind. Musical expressionism led to the abandonment of the major-minor scale system as composers explored atonality, music without a tonal center.

In the 1950s and 1960s composers experimented with electronic instruments like the theremin and synthesizer. Tape recorders were used to manipulate electronic, industrial, and natural sounds.

American composer John Cage (1912–1992) was music's greatest iconoclast. Cage's most famous composition is *4'33"*, in which the performer does nothing at all. Ambient noise—breathing and coughing, buzzing lights, and ventilation systems—provide the "music."

Perhaps the most popular style of later twentieth-century art music was minimalism, a reaction against the complexities of the intellectual music of the *avant-garde*, which came to the fore following World War II. Minimalism is characterized by harmonic consonance, steady pulse, and the slow, hypnotic transformation of musical phrases.

DID YOU KNOW?

MUSIC'S NEGATIVE EFFECTS: TURN DOWN THE VOLUME!

Repeated exposure to loud sounds can affect our health and psychological well-being. Loud sounds cause hearing loss. They also raise blood pressure, cause heart disease, increase the breathing rate, disturb digestion, and even contribute to low birth weight, birth defects, and premature birth.

Volume levels are measured in decibels (dB). Sounds louder than 80 dB are considered dangerous; those louder than 120 will cause pain and perhaps even permanent hearing loss. In the fall of 2007, students at Johns Hopkins University were given an assignment to calibrate noise levels in their environment. Surprisingly, they found that the highest noise levels were neither on a busy highway during rush hour nor at a symphony orchestra concert. Instead, the highest dB levels came from listening to music with earbuds. These levels often far exceeded the danger point.

QUESTIONS FOR THOUGHT

- Why do you enjoy some musical styles more than others?
- A national anthem is one obvious way in which people use music to express identity. What are some additional examples?
- The media often talk about different American cultures. What are some of them?
- Is all music associated with culture?

CONCLUSION

In this first chapter we have discussed ways in which music has a fundamental role in physiology, consciousness, and social identity. In the two chapters that complete our music fundamentals section, we introduce basic theoretical concepts and terminology that will give us the tools to analyze and discuss musical components and forms. After that, we will shift our focus to the role music plays in social experience. Our examples are wide ranging. They are drawn from around the world and across centuries of time. This makes for striking juxtapositions. For example, by organizing our study according to broad social categories—such as love and war, ethnicity, gender, politics, and religion—we are able to place music from the distant past alongside music of today. These pairings demonstrate connections between time and place that are not always apparent using chronological and monocultural approaches to understanding musical experience.

Finally, although we study a collection of wonderful music, this text is not primarily concerned with identifying and teaching an era's or society's greatest "masterpieces" or most popular works. Instead, we strive to give you tools for listening and for understanding music's place within the human experience. With these skills, the world will become your playlist.

CHAPTER GOALS

- To develop tools for listening.
- To understand the basic elements of music.
- To develop a vocabulary of musical understanding.
- To explore the relationships between musical sound and musical meaning.

QUESTIONS FOR THOUGHT

- How does music communicate meaning?
- How might a composer portray heartbreak? Joy? Fear? Surprise?
- How might a composer create coherence in a long piece?

Active Listening

Music is not a universal language. Rather, it is a culture-specific system of communication. Each musical culture has its own particularized grammar and syntax. Thus, sounds that are important in one musical system may not be meaningful in another. As with their first spoken language, children learn to make sense of music without much conscious effort. To understand music's complexities, however, we have to actively train, or "tune," our minds to respond to the proper audible stimuli.

This process is complex, yet relatively easy to understand. The ear itself takes in the enormous range of information from the soundscapes in which we live. But the mind quickly discovers that not all sounds—as is true with the information from our other senses—are equally important. Gradually, we learn to identify relevant sound patterns while disregarding the irrelevant ones. This is how we learn to speak a language. It is also how we learn to understand music.

The key is to actively listen. By focusing on a specific sound source or pattern of sounds, for example, we can follow a single conversation in a crowded room. Likewise, a trained musician can distinguish the second clarinetist's melody amidst the sonic commotion of a full orchestra. We can also train ourselves to simultaneously follow multiple musical ideas (or conversations).

Active listening is an acquired three-step skill that involves attentiveness, analysis, and interpretation. First, the active music listener pays careful attention to the sounds being played. Second (and often simultaneously with step one), she organizes the sounds into meaningful components. Finally, she constructs an interpretation of the performance. Hearing is easy—our eardrums do that automatically. But *active* listening takes work and requires careful attention. It is also hugely rewarding.

In order to get a better understanding of active listening, think back to a recent conversation you had with a friend. You listened to words for their meanings, of course. But you also listened to much more. You took notice of the speaker's tone of voice, tempo of speech, choice of words, and perhaps even the grammatical syntax. From these clues you attempted to deduce additional meanings that may have been hidden behind the words— for example, if the speaker was confident or nervous, honest or conspiratorial. All of this helped you to develop a rich interpretation of the speaker's true intent.

Compared with speech, music listening is more abstract, although the general process is the same. We pay attention to the instruments used and their sound qualities, as well as the melodic contours and rhythmic inflections. We listen for repeated patterns and musical phrases; perhaps we even tap a foot to help find the proper rhythmic groove. Then we process this information in an attempt to figure out what the composer and musicians are up to—what they are trying to express, and what they want us to think and feel.

The Elements of Music

Performers rely on sonic road maps to navigate their way through a composition. This is true for every musical genre or style. Listeners use road maps too. The biggest difference between a performer's road map and a casual listener's road map is the level of complexity. A performer's map is necessarily intricate and multifaceted. It consists of interrelated informational layers that

> "Music is the art of thinking with sounds."
> —Jules Combarieu
> (1859–1916)

are accessed to different degrees according to the demands of the music. These layers include such basic elements as melody and harmony, rhythm and texture, and others. By comparison, a listener's map might initially include only general outlines and expectations—perhaps just the lyrics of a song, or the overall emotional feeling it projects, or the dance beat. It takes active listening to fill in the details of a musical landscape.

Active listening requires mental work. But it is also satisfying work. After all, if you like music now, but are only taking in a small part of the information, just think how satisfying the experience will be when you are processing much more.

So how does one build a road map? You need specific tools, which we will learn to use in the following pages. Musical road maps can be extremely complex, of course. Do not worry about that. Like a house made of bricks, complexity is built by combining relatively simple ideas. These ideas, or building blocks, constitute the six major "elements" or "fundamentals" of music.

1. Melody
2. Rhythm
3. Harmony
4. Timbre
5. Texture
6. Form

In this chapter we focus on each element individually. In the next chapter we will look at three different compositions in order to see how all of the elements work together to form musical meaning. As you read about each of the six elements, be sure to use the associated mysearchlabs in order to hear the examples discussed.

Melody

At the most basic level, **melody** can be understood as a unit of distinctly ordered **pitches** (or **tones**) sounding successively through time. Stated in a more natural fashion, one might say that melody is the tune; it is the part of a **song** or **composition** you go away singing.
mysearchlab 2.1

Melodies can portray many different emotions. For example, a melody that moves by step (**conjunct motion**) from one pitch to the next and is narrow in **range** (the distance between highest and lowest pitches) might represent calmness. In contrast, one that has many leaps between high and low pitches (**disjunct motion**) might represent vigor or anxiety.
mysearchlab 2.2 Melodies that progress

slowly downward from high to low often project relaxation, melancholy, or even sadness. Melodies that move upward often represent resolve or optimism. (Experiment with these ideas by humming a favorite song. Pay attention to how the melody fits with the lyrics.)

Think of a melody as a sentence in tones. As you know from studying English grammar, sentences embody complex ideas that are organized into phrases and held together by periods, commas, and other punctuation. Nouns are stable; verbs suggest action. Still other words function as articles and prepositions, adjectives and adverbs. In a well-constructed sentence, every word has a function—a place in the grammatical whole. So too is the case with the various tones that comprise melodies.

The Western melodic system is built upon the principle of tension and release. Each of the seven tones of the **major scale**—do, re, mi, fa, sol, la, ti, (do)—embodies a different emotional tendency. "Do" (the home tone or **tonic**) and "sol" (the **dominant**) represent stability and rootedness (like nouns). Other scale degrees, particularly "ti" and "re," are relatively unstable and have action tendencies (like verbs). They generally create tension, such as a longing to return to "do." So it is with every scale tone. Each has its own distinct personality, like the different colors of a rainbow or the green/yellow/red of a traffic signal.

The term "scale" comes from the Latin *scala*, meaning ladder. Like a ladder, musical scales consist of ascending and descending steps; on each step resides a tone.
mysearchlab 2.3

The Western scale is divided into 12 equidistant steps called half steps (or semitones). A scale that contains all 12 notes is called a **chromatic scale** (see Figure 2.1).

```
              do
         ti        ti
         li        te
         la        la
        si          ley
        sol        sol
        fi          sey
        fa          fa
        mi          mi
        ri          may
        re          re
        di          ra
        do          do
```

FIGURE 2.1 Chromatic scale

Most pieces of Western music use either major or minor scales, which consist of specific patterns of whole steps and half steps. The pattern of the major scale is shown in Figure 2.2.

FIGURE 2.2 Major scale

Ascending							Descending					
do	re	mi^fa	sol	la	ti^do		do^ti	la	sol	fa^mi	re	do
W	W	H	W	W	W	H	H	W	W	W	H	W	W

Minor Scales   In the Western melodic system there are three types of minor scales: natural, harmonic, and melodic. All three use a lowered third scale degree whereby "mi" becomes "me." The differences among the three are in the raising and lowering of the sixth and seventh steps. We present the simplest of the three, the natural minor scale, which has a lowered sixth degree ("ti" becomes "te"; see Figure 2.3).

Both major and minor scales consist of seven tones that eventually repeat as the pitches extend higher or lower. The interval (or distance) from one tone to its upper or lower repetition (for example, "do" to "do" or "sol" to "sol") is called an **octave**. In Western art music, some hear the major scale as joyful, the minor scale as sorrowful. We shall see that this connotation is not always the case, but you might think of major tonalities as bright in color and minor tonalities as dark. Remember, though, that these descriptions are stereotypes. They serve only as a starting point.

FIGURE 2.3 Natural minor scale

Ascending						Descending					
Do	re^me	fa	sol	la^te	do		Do	te^la	sol	fa	me^re	do
W	H	W	W	W	H	W	W	H	W	W	W	H	W

DID YOU KNOW?

WESTERN MUSICAL NOTATION

Western musical notation developed in Europe during the ninth to fifteenth centuries. Pitch is indicated by placing symbols (called notes) on a five-line **staff**. Different clefs—treble and bass are most common—indicate the overall range of the staff. There are various ways to indicate the duration of notes. Notes of longer duration have white noteheads, shorter ones are black. Very short notes add "flags" on the stems. The more flags, the shorter the note. A time signature shows the meter (top number) and which type of note gets the beat (bottom number).

A more detailed discussion of notation can be found on **mysearchlab 2.4**.

The original 1935 production of *Porgy and Bess*.

Melody in the Western World: "Summertime" from *Porgy and Bess* Listen to the first verse of "Summertime" from the **opera** *Porgy and Bess* (1935) composed by George Gershwin (1897–1937). **mysearchlab 2.5** Pay special attention to the words of lyricist DuBose Heyward (1885–1940). The setting is a steamy evening along Catfish Row in Charleston, South Carolina. The verse divides into four complete sentences. The first three are strangely lethargic, lacking a tendency for action. Each requires more context. When we hear, for example, in the first line that the "livin' is easy," we do not really know what to make of this news. Is easy livin' good? Bad? Indifferent? Why should we care?

We have similar emotional responses to the second and third lines. We know about jumping fish, the successful cotton crop (which tells us it is mid summer), and a pretty mamma and rich daddy. But what to do with the information? Resolution finally arrives in the fourth sentence, "So hush little baby don't you cry." Now we have context. This is a lullaby. And yet, with that knowledge we perhaps feel some inner disquiet. Why spill tears in an opera's opening scene if life is so placid?

Maybe it is not.

If you are listening actively, and thinking symbolically, you realize that Heyward has created a scene of social disquiet.

Now let's listen to the melody. Mirroring the poetry, Gershwin divides the music into four melodic sections or **phrases**. After each, there is a short pause, allowing time for the singer to breathe and time for the listener to reflect.

Notice that the first and third phrases are virtually identical in terms of melodic contour. For purposes of analysis, we will label them as "A" phrases. Also notice that the A phrases meander downward in the same easy manner.

Relaxed though they are (and like the lyrics they enhance), the phrases do not provide a sense of resolution. Why? Because the phrases end on the pitch "sol," the dominant, rather than "do," the tonic. The listener is left hanging.

The second phrase (the "B" phrase) is similar in shape and downward direction to the A phrases, but the range is narrower. As B begins, we wonder if it will provide the anticipated resolution to the A phrase, but by ending on "re," it does not. Once again, there is no resolution.

Do you see how Gershwin (as did Heyward) is delaying satisfaction? He makes us continue to listen to the complete story.

The awaited resolution finally comes with the fourth phrase (the "C" phrase), which begins on the same low pitch that ended the A phrases. Notice that in contrast to the first three phrases, which all began on the same pitch and moved downward, the C phrase has a generally upward direction, though in the end it relaxes downward to "do," the tonic.

Figure 2.4 shows a simple map of the melodic structure of "Summertime."

Notice the tidy balance of the ABAC format. Four distinct sections divide neatly into two main groupings: AB and AC.

Now let's fully consider the relationship between melody and words. Hearing the melody without the words, one might characterize the emotional content as beautiful, but lethargic . . . perhaps even sad.

What about the meaning of the lyrics? At first they seem rather optimistic, don't they? Living is easy; Daddy is rich; Mamma is good-looking. But then Heyward stirs the crying child into the mix.

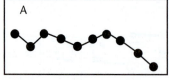

Summertime and the living   is   easy

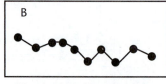

Fish are jumpin' And the cotton is high

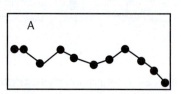

Your daddy's rich and your mamma's good lookin'

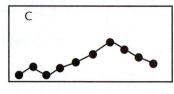

So hush little   baby   Don't   you cry

FIGURE 2.4   Melodic map of "Summertime"

When words and melody are combined, perhaps intuitively we become aware that something is not quite right. We note the eerie calm that precedes a terrible storm. Maybe daddy is not so rich after all. And maybe Mamma's good looks are going to bring a heap of trouble.

Take a moment to consider what a strange, wonderful, and emotionally complex world the composer and lyricist have created. It is as if the plain meanings of everyday life have been suspended in a dream, the meaning of which is just out of conscious reach. Such is the power of a well-constructed song.

Melody in the Non-Western World: An Example from South India   We have seen that Western melodies are built on specific concepts and expectations. Composers engage those ideas when writing music. The Western system is not universally employed, however. In the classical music of India, for example, melodies are based on collections of pitches called *ragas*.

Ragas may be compared to Western scales in that both comprise a specific set of pitches. In both systems, these individual pitches have particular personalities, including tendencies toward stability or motion. But there are also important differences. **mysearchlab 2.6**

- Even though two ragas may contain exactly the same pitches, one might be distinguished from another:
  - by emphasizing different pitches.
  - by employing characteristic turns of phrase.
- Individual ragas are associated with specific emotions or spiritual states. Some are associated with particular times of the day or night.
- The Western system employs just a handful of scales; thousands of ragas are theoretically possible.

Like the Western major and minor scales, ragas use a system of seven syllables to distinguish the *svaras* (tones): sa-ri-ga-ma-pa-dha-ni-(sa). The intervallic relationships between the tones, except for the fixed foundational interval between the "pillar tones" of "sa" and "pa," may be slightly larger or smaller from one raga to the next. Thus a raga's tones, which might fall between the measured half and whole steps of the Western scale, sometimes sound unusual to the Western ear.

Krishna and his consort Rahde.

Generally speaking, classical Indian music begins with an improvised and rhythmically free section known as *alapana (alap)*. Within the alap, the raga's various tonal, melodic, and emotional characteristics are introduced. In the next listening guide, we will listen to a brief alap excerpted from a longer performance by South Indian *venu* (bamboo flute) player Dr. N. Ramani. As you listen, notice the general melodic outline as first the instrument's lower range, then upper range, are explored. Notice as well the melody's mercurial quality.

Rhythm

Rhythm refers to the ways in which music is organized into distinct time units. **mysearchlab 2.7** To illustrate this, we will study the hymn tune, "Amazing Grace," the rhythm of which is built on a general pattern of short and long tones (see Figure 2.5).

short	long	short	long	short	long	short	long
A-	**ma-**	zing	**grace;**	how	**sweet**	the	**sound.**

FIGURE 2.5   "Amazing Grace" rhythm pattern

LISTENING GUIDE

CD I/Track 2
Download track 2
mysearchlab 2.6

EXCERPT FROM *MANASU VISAYA* BY TYAGARAJA (NATAKURANJI RAGA AND ADI TALA)

Performed by Dr. N. Ramani (venu),
T. S. Veeraraghavan (violin)

A tambura.

ALAPANA

0:00	The music begins with the soft sound of the "tambura," a resonant string instrument that plays a **drone** on "sa" and "pa." The tambura, which continues throughout the composition, has the essential role of providing the tonal backdrop against which all other pitches are understood. Even so, once the other instruments enter, the tambura is hardly noticed.
0:09	The venu enters and begins the essential process of unpacking and exploring the raga. Notice that Dr. Ramani immediately establishes his independence from the raga's pillar tones ("sa" and "pa") by entering on "ga." He stays on that single tone for nearly five seconds before relaxing downward and oscillating between "sa" and "dha." There is a sense of resolution when "sa" becomes the focus beginning at 0:18 and continuing through 0:26. Then the melody momentarily drops down to "ma" before rising (at 0:35) to a second held tone on "ga" (the same pitch as the opening). A violin follows the flute. Sometimes it follows the melody exactly; other times it plays the melody in a slightly different version or holds a single steady tone.
0:38	Though melodic movement is both up and down, there is a general upward movement as the flute's upper range is explored. The upper pillar tone "sa" is reached at 1:03 and finally "ga" (one octave above the melody's opening tone) and its upper neighbor "ma" are reached at 1:36. This is the high point of the alap. From here the movement generally relaxes downward, a sign that the section is moving toward its completion. Notice that phrases now tend to end on "sa," the raga's home tone.
1:57	The flutist introduces a brief motive that foreshadows the precomposed song that follows the alap. To the informed listener, this is another clear sign that the alap is nearly finished.
2:31	There is a sense of relaxation as the flute improvisation comes to a final end on the tone "sa." Now the violinist briefly explores the raga's tones and brings the alap to its conclusion.

ACTIVITIES AND ASSIGNMENTS

- Take a familiar piece and map its melodic phrases. Which phrases sound final? Which sound incomplete? On what pitch does the melody want to end? Where in the phrases are the highest notes? The lowest? Is the melody conjunct or disjunct? Is the range narrow or wide? How do these characteristics affect your emotional response?
- Using an online video source, find examples of traditional music from non-Western cultures. Does the melodic language sound different from what you are used to? Describe the differences using the previous concepts.

A crucial element of rhythm is pulse, or the **beat**. Understanding the beat is simple; it's what you tap your foot to, what you step to when you dance, and what soldiers march to. Some think of pulse as the musical heartbeat that underlies the musical flow.

Beats are generally organized into repeated groups (**measures**, or "bars") of strong and weak pulses. In most Western music, the first beat of every measure (the **downbeat**) is strong. The number and accentuation of beats in each measure determines a composition's **meter**. Meter is a fundamental organizing principle, a temporal yardstick that organizes rhythm's various elements into a cohesive whole.

To find the beat in "Amazing Grace," recite the previous lyrics and tap out a steady pulse that gives one tap to the "short" tone and two taps to the "long" tone. When long and short patterns are thus combined we get a repeating pattern of three pulses, called triple meter. Music that groups into two beats per measure is called duple meter; four beats per measure is quadruple meter.

So far, the concept of rhythm seems pretty simple. But there is one more issue to tackle. Where does the meter begin? On which pulse? As a general rule, begin your metric analysis with a strong pulse. That will be the downbeat. Thus in "Amazing Grace," the meter begins not with the vowel "A-," but with the accented syllable "ma," a fact we have indicated by using bold typeface. The syllable "A" is a **pickup** beat to the meter's beginning (see Figure 2.6).

short	long	short	long	short	long	short	long
A-	**ma-**	zing	**grace;**	how	**sweet**	the	**sound.**
3	1	2	3	1	2	3	1	2

pickup
note

FIGURE 2.6 "Amazing Grace" metric analysis

Notice that lyricists generally place the most important words or naturally accented syllables on strong beats. Thus in "Amazing Grace" the accented syllable "ma" is placed on the strong beat one, as are the colorful words "sweet" and "sound."

The last aspect of rhythm we need to discuss here is **tempo**. Simply put, tempo refers to the pace at which the beats go by. It is fine to refer to tempos as fast or slow, but classically trained musicians, who follow a European system developed over centuries, often use Italian terms, such as *adagio* (at ease), *andante* (walking tempo), and *allegro* (lively). **mysearchlab 2.8** These are the words you will generally see in the program book for a recital or symphony orchestra concert, even in English-speaking counties.

Tempo might stay steady throughout an entire work, or it might vary. Tempo can change gradually or suddenly. Often tempo changes signify a shift in emotional focus, or a shift from one musical section to another.

MUSICAL THEMES
THE *RAMAYANA*

The *Ramayana* (*Rama's Journey*) is an epic Sanskrit poem of 24,000 verses. Its authorship is attributed to the poet Valmiki, who lived during the fourth century BCE.

Valmiki tells the story of Rama (a worldly incarnation of the Hindu deity Vishnu) who lives on Earth unaware of his divine heritage and worldly mission. Throughout his life, Rama endures hardships and learns many difficult lessons.

Rama's greatest trial begins when his wife Sita is kidnapped by the many-headed demon Ravana, who desires Sita for himself. With the help of the monkey god Hanuman (an incarnation of Shiva) and Hanuman's monkey army, Rama is eventually able to defeat Ravana, an act that brings peace to the world.

Rhythm in the Non-Western World: An Example from Southeast Asia   Just as concepts of melody vary from culture to culture, rhythmic organizations also differ. A contrasting approach to rhythmic organization can be found in Bali, Indonesia, an island famous for its physical beauty, brass **gamelan** orchestras, and interlocking rhythms. **mysearchlab 2.9**

A kecak performance photographed in Bali.

These interlocking patterns are demonstrated here in kecak (pronounced ké-chak), a composition for narrator and men's chorus.

Drawing from the Hindu epic the *Ramayana*, the narrator tells a story from Rama's battle against Ravana. As he tells the story, perhaps acting out various roles along the way, the men's chorus takes on the role of the monkey "army," which chatters away. To achieve this effect, the men divide into groups and shout out monkey-like sounds ("cak") in interlocking rhythms that include short spaces for breathing. The Balinese call this interlocking technique **kotekan**, a central rhythmic foundation of Balinese music. It may be performed vocally (as in this example) or, more commonly, on the instruments of the gamelan.

A standard kotekan pattern for three groups of kecak performers appears in the following diagram. Form a trio (or larger group with two or more on each part) and try performing it. Reading horizontally from left to right, sing the patterns while clapping the beat. First, have everyone sing the same line together. Then, divide the parts so that each person (or group) sings a different line. You will notice that all the patterns have the same exact sequences of sounds and silences, but because each pattern fits differently against the beat, each feels different. When the patterns are performed together, every temporal subdivision is filled with a sound. (This is also the case when either patterns one and two or patterns two and three are performed together; see Figure 2.7.) **mysearchlab 2.9**

Harmony

Harmony occurs when at least two different pitches sound at the same time, such as when two people sing together with different material or when a musician strums the strings of a guitar. Harmonies that sound pleasing to our ears are said to be **consonant**. Those that sound harsh or clash are said to be **dissonant**. As a general rule, dissonant harmonies are used to produce feelings of anxiety or tension. **mysearchlab 2.10**

Different cultures and time periods have different standards of what is consonant and dissonant. A musician in the twelfth century, for instance, would likely find the works of Wolfgang Amadeus Mozart (1756–1791) to be jarringly dissonant. Today, however, we consider Mozart's music to be quite consonant.

In Western art music, three or more pitches that sound at the same time create a **chord**.

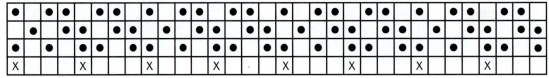

Each square represents a steady pulse
Clap the beat on X
● Represents "cak"
☐ Represents silence

FIGURE 2.7   Kotekan pattern

QUESTIONS FOR THOUGHT

- What would a composite diagram of all the kotekan parts look like?
- Notice in "Amazing Grace" that the full syllable is "maz," but that when sung the "z" is moved back and attached to the "ing." Experiment singing the phrase both ways. Why does the "z" get moved?
- How do you identify meter in music without words? What are the cues?

ACTIVITIES AND ASSIGNMENTS

- Tap out the beats to a song you know. Is there a pickup beat? Do the beats group into twos/fours (duple/quadruple) or threes (triple)? Have one person clap the rhythm of the piece and one person tap the beat. What's the difference between the rhythm and the beat?
- Compose an interlocking pattern for two people. Perform it for the class.
- Find a video of kecak on the Internet. Can you hear a pulse?

mysearchlab 2.11 Chords are built according to specific rules. The most basic rule is that a simple three-note chord, or **triad**, is built upward from its root in alternating scale tones. A triad built on "do" (remember the scale tones: do, re, mi, fa, sol, la, ti, do) will skip "re," include "mi," skip "fa," and end on "sol." The resulting triad will be do-mi-sol.

Chords function in a manner similar to melodic scale tones in that they too have varying degrees of stability. A chord built on the first scale degree (do-mi-sol) is the most stable. This is called the "tonic" or [Roman numeral] I chord. Most pieces in the Western tradition begin and end on the tonic chord. The "dominant," or "V" chord, is second in foundational importance to the tonic chord. It is built on the fifth scale degree (sol-ti-re). The dominant chord is slightly less stable than the tonic chord and has a tendency to return home to the tonic. Third in foundational importance is the "**subdominant**," or "IV" chord (fa-la-do). The subdominant tends to move either to the tonic or the dominant (see Figure 2.8).

FIGURE 2.8   I-IV-V chord progression

These three chords make up the harmonic backbone of Western music. If you string these together [subdominant (IV), dominant (V), and tonic (I)] you get a common ending formula known as a **cadence. mysearchlab 2.12**

Listen to the chorus of "Hang on Sloopy," a 1965 #1 hit song by The McCoys. Notice the repeating I, IV, V, harmonies accompanying the melody. Focus on the bass tones that sound the bottom notes of the chords. Instruments introduce the harmonies: I, IV, V, IV and repeat the progression after every line of text (see Figure 2.9).

Although harmony is central to most Western music, it is not a universally employed device. Traditional music cultures in the Middle East, India, Asia, and Native America do not use harmony.

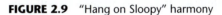

I	IV	V	IV		I	IV	V	IV

Hang on Sloopy; Sloopy hang on   (instruments)

FIGURE 2.9   "Hang on Sloopy" harmony

"Hang on Sloopy"
CD I/Track 3
Download track 3
mysearchlab 2.13

Timbre

Every sound has a particular tone color or **timbre**. It is through timbre that you can tell the difference between your grandmother's voice and your girlfriend's, a flute and a violin, and even one violin from another. During the course of the semester we will find that timbre can identify not only the individual or instrument producing the sound, but perhaps also the particular culture from which the music derives. In vocal music, for example, certain cultures value purity of tone whereas others value tones that are grainy or strongly nasal. So too, some instruments have a harsher quality than others. An instrument's timbre depends on a combination of three factors: (1) the size of the instrument, (2) the material from which it is made, and (3) how the sound is produced (see sidebar, Musical Instrument Classification Systems). Playing styles can also influence instrumental timbre.

A symphony orchestra (sometimes just called "symphony," "orchestra," or "philharmonic") is a Western art music ensemble consisting of strings, woodwinds, brass, and percussion instruments. In the eighteenth century, when these ensembles were first established, the typical orchestra rarely had more than 30 players. Over the years, as concert halls became larger and as composers imagined new textures and timbres, the orchestra grew. Today's ensembles may include 100 or more instrumentalists.

Most large cities have a resident symphony orchestra. In the United States alone there are nearly 2,000 such ensembles, ranging from unpaid community groups to prestigious full-time ensembles employing some of the world's finest musicians. In the 2008/2009 season over 25 million people attended a symphony orchestra concert.

**"Kyrie eleison"
CD I/Track 4
Download track 4
mysearchlab 2.15**

Texture

The ways in which different musical parts fit together is called **texture**. Music can have different textures. A large orchestral texture might be thick, like velvet, whereas a solo flute might be silky thin. Music theorists categorize texture according to the following four characteristics.

1. Monophony
2. Polyphony
3. Homophony
4. Heterophony

Monophony consists of a single musical line without accompaniment. Even though many voices or instruments might be heard, as long as all are sounding the exact same line, the texture is monophonic.

This "Kyrie eleison" is an example of a monophonic, sacred chant from the Middle Ages (see chapter 6: Music and Spirituality). Notice that all of the voices are singing the same melody.

ACTIVITIES AND ASSIGNMENTS

- Have students who play instruments bring them to class to demonstrate. After hearing them played, try to describe their sound.
- Make an idiophone with things in your backpack or on your desk. Can you make a chordophone? An aerophone?
- Notice how people change the timbre and pitch of their voices when talking to babies, yelling at a sports referee, or talking in front of a crowd. How and why do you change the timbre of your voice?
- As you listen to the pieces discussed in later chapters, describe the timbre of the instruments you hear (nasal, clear, rough, etc.). Then consider how the timbre affects the meaning of the work.

Standard symphony orchestra seating arrangement.

QUESTIONS FOR THOUGHT

- Where does an acoustic instrument leave off and its electric counterpart begin? Rock guitarists, for example, create many new sounds through electronic effects.
- Theater companies, as well as TV and movie producers, try to save money by reproducing the sounds of instruments electronically rather than paying musicians. What effect does this have on the music? On the musicians?
- In the seventeenth and eighteenth centuries, the trombone was associated with the underworld and death. Are certain instruments associated with particular ideas today?

Polyphony involves several independent lines sounding simultaneously. The simplest kind of polyphony is a round (also called a canon). A good example is the children's song "Row, Row, Row, Your Boat" in which everyone begins singing the melody at a different time.

In more complex examples of polyphony, the independent melodies are not necessarily the same tune. Instead, complementary lines are woven together like threads in a tapestry. Much of the music of the Renaissance and Baroque periods was written polyphonically, and composers relied on a strict set of rules to combine the different lines. Later composers often used polyphony to indicate a "learned" or elevated style of music.

Listen to a six-voice polyphonic setting of a Kyrie eleison text by the Renaissance composer Giovanni Pierluigi da Palestrina (ca. 1525–1594). Notice how each voice enters separately, one after the other (see Figure 2.10 and chapter 6: Music and Spirituality).

FIGURE 2.11   Vocal shape and chord accompaniment for "Amazing Grace"

soprano	1	_____
alto	2	_____
tenor 1	3	_____
tenor 2	4	_____
bass 1	5	_____
bass 2	6	___

FIGURE 2.10   Diagram of voices in Palestrina's "Kyrie eleison"

Homophonic texture consists of a melody plus chordal accompaniment, such as a folk singer accompanying herself on guitar. The basic idea behind homophony is that the tones sound together as a whole rather than as individual parts. For example, when a musician strums a six-string guitar, the listener hears a single event comprised of six tones, rather than six individual melodies each with its own particular identity. In the Western tradition, the vast majority of hymns, folk tunes, and popular songs are set in a homophonic texture. Listen to the Robert Shaw Festival Singers singing "Amazing Grace." Concentrate on the texture, particularly the relationship between the melody and the accompanying chords (see chapter 6: Music and Spirituality).

MUSICAL TERMS

DYNAMICS

Dynamics refer to the volume of a note or passage of music. In Western music, Italian terms are used to indicate how loudly or softly to play.

Forte (*f*) = loud
Piano (*p*) = soft

Other dynamic markings include:

fortissimo (*ff*), louder than *forte*
mezzo-forte (*mf*), moderately loud
mezzo-piano (*mp*), moderately soft
pianissimo (*pp*), softer than piano

The term "crescendo" means to get louder, whereas "decrescendo" means to get softer.

Heterophony pertains to the same melody being performed slightly differently by two or more performers. For instance, one singer/player might add embellishments to his version of the melody in order to differentiate it from the main tune. Or, he might perform it with slightly different rhythms or a slightly different tempo from the other performer. This texture is uncommon in Western music, but is used quite often in Middle Eastern and Native American cultures.

Listen to "His First Hunt," sung by an Inuit couple from Repulse Bay, Canada. In this example you hear the singers each sounding a slightly different version of the same melody. Notice that one performer sings just a bit behind the other, and at times interprets the melody slightly differently. They sing together, but maintain independent musical voices.

"On his first hunt
He killed a fine seal
Even in the dark"

"Palestrina's Kyrie from the Pope Marcellus mass"
CD I/Track 5
Download track 5
mysearchlab 2.16

"Amazing Grace"
CD I/Track 6
Download track 6
mysearchlab 2.17

"His First Hunt"
CD I/Track 7
Download track 7
mysearchlab 2.18

ACTIVITIES AND ASSIGNMENTS

- With a partner, read the following words aloud in exact unison: "Monophonic music requires perfect blend." If you succeeded in being in unison, you performed in a monophonic style. Now, choose a new sentence that your partner does not know. Say it aloud and have your partner repeat what you say as she hears it. Inevitably, she will speak her words slightly behind yours, and maybe even leave out or change a word. This is heterophony.

MUSICAL TERMS

GENRES

The word "genre" means "type" or "kind." Most cultural artifacts (art, literature, cinema, music, etc.) are labeled according to genre (novel vs. poem; watercolor vs. oil painting, for example). The following list includes the more common genres of Western art music (i.e., those you are likely to encounter in a concert setting).

Song: a work for a solo vocalist, usually with piano accompaniment (note that the term "song" is not a generic term for all pieces of music).

Symphony: a large-scale work written for a symphony orchestra, usually consisting of three or four separate sections called movements.

Concerto: a work for a solo instrument accompanied by a symphony orch0estra, usually in three movements.

Sonata: a multi-movement piece either for solo piano or for piano plus one other instrument. For instance, a violin sonata would be for violin and piano.

Opera: a staged drama told in music.

Chamber music: any number of instrumental combinations written for nine or fewer players. The most prevalent is the string quartet, written for two violins, viola, and cello.

Form

Form refers to the overall shape or structure of a piece of music. Composers generally have a basic form in mind before starting to write. Sometimes the form is the composer's invention, but often it conforms to a traditional structure. Examples of traditional Western art music forms include **binary** (two parts); **ternary** (three parts); and **rondo**, in which a familiar **refrain** alternates with new material. Forms common to Western popular music include 32-bar song form and 12-bar blues. Composers use their full arsenal of musical elements to distinguish different sections of a form, including melody, rhythm, harmony, texture, and timbre. Through repetition, contrast, and development, composers can both set up and thwart expectations; they can create tension or relaxation, chaos or order.

mysearchlab 2.19

ACTIVITIES AND ASSIGNMENTS

- Find artworks or poetry (or create your own) that illustrate the equivalent of binary, ternary, and rondo forms. How are the different sections delineated?
- Experiment with writing your own music using software on mysearchlab. [www.noteflight.com/login] Try to incorporate aspects of each of the musical elements discussed in the text.

CONCLUSION

This chapter equipped us with a vocabulary comprising the basic tools used to describe, order, and analyze listening experience. In subsequent chapters we put these tools to use in making sense of our musical world. The repertoire is fantastically diverse, but our general analytical techniques can be applied universally. With practice we will hear new complexities within single compositions, as well as connections between different musical genres, musical cultures, and historical eras.

■ To demonstrate how the ideas introduced in chapter 2 can apply to musical examples from three different musical traditions.

QUESTIONS FOR THOUGHT

■ What first attracts you to a piece of music? The lyrics? The beat? The melody? The timbre? Why?
■ How might the above elements convey social meaning?
■ Can the social meaning of a piece of music change? If so, think of an example. How and why did its meaning change?

"When I don't like a piece of music, I make a point of listening to it more closely."

—Florent Schmidtt (1879–1958)

In chapter 2 we undertook a general overview of musical terminology. Now we apply these tools by studying three compositions. Each is from a different time and culture; in addition, each has a different social purpose. As you listen to the examples, keep in mind the various musical elements and how they express meaning.

"Bourrée" by J. S. Bach

If during a eulogy for German composer Johann Sebastian Bach (1685–1750), someone had stated that 250 years after his death the composer would be considered one of a handful of giants in Western art music, the Protestant mourners, though sure to remain respectful, would have found the idea incomprehensible. Bach was a skilled musician to be sure, but others, now mostly forgotten, were more highly regarded. Nevertheless, the eulogist's words would have been true. Few composers have cast a shadow as broad and enduring as J. S. Bach.

Bach lived his life within a limited geographical area. **mysearchlab 3:1** He was born in the town of Eisenach, spent most of his life in small towns, and never left Germany. Bach was content to labor in the background. He considered himself a craftsman and a hard worker. Neither fame nor fortune interested him. In fact, four of his sons were far more prominent composers than he.

Bach was best known as a skilled improviser and keyboardist. As a Lutheran church organist he was accustomed to inventing preludes and elaborating on hymn tunes for church services. These, however, were skills expected of any reasonably accomplished church musician.

How good an improviser was Bach? In May of 1747 he visited the Potsdam court of Frederick II of Prussia (Frederick the Great, 1712–1786), who was himself an accomplished amateur musician. During an evening of chamber music, the king presented Bach with a melody he had composed. Bach took the tune, sat down at the keyboard, and effortlessly improvised an intricate polyphonic composition called a **fugue**. The melody continued to hold Bach's attention. He went on to write 13 pieces, each a complex elaboration of the original melody. Bach dedicated the collection, known as *The Musical Offering*, to Frederick II.

Bach's compositional output was extraordinary. The catalog of his works (*Bach-Werke-Verzeichnis*, or BWV) lists over 1,000 compositions; the complete recorded set fills 153 CDs. Bach wrote for nearly every imaginable combination of instruments and voices. From works for solo violin to massive pieces for chorus and orchestra, Bach's output was of universally high quality. Many of his compositions—such as his sonatas and partitas for violin solo, *The Well-Tempered Clavier*, the *Brandenburg Concertos*, to name just a few—are considered among Western art music's greatest achievements.

German cities where J.S. Bach lived and worked.

Bach's first important job came in 1708 when the Duke of Weimar hired him as organist, chamber musician, and later as first violinist in the court orchestra. Six of his 20 children were born in Weimar. It was there that Bach wrote the first of his didactic works, the *Little Organ Book*, for his eldest son and future composer, Wilhelm Friedemann Bach (1710–1784).

Bach left Weimar nine years later to accept a position in the court of Prince Leopold of Cöthen. The transition was not easy, however. At first the Duke of Weimar refused Bach's resignation and even imprisoned him for "too stubbornly forcing the issue of his dismissal." After nearly four weeks in detention. Bach was granted an "unfavorable discharge" and allowed to move his family to Cöthen.

Once there, work went well. The prince was an amateur musician who enjoyed having music at court, but he was also a Calvinist, with little use for music in worship. Therefore, Bach's Cöthen output was mainly secular. He wrote mostly instrumental works for members of the court orchestra, including his six Brandenburg concertos.

In 1723 Bach moved his family to Leipzig, a cosmopolitan city of 30,000 that was also the site of the world's most prestigious German-speaking university. Bach spent the last 27 years of his life in Leipzig serving as music director at St. Thomas Church and as the city's Director of Music. His duties included composing, rehearsing, and performing music for the four main churches in Leipzig; overseeing music for the town council and university; and providing musical training for the 50 to 60 boys at the boarding school attached to St. Thomas Church.

| Johann Sebastian Bach.

As much as we now revere Bach's music, it was rarely performed in the years immediately following his death. Bach lived at a time when audiences were more interested in what was new; the past was invariably out of fashion. That attitude took a seismic shift in 1829 when 20-year-old German composer and conductor Felix Mendelssohn (1809–1847) put together a performance of the *St. Matthew Passion*, one of Bach's most important works (see chapter 6: Music and Spirituality). The audience was moved and intrigued by what it heard. Thus began not only the reintroduction of Bach's music to the public but also an interest in historical music in general.

LISTENING GUIDE

CD I/Track 8
Download track 8
mysearchlab 3.2

"BOURRÉE" FROM SUITE IN E MINOR, BWV 996   *by Johann Sebastian Bach*

Though the bourrée originated as a seventeenth-century French folk dance, by the mid-eighteenth century it was commonly danced by the nobility. Used both as a social courtship dance and in theatrical entertainments, bourrées were cheerful and lively, in duple meter, and began with a pickup beat. The dance opened with a plié (a slight bending of the knees), which provided the impetus to rise gracefully onto the balls of the feet and flow into a variety of gliding steps. Gentle leaps and hops often separated the steps.
mysearchlab 3.3

Bach and other composers of the Baroque period wrote bourrées (as well as other popular dances) and included them in instrumental **suites**. Comprising four to six different dances, a suite was meant for listening only. Even so, each dance retained its representative meter and character, thus reminding listeners of the social dances they knew so well.

(Continued)

LISTENING GUIDE (*Continued*)

Part 1 (A)

0:00	Phrase one (a)
0:05	Phrase two (b)

Part 1 (A) Repetition

0:11	Phrase one (a)
0:17	Phrase two (b)

Part 1 (A) consists of two angular phrases. Both begin in the upper register on "do," ascend to "me," and then meander up and down, eventually heading toward the bottom of the melody's range. The first phrase ends on "do," an octave below the first note of the phrase. Notice the octave leap that results when moving to phrase two. The second phrase begins like the first, but ends on "me." This and the relatively unstable harmonic underpinning propel the listener either back to the beginning (for the repeat) or on to the next section.

Try clapping the beat. Or better yet, walk to the beat so that you can feel the rhythm in your entire body. How quickly should you clap/step? Let your body and intuition tell you which rate is most appropriate. Perhaps you have noticed that the rhythm is extremely repetitive—short-short-long, short-short-long, and so on—and also extremely propulsive. Notice how the two quick tones push the melody (and your stepping body) forward.

Part 2 (B)

0:23	Phrase one (c)
0:29	Phrase two (d)
0:35	Phrase three (e)
0:41	Phrase four (f)

The B section is longer, with four separate phrases whose melodies differ from those in the A section. The short-short-long rhythmic motive carries over from the first section, but here the melodic contours are more jagged, or disjunct. The harmonies are also less stable than in the A section, creating a unified drive to the end of the last phrase. This section is then repeated.

Part 2 (B) Repetition

0:47	Phrase one repeated (c)
0:53	Phrase two repeated (d)
0:59	Phrase three repeated (e)
1:04	Phrase four repeated (f)

The overall form of this piece is AABB, or more simply, AB, known as binary form. There are many ways form can be delineated, but usually it is based on the concept of "same" and "different." Our brief example is organized according to same/different melodies. In the case of large-scale works, many more musical elements would work together to delineate the different sections.

So far we have concentrated on the music's melody, rhythm, and form. What else is happening? Below the melody is another line of music. It has less rhythmic interest than the top part and mostly moves along by keeping a steady beat. It does, however, have its own melodic character and could function independently as a separate tune, albeit a less interesting one. As we have learned, when two or more independent lines sound together, the resulting texture is polyphony.

Finally let's return to the social context of Bach's "Bourrée." How might this piece remind listeners of the dance? Can you envision the steps and hops? Why did Bach choose to emphasize the short-short-long rhythmic pattern? And considering that the bourrée was a cheerful dance, why did Bach write this work in a minor key? Here is a case where the minor scale does not correspond to its oft-associated "sad" affect. Perhaps Bach was trying to portray a more serious bourrée, one befitting the nobility rather than the folk. Or perhaps Bach's bourrée is more reflective than cheerful—evoking the reminiscence of the dance, rather than the dance itself.

The instrument playing is a guitar, but Bach actually wrote the piece for a keyboard instrument. Today, one can hear this composition on almost any instrument and in a variety of styles. It was a favorite of Led Zeppelin guitarist Jimmy Page (b. 1944), who often attached it to his improvised solo in the song "Heartbreaker." It was also a favorite of Ian Anderson (b. 1947), flutist in the 1960s rock group Jethro Tull. It is one of Bach's most recognized pieces. **mysearchlab 3.4**

Music from Japan

Our discussion of the Bach "Bourrée" demonstrated some basic principles in the composition of Western art music. Many of those principles are employed in traditions around the world . . . although not all, of course. Our next example, a composition for the Japanese *shakuhachi* bamboo flute, offers a different set of compositional principles and aesthetics.

First, however, we provide some history. Though long associated with Japan, the shakuhachi was invented in China, where it was known as the *chiba*. The instrument was brought to the Japanese islands in the eighth century as part of a mixed instrumental ensemble used to accompany the courtly music and dance genre, *gagaku*. **mysearchlab 3.5**

Though gagaku has continuously thrived in Japan, the shakuhachi apparently did not. The marriage of instrument to genre ended by the tenth century. At that point, the shakuhachi mostly disappeared from the historical record for some 500 years.

During the late seventeenth and eighteenth centuries, the shakuhachi again rose to prominence. It was also during this time that it attained its contemporary physical form. The modified instrument was thicker and heavier than earlier versions and had a slightly flared end.

Perhaps these were aesthetic choices. Equally possible was that the changes accommodated the instrument's double use as a defensive weapon when carried by monks of the Fuke sect of Zen Buddhism. Wearing basket-like hats (*tengai*) over their heads to hide their identities, these monks, many former samurai warriors, walked the dangerous countryside playing their shakuhachis and begging for alms. Also, or so it is believed, they worked as spies on behalf of the government.

Whatever the monks' political motives, they apparently became formidable instrumentalists. Primarily, they played the instrument as a meditative exercise, as a way to focus breathing and discipline the mind. It was also during this time that a standard repertoire developed. Many of these compositions were written down and preserved. They are still taught today.

The Meiji Restoration of 1868, which ended nearly seven centuries of Japanese feudalism, centralized government and initiated waves of cultural reform. Two such reforms were the banishment of the Fuke sect and a proscription against using the shakuhachi for religious purposes. Again, the instrument was adapted to fit new interests. The repertoire was secularized and music notation improved. New theoretical ideas were developed, and compositions began to be written for ensembles of different-sized instruments.

This last development might seem strange, since the word shakuhachi specifically refers to the instrument's size. A *shaku* is a little less than one foot in length; *hachi* stands for 8/10 of a *shaku*. Thus, a shakuhachi equals a length of just under 1.8 feet. Today, while this size

A shakuhachi.

LISTENING GUIDE

CD I/Track 9
Download track 9
mysearchlab 3.6

"NEZASA SHIRABE"   *Performed by Tadashi Tajima*

"Nezasa Shirabe," like nearly all traditional shakuhachi music, is built on a **pentatonic** (five-tone) scale: do-re-me-sol-ley, which, to the Western ear, gives the impression of a minor tonality. **mysearchlab 2.3**

As you listen to the piece, try to breathe in sync with the musician. Notice how long your breaths become, perhaps how time itself seems to expand. The music has no pulse, no meter. Instead it seems to float alongside the slow rhythm of the breath.

Nezasa is a branch of northern Japan's Kinpû school; a *shirabe* is a short introductory piece, generally of a meditative character. Sometimes shirabe stand alone; other times they are attached to the beginnings of longer compositions. The music is designed to warm up both shakuhachi and performer. A particular trait of this piece is the *komibuki* (pulsating breath), a technique designed to focus the mind.

0:00	The opening gesture is a downward movement: a short upper **grace note** followed by a long held tone (sol-re). We cannot know it yet, but the gesture lands on the lowest pitch in the composition. It will also be the tone on which the music concludes. Notice how Tajima colors the tone by constantly changing its inflections through komibuki, vibrato, dynamics, and subtle pitch bending.
0:12	The second gesture is more or less opposite the first in that it leaps up to, and then sustains, the same tone that served as the grace note at the music's beginning (sol-re-sol).
0:21	A movement to "ley" (though only the third of five possible pitches) gives complete shape to the pentatonic scale, which an experienced listener will now hear in his inner musical road map. "Do," a new high point in the melody, is briefly sounded, then a return down to "sol."
0:47	As Tajima continues his slow upward exploration, it seems as if every movement upward is followed by another small one in the opposite direction. He reaches a new high pitch, "re," then settles back down to "do" before continuing to move upward to "me" at 0:56, "sol" at 1:13, and "ley" at 1:20.
1:25	The composition, just short of halfway complete, reaches its upper limit sitting on the tones "do" and then "re" at 1:35. This is the music's climax, which is followed by a meandering descent to the original pitch area.
2:33 – 2:42	Finally, repeating the gestures with which the composition began, the melody returns to its opening tones. The return signals the music's end.

We have heard that the piece unfolds along an undulating arc moving generally from low to high and back down again. We have also noticed that the same melodic and rhythmic gestures open and close the composition. How else might you describe the music? Meditative? Austere?

Finally, notice that many of the skills used to understand Bach's "Bourrée" are useful in understanding "Nezasa Shirabe." In both we hear the outlines of organized form, the use of repeated melodic gestures, and applications of rhythmic gestures. Despite the many obvious differences in mechanical application, social use, and emotional effect, the pieces also have much in common.

remains common, shakuhachis come in a variety of sizes.

The shakuhachi proves that simplicity of design is no indication for ease of performance. It is notoriously difficult to play. Breath control can takes years to master. Pitch inflection, which is achieved by changing the angle of the breath and by partially uncovering any of the five finger holes, is a subtle and essential aspect of performance.

Japan today has a number of shakuhachi playing schools. Each is associated with a characteristic style and a particular lineage of teachers. Although the instrument has lost many of its sacred connotations, links to Zen Buddhism remain. This can be heard in the slow unfolding tempo of performance and the common practice of focusing on just a single extended tone, despite the instrument's range of about three octaves.

Understanding American Popular Song: "Over the Rainbow"

In 1938, at the age of 16, child film star Judy Garland (1922–1969) was cast as Dorothy Gale in the Metro-Goldwyn-Mayer film *The Wizard of Oz* (1939). It was the role of a lifetime for a young woman with a once-in-a-generation voice. "Over the Rainbow," by composer Harold Arlen (1905–1986) and lyricist E. Y. Harburg (1896–1981), became an American standard and one of the most recorded songs in history.

We close this chapter by analyzing two different "Rainbow" recordings. The first is Garland's original from the motion picture soundtrack. The second was recorded by jazz pianist Art Tatum (1909–1956). The performances, which could hardly be more different, give an idea of the interpretive range that skilled musicians bring to their work.

LISTENING GUIDE

CD I/Track 10
Download track 10
mysearchlab 3.7

"OVER THE RAINBOW" BY HAROLD ARLEN AND E. Y. HARBURG

Recorded in 1938 with vocalist Judy Garland

We begin with the Garland version, not just because it came earlier, but also because it is by far the easier performance to understand. Listen to the first verse and its graceful melody.

The melody begins on the word "Somewhere" with the inspirational upward leap of a full octave from "do" to "do." It is a lovely beginning, an affirmation of a young girl's dreams of the world she hopes some day to see. From there, the melody loops downward slightly but finishes the line ("rain*bow*") back at the upper tonic. The second half of the phrase ("Way up high") also begins on "do" but lacks the energy of the full octave leap. Instead it jumps to "la" before settling on "sol" with the word "high." It seems that "high" is not so high after all, at least not as high as Dorothy's dreamy "Some*where*."

The pause on "sol" is structurally important. It sets up a downward near-octave fall from one phrase to the next—that is, from the word "high" to "There's" on the pitch "la" below the opening "do." With that tone Arlen has given the limits of the song's melodic frame, nearly an octave and one-half. Also notice the symmetry—the leap upward to the song's highest note has been balanced by a fall downward to its lowest note. With the final syllable of "lullaby" the melody ends back home, on the same pitch that it began.

What about the accompaniment? Soft tones from orchestral strings and winds contribute to the dreamy atmosphere. There are no stark lines; there is little sense of meter. A clarinet, which is hardly noticeable within the texture, plays a counter melody to Garland's.

Now take notice of Harburg's equally well-crafted lyrics. Stanzas one, two, and four begin the same, with the line "Somewhere over the rainbow." All three stanzas also rhyme lines two and four (high/lullaby, blue/true, fly/I), creating a rhyme scheme of ABCB. Notice also that stanza four returns to the rhymes of stanza one, yet another one of the song's many symbols of returning home.

Contrast stanzas one, two, and four with stanza three, which is the odd one out. Here the words come faster and the rhymes are more complex. The opening line's closing word "star" is rhymed with an interior word "far" in the following line. This allows Harburg to complete the rhyme scheme with "me"/"me" and "drops"/"tops," thus creating a stanza rhyme scheme of A(A)BCCB.

You have probably noticed that stanzas one, two, and four all have the same melody and that stanza three is different. Building from this we can analyze the large-scale melodic material of the four stanzas as fitting a model of AABA.

Listen to the song again and tap a beat along to the melody. You will notice that all four stanzas are exactly the same length, eight complete measures. Your beats should fall in the following places:

beats 1 and 2 (Some . . .), beats 3 and 4 (where . . .) = one measure

Continue to map out the measures and place the words underneath the appropriate beats.

Now, finally, we are in a position to give the song's structure a name. It is 32-bar song form, consisting of four equally sized sections of eight measures in the melodic framework of AABA. Many thousands of songs have been written in this form, from nineteenth-century art songs to rhythm and blues.

Perhaps you have noticed that the 32-bar song form seems to ignore the song's final two lines. These lines are an optional addition to the form, called a **coda** ("tail"). If a performer were to expand on the general 32-bar form, perhaps with improvisation or by adding additional stanzas, the coda would not be played until the song's end.

What other things might you choose to listen for? We suggest you listen to Garland's voice, to the way she inflects the melody, to her use of vibrato, and to the general character of her voice. Is she convincing in her delivery? Does she sound like a young girl?

LISTENING GUIDE

CD I/Track 11
Download track 11
mysearchlab 3.8

"OVER THE RAINBOW"

Performed by Art Tatum

"I used to close my eyes when we worked together, thinking that maybe if I couldn't see, I might learn to hear like Art."
—jazz vocalist Jon Hendricks (b. 1921)

Cursed with near blindness from early childhood but blessed with perfect pitch, pianist Art Tatum (1909–1956) was an iconic and controversial figure in the world of jazz. Fans and fellow musicians found his vivid and eclectic musical imagination unsurpassed. So too were his technical skills. No jazz pianist, before or since, has gotten around the piano keyboard with a more formidable combination of spontaneity, power and lightness, speed and groove. Curiously, Tatum's critics found fault with the same qualities his supporters admired. They found his imagination rich, but undisciplined, and his technique so intrusive as to overwhelm the music itself. Although these controversies continue, today Tatum's large catalog of recordings, the vast majority done on a single take, serves as a sonic textbook for both aspiring and well-established musicians.

A child prodigy, Tatum was born and raised in Toledo, Ohio. And like so many successful black American musicians, he grew up in the shadow of the church. Both parents were musically involved at Toledo's Grace Presbyterian Church, where his mother was the pianist. Tatum learned to improvise on church hymns while still a small boy. Elsewhere, he received formal instruction in classical music, the results of which can be heard in his penchant for lightning-fast melodic runs, metric interruptions, and complex harmonizations—qualities also central to the music of Europe's nineteenth-century virtuoso pianist/composers, such as Frederic Chopin (1810–1848) and Franz Liszt (1811–1886).

However strong Tatum's early attraction to classical music may have been (he often improvised on classical melodies), those sounds could not offer a career path for African Americans in the 1920s. Jazz did. While still in his teens, Tatum got his own radio show. He was also a regular performer, often with Jon Hendricks, at the Waiters' and Bellmans' Club, the "black and tan" (that is, racially integrated) nightclub that formed the heart of Toledo's then vital jazz scene. Tatum moved to New York City in the early 1930s where he spent much of the rest of his brief life.

Stylistically, Tatum's music is hard to categorize. He performed mostly as a soloist. (Perhaps describing him as a one-man orchestra is

Jazz pianist Art Tatum, c. 1946.

most accurate.) Playing alone allowed Tatum the freedom to give his musical eccentricities and eclecticism their full range. Though he began his career as a "stride" pianist (a style in which the left hand moves quickly between bass line and chords) and he could "swing" as well as anyone. Tatum often abandoned stride's muscularity to insert lush chords and idiosyncratic runs. While he occasionally played the blues (see chapter 4: Music and Ethnicity), the pianist seemed most at home with the more intricate harmonies characteristic of the **American Songbook**, that is, music drawn from musical theater and film, and **Tin Pan Alley**.

"Over the Rainbow" is an American Songbook classic, of course. It was also a staple in Tatum's repertoire. He recorded the song on multiple occasions, each time performing it differently. The first surviving recording comes from a radio broadcast made just six weeks after the movie *The Wizard of Oz* was released. The version we have here, from sometime in the early 1950s, was recorded in a private home in Beverly Hills, California.

Listen to Tatum's recording. So thick are the textures and so extravagant the melodic additions and harmonic alterations that the first time through you may feel rather overwhelmed, if not altogether lost. Keep the original melody in mind and try to follow the AABA form.

(Continued)

LISTENING GUIDE (*Continued*)

0:00	First stanza	(A)
0:15	Second stanza	(A)
0:29	Third stanza	(B)
0:48	Fourth stanza	(A)

The performance begins in a relatively straightforward fashion. Tatum sounds an opening chord, reinforces it in the bass, and then plays the melody ("Somewhere, over the rainbow"). The song's original harmonies are embellished but the general rhythmic movement is forward. The line "Way up high," however, is much more embellished. The original melody is obscured under Tatum's improvisatory filigree. Notice how Tatum rushes through the final words of the stanza ("Once in a lullaby").

The same basic strategy is followed for stanza two. Throughout the song, Tatum keeps the beginning of the musical phrases relatively straightforward. The most extensive embellishment comes at a phrase's end.

In the B stanza ("Someday I'll wish upon a star . . ."), Tatum's improvisatory abstractions virtually subsume the original melody. Exotic harmonies are introduced; the tempo rushes forward only to pull back a moment later. Try to find the melody tones. Most of them are there, but they are hidden inside thick chords and sometimes displaced across octaves.

1:05	First stanza	(A)
1:24	Second stanza	(A)
1:44	Third stanza	(B)
2:04	Fourth stanza	(A)

Rhythmically, the performance divides into three main sections. The first time through the AABA form, Tatum repeatedly breaks the rhythmic flow to allow room for his melodic expeditions. The music has a stop-and-go quality to it. On first hearing Tatum, one might imagine that this sort of rhythmic discontinuity is a requisite part of the pianist's style, the only way to squeeze in his melodic and harmonic ideas. But the second time through the AABA form demonstrates that this is not the case. Here Tatum uses a left-hand stride technique that, though occasionally abandoned, propels the music forward. It is easy to tap your foot and never lose the beat. The final (partial) repeat of the form (an extended coda beginning at 2:25) returns to the generally nonmetric feel that opened the performance. Looking at the overall rhythmic structure, we can see that Tatum organized it in an AB(a) (that is, nonmetric/metric/nonmetric), or **rounded binary**, form.

2:25	Third stanza	(B)
2:47	Fourth stanza	(A)

One gets the impression that Tatum particularly enjoyed the B section of "Over the Rainbow," which receives some of the most extensive and lush harmonizations. Notice how in signaling the end of the performance he jumped directly to B. (Garland's coda did the same thing: "If happy little bluebirds fly . . ."). But while Tatum also makes the jump in coda-like fashion, rather than simply using the B section as closing material, he continues to explore new ideas. This move requires Tatum to add a final shortened A stanza to achieve a balanced sense of completion.

CONCLUSION

We have seen that while musical compositions are extremely complex in the aggregate, they are built from many separate, and relatively simple, elements. By investigating these elements individually through careful listening and thoughtful analysis, even highly intricate music becomes understandable.

In the following chapters we will look at many different kinds of music. We will explore the technical make-up of representative works in order to understand how they were conceived and composed. We will also study how music influences and reflects the social world in which it is created and performed. We will learn that musical sounds and functions vary considerably according to time and place, social identity and aesthetics. Finally, we will come to understand how exploring our musical world offers rich insights into the human condition.

CHAPTER GOALS

- To investigate the ways in which music reflects ethnic identity and values.

- To investigate the ways in which musical ethnicity crosses cultural and social boundaries.

- To become familiar with musical expressions of ethnicity in a few selected times and places.

QUESTIONS FOR THOUGHT

- What is your ethnic background or heritage? Does your family express this background in particular ways, such as through music or dance, or perhaps cooking styles or fashion? If so, when and how?
- Have you ever spent a holiday or special occasion with a family whose ethnicity is different from your own? How did this experience compare with the way things are done within your own home?
- How many different ethnicities are formally represented at your school? Do they ever sponsor special activities or events? If so, what is the music like?

Perrysburg, Ohio

Buffalo steaks sizzle on grills as crowds stroll toward the sounds of Sioux-style singing and drumming emanating from the nearby performance ring. The dancers, who have come to the powwow from cities and towns across North America, wear the traditional clothing of their various ethnic groups, including Cherokee, Seminole, Ojibwe, Navaho, and many more. Later, a blond-haired, blue-eyed dancer tells the audience that she is Native American. It is our experiences and worldview, not genes, that make us who we are, she says.

This chapter is the first of three chapters that explore the ways in which music reflects and gives shape to social identity. Here we focus on the concept of ethnicity, a central building block in the establishment of one's sense of self, home, and community.

What do we mean by "ethnicity"? According to textbook definitions, ethnic groups are bound by shared identity and common ancestry, that is, by a combination of lived experiences and genetic materials. But as our blond-haired dancer would argue, today's social realities are not so easily encapsulated. Ethnic borders are often porous and difficult to delineate.

In order to develop a better understanding of ethnicity in general and of "ethnic music" in particular, we draw examples from a tiny sampling of the world's many ethnic groups. As we do so, you might sense that the distinctions between ethnicity and race are blurry. Perhaps you will even begin to wonder if you might best identify yourself as belonging to multiple ethnic groups.

As an activity:

- Go to **mysearchlab 4.1** and watch a video of fancy dancers performing at the 202nd annual Omaha Nation Powwow in Macy, Nebraska, in 2006.
- Attend a powwow.

The *Jalolu*: Musician/Historians of West Africa

Seated inside a family compound in The Gambia, West Africa, a *jali* (pl.: *jalolu*, Fr.: *griot*) remembers the life of a recently deceased elderly Mandinka chief. There is much to say. One by one, the chief's accomplishments are recounted. The jali's tale gradually expands outward to include the man's family and friends. Genealogies are traced, and life histories are expounded. Sometimes the praise singer's meaning is clear. Other times, words are cloaked in symbolism that only the elders understand. Such a performance might continue long into the night.

AFRICA

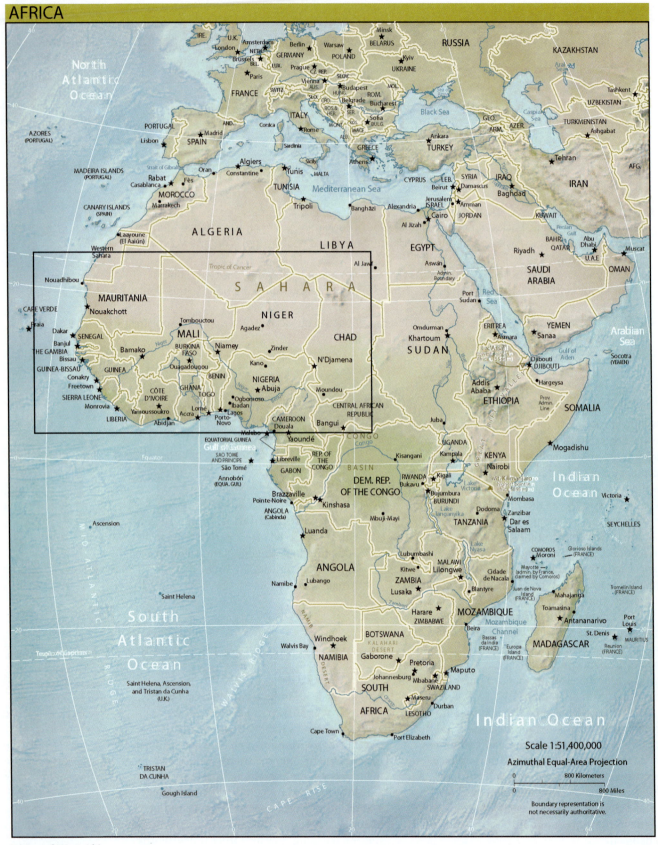

Map of West Africa.

Perhaps the jali tells the history of the Mandinka ethnic group itself, a tale that crosses centuries and details the rise and fall of civilizations. The jali might reach all the way back to the warrior/king Sundiata Keita (ca. 1217–ca. 1255), founder of West Africa's vast Mali Empire (1234–1600) and spiritual father of the Mandinka people. As the story unfolds, the jali links past to present, thus offering insights on how best to prepare for the future.

The jali accompanies himself with the *kora*, a plucked 21-stringed chordophone. With a range of three octaves, the kora's soft interlocking melodies provide a kaleidoscopic tonal foundation for song. Between vocal lines, the kora comes to the musical foreground, perhaps echoing a melody just sung, perhaps improvising sounds altogether new. Together, voice and kora form a balanced pair, each supporting the other.

Sometimes described as "casted bards," for at least 800 years the jalolu have sung the history of the Mandinka. They are born into their profession, and training begins in early childhood. Learning is a lifelong enterprise that involves memorization of social history, skill in rhetoric, and training as a singer and/or instrumentalist. A jali's most important characteristic, however, is integrity. A jali must tell the truth.

In the past, the jalolu were attached to chiefs. But with the political decline of chieftaincies, along with the rise of the nation-state and market-based social systems, the jalolu's clientele has broadened. Today's jalolu sing for politicians, businessmen, religious leaders, and community members. They perform at naming ceremonies, weddings, funerals, and all other socially important events. A number have developed successful careers in the commercial music industry.

The kora is the instrument that has most captured the imagination of Western listeners, but it is only one of a number of melodic instruments a jali might play. Others include the *balafon* (xylophone); the five-stringed *ngoni* lute; and the *bolon*, an arched harp. Traditional gender roles dictate that female jalolu generally do not play instruments, but they are considered excellent singers. Men provide instrumental accompaniment for women, other male vocalists, and themselves. Generally, a solo singer takes a leading role in presenting the historical narrative. Often, other jalolu support the soloist by singing a repetitive

African kora.

refrain. Music scholars call this solo/chorus song style "call and response."

Jalolu music making features sets of balanced oppositions: solo/chorus, song/narrative, male/female roles, and vocal/instrumental combinations. The vocal and instrumental aspects each divide into two styles. Instrumental playing comprises accompanimental (*kumbengo*) and soloistic (*birimintingo*) styles. Kumbengo melodies support song by providing a tonal backdrop. Because there is no singing during birimintingo improvisations, these virtuosic sections provide opportunities for listeners to reflect on the jali's story.

Jalolu divide vocal styles into the categories *donkilo* and *sataro*. Donkilo is the composition's basic tune, often consisting of a short phrase that is repeated time and again throughout the performance. If, for example, a jali were telling the story of Sundiata Keita, he might set to the donkilo melody the words, "the master of a hundred kings." With each donkilo repetition, the idea of Sundiata's power is reaffirmed. Over time that concept of power is woven inseparably into the story and into the listeners' minds. With words so closely associated to a particular melody, eventually the phrase's meaning will be "heard" in the melody alone, even if played by the kora.

Sataro is speech-like verse that includes proverbs, praise, and other commentary. It flows free of the kora's established melody and rhythmic meter. In sataro, information can be quickly distributed. Therefore, a jali will move to sataro when she/he has much to say, wants to move the story forward, or simply wants to increase the dramatic pace.

LISTENING GUIDE

CD I/Track 12
Download track 12
mysearchlab 4.2

"KELEFABA" AND "KURUNTU KELAFA" (MEDLEY)   *Performed by Foday Musa Suso*

0:00	(. . . recording begins in the midst of a performance.) Kora fades in with a series of kumbengo-style accompaniment figures. Listen to the repeating bass line that provides the foundation for the previous tones.
0:24	Improvisation in the birimintingo style
0:34	Kora begins simple kumbengo-style accompaniment figure
0:40	Foday Musa Suso sings in donkilo style the song "Kelefaba":

Mindolo banta. Malama la mindolo banta	The millet beer is finished, The millet beer is finished.
Kelefaba la mindolo banta.	The great Kelefa's millet beer is gone.

The song tells about the exploits of the nineteenth-century Mandinka mercenary Kelefa Sanneh, who fought along the Gambia River for the kingdom of Nyomi against neighboring Jokadu. Notice the general downward trend of the melody (do-ti-la-sol . . . sol-la-sol-fa-mi . . . and all the way down to "do").

1:16	Extended birimintingo solo
1:50	Short kumbengo section
2:00	Birimintingo
2:30	Kumbengo
2:36	Closing section of "Kelefaba" (Notice the same melody as at 0:40.)
2:52	New song: "Kuruntu Kelefa" ("Trailing Kelefa") Kora plays in the kumbengo style as the singer **riffs** in donkilo style on the phrase:

Mansa jalo kuma fo baga le,	The king's jali says,
"Kari siya jama, a kela man siya."	"Those who talk are many, but those who act are few."

3:02	Kora in birimintingo style

Legend says that this song was played by Kelefa's personal jali as he followed his master in various exploits.

ACTIVITIES AND ASSIGNMENTS

- Find jalolu performances on the Internet. Compare and contrast them.
- View Malian kora virtuoso Toumani Diabaté's *The Mande Variations*, available on the Internet. He demonstrates kumbengo and birimintingo. The video also includes a section on kora construction.

QUESTIONS FOR THOUGHT

- The sound of the kora is very beautiful in its own right. Imagine a jalolu kora performance without song. Would this be complete? Why or why not?
- Imagine that you are a jali. What would you sing about? How much of your own family's history could you tell? What about the history of the place where you live?
- Think about the music you know well. Can you identify any instrumental melodies to which you automatically hear the implicit words?

Ethnicity in a Changing World

We have presented the jalolu as representatives of the Mandinka, an ethnic group of some 11 million people found across West Africa in coastal countries stretching from Senegal to Côte d'Ivoire and inland to landlocked Mali. The Mandinka are bound together by common ancestry, language, and tradition. Farming forms the basis of their economy. Islam is nearly universally practiced, though it is generally infused with older beliefs and rituals. The Mandinka have their own language but no written script. Their oral histories, as sung by the jalolu, are some of the world's richest.

The Mandinka are an ethnic subgroup of a still larger group of West African people known as the Mande, which includes the Bafour, Malinke, Kpelle, Dyula, and other subgroups. Anthropologists generally speak of Mande as a cultural group made up of a variety of ethnicities.

In the section that follows we trace aspects of West African ethnic heritage across the Atlantic Ocean to the United States, where it was transformed to fit new surroundings, social needs, and personal interests. Eventually, we will return to Africa itself. From there, we present case studies of musical ethnicity in other parts of the world. In each example we will see how music is adopted and adapted according to specific needs of time and place, values and identity.

QUESTIONS FOR THOUGHT

- Ethnicity is often seen through the political lens of a nation. In the United States, for example, we speak of African Americans, Asian Americans, and so on. What sorts of differences do these terms imply? Are those implications accurate?
- Can you think of musical differences among American ethnic groups?

The African Diaspora: *The Blues*

Four and one-half centuries of trans-Atlantic slavery resulted in as many as 10 million Africans captured, chained, and transported to the Americas where they were sold as chattel. African slaves brought almost no material culture with them to the New World. What they did bring, however, was a rich and vital social culture. African ways of thinking and acting, of cooking and farming, and of making music and dance all took root across the Americas. In later chapters we will study African-derived New World religious and dance traditions. Here, we focus on the **blues**, a form that grew out of the African American experience in the Mississippi Delta.

The earliest blues reach back to the late nineteenth century. The genre began as a rural tradition with roots in African American work songs, field hollers, and spirituals. African aspects of these sources are apparent in social values (storytelling, group participation, and improvisation) and musical style (call-and-response, rhythmic groove, and sliding pitches). One hears echoes of the jalolu/kora tradition in the relationship between a blues singer and his guitar accompaniment.

In the 1920s and 1930s, singer/guitarists such as Lead Belly (1888–1949), Charlie Patton (1891–1934), and Robert Johnson (1911–1938) codified the blues into the form we know today. They honed their repertory in traveling shows and town squares, **juke joints**, and nightclubs. The emerging blues style was rough but distinctive. It was simple in form but capable of endless nuance. Like the jalolu an ocean away, blues artists focused on human experience. Songs spoke of everyday life, and often of broken love and troubled times.

The blues changed as its popularity grew and as it moved from the rural South to the urban North. The instrumental and vocal sounds remained muscular, but the packaging became sleeker. Performance formats grew from solos and duos to small ensembles. Arrangements became tighter, and improvisation more formalized.

There are a number of standard blues forms. The most common is the **12-bar blues**, which divides neatly into three sections of four measures (bars) each. Over the course of 12 measures, the song's lyrics go through a single cycle, as do the chords.

Generally, the lyrics of a 12-bar blues song contain two different lines of text. The first line is sung across the first four measures of the 12-bar cycle, then is repeated over the next four measures. The second line is sung in the final four measures. Thus, the lyric form is a simple AAB.

Consider the lyrics from "Cross Road Blues" by Robert Johnson. **mysearchlab 4.3** The first line sets the scene and serves to attract the listener's interest:

A. *Was standin' at the crossroad, tried to flag a ride*

   Think about the lyrics' implications and imagine the scene. Why a crossroad? Why is he hitchhiking? Where is he going? What does the crossroad look like? Rather than provide answers, Johnson repeats the line. As is common in the blues, he alters the words slightly:

A. *Ooo eeee, I tried to flag a ride.*

   Okay, but there must be more to the story. We want to know what happened. What was he doing there? Did anyone pick him up? With the B line, the singer partially satisfies our desire for more information:

B. *Didn't nobody seem to know me. Everybody pass me by.*

Certain themes pop up repeatedly in the blues. Songs are about hard times, social isolation, sex (mostly good), love (often gone bad), money (mostly needing it), and the patient endurance required in the face of hardship. The singers themselves are outsiders—roaming, rambling, living hand-to-mouth—and often seen as living outside social norms. These characters had a powerful effect on the American imagination. Robert Johnson and other early blues singers form the prototype for rebellious rockers from Elvis Presley (1935–1977) to Mick Jagger (b. 1943) to Kurt Cobain (1967–1994).

Lead Belly performing in Washington, D.C., c. 1946.

MUSICAL THEMES

"CROSS ROAD BLUES"

Robert Johnson's "Cross Road Blues" is a classic early blues song, covered countless times over the past 70 years. Listen to Johnson's recordings and you will notice that he does not follow the 12-bar form exactly. Some phrases are longer than expected; others are shorter.

What is the song about? Ask five people and you will probably get five different answers. Folk legend says that Johnson went to the crossroads to make a bargain with the devil—his soul for guitar virtuosity. Others say the crossroads is a religious symbol associated with *Legba*, a West African trickster spirit. Still others reject the African connections but like the idea that danger lurks at crossroads—places where ideas and people intersect, and where decisions (right or wrong) are made. Another theory argues that the song is about the danger that African Americans felt when traveling in the white South. Still others will say the song is simply about hard times, about trying to hitchhike when no one stops.

Perhaps there is truth to all of these interpretations. Blues lyrics are often ambiguous, open to a variety of readings. A good blues song invites you to reflect upon your own experiences or perhaps to compare and contrast your experiences against those of the singer.

For a very different interpretation of "Cross Road Blues," listen to "Crossroads" as recorded in 1968 by the British rock band Cream, which featured guitarist Eric Clapton (b. 1945). Footage of Cream performing "Crossroads" can be found on various Internet sites.

LISTENING GUIDE

CD I/Track 13
Download track 13
mysearchlab 4.4

"SWEET LITTLE ANGEL"   *by B. B. King (b. 1925)*

Listen to this classic 12-bar blues song by guitarist B. B. King. It begins with a 12-bar introduction, followed by 24 bars of vocals (two cycles), followed by 12 bars of the band playing riffs, then 12 bars of King soloing on guitar. Follow the chords (I-IV-I-I-IV-IV-I-I-V-IV-I-V), which fit one to a bar. To hold your place within the form, use the snare drum backbeat, which plays on beats two and four of each bar.

0:00	Instrumental introduction 12 bars
0:48	A (bars 1–4)
	(1) I've got a sweet little angel, (2). . . . . . .
	I IV
	(3) I love the way she spread her (4) wings
	I I
1:03	A (bars 5–8)
	(5) I've got a sweet little angel, (6). . . . . I love the
	IV IV
	(7) way she spread her wings. (8). . . . .
	I I
1:17	B (bars 9–12)
	(9) When she spreads her wings around me, (10). . . . . . . I get joy
	V IV
	(11) in everything. (12). . . . .
	I V

(Continued)

LISTENING GUIDE (*Continued*)

King exploits a variety of vocal timbres as he bends pitches and jumps back and forth between **chest voice** and **falsetto**. Listen to King's singing and compare it to his guitar playing. Are there any similarities?

The following are things to try with the music:

1. Sing the root (bottom) tones of the chord changes along with the recording

I	IV	I	I	//	IV	IV	I	I	//	V	IV	I	V
do	fa	do	do	//	fa	fa	do	do	//	sol	fa	do	sol

2. Sing the words along with King. Then, sing the words during the solos. See if you can hold your place inside the form.
3. Improvise your own solo. You might start small by singing little interjections against the words or the guitar.
4. Consider the meaning of the words. What sort of "angel" is this woman?
5. Write a verse about your own ideal "little angel."

QUESTIONS FOR THOUGHT

- Is social experience an important aspect of authentic blues? What does "authentic" mean? Are some blues less "authentic" than others? If a Japanese garage band covers "Cross Road Blues," is that still the blues, or is there a necessary social component to "authentic" blues?
- Robert Johnson used just his guitar to play the blues. B.B. King uses a band comprised of highly skilled sidemen. What effect did solo versus ensemble performance have on the blues form?
- Are words an essential part of the blues?
- Does the choice of musical instruments matter? Is the blues still "the blues" if performed by a symphony orchestra? "Composed" by a computer program?

American Popular Song

American music need not be in the blues format to reference African heritage. Consider the classic 1937 song "Caravan," which was written in 32-bar song form (see chapter 3, "Over the Rainbow") by Edward Kennedy "Duke" Ellington (1899–1974) and Juan Tizol (1900–1984). Even today, the song invokes an exotic atmosphere laced with feral danger.

How are these effects achieved? First, there is Tizol's restlessly chromatic and undulating melody. Behind this, Ellington adds harmonization that is simultaneously lush and dissonant. Finally, there is Ellington's **orchestration**. Then Ellington added accompanying instruments to deepen the effect: "African" tom-toms beat; a trumpet growls. Taken as a whole, "Caravan" presents a soundscape of unprecedented exoticism, one that seems to invoke America's deepest imaginings about the place Westerners once called the Dark Continent.

Using music to create powerful imagery was standard procedure for Ellington, who wanted his music to have what he called "representative character." Nearly everything he wrote—whether the subject matter was love, city life, dance, or spirituality—was meant to inspire a vivid sense of place and attitude. Invariably, Ellington's music reflected the life he lived and the world his audiences imagined.

Juan Tizol playing trombone with the Ellington band, c. 1943.

Part of Ellington's genius was that his music made use of the unique backgrounds, talents, and personal styles of his bandsmen. Each musician was encouraged to contribute his own individual personality. Some band members, such as drummer Sonny Greer (1895–1982) and trumpeter Arthur Whetsol (1905–1940), had been Ellington's childhood friends. Others brought to the group a wealth of regional styles. The earthy sounds of New Orleans can be heard in the playing of trumpeter Bubber Miley (1903–1932) and clarinetist Barney Bigard (1906–1980). Trombonist Joe "Tricky" Sam Nanton (1904–1946), along with trumpeters Miley and Charles "Cootie" Williams (1911–1985), specialized in "jungle" growls. Puerto Rico native Juan Tizol added Caribbean colors and grooves.

Ellington's songs often referenced African American heritage and culture. His early compositions include "Black and Tan Fantasy" and "Creole Love Call," both from 1927. His middle-era works included "Reminiscing in Tempo" (a 1935 ode to his recently deceased mother) and "Harlem Airshaft" (1940). In his later music, Ellington often took European themes and reshaped them to fit his own social world. Among these works was *Harlem Nutcracker*, a thoroughly adult dance suite drawn from Russian composer Pyotr Ilyich Tchaikovsky's (1840–1893) ballet, *The Nutcracker*

(1892). Ellington became increasingly religious in his later years, the period in which he wrote and performed a series of *Sacred Concerts*.

mysearchlab 4.5

Raised in Washington, DC, Ellington moved to New York City in 1923. In 1927 his all-black jazz orchestra successfully auditioned for a steady engagement at Harlem's prestigious Cotton Club, which, despite its location, served an all-white clientele. Ellington led his orchestra, soon to be the city's most important jazz orchestra, for 50 years, during which he helped revolutionize American music.

Although perceived as a jazz musician, Ellington did not like the label. His music, though inflected with a jazz sensibility, had extraordinary range. He wrote over 3,000 compositions, including music for Broadway, theatrical dance, and the concert hall. Few composers of any time or genre have been more productive or influential.

"Caravan" has a set of lyrics written by Irving Mills (1894–1985), but they are rarely sung. Perhaps this was because the words are not as strong as the melody they adorn. Perhaps, however, it is because the instrumental parts alone are enough to launch the listener's imagination. The lyrics, dreamy though they may be, lock the listener into one particular desert vision. The instrumental version, in contrast, offers endless imaginative possibilities.

LISTENING GUIDE

CD I/Track 14
Download track 14
mysearchlab 4.6

"CARAVAN"　　　　　　　　　　　*by the Duke Ellington Orchestra*

0:00	The recording begins with drummer Sonny Greer beating out "jungle" rhythms on the tom-toms. Cymbals and gongs punctuate each new two-measure cycle. At the end of the cycle, Ellington's piano chords replace the gongs.
0:09	A section Trombonist Juan Tizol enters with the song's chromatic main melody, a swaying Arabic-sounding tune that drifts across the pulse like shifting sands. Tizol's vibrato is fast and wide, filled with emotion. The melodic phrase itself is oddly unbalanced, consisting of seven alternating sections of held tones and movement—stasis, action, stasis, action, stasis, action, stasis. During the stasis sections, baritone saxophonist Harry Carney (1910–1974) interjects a counter melody. A trumpet growls as the section comes to an end.
0:26	A section Tizol repeats the melody.
0:42	B section Woodwinds sound held chords over which Tizol's solo continues.

(Continued)

LISTENING GUIDE (*Continued*)

0:59	A section Clarinetist "Barney" Bigard takes over the A section melody. The feel is lighter and jazzier than in Tizol's version. The accompaniment—now woodblocks and muted brass instruments—has changed as well. Bigard's improvised flourish at the end seems to abandon the melody altogether.
1:15	A section Trumpeter Cootie Williams has been growling in the background all along. Now he takes the lead with a jazzy solo that is both brisk and sharply punctuated.
1:31	A section Williams's solo continues, but now he exploits his plunger mute. The tones are longer and more flowing. It sounds as if he is telling a story with his trumpet.
1:48	B section The sequence of featured soloists is broken as the spotlight is given to the saxophone section as a whole. Musical individuality has been replaced by the voice of community.
2:04	A section Carney takes over the melody. The ensemble growls its approval. Greer moves back from woodblocks to tom-toms.
2:15	A section conclusion Tizol interrupts Carney. The band drops out. Rhythmic time stops while Tizol plays a short operatic-like cadenza. Notice the lack of tonal resolution in both melody and harmony. A gong strike closes the song, but one cannot help but feel that the stop is temporary, a moment of stasis between action.

QUESTIONS FOR THOUGHT

- "Caravan" is considered a highpoint of Ellington's "jungle" sound. Yet, the song seems to be referencing the nomadic life of the North African desert. What is jungle-like in the sound texture?
- Consider the song's trajectory from jungle to jazz to closing cadenza. What might the range suggest?
- Regional music styles are far less distinctive today than they were in the 1930s. Why might this be?

ACTIVITIES AND ASSIGNMENTS

- "Caravan" has been recorded over 1,000 times by artists ranging from pop crooner Bobby Darin (1936–1973) to Phish to the Jamaican ska band The Skatalites. The rapper Redman (b. 1970) samples "Caravan" in "Da Goodness." Search out these or other recordings and compare and contrast them to the original.
- Investigate the following site, which is sponsored by the Smithsonian Institution: http://americanhistory.si.edu/documentsgallery/exhibitions/ellington_strayhorn_4.html

Western Art Music: William Grant Still (1895–1978)

Known as the "Dean" of African American composers, William Grant Still successfully navigated his way through the socially conservative and, at the time, almost exclusively white realm of classical music. He was the first African American to conduct a white

Composer William Grant Still, 1949.

American orchestra; he was also the first African American composer to have a symphony performed by one. Early in his career, Still worked as an arranger for jazz orchestras and Broadway shows. He went on to compose eight operas, along with other classical works.

His most acclaimed composition is the "Afro-American" Symphony. Although written for a symphony orchestra—a medium of European heritage—Still sought a distinctly African American voice. He stated that his goal was to compose ethnic music that did not show a Caucasian influence. In his "Afro-American" Symphony, Still wanted to show that the blues, though "often considered a lowly expression, could be elevated to the highest musical level." Accordingly, he opened the symphony with a 12-bar-blues theme. The second theme has the quality of an African American spiritual, a genre that Still considered more Caucasian, less authentically African, than the blues.

MUSICAL TERMS

SONATA FORM

Sonata form, an instrumental form that developed in Europe in the eighteenth century, provided a grid upon which composers could lay out their musical ideas for easy understanding. It consists of three main sections:

- **Exposition**—where the composer introduces the main musical themes
- **Development**—where the main themes are developed
- **Recapitulation**—where the original ideas return

mysearchlab 2.19

LISTENING GUIDE

CD I/Track 15
Download track 15
mysearchlab 4.7

"AFRO-AMERICAN" SYMPHONY (1930)   *by William Grant Still*

Sonata Form

0:00	Introduction: melody played by English horn.

Exposition

0:22	Theme 1 (blues) begins and is played by a sultry muted trumpet.
0:54	Theme 1 repeats 12 bars later, this time with a clarinet taking the lead. Notice how the other instruments in the orchestra seem to answer.

(Continued)

LISTENING GUIDE (*Continued*)

1:25	The blues form evaporates. Still chops up and embellishes his thematic material. At 1:33 the full orchestra has one last go at thematic material before easing into theme 2.
2:05	Theme 2. For this inward-looking theme (an emotional quality typical of second themes) he borrows from the style of the spiritual. The music then proceeds through a series of transformations in style and attitude. Some is inward looking, and some is extremely jazzy and extroverted.

Development

3:23	Recasting of ideas from theme 2.

Recapitulation (Notice that the thematic order is reversed.)

4:28	Theme 2.
5:05	A jazzy version of theme 1. Listen to the conversation between the muted trumpets and the riffing woodwinds. It consists of 12 bars.
5:36	Coda. Expansion of theme 1 ideas.

QUESTIONS FOR THOUGHT

- Still wanted to compose an orchestral score free of Caucasian influence. Is this possible?
- Why do you think Still wanted to elevate the blues "to the highest musical level"? What do you think he meant by that idea? Do you think he succeeded?
- Who was Still's audience? What was he trying to say to them?
- In what ways might the blues be more African than a spiritual? (Consider both musical and social possibilities.)
- In the symphony's third movement, Still adds a banjo to the orchestration. Why?

MUSICAL THEMES
HARLEM RENAISSANCE

The Harlem Renaissance sought to give expression to the Afro-American experience. Important figures in the movement included sociologist W. E. B. DuBois (1868–1963), nationalist Marcus Garvey (1887–1940), philosopher Alain Leroy Locke (1885–1954), writer Langston Hughes (1902–1967), folklorist Zora Neale Hurston (1891–1960), composers Duke Ellington and William Grant Still, and many others. The movement, which coincided with the Great Migration of African American families from the South in search of work in the urban North, is generally dated from 1919 until the mid-1930s.

West to East: Return to West Africa

We have seen that the roots of African American blues and jazz are to be found in the ancient musical and social cultures of West Africa. It is important to realize, however, that connections across the African diaspora flow in multiple directions. In the 1960s, for example, soul singer James Brown (1933–2006) achieved superstar status in West Africa. His music served as a model for Nigerian musician/activist and afrobeat creator Fela Anikulapo Kuti (1938–1997) (see chapter 10: Music and Broadway). In the 1970s and 1980s, the revolutionary politics of reggae were heard across the African continent. In today's Africa, traditional and modern values continue to intersect and merge in ways both vital and unpredictable.

Malian Blues: Salif Keita (b. 1949)

Journey today through the dusty neighborhoods of Bamako, Mali, in West Africa and one is sure to come upon musicians. Although some have traded traditional instruments for guitars and amplifiers, their craft remains the same: musicians sing of the past to open doors into the future. Bamako is a center for West African popular music. The city has served as a base for singer Fanta Damba (b. 1938), singer/guitarists Ali Farka Touré (1939–2006) and Baubacar Traoré (b. 1942), kora player Toumani Diabaté (b. 1965), and many others.

It is also the home of Salif Keita (b. 1949), whose Mandinka family claims royal descent dating back to the thirteenth-century reign of Sundiata Keita. Normally, such a powerful lineage would prevent one from working in the relatively low-status profession of musician. After all, the traditional jalolu mission was to *serve* royalty.

Life dealt Keita a different set of rules, however. He is albino, a sign of bad luck among the Mandinka. An outcast in his home town of Djoliba and rejected in his own family, a teenaged Keita made his way to Bamako where he joined the Rail Band, one of the city's most popular groups. In 1972, Keita became a member of Les Ambassadeurs, which had a high profile all across West Africa. Keita

moved to Paris in 1984. Today he divides his time between Bamako and Europe.

Keita considers himself a pop musician, not a jali. His inspiration comes from traditional African styles as well as African American musicians such as Chuck Berry (b. 1926), Little Richard (b. 1932), and James Brown. But Keita generally delivers a more socially conscious message than his American models. Like the jalolu, he is committed to singing about social truth. His songs tell of the importance of love, justice, and community. He talks about the difficulties of making a living as an artist, the importance of values, and standing up for justice.

Keita's song "Baba" is typical of his general musical style and his socially complex approach to music making. The song tells of Malian millionaire Babani Sissoko, who is famous for giving money to impoverished musicians. Keita acknowledges that Sissoko has also been accused of being a swindler. Maybe he is; maybe he is not, says Keita. But even if he is, at least he shares the bounties with those less fortunate.

Salif Keita, Malian afro-pop singer-songwriter performing at the WOMAD Festival, 2010.

ASSIGNMENTS AND ACTIVITIES

- Numerous music videos of Salif Keita can be found on the Internet. Search them out and try to understand his approach to music making.
- Search the Internet for video clips of other Bamako pop stars. What do the videos share in common? How do they compare with American music videos?

Identity and Ethnicity in Twentieth-Century Europe

The affirmation of one's roots can be an empowering experience. But what about the weakening of one's roots? For some, this might

offer a sense of independence and freedom; for others, however, it might create a sense of unease, even inspire a search for identity. Drawing from the European experience, we now look at three examples of twentieth-century music making. Each can be understood as a different response to the complexities of ethnic identity. Each is represented by a distinctive flowering of musical ideas.

Maurice Ravel (1875–1937)

Composer Maurice Ravel's ethnic and cultural heritages drew from a variety of sources. Although his mother was Basque (an ethnic group residing in the Pyrenees Mountains along the border of Spain and France), she was raised in Madrid. His father was Swiss. Ravel was born in the Basque village of Ciboure but raised in Paris, at the time the world's most cosmopolitan city.

While still in his early teens, Ravel attended the Paris-based 1889 Exposition Universelle, a summer-long world's fair attended by over 30 million people. The event featured exhibits from cultures around the world, including a Cairo bazaar, a 400-person *village nègre* (Negro village), a Javanese gamelan orchestra, and Annie Oakley performing in Buffalo Bill's Wild West Show. The Eiffel Tower was one of many structures built for the exhibition.

As the success of the exposition suggests, *fin de siècle* Europe was fascinated with the "exotic" ways of distant ethnicities and cultures. Composers were quick to incorporate newly discovered cultures and soundscapes into their own work. For Ravel, that interest

would resurface throughout his creative life. He invoked ancient Arabia in his orchestral song cycle *Shéhérazade* (1903) and ancient Greece in his ballet *Daphnis et Chloé* (1909–1912). He drew ideas from Roma (Gypsy) musical culture in *Tzigane* (1924, for violin and orchestra), and the blues in his "Sonata for Violin and Piano in G Major" (1923–1927). Other compositions were influenced by the sounds of Spain, Asia, and Africa.

> ### *DID YOU KNOW?*
> #### HUMAN ZOOS
>
> Ethnic imaginings sometimes took bizarre turns. The 400-person village nègre of the 1889 Exposition Universelle was just one of hundreds of similar exhibits presented between the 1830s and the early 1900s. A 1906 exhibit at New York City's Bronx Zoo presented the caged Congolese pygmy Ota Benga (1883–1916) as the "missing link" in the evolution between ape and man. Other exhibits in other times and places have displayed Inuits and Apaches, Filipinos and Samoans. For a recent "human zoo" exhibit, see the film documentary *Couple in a Cage* (1997).

In the sciences, the dawning century heralded a time of new explorations. Some journeys involved traversing wide geographies; others unfolded in the mind. Scholars in the newly created field of anthropology searched the globe for "primitive" cultures within which they hoped to discover the secrets of the "pre-rational" mind. Psychologists stayed in their laboratories where, following Sigmund Freud (1856–1939), they traveled inward in hopes of mapping the unconscious. Meanwhile, physicist Albert Einstein's (1879–1955) theory of relativity revolutionized the most fundamental ideas of matter. The firm ground of eighteenth-century **Enlightenment**-era rationalism, which held that truth was immutable and accessible by reason alone, was crumbling.

Visual artists of the time were also intrigued by the idea of capturing events beyond everyday experience. Painters explored a style known as **Primitivism**. Their canvases were vivid, with thick textures. Subjects were often

Maurice Ravel at his piano.

taken from unsullied nature. Paul Gauguin (1848–1903), for example, traveled to Tahiti and other "exotic" lands to escape the "artifice" of European culture.

French artists who remained at home developed a new way of painting called **Impressionism**. Shimmering light, glistening pastels, and blurred edges characterize the style. From a distance, the brushstroke techniques appear relatively conventional. But as one gets closer, the viewer detects blotches of paint, bold individual brushstrokes, and striking juxtapositions of color. Artists such as Edouard Manet (1832–1883), Claude Monet (1840–1926), and Pierre-August Renoir (1841–1919) were considered radical for breaking with conventional painting methods.

Just as the visual artists experimented with color, Ravel and fellow French composer Claude Debussy (1862–1918) experimented with timbre. Both were deeply affected by the shimmering Javanese gamelan music they had heard at the Exhibition Universelle. Both attempted to recreate the aesthetic with Western instruments, thus developing what many have termed "Impressionist music." To achieve the desired sonic effects, Ravel and Debussy experimented with exotic scales, rich chordal combinations, and striking instrumental groupings that mirrored the iridescent colors of the gamelan.

Rapsodie espagnole (1907–1908): "Habanera"

Ravel's orchestral composition *Rapsodie espagnole* is a masterpiece of Impressionist imagery. It consists of four **movements**: "Prélude à la nuit," "Malagueña," "Habanera," and "Feria." Each movement (a prelude and three dances) is a study in tone color. Here we examine the "Habanera" movement, which is modeled on a Cuban dance genre of the same name. (We will return to the habanera when we take up the story of the operatic heroine Carmen; see chapter 5: Music and Gender.)

The habanera has a complex social history. It is known world wide as a Cuban dance, though it came to the island by way of French refugees escaping the early nineteenth-century Haitian wars of independence. Once in Cuba, the habanera was adopted by Afro-Cuban slaves who infused it with African rhythmic nuances. The dance soon became popular across Cuba with peoples of all ethnicities and social classes. From Cuba, it spread to South America and back across the Atlantic Ocean to Spain.

Ravel reframes the dance as if viewed through a tinted soft-focus sonic lens. Like Bach did with his "Bourrée" and Still would soon do with the blues, Ravel removes the music from its natural setting and places it in the concert hall. Dance takes place in the imagination alone.

LISTENING GUIDE

CD I/Track 16
Download track 16
mysearchlab 4.8

"HABANERA" FROM *RAPSODIE ESPAGNOLE*

by Maurice Ravel

0:00	Notice the texture's soft-edged and nonrhythmic ethereal quality. The tones of the muted strings evoke dreamy distance suggestive of the Impressionist aesthetic. Perhaps we also hear Ravel referencing the shimmering textures of Javanese gamelan.
0:22	A gentle pulsing melody begins in the oboes, English horn, and clarinets. Hear how the melody seems first to rush upward and then fall back (but always falling less than it rises). It feels as if the music is trying to get something started but cannot quite muster the energy.
0:53	The melody becomes more energized. Listen to the typical habanera rhythm (long/short/long/long). The energy quickly dissipates until . . .
1:08	The horns play a long drawn-out chord.

(Continued)

LISTENING GUIDE (*Continued*)

1:22	Clarinet and violins play the rising/falling melody heard earlier in the oboes, English horn, and clarinets. Melody and rhythms echo throughout the orchestra.
2:14	The habanera rhythm is expanded and developed with accents from a tambourine and snare drum. The woodwinds have the melody for two cycles . . .
2:24	Then the strings enter.
2:35	The opening texture returns. The music fades away like perfume in the wind.

Béla Bartók (1881–1945)

A similar fascination with ethnicity pervaded the thinking of Ravel's near contemporary, the Hungarian composer and pianist Béla Bartók. Yet Bartók's response could hardly have been more different from Ravel's. As we have seen, Ravel was working in Paris at the powerful and outward-looking center of the European world. From that socially confident perch he tried on a variety of musical ethnicities with the ease of one being fitted for an elegant new suit.

Bartók, working at Europe's eastern periphery, did not share Ravel's confidence in eclecticism. Instead he, like his Hungarian contemporary Zoltan Kodaly (1882–1967), decided it was important to champion his own ethnic background within the international style of Western European art music. The aim was simple enough, but there was a problem. "Real" Hungarian music—that is, the pure ethnic music of the Hungarian "folk"—was no longer heard in urban Hungary. Bartók, though attracted by the idea of ethnic music's social purity and potency, was not even sure what an "authentic" Hungarian tune sounded like.

In 1904, at age 23, he decided to find out. The plan, he wrote to his sister, was "to collect the finest Hungarian folksongs and raise them . . . to the level of art-song." In the process, he would find his own musical voice; it would be grounded in the songs of the common people.

Thus began for Bartók a decades-long process of song collection, analysis, and musical transformation. Equipped with pencil and paper, and sometimes also with hundreds of pounds of primitive recording equipment, he documented peasant musical life, collecting thousands of songs and dances. In addition,

Béla Bartók, c. 1941.

he arranged some of them for the concert hall.

Virtually all of Bartók's composition was influenced by the folk music he collected. His music was filled with locally derived scales, brash dissonances, and regional dance rhythms. The harmonic style was spare and dissonant. Rhythms reflected the agogic accents of the Hungarian language. Sometimes they pounded violently, as if animated by the vigorous cadences of life lived close to Earth. All of this is heard in Bartók's "Allegro Barbaro" (1911) for solo piano.

LISTENING GUIDE

CD I/Track 17
Download track 17
mysearchlab 4.9

"ALLEGRO BARBARO" (1911)

by Béla Bartók

0:00	Hammering alternating chords create a relentless rhythmic **ostinato** (repeated phrase).
0:03	Theme 1 sounds over the ostinato.
0:11	Theme 1 is heard again, this time at a higher pitch level and in a more expansive form.
0:29	Ostinato alone appears as in the beginning, only on a lower pitch.
0:33	Theme group 2, four ideas derived from theme 1's extension material. Each idea is separated by the ostinato figure growling away in the low register. The ostinato gradually disintegrates.
0:59	Theme 1 returns, now with a thinner texture.
1:19	Theme 2 ideas intermingle with the ostinato but finally come to a halt around 1:35.
1:35	Theme 2 material in the lower register joins with the ostinato and theme 1 extension material.
1:48	Right-hand flourishes momentarily disrupt the obsessive pounding of the ostinato.
1:57	Theme 2 material restarts the rhythmic engine.
2:12	Ascending scalar passage appears, a final statement of the ostinato pattern.

MUSICAL THEMES

THE PIANO

The piano was invented in the early eighteenth century as an "improvement" on the main keyboard instrument of the day, the harpsichord. Nineteenth-century composers in particular were enamored with the piano. Hungarian Franz Liszt (1811–1886) and Polish-born Fryderyk Chopin (1810–1849) wrote virtuosic music that greatly expanded the instrument's expressive range. Both incorporated elements of their respective ethnic homelands into their music.

QUESTIONS FOR THOUGHT

- How do Ravel's and Bartók's musical languages differ from one another? Might this be a reflection of ethnicity?
- Bartók and Still both sought to infuse art music with their ethnic heritage. How else might they be seen as similar? How might they contrast with Ravel?
- What might make a musical style authentic? What might make it inauthentic?

ACTIVITIES AND ASSIGNMENTS

- Investigate the sounds of Hungarian folk songs. What characteristics of this music do you hear in Bartók?
- For more on the Exposition Universelle, see the following Web site: www.nga.gov/resources/expo1889.shtm

Klezmer

The setting is Anatevka, a *shtetl* (village) in Czarist Russia. Life is hard for the Jews who live there. Tevye the milkman struggles to support his wife and five daughters. His horse is lame; money is short. Keeping one's footing is precarious in such a world—like a fiddler on the roof, he says.

All this we learn in the first minutes of composer Jerry Bock (b. 1928), lyricist Sheldon Harnick (b. 1924), and author Joseph Stein's (b. 1912) 1964 Broadway musical *Fiddler on the Roof*. By show's end, Tevye's three eldest daughters have married, mostly against their father's wishes, and the Jewish populace has been forced to leave Anatevka. Yet even amidst the setbacks and failed hopes, life goes on. Tevye and his wife will start again, in America, the land of immigrants in which everyone, or so Tevye hopes, is given a fair chance, whatever his ethnicity.

Tevye and Anatevka were fictitious, of course. But the Jewish experience that the show describes was not. Nor were the distinctive sounds that made this Broadway show so memorable. Bock drew his materials from the traditions of the Ashkenazic **klezmer** musicians of Eastern Europe. The style's raucousness was softened for Broadway, but the plaintive appeal of its harmonic and melodic language remained.

Klezmer is a Yiddish term. It refers to both Jewish professional musicians and the music they play. The word derives from two Hebrew words, *kley* (instrument) and *zemer* (song). Klezmer came to the United States with waves of Eastern European Jewish immigrants in the early decades of the twentieth century. The music was essential at Jewish weddings and other celebratory events.

Klezmer music virtually disappeared in Europe during the years of the NAZI-driven Holocaust. In the United States during the same period, klezmer faded as immigrants and their descendants assimilated into American culture. Even so, the Jewish sound prevailed in other ways. Echoes of klezmer's exuberance and tonal personality can be heard in the improvisations of jazz clarinetist Benny Goodman (1909–1986), the melodies of George Gershwin and Irving Berlin (b. Israel Baline, 1888–1989), and countless other Jewish American performers and composers.

Today, klezmer music is undergoing a resurgence across both Europe and North America. Although the musical sound remains closely connected to Jewish culture, contemporary performers come from a variety of ethnic backgrounds. Klezmer is also an important category in the rapidly growing "World Music" commercial genre.

In the past, the violin formed the heart of a klezmer ensemble. Today that role is often taken by the clarinet. Other popular instruments include the **cimbalom** (hammered dulcimer), bass or cello, flute, accordion, trumpet, trombone, drums, and most any other instruments that might be available.

Today's klezmer ensembles tend to be highly eclectic in both membership and musical approach. Consider, for example, the New York City-based group, The Klezmatics. Formed in 1986, the ensemble forged its sound by emulating klezmer recordings from the 1930s and 1940s. To this they added a dash of social activism, a pinch of Jewish mysticism, and sounds (from jazz to punk) of the city in which they live and perform. The ensemble has collaborated with artists ranging from folksinger Arlo Guthrie (b. 1947) to classical violinist Itzhak Perlman (b. 1945) to "Beat" poet Allen Ginsberg (1926–1997). When not playing klezmer music, band members are busy following other endeavors. Some compose for theater, film, and television. Others perform in a variety of ethnic music styles from North America, the British Isles, and Eastern Europe.

A scene from *Fiddler on the Roof*.

LISTENING GUIDE

CD I/Track 18
Download track 18
mysearchlab 4.10

"PERETS-TANTS"

Performed by The Klezmatics

Form: Intro / AA / BB / CC / DD / CC / DD / E / AA / BB / CC / DD / CC / DD

0:00	Introduction. The music opens with a vamp-style dialog between trumpet and violin over an animated rhythmic groove and static harmony from the accordion and clarinet. Listen to how the two solo instruments trade ideas back and forth, sometimes even overlapping.
0:25	A new section begins with the entrance of drums. This is a four-measure phrase that repeats. Since it is the first material of the main body of the piece, let's call it A. Since it repeats (at 0:32), the entire section is AA.
0:39	Section B. Notice that the complete phrase of four measures is actually two contrasting sections of two measures. It might seem like nitpicking to be so exacting, but it is not; there is a reason for the distinction. The musicians shortened the phrase length to speed up the sequence of events. Increased pacing translates into increased excitement. The B phrase repeats at 0:45.
0:51	Section CC. Call this the "stop-time" section; the rhythm instruments play accents. Notice the countermelody embellishment the second time through (repeat begins at 0:58).
1:04	Section DD. Violin and trumpet exchange four-measure solos.
1:17	Section CC. Similar to the original CC, the drummer plays on a woodblock.
1:30	Section DD. Violin and trumpet play together.
1:43	Section E. This section is 16 bars. So now the pace of musical change has been slowed down. A saxophone solo occurs. The section serves as a bridge back to the beginning of the form.
2:09	Return of AA, slightly embellished.
2:22	Return of BB, slightly embellished.
2:35	Return of CC, slightly embellished.
2:48	Return of DD. The violin and trumpet exchange four-measure solos.
3:01	Return of CC, slightly embellished.
3:14	Return of DD. The violin and trumpet play together.

ACTIVITIES AND ASSIGNMENTS

- Interview an elderly family member and ask about ethnic heritage. Do any pre-American cultural traditions survive today? Recipes? Holiday songs? Were any practiced when your interviewee was a child?
- Interview a student from another country. Ask about the kinds of music he or she listens to. Ask about the music his or her parents and grandparents listen to. Ask if his or her musical tastes have changed since coming abroad.

CONCLUSION

When considering ethnic music in the United States, we tend to think of sounds produced by people outside the Western European core upon which the early nation developed. But consider a symphony by Aaron Copland or a song by Madonna. Might these also be ethnic music? Your answer depends at least in part on the lens you use for analysis.

Ethnicity has always played a role in American social consciousness. Communities often formed along ethnic divisions. Majorities oppressed minorities along lines of skin color, language, cultural heritage, and religion. For many, the easiest way to avoid discrimination was to assimilate. Children learned English—the language of public school education—and wore the local fashions. Old World traditions were replaced. Achieving a certain level of conformity may have been an essential ingredient for building national identity, but much was lost.

Today, many Americans are searching for ethnic roots that have been nearly forgotten. Family trees are constructed, old recipes tried, and songs rediscovered. In some cases, second-, third-, and even fourth-generation Americans hold to Old World traditions, even as those still living in the original "homeland" have moved on. A Polish visitor to the United States, for example, might not recognize the "authentic" dances and songs performed at the local Polish American heritage festival.

We have seen that music is one way in which people express ethnic identity. Sometimes that expression is conscious; often it is not. In the following chapters we explore other ways in which music shapes and is shaped by other sorts of cultural and personal perceptions of identity.

Music and Gender

CHAPTER

5

"I won't forget when Peter Pan came to my house, took my hand. I said I was a boy; I'm glad he didn't check."

—folksinger Dar Williams (b. 1967)

Introduction: Understanding Gender

Author J. M. Barrie (1860–1937) conceived Neverland as a boy's playground, an island populated with pirate hoards and mermaids, fairies and Indian bands. Neverland is home to Peter Pan, for whom life is little more than an endless series of adventures. Sometimes, when Peter is lonely, he visits our world. Should Peter arrive at your window some night, let him in. If he likes you, he might even take you to Neverland. If he does, and you are a boy, all of his adventures will be yours. But if you are a girl, he will expect you to play the mom.

Peter Pan lives in a gendered world, like the ones inhabited by all our fairytale heroes and heroines. As a child you might have learned the story of Little Red Riding Hood and how she needed a beefy woodsman to save her. You might have read about Sleeping Beauty, who remained dead to the world until kissed by a charming prince. Perhaps as a child you experimented with gender roles by playing with Barbie dolls or G. I. Joes.

Gender roles are learned. They differ from one culture to the next, sometimes even from one generation to the next. In a future telling, maybe it will be the charming prince who helplessly awaits a woman's animating touch. Likewise, maybe a woodsman will need Red to come to the rescue. After all, G. I. Jane already made her popular culture debut in a 1997 movie starring Demi Moore.

Gender is performed. We place gender on display when we put on pants or dresses, shirts or blouses, aftershave or perfume. We perform our gender through the way we carry our body when we walk or sit, through the ways we use our hands, and through the ways we speak and interact.

Gender is stamped into our earliest experiences. Baby girls are often dressed in pink, boys in blue. Breaking gender rules comes with a price. As country and western singer/songwriter Johnny Cash (1932–2003) correctly observed, life is sure to be tough for "A Boy Named Sue" (1969).

We opened this chapter with a quote from folksinger Dar Williams's song "When I Was a Boy" (1993). Williams sings of the increasingly stringent gender restrictions that confine us as we grow from childhood toward adolescence and on into adulthood. She sings of a childhood relatively unconstrained by gender, of a time when she could be herself, even if hers was "boy" behavior. She played pirate games, climbed trees, and even rode her bike without a shirt.

DID YOU KNOW?

GENDER OR SEX?

There is a world of difference between sex and gender. While sex has to do with our biological makeup, gender is contextual. It is dependent on a combination of societal expectations and individual preferences. Social scientists consider masculinity and femininity to be performed aspects of our personality, as opposed to being essential parts of our nature.

Listening in, we feel for Williams—and perhaps also for the freedoms of our own lost childhood. The song's kicker comes at the end, when she includes the perspective of her male friend. He too, it turns out, once enjoyed a time unconstrained by gender restrictions.

Gender norms are constantly evolving. From college classrooms to the pages of *Vogue*, women's fashion continues to explore domains once reserved for men. Women in pants? No problem. But is it considered appropriate to see a man in a dress?

In the Middle East, American women are involved in combat-related activities that would have been unthinkable a generation ago. By comparison, male behavior has been relatively resistant to change. Today's working women are highly respected. But dads who quit their jobs to raise children are fodder for television comedies.

Not surprisingly, gender pervades musical sounds and music-related activities. Composers use strings and woodwinds to express the "gentle" feminine. In contrast, brass and percussion instruments represent the "brawny" masculine. In many places, we also encounter gender-restricted music making. It was not until 1997 that the Vienna Philharmonic allowed a woman into its membership. Women have been barred from playing ritual drums in some Sub-Saharan African cultures, barred from playing in the Balinese gamelan ensemble, and barred from playing the **didgeridoo** in Australian Aboriginal ceremonies. Men face proscriptions as well. Musical activities controlled exclusively by women include singing laments in Eastern and Northern Europe and the *Muheme* drumming tradition in Tanzania.

In the following pages we look at the ways in which music gives voice to gender. We listen to "masculine" and "feminine" music and study how each reflects and shapes cultural ideals. We learn about individuals whose expressive lives were stunted by gender restrictions. We encounter others who confronted these restrictions head on and forced society at large to reevaluate fundamental notions of identity.

ACTIVITIES AND ASSIGNMENTS

- Seek out songs that take a stand on gender. Examples might include Bo Diddley's (1928–2008) "I'm a Man" (1955), Helen Reddy's (b. 1941) "I Am Woman" (1972), and Ciara's (b. 1985) "Like a Boy" (2006).
- Make a list of music-related gender expectations that you have experienced in your own life.

Female Composers of Western Art Music

Until the last half of the twentieth century, there were few women composers of Western art music. Musical training for "ladies" was usually limited to the home or convent. Playing wind and percussion instruments was considered unfeminine. Some thought too much creative work might affect a woman's sanity. In addition, those women who did make significant contributions to art music's development were largely ignored by historians. Restoring these women to the historical narrative is called **reclamation history**.
mysearchlab 5.1

Important women composers include Hildegard of Bingen (1098–1179), Comtessa de Dià (flourished in the late twelfth–early thirteenth century), Isabella Leonarda (1620–1704), and Elisabeth Claude Jacquet de la Guerre (ca. 1666–1729). Hildegard of Bingen, a German abbess, wrote sacred works exclusively for the women in her convent. She also composed the first musical drama, *Ordo Virtutum*, a play about a young soul who wrestles with good versus evil. Isabella Leonarda, also a nun, was the first woman to publish a collection of instrumental sonatas. Jacquet de la Guerre came from a family of prominent musicians. She was both a composer and **virtuoso** harpsichordist at the court of Louis XIV.

In the nineteenth century, artistic skill was expected for young women of the upper middle class. Their performances and compositions were generally confined to the home's parlor, however. This was the case for Fanny Mendelssohn Hensel (1805–1847), sister of composer Felix Mendelssohn (1809–1847). Few of Hensel's compositions were published during her lifetime but many were performed at the family's salon—a domestic gathering of intellectuals and artists where talented women could respectably display their talents. One woman who ventured into professional

"Perhaps for Felix music will become a profession, while for you it will always remain but an ornament; never can nor should it become the foundation of your existence."

—Abraham Mendelssohn in a letter to his daughter, Fanny

music making was German composer and pianist Clara Wieck Schumann (1819–1896). Schumann came from a middle-class family, which allowed her more professional leeway than her upper-class contemporaries. She began concertizing at age 9 and eventually became one of Europe's greatest virtuosos.

By the late nineteenth century, music conservatories were matriculating women. This and other social reforms gradually opened new artistic opportunities. Though still a minority, a few of today's prominent women composers are the Russian Sophia Gubaidulina (b. 1931) and Americans Pauline Oliveros (b. 1932), Joan Tower (b. 1938), and Ellen Taaffe Zwilich (b. 1939).

Gender in Popular Music

With the rise of television in the years immediately following World War II, American popular music became nearly as visual as sonic. It has also been controversial. Perhaps Elvis Presley (1935–1977) was the catalyst. In mid-1950s television appearances, the singer's gyrating hips and spaghetti legs dazzled teens and worried parents. His 1956 performance on the *Milton Berle Show* was "tinged with a kind of animalism," said New York's *Daily News*.

Some thought Presley was hypermasculine. Others found him effeminate and a dangerous role model. For Presley, the display proved a formula for success. Those watching on TV took notice. Ever since, the popular music industry has made the performance of gender a central aspect of an artist's public persona.

Early rock 'n' roll was dominated by white male performers, writers, producers, and, to a certain extent, even audiences. A milestone in the early 1960s was the introduction of "girl groups." Typical girl groups were ensembles of three to six vocalists, sometimes teenagers and often black. The girl group run was short but significant, in particular because these women appealed to both black and white markets at levels that only a few black men—such as Little Richard (b. 1932), Chubby Checker (b. 1941), and Chuck Berry (b. 1926)—had previously achieved.

Most girl groups were careful to conform to the period's gender expectations. Marketed as "girls" rather than "women," even their names were diminutives. There were, for example, The Bobbettes, The Ronettes, The Marvelettes, and The Primettes (the original name of The Supremes). These "girls" also

knew their place. Song lyrics portrayed a restrictive social world of carefully constructed gender roles. The focus was often on a teenaged girl's romantic fantasies. Self-worth was often measured by whether or not she had a boyfriend. Girls were depicted as dependent on, even reverential toward, their boys. Boys also met a wall of expectations. The girls wanted them strong and faithful. Often they were neither.

Consider the lyrics to the first number one *Billboard* hit by an all-female group, The Shirelles' "Will You Still Love Me Tomorrow?" (1961). On the one hand, the piece is an admission of a teenage girl's sexual desires—a groundbreaking topic for teen music in the early 1960s. At the same time, however, premarital sex is coupled with the fear of abandonment. The young woman, who has far more to risk from a sexual encounter than her fancy-free boyfriend, is anxious and apprehensive.

A similar perspective is heard in the record debut of 16-year-old Lesley Gore (b. 1946), whose single "It's My Party" (1963) reached number one on the *Billboard* pop music chart. The song tells the story of a girl who watches her boyfriend leave her birthday party with a rival. Abandonment has become a reality.

In the early 1960s less than a quarter of the number one hit songs were sung by women, and most of them expressed a dependence on men, even men who hurt, abandoned, or ignored them. But gender roles were changing, and soon teenage girls would have more options for the future than their 1950s and early 1960s counterparts.

The same year that "It's My Party" was released, social activist Betty Friedan (1921–2006) published *The Feminine Mystique*, a book that helped spark **Second-Wave Feminism** of the 1960s and 1970s. During this period, women made important and lasting inroads into male-dominated professions and institutions. Harvard, Yale, and Princeton became coeducational, and women began to insist on economic equality and reproductive freedom.

Over the next decade, the women's movement would gain momentum with the 1966 formation of the National Organization for Women (NOW), protests at the 1968 Miss America Pageant, a 1970 sit-in at the headquarters of the *Ladies Home Journal*, and the establishment of *MS Magazine* (1971). Yet Women's Lib, as it was called then, did not meet with unanimous popularity. Some saw it as a threat to traditional values, as well as the American way of life.

In spite of the social advancements made by second-wave feminists, the movement is often criticized for ignoring the experiences of African American women. Perhaps it did, but African American women had their spokespersons, including the hugely influential Aretha Franklin (b. 1942).

No diminutive "ette" would ever contain this singer. The daughter of Detroit-based civil rights leader C. L. Franklin, Aretha grew up singing in the New Bethel Baptist Church, where her father was pastor. She also grew up fast, becoming the mother of two by age 15.

In the mid-1960s Franklin signed with the R&B-oriented Atlantic Records and shifted her attention from gospel to soul. Working with producer Jerry Wexler, Franklin recorded a string of hits that blended gospel's soulfulness with pop music's funky sexuality. These included "I Never Loved a Man (The Way That I Love You)," "Respect" (which won two Grammy Awards), "Chain of Fools," "Think," and many others. She never totally left singing for the church. Her *Amazing Grace* album (1972) became the biggest-selling gospel record ever.

In 1967 she recorded one of her greatest commercial hits, the song "Respect," written by rhythm and blues singer/songwriter Otis Redding (1941–1967). Redding, who was the first to record the song in 1965, also achieved considerable success as a performer in the African American market. But in a time when race was a powerful social divider, Redding's version hardly crossed over into the white market.

Aretha Franklin, in performance in 1973.

As sung by a man, "Respect" replays topics often covered in blues songs—infidelity, disillusionment, and love on the rocks. Redding portrays a man on the defensive. He cannot control his cheating woman; neither can he find the strength to leave her. Franklin's recording transformed the song's gender assumptions. She and her backup singers oozed authority. They projected the antithesis of "girl group" dependency. In Franklin's version, it is the woman who earns the money. And now she is taking charge of the domestic life. Her man may have been messing around in the past, but that was going to stop. Now. Or else.

MUSICAL LIVES

STEFANI GERMANOTTA (b. 1986)

The world knows her as Lady Gaga. In 2008 her debut album, *The Fame*, placed her in the express lane to superstardom. Two of the album's singles, "Just Dance" and "Poker Face" (co-written by Gaga and her Moroccan, Los Angeles-based producer Nadir Khayat (a.k.a. RedOne)), topped the *Billboard* Hot 100 as well as pop charts throughout the world. By 2010 she had risen to number four on *Forbes* magazine's list of the world's most popular celebrities.

Gaga's reputation lies as much in her outrageous fashions as in her music. Her tamest costumes resemble lingerie but she's also sported "dresses" made of Hello Kitty dolls, bubbles, Christmas tree lights, and meat, to name a few. After Madonna made cone-covered breasts *de rigueur*, Gaga added sparklers.

Lady Gaga credits her early success to a large gay following, a fan base that began when she played lower Manhattan's cabarets and gay bars. Like Judy Garland, Barbra Streisand, and others, Gaga has become a "gay icon." She revealed her own bisexuality in the lyrics of "Poker Face," which she explains is about being with a man while dreaming of a woman. In a December 2009 interview with Barbara Walters, Lady Gaga put to rest a rumor that she was a hermaphrodite. But she does claim to "blur the boundaries," and much of her inspiration comes from the gender-bending aesthetics of glam rockers David Bowie and the rock group Queen (she took her name from Queen's hit single from 1984, "Radio Ga Ga").

Detractors are quick to point out Gaga's debt to artists such as Madonna, Gwen Stefani, and Christina Aguilera, but fans (her "Little Monsters") see her as an eccentric and provocative voice that has revolutionized pop music.

LISTENING GUIDE

CD I/Track 19
Download track 19
mysearchlab 5.2

"RESPECT"   *Composed by Otis Redding and recorded by Aretha Franklin in 1967*

0:00	Introduction: Four-measure instrumental introduction. The wind instruments trade riffs with the electric guitar across a two-measure cycle. The drummer plays a strong 2 and 4 backbeat on the snare drum. As the second two-bar cycle concludes, the drummer's riff signals the vocal entry.
0:09	*Verse 1:* Franklin's trio of backup singers lead off with the **vocable** "oo." The sound is placed hard on the downbeat, taut yet sweetly aggressive. Franklin enters and the backup singers continue their pressure. "Listen up," they seem to be saying. (Could "oo" stand in for "you"?) When Franklin demands respect, the trio echoes the demand. They scold with, "Just a little bit. . . . Just a little bit." Listen carefully to Franklin's authoritative and expressive voice. On occasion she breaks into a kind of sung shout, as with the word "need" in the second line. Franklin is audacious. She takes risks and holds nothing back. Pop music tends to unfold in eight-bar phrases. "Respect" could easily fit that mold, but each sung verse tacks on an additional two measures. The change allows the backup singers time to fully reinforce Franklin's demands. Count through all 10 bars so you internalize the unbalanced form.
0:29	*Verse 2:* Same format, though the backup singers do not enter at the verse's beginning.
0:52	*Verse 3:* Notice how the trio's words ("just a, just a . . .") are being used for their color and rhythmic energy.
1:13	*Interlude:* Saxophone solo. The saxophone, though easily conceived as a powerful "male" instrument, sounds thin when juxtaposed against Franklin's commanding vocal presence. Thus, even the saxophone's timbre reinforces the song's message of female strength. Without the backup chorus's scolding, there is no need to extend the section to 10 bars. It is only eight bars long.
1:29	*Verse 4:* Franklin opens with a long "oo." The vocable works in two ways. First, it echoes the language of the backup singers. (These women are united.) Second, it slows the dramatic pace of the lyrics, as if Franklin also had time to reflect during the saxophone solo.
1:50	*Break:* In case her backsliding man still does not get it, Aretha literally spells it out for him. This section is a Franklin addition that does not appear in the Redding original. (The chorus sings: "Sock it to me. Sock it to me . . ."; as the song fades out, they chant: "Re – re – re – re.") Like the "oo" at the song's beginning, the "Re" has a double meaning. The chorus is clearly chanting the opening syllable of "Respect." But they also seem to be chanting (A)*re*(-tha). And why not? No other pop song came close to portraying women in so powerful a light.

Franklin was not alone in challenging quickly evolving sexual mores and gender roles. In 1968, the San Francisco rock band Jefferson Airplane recorded David Crosby's (b. 1941) "Triad" in which lead singer Grace Slick (b. 1939) suggested to her men, with their "long hair flowing," that they "try something new."

Musicians continued to play with sexuality and gender, but it was becoming harder and harder to shock. Just four years after "Triad," New York City-based singer/songwriter Lou Reed (b. 1942) released "Walk on the Wild Side." Reed devoted each verse to a different real-life person associated with pop artist Andy Warhol's (1928–1987) infamous New York production studio, The Factory. Despite unmistakable references to transsexuality, drugs, and prostitution, the song garnered considerable radio airplay and even became a Top 40 hit.

Reed's song coincided with the early 1970s emergence of glam rock, a movement that continued the curious and ironic journey toward androgyny that Elvis Presley and his contemporaries began. Performers like David Bowie (b. 1947) wore makeup and jewelry, sported long carefully coiffed hairdos, and sometimes pranced about the stage in platform shoes.

Cultural theorists have offered various explanations for the look, including shock value, an attempt to portray an "alien" and exotic persona, and a symbolic rejection of capitalist society (even as the musicians raked in millions of dollars). Perhaps all of these factors contribute to the answer, but there has to be more to it. Maybe these guys were popular because they were just plain sexy, a status they achieved by daring to live outside social norms and within the ever-perilous world of gender ambiguity.

QUESTIONS FOR THOUGHT

- Choose a favorite song. Can you identify masculine and/or feminine elements in the music? How do these sounds reinforce the lyrics?
- Have your own evolving musical tastes reflected changing ideas about gender?
- Make up some diminutive names for 1960s "guy" groups. How do the name changes affect our perception of their masculinity? "The Four [Small] Tops"? "The [Minor] Temptations"? "Temptation[ette]s"? "The Rolling Pebbles"? What about "Little Stevie Wonder"?
- How are gender issues expressed in popular music today? Do certain styles of music reflect general worldviews?

ACTIVITIES AND ASSIGNMENTS

- Get on the Internet and view one of Elvis Presley's early performances. Do you find the performance gendered? Why or why not? Some critics found Presley effeminate. How do you see him?
- A fascinating song from the 1960s is Nancy Sinatra's "These Boots Are Made for Walking." Search the Internet for a video of a performance. Compare it with Jessica Simpson's video of the same song.
- Survey your class members to see what types of music they like. Are there gender-delineated trends?
- Watch *Dreamworlds 2: Desire, Sex, and Power in Music Video* (1995 by Sut Jhally). Does Jhally's premise hold true today?
- Compare and contrast Motley Crue's "Girls, Girls, Girls" with Shakira's "Hips Don't Lie."

Gender in the World

Balinese Gamelan

Earlier in the chapter we noted that a person's sex can limit his or her musical activities. Such is the case in Bali. **mysearchlab 2.9** There, playing the gamelan is considered men's work.

Although Indonesia as a whole has the largest Muslim population in the world, nearly all on the island of Bali practice Hinduism, a religious philosophy that requires a delicate balance of male and female energies. Many aspects of Balinese culture reflect that balance. For example, while men care for cattle, buffalo, and ducks, women care for chickens and pigs. Trades and crafts are generally the province of men, but making certain kinds of religious offerings is a task exclusively for women.

Gamelan instruments are arranged in complementary pairs of male and female. Female instruments are tuned slightly lower, whereas male instruments are tuned higher. Some say this reflects women's closeness to Earth. Whatever the reason, both male and female instruments must sound together in order to attain the desired shimmering effect that is essential to the gamelan's sound.

Until recently, women have been prohibited from playing the gamelan. One of the reasons for this is a concept that the Balinese call *gaya* (style). Gaya is a projection of energy, showmanship, and vigor, which the Balinese consider to be a masculine quality. Furthermore, gamelan playing is essential in Hindu temples, where anyone bleeding is forbidden to enter. Because of their menses, women often must remain outside.

Beginning in the early 1980s, however, women began forming their own ensembles. Several factors contributed to this, most notably a government-sponsored mandate for coeducation. Suddenly, music students at both the high school and university levels found themselves playing in mixed ensembles. Greater exposure to Western ideas of sexual equality probably also helped open doors. At first, women played for personal enjoyment or for tourists. Slowly emboldened, they began to set up gamelans around temple perimeters in order to participate in religious festivals. Yet even today, women's gamelans do not enter the temple.

Women's and men's gamelan performances are quite different. The women play more slowly, are apt to make more mistakes, and often have less-polished performances. There are reasons for this. First, boys are initiated into playing gamelan at a very young age, often by sitting on their father's

laps. Girls start much later. In addition, gender norms dictate that women conduct themselves demurely and modestly. Flashy expressions of gaya are socially inappropriate for women. Faced with such a paradox, women may prefer to sacrifice showmanship for propriety. The area in which female performance aesthetics do dominate is in dance. Many dances are meant specifically for women, whose controlled and elegant motions are highly valued.

Girls dancing Tari Kelinci (rabbit dance) during a women's gamelan performance.

LISTENING GUIDE

MEKAR SARI, WOMEN'S GAMELAN

mysearchlab 5.3

This video was taken in the summer of 1997 on a research trip to the town of Peliatan, Bali. Featured is *Mekar Sari* (Essence of Flower), a women's gamelan that performs weekly for tourists in an outdoor pavilion. Notice that while there is a protective roof, there are no walls. Performances are informal by Western standards. The audience is free to come and go, wander around, and even talk. Sounds of traffic and gamelan intermingle.

Scene 1 0:00	Pre-concert preparations. Performers ready the stage by distributing offerings to the Hindu gods; water is sprinkled in order to purify the performing area. A boy (one of the performers' sons) slips on stage and plays the reyong. (*fade out*)
Scene 2 2:08	The warrior dance *Baris*. Usually the warrior is danced by a grown man. But since the women usually perform with children, a boy takes the role. His gestures and poses are typically male. The dancer's movements also control the orchestra, which follows danced cues. (*fade out*)
Scene 3 5:59	Tari Kelinci (rabbit dance). This is one of several dances that became popular in the 1990s. Movements portray a variety of animals, including deer, birds, and, in this case, rabbits. Tari Kelinci is danced by prepubescent girls, usually ages 6 to 9. Girls have always been essential to the dance tradition. (*fade out*)

MUSICAL TERMS

ETHNOMUSICOLOGY AND FIELDWORK

Ethnomusicology, a scholarly discipline closely related to anthropology, seeks to understand music from a cultural perspective. Often, but not always, the object of study is a living tradition outside of Western art music. In the early years of the field, the focus was on collection. Ethnomusicologists—armed with wax cylinder recording devices, pencils, and paper—journeyed to far-away places where they sought to document and catalog the world's music.

Our Bali video is a field recording. Although not exactly technologically "primitive," like a wax cylinder audio recording, the picture quality is low in comparison to today's high-definition digital recordings. Fieldwork documentations often suffer from bumps given from bystanders, ambient noises, and visual impediments. In addition, since the cinematographer in this case is usually a scholar rather than a trained videographer, experience is a factor as well.

Women's Laments

Songs relating to life-cycle transitions—birth, puberty, marriage, or death—are often the province of women. Songs specifically associated with death are called **laments**. Typically, laments are passed on by **oral tradition** and in many parts of the world are performed by female relatives of the deceased. If no relative is available, a professional lamenter might be hired. In the Middle East, hired lamenters are the norm since it is believed that having a relative lament a death would question God's perfect will.

Lamenting practices vary throughout the world. Stylistic characteristics are closely tied to geographic region. Some trace their roots back to ancient classical Greece and Egypt.

Others, like the Finnish–Karelian laments from Northern Europe and Russia, exhibit vestiges of ancient female-centered folk religions.

Laments of Eastern Europe are sung for practical reasons. For the living, they facilitate mourning and celebrate lives well lived. For the dead, they are believed to assist the soul's transition from life to afterlife. Accordingly, singers are often said to possess magical or shaman-like powers.

Laments often provoke emotional catharsis. Performers utilize wailing, sobbing, speech-like song, and nontonal pitch inflections. In the Finnish–Karelian tradition, lamenting is called "crying with words." Romanian lament singers are expected to perform with tears in their eyes.

LISTENING GUIDE

CD I/Track 20
Download track 20
mysearchlab 5.4

"MĂ GUARIȚĂ," ROMANIAN LAMENT FOR A DEAD BROTHER

In Transylvania (a region of Romania), laments are called *bocete* (singular, *bocet*, pronounced "BO-chet"), which literally means "to cry with tears." Bocete are performed by close female friends or relatives of the deceased during the first three days following death. They may be sung in the home, in the funeral procession, or at the burial. They are also performed on subsequent visits to the cemetery and on special days designated to remember the dead. Bocete are fully or partially improvised, but follow a recognizable formula. Sometimes, as in this case, mourners will mumble or elide words and mix crying with singing.

This example consists of 15 short melodic phrases separated by pauses. All of the phrases end on the same pitch, with a vocal "ah" sound at the end, sounding much like a sigh. The melody is simple and **modal** and uses just four pitches. Phrases follow a general pattern of falling from the fourth scale degree stepwise to the tonic. The "ah" vocable falls to the lowered seventh degree. The text setting is **syllabic**, as if the lamenter is half speaking, half intoning her thoughts. Some of the phrases are ornamented with oscillating pitches, especially those that call out the name of the deceased, Guariță (Georgie). Not all the words, or their meanings, are clear.

0:00	Mă Guariță draga	You Guariță, dear
0:05	Guariță, Guariță fratele meu drag	Guariță, my dear brother

LISTENING GUIDE (*Continued*)

0:13	Spune-mi dragă spune-mi cum ai mai facut	Tell me dear how were you?
0:21	Mă Guariță mă . . .	You Guariță, you
0:27	Pînă la Brasov mă Guariță mă	All the way to Brasov [town in Transylvania], you Guariță
0:34	Că . . . te-ai mai dus pe . . .	You indeed took me on . . .
0:41	Pînă la coadra, Guariță, Guariță	All the way to [the forest?], Guariță, Guariță
0:48	Cine . . . apa	Who . . . water
0:54	La ceasul morții mă Guarița mă	The hour of death. You, Guariță, you
1:01	Gata lumea dragă toată la . . .	[You] are finished with the whole world
1:08	De pe lumea . . . Guariță dragă	From this world . . . Guariță, dear
1:15	Vino dragă vino vino noaptea in vis	Come dear, come at night in dream
1:23	Sa te . . . sa mă racoresc	To . . . cool me off [soothe me]
1:29	Mă Guariță Mă ia . . .	You Guariță, you, take . . .
1:36	Pînă la coadra sa-mi vin si ea dragă. (repeat)	All the way to [the forest?] for me to come as well, dear. (repeat)

ACTIVITIES AND ASSIGNMENTS

- Listen to a piece of music by a woman composer. Would you be able to tell the sex of the composer if you didn't know?
- "History is written by the winners," wrote author Alex Haley (1921–1992). How might that idea be reflected in the historical discourse on women in music in both the nineteenth century and today?
- Watch the film *Songcatcher* (2001), a fictional portrayal of a woman ethnomusicologist from the early twentieth century who documents English ballads in Appalachia. Note the style of singing, the use of wax cylinders, and the moral conflict inherent in "taking" other peoples' traditions for one's own gain.
- Find a video of a men's Balinese gamelan on the Internet. Compare the concept of gaya in the male ensemble to the women's group above.

QUESTIONS FOR THOUGHT

- Are some kinds of music considered to be more "feminine" or more appropriate for women to perform/compose? Are any styles off limits for one sex or the other?
- Why do you think it might be more socially acceptable for women to sing laments rather than men?
- What ethical issues might arise when recording a woman singing laments?

Gender on Stage

In opera, gender issues are worked out on stage. Nonconformity often leads to disaster. Witness the case of poor Lucia Ashton in the opera *Lucia di Lammermoor* (1835) by Italian composer Gaetano Donizetti (1797–1848). Lucia, who has secretly sworn herself to another, is forced to marry a family ally. Driven mad by guilt and shame, she pulls out a knife and murders her unwelcome mate in their bridal chamber. Moments later, crazed and bloodied, she appears center stage, sings an **aria**, then drops dead, presumably the victim of vapors, hysteria, and other overwrought emotions common to nineteenth-century women. Lucia's fate was not an isolated case. She is just one of many female characters who rebel against social imperatives and pay for it with their lives.

mysearchlab 5.5

Take, for example, Carmen, perhaps opera's most sensuous leading lady. *Carmen* (1875) was composed by Frenchman Georges Bizet (1838–1875), with **libretto** by Henri Meilhac and Ludovic Halévy. The opera tells the story of a sultry gypsy who works in a Seville tobacco factory. Carmen is the ultimate free spirit, equally comfortable seducing members of the local militia or traveling with a band of renegade smugglers.

These associations provide for colorful crowd scenes and lively choruses, but the real drama has to do with Carmen's tempestuous relationships with two lovers, the sturdy (though thick-skulled) soldier, Don José, and the passionate matador, Escamillo. As one might expect, things go poorly for Don José after he falls for Carmen. He lands in jail, deserts his regiment, rejects the entreaties of the faithful Micaela, and

| Georges Bizet.

is finally humiliated and scorned by Carmen and her gypsy clan. In the opera's final scene, Don José takes vengeance on the object of his desire, fatally stabbing Carmen as she attempts to enter the bullring where Escamillo is performing.

Listen to the **chromatically** inflected and rhythmically seductive habanera ("L'amour est un oiseau rebelle que nul ne peut apprivoiser"), the music that first introduces us to Carmen and her cigarette girls.

CD I/Track 21
Download track 21
mysearchlab 5.6

LISTENING GUIDE

"HABANERA" FROM THE OPERA, *CARMEN* (1875)

Carmen's aria begins with a brief introduction featuring the hypnotic rhythm of the Cuban habanera (see chapter 4: Music and Ethnicity). For French audiences of 1875, the opera's Seville setting was sure to convey a sense of mystery, and perhaps even social danger. More provocative still would have been the habanera, with its boundary-crossing Afro-Cuban genesis. Bizet's habanera is laden with sensuality.

As the scene unfolds, Carmen is flirting with the young men gathered in the town square. Soon, however, her attention focuses on the hapless Don José, who, once locked into Carmen's siren-like sights, is destined to fall. Note the interjections of the cigarette girls. In warning bystanders to beware of Carmen's love, they function much like the all-knowing choruses of ancient Greek tragedy.

Carmen represents the ultimate *femme fatale*. Her character is mirrored in the music through a combination of rhythmic, melodic, and textual elements. Just as the habanera's sensual lilt invites physicality, the falling chromatic melody suggests seduction. Then there are the lyrics. Love, says Carmen, is untamable, flighty like a bird, and not subject to any law. And so is she.

LISTENING GUIDE (*Continued*)

0:00	*Carmen:* L'amour est un oiseau rebelle Que nul ne peut apprivoiser, Et c'est bien en vain qu'on l'appelle S'il lui convient de refuser Rien n'y fait, menace ou prière, L'un parle bien, l'autre se tait Et c'est l'autre que je préfère; Il n'a rien dit, mais il me plaît.	Love is a rebellious bird That nobody can tame, And it's simply no good calling it If it suits it to refuse; Neither threat nor prayer will prevail One of them talks, the other holds his peace, And I prefer the other one! He hasn't said a word, but I like him!
0:40	*Chorus:* L'amour est un oiseau . . .	Love is a rebellious bird . . .
0:42	*The chorus continues in the background with Carmen's melody while Carmen sings:* L'amour! L'amour! L'amour!	Love! Love! Love!
0:57	*A reduced orchestra with pizzicato strings centers the focus on Carmen:* L'amour est enfant de Bohème, Il n'a jamais connu de loi Si tu ne m'aimes pas, je t'aime; Si je t'aime, prends garde à toi!	Love is a Gypsy, It has never been subject to any law. If you do not love me, I love you If I love you, take care!
1:14	*Chorus (a bold and cautionary interjection, with full orchestra):* Prends garde à toi! . . .	Take care! . . .
1:16	*Listen to Carmen dwell on "pas":* Si tu ne m'aimes PAS, je t'aime;	If you do NOT love me, I love you
1:22	*Chorus:* Prends garde à toi! . . .	Take care! . . .
1:24	*Carmen:* Si je t'aime, prends garde à toi!	If I love you, take care!
1:37	*Chorus:* L'amour est enfant de Bohème . . .	Love is a Gypsy . . .
1:52	Prends garde à toi! . . .	Take care! . . .
1:54	*Carmen:* Si tu ne m'aimes pas, je t'aime; Si je t'aime, prends garde à toi!	If you do not love me, I love you If I love you, take care!
2:02	*Carmen and Chorus:* Si tu ne m'aimes pas, je t'aime; Si je t'aime, prends garde à toi!	If you do not love me, I love you If I love you, take care!

2:21	*Here the music from the beginning repeats.* *Carmen:* L'oiseau que tu croyais surprendre Battit de l'aile et s'envola; L'amour est loin, tu peux l'attendre; Tu ne l'attends plus, il est là! Tout autour de toi vite, vite, Il vient, s'en va, puis il revient Tu crois le tenir, il t'évite; Tu crois l'éviter, il te tient!	The bird you thought to surprise has spread its wings and flown; Love is far away, you may wait for it; When you've given up waiting, it is there! All around you, quickly, quickly It comes, goes, and comes again. You think you've caught it, it escapes you; You think to escape it, you are caught!
2:55	*Chorus:* Tout autour de toi . . .	All around you . . .
3:11	L'amour est enfant de Bohème . . .	Love is a Gypsy . . .
3:28	*Chorus:* Prends garde à toi! . . .	Take care! . . .
3:20	*Carmen:* Si tu ne m'aimes pas, je t'aime;	If you do not love me, I love you
3:36	*Chorus:* Prends garde à toi! . . .	Take care! . . .
3:38	*Carmen:* Si je t'aime, prends garde à toi!	If I love you, take care!
3:51	*Chorus of Girls:* L'amour est enfant de Bohème . . .	Love is a Gypsy . . .
4:17	*Carmen and Chorus:* Si je t'aime, prends garde à toi!	If I love you, take care!

A Leading Man: Siegfried

How might opera portray a strong, virile man? For this, we look to German composer Richard Wagner's (1813–1883) epic four-opera cycle, *Der Ring des Nibelungen* (*The Ring of the Nibelungen*), which was first performed in its entirety in 1876, one year after *Carmen*'s premier. Thirty years in the making, the cycle is the culmination of the composer's philosophies concerning drama. Wagner believed that opera was the greatest of the art forms and that it should strive not only to unify all of the arts (music, visual art, drama, and poetry), but also to portray the inner psychological workings of humankind. *The Ring Cycle* (as it is called, or sometimes just *The Ring*) is an attempt to realize that ideal.

The complex story was drawn from Northern European epic poetry and mythology.

Characters include gods and humans, heroes and thieves, dwarves and dragons. The plot centers around the magic gold of the Rhine River. Whoever controls this magic gold has power over the entire world. But there is a catch. One can only obtain the gold by renouncing love; this is the metal's corrupting curse. The gold is stolen, then forged into a ring of power. Thereafter—and amidst murder and mayhem—the ring is vied for by gods, humans, and even a dragon. In the end, Brünnhilde (the famous opera character who wears the winged helmet) sacrifices her immortal life in order to return the ring to the Rhine River. With that act, the reign of the gods is ended. The era of man begins.

In accordance with his desire to unify all of the arts, Wagner expanded the expressive range of the orchestra. He increased and

Siegfried slaying the dragon.

became a storyteller, capable of foreshadowing and revealing ideas and happenings of which even the characters on stage were not always aware.

Wagner accomplished this trick in part through the use of **leitmotives**, short musical motives representing people and places, things and ideas. Because of their brevity, leitmotives are easily folded into the orchestral texture where they enhance the story being acted out on stage. Wagner manipulates and juxtaposes the motives so that they take on considerable dramatic significance.

The third of the four *Ring* operas is titled *Siegfried*. It tells the story of the half-human grandson of Wotan, the most powerful of the gods. Siegfried is naïve in the ways of mankind, but he is fearless. As the opera opens, Mime (*Mee-muh*), Siegfried's surrogate father, is attempting to forge a sword powerful enough to slay Fafner the dragon, who currently possesses the ring. Mime hopes to coax Siegfried into killing the dragon, then murder him. He will half succeed. Sword in hand, Siegfried heads off toward the dragon's lair. He blows his horn to awaken the beast and the battle begins.

diversified the instrumentation, and employed a bold, even revolutionary, harmonic language. Thus fortified, the orchestra gained a status equal to that of the voice. The orchestra itself

LISTENING GUIDE

CD I/Track 22
Download track 22
mysearchlab 5.7

ACT II/SCENE 2, FROM THE OPERA, *SIEGFRIED* (1871)

Siegfried plays his famous horn tune. It is a call to battle, a leitmotive representing Siegfried's youth and boundless energy. We hear the motive three times. Then Siegfried switches to a more personal tune, one that was first heard at the beginning of the opera. The melody differs from the initial horn call in that it is contemplative, dark, and less youthful. Perhaps this represents the tragic Siegfried who, despite all of his bravery and good intentions, is destined to succumb to deception and a murderous end.

0:00	Horn call
0:09	Horn call (echo, extended)
0:20	Horn call, elaborated
0:35	Siegfried's motive, twice
1:21	Horn call again, elaborated
1:38	Tubas, Fafner awakens; the orchestra enters with Fafner's awakening. The music is thick, ominous, and tonally unstable. A chromatic melody creeps upward as Fafner drags himself up from the bowels of Earth. The music tells us that the creature is feral and brutal. Perhaps it deserves the death that Siegfried plans. Contrast these sounds to the tonal clarity of Siegfried's horn call. The horn, an instrument of the hunt and the military, represents a socially acceptable show of masculine power. It soars above Fafner's mucky sludge.

2:33	*Siegfried*: Haha! Da hätte mein Lied Mir was Liebes erblasen! Du wärst mir ein saubrer Gesell!	Just look, my tune has Brought me something lovely. You would be a pleasant friend for me.
3:11	*Tremolo in the strings and timpani alert the audience to trouble, though Siegfried is still fearless.* *Fafner*: Was ist da?	What is that?
3:54	*Siegfried*: Bist du ein Tier, Das zum Sprechen taugt, Wohl ließ sich von dir was lernen? Hier kennt einer Das Fürchten nicht Kann er's von dir erfahren?	Well, now, if you're an animal That's learned talking, Perhaps I can find out something from you. Someone here knows Nothing about fear: Can he learn it from you?
4:08	*Fafner*: Hast du Übermut?	Are you being arrogant?
4:14	*Siegfried* Mut oder Übermut, Was weiß ich! Doch dir fahr' ich zu Liebe, Ehrst du das Fürchten mich nicht!	Brave or arrogant— How do I know? But I'll cut you to shreds, If you don't teach me fear.
4:26	*Fafner*: Trinken wollt' ich: Nun treff' ich auch Fraß!	I wanted a drink: Now I've found food, too.
4:44	*Siegfried*: Eine zierliche Fresse Zeigst du mir da, Lachende Zähne Im Leckermaul! Gut wär' es, den Schlund Dir zu schließßen, Dein Rachen reckt sich zu weit!	That's a pretty maw You're showing off; Teeth laughing In a dainty mouth! It would be a good thing To stop the gap for you. Your jaws are gaping too wide.
4:59	*Fafner*: Zu tauben Reden Taugt er schlecht: Dich zu vershlingen, frommt der Schlund	At empty chatter They're no good. But for gobbling you up My throat is just right.
5:18	*Siegfried*: Hoho! Du grausam grimmiger Kerl! Von dir verdaut sein, Dünkt mich übel: *Secisive, quick string chromatic scales:* Rätlich und fromm doch scheint's Du verrecktest hier ohne Frist	Ho ho! You gruesome Angry fellow! Being digested by you Seems to me a bad idea. But it seems sensible and decent For you to drop dead without delay.
5:31	*Fafner*: Pruh! Komm, Prahlendes Kind!	Bah! Come on, Bragging child.
5:38	*Siegfried*: Hab acht, Brüller! Der Prahler naht! *Siegfried wields his sword and, with crash of cymbal, plunges it into Fafner's heart:* Da lieg, neidischer Kerl Notung trägst du im Herzen!	Watch out growler. The braggart is coming. Lie there, hateful fellow! You've got Notung [the sword] in your heart.

Gender Confusion: Castrati and Pants Roles

What is the ideal masculine voice? A stentorian bass? A soaring tenor? How about a golden soprano? The latter was once Europe's heroic timbre of choice. But how is a man to get one? The obvious way to preserve a boy's soprano voice is to deny puberty, which is accomplished through castration. Such was the fate of more than a few seventeenth- and eighteenth-century boys who showed exceptional vocal promise.

The greatest castrati—accounts tell of powerful, brilliant, and even "unearthly" voices—achieved fame and fortune singing both male and female operatic roles.

Although the practice of castration had generally ended by the early nineteenth century, there were a few castrati singing in the Catholic church up into the early twentieth century. Today, castrati roles are sung either by women or **countertenors** (men who have developed their falsetto range).

MUSICAL LIVES
FARINELLI

The castrato Farinelli (stage name of Carlo Maria Broschi, 1705–1782) attained superstar status singing on operatic stages in Italy, France, and England. In 1737, he gave up the stage to work for Philip V of Spain. The king, who was plagued by depression, required Farinelli to sing to him every evening. In addition, Farinelli directed the king's chapel music and staged Italian operas. Farinelli remained in Spain for over 20 years, then retired to a villa in Bologna, Italy.

A fictional account of Farinelli's story was celebrated in the French film *Farinelli* (1994) directed by Gérard Corbiau. The task of creating the castrato sound was given to the Institut de Recherche et Coordination Acoustique/Musique (IRCAM), an organization otherwise known for its pioneering efforts in electronic music. After much experimentation, IRCAM digitally blended the voice of a male countertenor with a female **coloratura** soprano to replicate the imagined castrato sound.

Another common operatic practice was composing male roles designed to be sung by women. The classic "pants," or **"breeches role,"** character is a handsome boy at the cusp of manhood, his hormones raging. Usually, he is a character of relatively low status, perhaps a servant or court page, and is hopelessly in love with a leading lady who treats him as the mere boy he is. Female characters adore him for his gentle beauty and naïve charm; adult male characters are understandably less enthralled.

For the story's action, of course, the character's gender is not in question. Things are not so clear in the audience, however. Theater, after all, is artifice. Although we may enter fully into the characters we watch, sophisticated viewers are simultaneously engaged with the actor/actress playing the role. This being the case, what should one make of the allure of a lovely boy/man who is actually a woman? All of this provides tantalizing ground for composers and audiences alike.

MUSICAL LIVES

WOLFGANG AMADEUS MOZART AND *THE MARRIAGE OF FIGARO*

The Salzburg, Austria-born Mozart was a child prodigy—an accomplished harpsichordist and violinist at age 4, a composer at age 5, and a guest of both France's Louis XV and England's George III by age 8. As an adult, however, Mozart struggled. He pasted together a successful career by working as a performer, teacher, and composer but was often in debt. He wrote over 600 compositions, including symphonies, concertos, sacred works, string quartets, and other chamber pieces.

His 20-some operas reveal a musical and dramatic imagination that is unsurpassed. *The Marriage of Figaro*—based on a 1784 play by Pierre Beaumarchais (1732–1799)—is the first of three operas on which Mozart collaborated with librettist Lorenzo da Ponte (1749–1838). Beaumarchais's play, which satirized the aristocracy during a time of political instability (the French Revolution was just a few years away), was banned in Vienna. The opera, however, with its charming melodies and toned-down politics, premiered there successfully on May 1, 1786. Two hundred years later, the overture was used in another comedic satire about social class, the film *Trading Places* (1983), starring Eddie Murphy and Dan Aykroyd.

Young Mozart instructing a singer who is rehearsing one of his works.

One of the greatest pants role characters is Cherubino ("the little cherub") from Wolfgang Amadeus Mozart's (1756–1791) *Le Nozze di Figaro (The Marriage of Figaro,* 1786), with libretto by Lorenzo da Ponte (1749–1838). Cherubino is a stock character: the classic hormonally driven adolescent. Time and again, the poor fellow, a page in Count Almaviva's court, is overwhelmed by his desires and fantasies. "Any woman makes me change color; any woman makes me quiver," he confesses in the aria "Non so piu cosa son." From the get-go, Cherubino's antics offer plenty of gender mayhem to all the characters on stage. The Countess and Susanna (Figaro's bride-to-be) treat him as little more than a doll, even dressing him up as a young lady.

LISTENING GUIDE

CD II/Track 1
Download track 23
mysearchlab 5.8

"NON SO PIU COSA SON," ACT I FROM THE OPERA *THE MARRIAGE OF FIGARO* (1786)

Listen to the orchestra accompaniment and the syncopated rhythms of the violins, which are perhaps a mirror of Cherubino's racing heartbeat. His vocal line is quick with excitement, almost breathless, and in an upper range. It rises even higher with the line "any woman makes me quiver."

0:00	*Cherubino*: Non so piu cosa son, cosa faccio, Or di foco, ora sono di ghiaccio, Ogni donna cangiar di colore, Ogni donna mi fa palpitar	I don't know any more what I am doing, Now I'm fire, now I'm ice, Any woman makes me change color, Any woman makes me quiver.
0:19	Solo ai nomi d'amor, di diletto, Mi si turba, mi s'altera il petto, E a parlare mi sforza d'amore Un desio ch'io non posso spiegar	At just the names of love, of pleasure, My breast is stirred up and changed, And a desire I can't explain Forces me to speak of love.
0:47	*Non so piu . . .Here Cherubino pours out his heart. Notice the dramatic pauses, the melodic peaks, and the repeated phrases, all of which suggest adolescent exuberance and yearnings. In the last two lines, Cherubino echoes the near universal fate of love-struck adolescents, "And if there's nobody to hear me . . . I speak of love to myself."*	

LISTENING GUIDE (*Continued*)

1:07	Parlo d'amore vegliando,	I speak of love while awake,
	Parlo d'amor sognando,	I speak of love while dreaming,
	All'acqua, all'ombra, ai monti,	To the water, the shade, the hills,
	Ai fiori, all'erbe, ai fonti,	The flowers, the grass, the fountains,
	All'eco, all'aria, ai venti,	The echo, the air, and the winds
	Che il suon de'vani accenti	That carry away with them
	Portano via con se.	The vain words.
	Parlo d'amore vegliando . . .	I speak of love while awake . . .
	E se non ho chi m'oda,	And if there's nobody to hear me,
	Parlo d'amor con me!	I speak of love to myself!

DID YOU KNOW?

MEN WITH HIGH VOICES

The era of castrati is long over, but we still enjoy listening to men sing in falsetto. Some of these artists are simply goofy, such as scraggly haired, ukulele-strumming Tiny Tim (born Herbert Khaury, 1932–1996). Others, such as Little Richard, Brian Wilson of the Beach Boys, Michael Jackson, David Ruffin of The Temptations, Bobby McFerrin, Usher, and Justin Timberlake, have become teen idols.

ACTIVITIES AND ASSIGNMENTS

- Is there such a thing as nongendered music? Find a piece or song that you think is nongendered. Be sure to take its historical context into account.
- Are any of the gender concepts discussed in the previously noted operatic examples found in contemporary music videos?
- Gender confusion reigns in the romantic comedy *Tootsie* (1982), which starred Dustin Hoffman as an actor pretending to be a woman in order to land a television role. Watch the movie and pay particular attention to the song "It Might Be You." Part of the song's considerable charm stems from the fact that the lyrics give no clue to the many romantic possibilities the movie presents.

Lesbian and Gay Issues

We would all agree that signifiers such as ethnicity, gender, religion, and nationality are part of a person's identity. What about sexual orientation? Is Russian composer Pyotr Ilyich Tchaikovsky's (1840–1893) homosexuality audible in his music? What about Elton John's (b. 1947)? In many parts of the world, gays and lesbians continue to endure cultural oppression that ranges from exclusion to outright violence. How does this affect their artistic voice? American anti-homosexual sentiments in the 1950s and 1960s kept many gay composers close to the closet. Aaron Copland's (1900–1990) homosexuality was not widely known until after his death.

Important gay or bisexual American composers of the succeeding generation included John Cage (1912–1992), Samuel Barber (1910–1981), and Leonard Bernstein (1918–1990).

In the pop music world, there are many more "out" lesbian and female bisexuals than openly gay males. Melissa Etheridge (b. 1961), k.d. lang (b. 1961), Indigo Girls, and Ani diFranco (b. 1970) have provided lesbians and bisexuals with a level of visibility unknown in previous generations. (Lesley Gore came out in 2005. "You Don't Own Me" is now a favorite at gay-pride celebrations.)

One of the ways that gay musicians, especially those in the popular realm, have expressed their sexual orientation is through a specific kind of humor known as "camp." Camp can be difficult to define, though it may include elements such as self-mockery, theatricality, exaggerated gendered mannerisms, absurdity, vulgarity, silliness, and banality. Camp has often served as a code, safely signaling homosexual themes for those in the know while leaving others oblivious to the subtext. Musical examples include female impersonator Jean Malin's (1908–1933) Columbia recording "I'd Rather Be Spanish (Than Mannish)" (1933), Cole Porter's (1891–1964) "Anything Goes" (1934), and Little Richard's "Tutti Frutti" (1955).

One of the most openly gay musical activities is the gay and lesbian chorus movement, which began during a vigil following the murder of San Francisco councilman Harvey Milk (1930–1978). Today there are over 200 gay and lesbian choruses, with over 10,000 singers involved internationally. The choruses are civic as well as musical organizations. Members work to promote tolerance and generate social awareness.

Preceding the gay choral movement by two years was the Michigan Womyn's Music Festival (MWMF). (Womym, with a "y," implies there are no "men" in womyn.) For one week every August, the MWMF is home to over 4,000 women who collectively run and maintain the campgrounds, support systems, and entertainment. The festival has a strict and controversial women-born-women policy: men, transgendered, and transsexual women are not allowed on the grounds. The belief is that being born in a female body is essential to understanding patriarchal oppression.

On a cold evening in April 2008, the ethics surrounding the MWMF exclusion policy played out on Main Street in Bowling Green, Ohio, a small college town. The folk-rock/alternative performer/activist/actress/poet/bisexual Bitch, who is also a regular performer at the MWMF, was set to appear in one of the downtown bars. On arrival, Bitch found sign-carrying protesters in front of the bar. The protesters—most of whom were transgendered male-to-female—were asking people to boycott her performance because she supports MWMF.

Bitch went outside to speak with them. The demonstrators stressed their need for a safe place to be immersed in women's culture. They pointed out the hypocrisy of the MWMF

DID YOU KNOW?
THE AIDS SYMPHONY

Inspired by seeing "The Quilt," Pulitzer Prize-winning composer John Corigliano (b. 1938) composed his Symphony No. 1 (The AIDS Symphony) as an elegy to friends who had died of the disease. The piece was commissioned by the Chicago Symphony Orchestra and received its first performance in 1990. Since then it has received over 1,000 performances by orchestras all over the world.

MUSICAL LIVES
BILLY (NEE DOROTHY) TIPTON: PERFORMING GENDER

Jazz pianist and saxophonist Billy (nee Dorothy) Tipton (1914–1989) performed at a time when finding employment as a female jazz instrumentalist was extremely difficult. In order to live her dream, she decided to cross the line. At age 19, Dorothy became Billy.

At first, Tipton's male identity was more of a disguise than a lifestyle; her friends knew "he" was a she. But as Tipton moved from job to job and city to city, she gradually assumed a full-time male identity. She bound her breasts and claimed that a car accident had resulted in both sterility and permanently unhealed ribs. Throughout the 1930s and 1940s Tipton played with various West Coast dance bands. In 1954, he formed the Billy Tipton Trio and led the group for more than 10 years. Eventually, Tipton moved to Spokane and worked as an entertainment agent. He and his fifth wife adopted three sons. The couple led a typical family life. Tipton even served as a scoutmaster.

In the end, however, Tipton's life was marked by poverty and isolation. The marriage broke up and Tipton's health declined. Having avoided any kind of paperwork that would reveal his sex, Tipton was unable to collect Social Security or Medicare benefits. He avoided physicians. At age 74, Tipton collapsed in his trailer. As his son looked on, paramedics undressed the musician to administer CPR. Tipton's longest and most remarkable performance was finally over.

women-born-only policy. How was it that a female-to-male transgendered person could attend the festival, but they, now women, were excluded? If Bitch were a true feminist, they argued, she would show her support by boycotting the MWMF.

Bitch sympathized with the demonstrators' position on MWMF, but refused to boycott the festival. "The festival changed my life. It would break my heart not to play there," she said. In the end, Bitch seemed to concede that the festival's rule was problematic, but also pointed out that she did not set the policies. Eventually, the protesters went home; Bitch performed as scheduled.

Womyn's music is often characterized by an emphasis on social justice and peace. The encounter on Main Street was certainly peaceful, with respectful dialogue on both sides. But the question of social justice remains open. Who decides what is just and for whom? What does it mean to be a woman or a man? And what are the costs for those who cross the boundaries?

ACTIVITIES AND ASSIGNMENTS

- In the film *Arizona to Broadway* (1933), Jean Malin played the character of actor Ray Best, whose stage show is an obvious send-up of sexpot comedienne Mae West (1893–1980). In the 1960s, actor Flip Wilson played the popular character Geraldine in the comedy television show *Laugh-In*. Search out other cross-gender impersonators.
- Compare the women-only ideology of the MWMF with Dar Williams's point of view in "When I Was a Boy." Would it surprise you to know that Williams opened the festival in 2007?

CONCLUSION

We opened the "Gender in Popular Music" section of this chapter with a discussion of Elvis Presley, "girl groups," and changing social norms from the 1950s into the 1970s. Perhaps as you read that section you were thinking of songs or musicians that broke with the general trends we outlined. Perhaps you thought of Roy Orbison's (1936–1988) plaintive ballad "Crying," (1961) which tells the story of a man who cannot stop loving the woman he has lost. The song broke the social norms of the time. Girls cry, not men.

If that was a problem, audiences did not seem to notice. Orbison was an enigmatic figure. His voice ranged from deep baritone to falsetto, and was warmed with a rich vibrato. On stage, he presented the quiet, yet stalwart, and even tragic persona of someone who could cry without endangering his manhood.

There is not much of a story to glean from the lyrics to "Crying." Orbison has lost his lover, but we do not know why. He sings a soliloquy in which he describes a world imploding.

In 1987, Orbison re-recorded the song with feminist, activist, and out-lesbian k.d. lang. **mysearchlab 5.9** Watch the video of this remarkable collaboration between Orbison (the feminized male) and lang (the masculinized female). Are they simply two lonely voices in the night, bound by hurt but noth-

Roy Orbison in performance at the London Palladium in 1965.

ing else? Or might they be singing about the same woman? Or perhaps, could Orbison and lang themselves be the unhappy couple? The social ambiguities only add to the song's despair.

Throughout this chapter we have seen that music is rarely, if ever, gender neutral. Indeed, it is through subtle (and sometimes not so subtle) projections of gender that much of music's emotional power is cultivated. This should not be surprising. After all, gender is a cornerstone of personal and social identity. Composers and performers inevitably (though not always consciously) reflect that identity in their music. Sometimes they do so by reinforcing accepted social constructions. Often, however, their music challenges social norms. As sensitive listeners, conceptualizing these various representations gives us a wealth of opportunity through which to re-imagine the gendering of our own inner and social lives.

Music and Spirituality

CHAPTER GOALS

■ To understand how humankind uses music to express spirituality.

■ To investigate musical relationships between the sacred and the secular.

■ To become familiar with select works that exemplify spiritual traditions in music.

QUESTIONS FOR THOUGHT

■ Are there particular types of music that you consider to be spiritual?
■ Are there any styles of music you believe to be inappropriate for religious services?
■ Does music need to have religious text in order to be sacred?
■ Is there a difference between spiritual music and religious music? How so?

> "Music is the harmonious voice of creation; an echo of the invisible world."
>
> —Giuseppe Mazzini
> (1805–1872)

Tibetan Buddhist Chant

Clothed in their high-crested yellow hats and flowing red robes, the Gelug monks chant ancient Buddhist texts. The sound is strange to the Western ear—they chant deep bass tones over which high-pitched harmonics float like wind-borne angels. The monks' goal is not to make music as such. Instead, they chant to center the mind, to quiet desire. They seek enlightenment, the awareness of the divinity of all things.

Oftentimes, the monks employ a type of **harmonic singing**. The technique is relatively simple. Upon sounding the fundamental tone in the vocal cords, the vocalist shapes his oral cavity to accentuate overtones. **mysearchlab 6.1** When the proper shape and resonance are achieved, experienced singers can produce up to three simultaneous pitches.

The monks' vocal technique is easily described in mechanical terms. But how might their chanting be spiritual activity? Here are some initial ideas to consider.

■ First, the texts deal with sacred topics. Thus, chanting, which "performs" the sacred, is a type of meditation.
■ Second, the chanting technique requires considerable focus, which stills the mind and removes it from the worries and interests of everyday life.
■ Third, the technique slows the breathing, which may have a calming effect.
■ Fourth, the chanting is highly repetitive, which allows the mind to entrain to a single idea.

Surely you can think of additional ways in which chanting might focus consciousness. But are these physical acts the keys to Tibetan spirituality? No, say the Gelug. While these techniques might help prepare one for a spiritual experience, they are not the experience itself. That can only come from right thinking. Thus, chanting is best understood as the vehicle, not the destination.

The monks' texts are subtle and often capable of multiple interpretations. Consider the oft-chanted phrase "Om mani padme hum," the words of which are both enigmatic and recursive. According to Tenzin Gyatso (the fourteenth Dalai Lama and current leader of the Gelug order), the single syllable "om" is a tripartite reference to body, speech, and mind of both the desire-bound devotee and the enlightened Buddha. "Mani" embodies the "jewel" of altruism, whereas "padme" embodies the "lotus-flower" perfection of wisdom. "Hum" represents the idea of unity or indivisibility. Taken as a whole, the phrase presents the idea that impurities of existence can be overcome through the unifying power of altruism and wisdom. "Om" simultaneously represents the devotee's starting point and final goal.

The Gelug order was founded by the Tibetan monk Je Tsongkhapa in the early

Gelug monks playing music on a rooftop overlooking the Tikse Monastery in Ladakh, India.

fifteenth century. Known as the Yellow Hats, these monks have resided in India since 1959, when they fled Tibet following the Chinese military's suppression of the Lhasa uprising, a grassroots protest against the Chinese occupation that began in 1950. Today, the monks make their home in Dharamsala, a town at the edge of the Himalayan Mountains. Since the 1960s, the Gelug tradition and numerous other Buddhist orders have made performance tours in the West, followed by critically and commercially successful audio recordings. In fact, a recording made by monks from the Tai Situpas lineage won a 2004 Grammy Award.

LISTENING GUIDE

CD II/Track 2
Download track 24
mysearchlab 6.2

YAMANTAKA (EXCERPT)

chanted by the Gyuto Monks

Produced by Dutch jazz musician/composer/arranger Chris Hinze (b. 1938), this recording was inspired by Hinze's conversations with the Dalai Lama during a 1994 concert tour of India. The meditation, a small portion of which is presented here, honors the Tibetan deity Yamantaka, the conqueror of death. The monks' invocations are meant to rid human beings from the failings of anger, lust, greed, and envy, so that self-realization may be attained. In the recording studio, Hinze subtly enriched the texture of the original meditation by adding synthesized drone tones in the upper register.

Monastic rituals that employ this type of chanting might last several days and include the construction of a mandala, which the Gyuto construct by pouring colored sand. Mandalas illustrate the perfect relationship between god and mankind, between spirit, mind, and body.

0:00	A single monk begins the meditation. Notice the gravelly, deep vocal quality.
0:12	He is joined by the rest of the group. Listen for the very low fundamental and the shimmering, electronically enhanced overtones vibrating above. For the most part, the monks breathe.
0:37	A bell occasionally sounds. Its resonant tone warns evil spirits to stay clear of the sacred space. (Bells are also said to represent the teachings of Buddha.)
3:27	Fade out.

DID YOU KNOW?

SAND PAINTING

Chanting is just one of numerous meditative endeavors undertaken by the monks. Another is the construction of sand **mandalas**, geometrically shaped images designed to create sacred spaces where enlightenment can occur. Although a mandala can take many days to create, it is destroyed shortly after completion. For the monks, the process of creation and destruction is a meditation in itself, a days-long rumination on life's complexity and impermanence.

QUESTIONS FOR THOUGHT

- Do you think Buddhist chant is sacred when performed as part of a ritual ceremony? What if the same chant were performed in New York City's Carnegie Hall as part of a Free Tibet fundraising concert?
- There are dozens of versions of "Om mani padme hum" available on the Internet. Compare and contrast some of them.
- Adam Yauch of the Beastie Boys is Buddhist. In 1995, the group released "Bodhisattva Vow." Might this be characterized as spiritual music? (A *bodhisattva* is an enlightened individual who serves humanity.)

Music and Spirituality

In this chapter we investigate the ways in which music is used to enhance spiritual experience. We will discover tremendous variation. Some religions use music to quiet mind and body; others use it to excite. Some traditions focus on words, others on melody, and still others on rhythm. Invariably, however, music is used as a lens to focus experience.

First we take up an exploration of the Christian **hymn** "Amazing Grace." We examine three different musical performances, each of which reflects distinct social values. From "Amazing Grace" we travel back in time to the Middle Ages and Renaissance where we study the early development of Christian church music and, by extension, the roots of Western art music. Then we explore music from the Yoruba, Sufi, and Jewish traditions.

"Amazing Grace"

Many consider "Amazing Grace," with its sturdy **diatonic** melody and message of personal transformation, to be the ultimate musical testament to the Christian doctrine of salvation.

Though commonly sung in church services, the hymn is also performed at commemoratory events, particularly funerals. In 1838, for example, it was sung on a near daily basis during the notorious "Trail of Tears" march, when thousands of Cherokee Indians died during forced relocation to Indian Territory. Today in San Francisco's Chinatown, traditional funeral processions open with the hymn, which is performed by the Green Street Mortuary Band. Following the deadly New York City terrorist attacks of September 11, 2001, the city's police and fire department bagpipe ensembles repeatedly played the hymn during ceremonies honoring their fallen comrades.

> *Amazing grace, how sweet the sound*
> *That sav'd a wretch like me!*
> *I once was lost, but now am found,*
> *Was blind, but now I see.*

The hymn's text was written by John Newton (1725–1807), an English slave trader who, after surviving a violent storm at sea, converted to evangelical Christianity at age 23. It is often told that Newton's near-death experience immediately convinced him of the sins of slavery and that he wrote "Amazing Grace" in response to that conversion. But that story is false. In fact, Newton became an abolitionist only late in life. "Amazing Grace" was written in 1772 for his own use in a sermon, and possibly also as an entry for an informal hymn-text writing competition. In addition, Newton did not compose the melody. He would have expected a congregation either to speak the words or to sing them to any commonly known melody that might have fit. It was not until around 1835 that text and music, a tune called "New Britain," became inextricably bound.

We now compare and contrast recordings of the hymn by Bernice Johnson Reagon (b. 1942), the Robert Shaw Festival Singers, and American **shape-note** singers. Each performance promotes the same message of redemption, but the styles are vastly different.

"Amazing Grace," Performed by Bernice Johnson Reagon The daughter of a Baptist minister, Bernice Reagon was born and raised just outside of Albany, Georgia. Through her involvement in the civil rights movement she became, at age 20, a founding member of the SNCC (Student Non-violent Coordinating Committee) Freedom Singers. In 1973 she founded the singing group Sweet Honey in the Rock.

For Reagon, music is a link to heritage. In this recording she demonstrates a technique called **lining out** in which the song leader introduces the words and tune that the choir will then sing. Lining out, an essential choral technique in nonliterate America, is still used in some churches today.

Freedom Singers (Bernice Johnson Reagan third from right).

LISTENING GUIDE

CD II/Track 3
Download track 25
mysearchlab 6.3a

"AMAZING GRACE"

Performed by Bernice Johnson Reagon

Reagon performs the song's first verse only, which she divides into two parts. She lines out the first two halves of the stanza and then, taking the part of the choir, repeats it in an embellished fashion, as an African American Baptist chorus or congregation might. Then she follows the same process with the last two lines. When lined out, the words are presented in a simple syllabic style with a narrow melodic range. The repetitions are melismatic with greatly expanded melodic flow. The performance is nonmetric; Reagon offers only hints of the song's commonly known melody. Finally, the text is slightly changed—"sound" becomes "Son."

0:00	Reagon lines out the lyrics: Amazin' grace, how sweet the Son That save[d] a wretch like me.
0:11	Lines are repeated in expanded form.
1:11	Reagon lines out the final two lines: I once was lost, but now I'm found. Blind, but now I see.
1:21	Lines are repeated in expanded form.
2:16	Reagon hums. One can imagine the words implied in the melody: (Amazin' grace, how sweet . . .
2:27	That save a wretch like me.
2:33	I was lost, but now . . .
2:41	Blind, but now I see.
2:48	Amazin' grace.)

MUSICAL LIVES

THOMAS DORSEY (1899–1993)

Paving the way for the gospel sound was Thomas Dorsey, the "father of gospel music." Dorsey, like Reagon, grew up in his father's Baptist ministry before going on to a successful career in secular music. When a nervous disorder interrupted his jazz career, however, Dorsey returned to sacred music. In 1931 he founded the Thomas A. Dorsey Gospel Songs Music Publishing Company, the first African American gospel music publishing house. At the time, African American church music was marked by an increasingly restrained vocal style. Dorsey interrupted that trend by infusing his music with a rhythmic aesthetic built on improvisation, spontaneity, and heartfelt emotion.

Dorsey's gospel masterpiece is "Take My Hand, Precious Lord," which he wrote in a hotel room in 1932 after receiving a telegram stating that his wife and infant had died in childbirth. The words came "like drops of water from a crevice of a rock above," said Dorsey. Over time, "Precious Lord" not only attained a central place in the African American church but became an anthem for the 1960s civil rights movement. Mahalia Jackson sang the song at the funeral of her friend, Dr. Martin Luther King Jr.

"Amazing Grace," Performed by the Robert Shaw Festival Singers   Now let's compare Reagon's solo performance with a choral performance led by conductor Robert Shaw (1916–1999). Under Shaw's direction, improvisation is replaced by order, individuality by the concordant blend of unified forces.

Shaw served as music director of the Atlanta Symphony from 1967 to 1988, but he made his mark as a choral music conductor, for which he earned 14 Grammys and the National Medal of Arts (1992). Vocalists on this recording are music professionals in residence at the Robert Shaw Institute. Though in session for only a few weeks in the summer, the Institute drew choral music professionals seeking advanced training under Shaw's guidance. Each residency culminated in the recording and release of an album under the name of the Robert Shaw Festival Singers.

LISTENING GUIDE

CD II/Track 4
Download track 26
mysearchlab 6.3b

"AMAZING GRACE"   *Performed by the Robert Shaw Festival Singers*

The performance is **a cappella** (voices only) and the form is **strophic**, that is, the melody for each verse remains essentially the same. Notice the characteristics of the professionally trained voices: vibrato and careful text articulation.

0:00	*Verse 1.* A tenor soloist sings the melody with chordal accompaniment provided by the chorus's tenors and basses.
0:43	*Verse 2.* The full chorus enters.
1:25	*Verse 3.* The tenor soloist returns.
2:08	*Verse 4.* The full chorus sings again.
2:50	*Verse 1.* The tenor soloist sings the words to verse 1 again, slightly varying the melodic line.
3:39	*Coda.* The chorus's male voices conclude the hymn by repeating the last two lines of the verse.

Notice the symmetry in the arrangement. The tenor soloist presents verses one, three, and five. The full chorus is featured in verses two and four.

"Amazing Grace," Performed by the Old Harp Singers of Eastern Tennessee
Finally, we listen to an arrangement of "Amazing Grace" as performed by sacred

harp singers from rural Eastern Tennessee. Sacred harp, also called "shape-note" singing, is an American folk tradition dating back to the late eighteenth century when friends would gather at the local church or meeting hall to socialize and sing hymns. They used song books that facilitated music reading by having different-shaped notes represent different pitches (for example, "mi" = ◇, "fa" = ◿, "sol" = 𝒪, "la" = □), hence the term "shape-note" singing. **mysearchlab 2.4** The earliest of these books were used as teaching tools in New England singing schools—America's first musical training institutions.

Sacred harp singing emphasizes the natural voice (the "sacred harp"). The vocal timbre is untutored and often strident. No instruments are used and the melody line is often sung by tenors, or tenors and sopranos an octave apart. Singing focuses on face-to-face interaction, with vocalists sitting along the perimeter of an open square and facing the middle. Participants take turns leading from the center. Community spirit and honest expression are their most valued qualities.

Historically, sacred harp flourished primarily in the South, where in rural areas the tradition survives relatively unchanged. It is currently enjoying a revival in urban centers across the country. Those who participate do so for the love of singing. They remark upon the physicality of facing one another, singing in a full voice, and feeling the great waves of sound reverberate throughout the room. With most of today's shape-note singing there is no denominational association. Even so, participants often remark on the deeply spiritual emotions engendered by the experience.

LISTENING GUIDE

CD II/Track 5
Download track 27
mysearchlab 6.3c

"AMAZING GRACE"

Performed by the Old Harp Singers of Eastern Tennessee

In a fashion reminiscent of Reagon's lining out, the leader begins each verse slightly before the rest of the singers. The choir quickly joins in and all sing together. Voices are untrained and uninhibited; some even stand out as shrill and nasal. Enthusiasm is valued over blend. Singers tend to slide from one note to the next.

The hymn is sung in four-part harmony, but the texture sounds even thicker. This is because the various lines are being sung by men and women alike. Thus, the bass part is doubled up an octave by the women and the soprano is doubled down an octave by the men. The triple meter pushes forward with soldier-like regularity (one . . . three one . . . three one . . .).

0:00	Verse 1.
0:38	Verse 2.
1:15	Verse 3.
1:53	Added verse. (Not original to John Newton; first connected to "Amazing Grace" by Harriet Beecher Stowe in her 1852 antislavery novel *Uncle Tom's Cabin*.) *When we've been there ten thousand years,* *Bright shining like the sun,* *We've no less days to sing God's praise* *Than when we first begun.*

Take some time to compare and contrast the three performances. Some listeners will find that Reagon' improvisatory style speaks directly to the heart, to the needs of the individual in the here and now. Others, however, will find the Festival Singers' somber aesthetic to be quintessentially worshipful. Others might label the sound too polished and prefer the shape-note singers. Can any of them be considered "better" or "more sacred" than the others?

It is remarkable that all three of these examples, different as they are, come from contemporary American traditions. Imagine how differences will magnify as we travel back in time or to different cultures and religious practices. This is the journey we now undertake.

As we move through the rest of this chapter, keep in mind the people for whom the musical examples are meant. What is their worldview? What is their spiritual view? What are their particular needs and desires? And especially, how does music represent and fortify their spiritual understandings?

ACTIVITIES AND ASSIGNMENTS

- Is there such a thing as a "definitive" recording of "Amazing Grace"? Can one performance be more "correct" than another? If so, what might be the criteria?
- How many different performances (recordings, movies, TV shows, Internet videos) can you find of "Amazing Grace"? How do these different performances reflect the values of their audiences?
- Think to a time in a religious service (or perhaps during the singing of "The Star-Spangled Banner" at a sporting event) when the person next to you sang horribly out of tune. (Perhaps you were that person.) What did you think of the performance? Would you have rather she or he did not sing at all? Should "bad" singers be barred from participation? What is most important, sound or intention?
- Look on the Internet for shape-note singing events near you. Consider attending one. Document your own personal experience or interview a participant.

Music in the Early Christian Church

From the early Middle Ages up until the early 1960s, most of the individual elements (collectively called the **liturgy**) in the Catholic **Mass** were chanted. Chant (or plainchant) ranged in style from simple text recitation on just one or two notes to long, soaring, and undulating melodies. Most chant was sung by clerics (men or women who had taken holy orders) in churches, monasteries, and convents. As with the chanting of the Gyuto monks, plainchant was a tool for connecting with the sacred.

Chant was originally performed for voice alone, which was thought to be God's "perfect instrument." The language was Latin, and the melodies were monophonic and rhythmically free. Chants usually had smooth melodic contours and sounded in one of the eight church melodic **modes** (rather than in the major and minor scales we use today). **mysearchlab 2.3** Plainchants were composed anonymously and passed on by oral tradition. They were first written down in the ninth century as Western musical notation began to develop in European monasteries. **mysearchlab 2.4**

Listen to a plainchant of *Kyrie eleison*. The text is Greek, a vestige from the early Byzantine church, and the only part of the Mass that is not in Latin.

CD I/Track 4
Download track 4
mysearchlab 6.4

LISTENING GUIDE

KYRIE ELEISON, PLAINCHANT

PLAINCHANT: *KYRIE ELEISON* (FROM MISSA "CUM JUBILO")

0:00	Kyrie eleison (3 times)	Lord have mercy
0:36	Christe eleison (3 times)	Christ have mercy
1:03	Kyrie eleison (3 times)	Lord have mercy

Notice that the words are set melismatically. The "e" of the final "eleison" spans nearly 40 pitches. This technique of stretching the words allows the listener time to assimilate the spiritual message. The rhythm is without meter, free and flowing. The melodic contour is conjunct and forms gentle arches. Each line of text is repeated three times, creating a symbolic representation of the Trinity.

The Renaissance Mass

By the Renaissance, composers were writing polyphonic settings for the **Ordinary** of the Mass—the parts of the liturgy in which the texts never changed: the Kyrie, Gloria, Credo, Sanctus, and Agnus Dei. The rest of the Mass, the **Proper** (with texts that changed from day to day), continued to be chanted. Polyphonic Mass settings peaked during the Renaissance, but even today composers set these traditional texts.

MUSICAL TERMS

GREGORIAN CHANT

There are many plainchant traditions. Gregorian Chant, the most recognized type today, developed in Western Europe in the eighth century. As nearly as scholars can tell, it was probably a mixture of two earlier chant traditions, Old Roman and Gallican. It is likely that the repertory developed because Charlemagne (747–814), the first Holy Roman Emperor, wanted to unify his territory and strengthen ties with Rome. The chant was named for Pope Gregory I (ca. 540–604), who supposedly received the chants from the Holy Spirit (symbolized in literature and painting with a dove). Charlemagne apparently used the story to convince his Frankish countrymen to switch to Roman chant. With the merging of Roman and Gallican chant, "Gregorian Chant" was born. Thus, one of Catholicism's most sacred musical genres likely developed from political aspirations rather than purely religious intentions.

Gregorian Chant was used in the Catholic church until the Second Ecumenical Council of the Vatican (known as Vatican II), held from 1962–1965. In many Catholic churches, especially in North America, folk-style music replaced the Latin chants. In 2007, however, Pope Benedict XVI suggested reviving the pre-Vatican II plainchant Mass.

LISTENING GUIDE

CD II/Track 6
Download track 28
mysearchlab 6.5

KYRIE FROM THE POPE MARCELLUS MASS
by Giovanni Pierluigi da Palestrina

Palestrina (1525/26–1594) lived during the Counter-Reformation, a time when the Catholic church was responding to the Protestant Reformation. Leaders of the Counter-Reformation sought a return to religious basics. For music, that meant purging from the Mass secular tunes that had infiltrated the polyphonic texture and making sure the sacred text could be understood. Palestrina's music was held up as a good example of reform aesthetics.

This excerpt is the first part of his *Pope Marcellus Mass*, named for Pope Marcellus II, who died in 1555 after just three weeks in office. The Mass is written for six independent voice parts and is performed a cappella. The six voice lines are soprano, alto, two tenors, and two basses. Palestrina's Kyrie divides into three sections dictated by the text. Each section begins with a thin texture that increases as more voices enter. The text is repeated as melodic lines are echoed and reshaped throughout the music. The feeling is calm, but metered, and forward in its rhythmic direction.

0:00	*Kyrie eleison*	Lord, have mercy upon us. The voices enter in the following order: tenor 1, soprano, bass 1, alto, tenor 2, and bass 2. Listen for the distinctive upward leap in each voice. It is easiest to hear in the soprano, but all of the voices are singing it.
1:11		All of the voices gradually converge on a sustained chord that signals the end of the section.
1:19	*Christe eleison*	Christ, have mercy upon us. This section begins with three of the voices singing homophonically (all together, not imitatively). Soon, however, more voices enter and the texture once again becomes polyphonic with independently moving lines intertwining one with another.
2:38		Once again, the voices cadence on a long note to signal the end of the section. This chord does not sound resolved, however, so we know the piece is not over.
2:45	*Kyrie eleison*	

Music of the Protestant Reformation: From Luther to Bach

In 1517, the Catholic monk Martin Luther (1483–1546) nailed his "Ninety-Five Theses" to the door of the Wittenberg Castle Church in Saxony (now Germany). The document, which criticized the Catholic policies on purgatory and selling indulgences, began the Protestant Reformation.

Some reformers thought that music represented luxurious excess and limited its use. Not Luther, who used music to instruct and to worship, and who wrote that "next to the Word of God, the noble art of music is the greatest treasure in the world." Instead of plainchant, however, the Lutheran church used German chorales: strophic congregational songs with singable tunes. Luther himself wrote many chorale texts and a few tunes. Some chorales had their roots in the Catholic church and even in secular works. Both were the case with "O Sacred Head, Now Wounded."

The chorale's text dates back to the twelfth century. Originally in Latin, the text is attributed to Bernard of Clairvaux (1091–1153), an influential monk remembered for his elegant sermons, theological treatises, and hymn texts. The music, if there was any, no longer exists.

The text was translated into German (*O Haupt voll Blut und Wunden*) for use in the early Lutheran church. It was paired with the melody of a secular love song. "O Sacred Head, Now Wounded" is now a standard hymn in many Christian denominations.

St. Matthew Passion (1739), by J. S. Bach

Two hundred years after the actions of Martin Luther, Johann Sebastian Bach would spend most of his career working within the Lutheran church. Many of his works make use of traditional chorale tunes. The melody of "O Sacred Head, Now Wounded," for example, appears in at least seven works, most notably in the *St. Matthew Passion* (1739).

The *St. Matthew Passion* is an oratorio, an unstaged and uncostumed musical play. Specifically, it is a *passion* oratorio, which tells the biblical account of Jesus's last days. The narrative is told through the evangelist—additional soloists sing the parts of Jesus, Pilate, Judas, and other characters; two choruses take the parts of the soldiers, the disciples, and the crowd. The composition takes almost three hours to perform.

For Bach, the *St. Matthew Passion* functioned as both a way to tell the historical narrative of Christ's suffering and as a vehicle for spiritual reflection. The insertion of chorale tunes signified the music's specifically Lutheran origins.

Today, this work exists in the concert hall, though in keeping with its original purpose it is often performed just before Easter. Thus, the *St. Matthew Passion* now functions on even more levels than it did in Bach's time. One may simultaneously see the work as:

- Bach's individual testament of religious faith.
- An example of eighteenth-century Lutheran spirituality.
- A vehicle for personal religious reflection.
- One of the greatest examples of late-Baroque artistic achievement.

Martin Luther burning the papal edict that condemns his actions while university officials and townspeople watch; in the background is the town of Wittenberg.

LISTENING GUIDE

CD II/Track 7
Download track 29
mysearchlab 6.6

ST. MATTHEW PASSION   *by J. S. Bach*

Listen first to the chorale, "O Sacred Head, Now Wounded" (AABC form). The first two musical phrases are the same (AA), ending without resolution on nontonic chords. The melodic leap at the beginning of each phrase (perhaps a metaphor for the desire for heavenly ascent) gives the melody a yearning quality, as does the even larger leap in the middle of the phrase. To add contrast, as well as increasing dramatic motion, the last two phrases are different (BC). While both begin in a high melodic range and descend to the same ending pitch, their respective harmonizations present different emotional qualities. The B phrase sounds bright, but incomplete. The C phrase, in contrast, offers conclusion.

	Phrase 1 (A)	**[familiar English version]**
0:00	O Haupt voll Blut und Wunden, / Voll Schmerz und voller Hohn	O sacred Head, now wounded, / With grief and shame weighed down,
	Phrase 2 (A)	
0:15	O Haupt, zum Spott gebunden / Mit einer Dornenkron,'	Now scornfully surrounded / With thorns, thine only crown:
	Phrase 3 (B)	
0:31	O Haupt, sonst schön gezieret / Mit höchster Ehr' und Zier,	How pale thou art with anguish / With sore abuse and scorn!
	Phrase 4 (C)	
0:46	Jetzt aber höchst schimpfieret; / Gegrüßet sei'st du mir!	How does that visage languish / Which once was bright as morn!

The chorale melody appears five times in Bach's *Passion*, all in the second half, where the focus is on Christ's trial and crucifixion. The following excerpt begins with the evangelist describing the last minutes of Christ's life. As darkness settles over the land, Jesus cries his famous words, "My God, my God, why have you forsaken me?"

0:00	EVANGELIST As the narrator, the evangelist sings in recitative style. The organ accompanies him, beginning with a chord that gives the first pitch. Then he sings alone in a speech-like manner, with organ interjections. The organist sounds a clear cadence at the end of the sentence. Und von der sechsten Stunde an war eine Finsternis über das ganze Land, bis zu der neunten Stunde.	Now from the sixth hour there was darkness all over the land until the ninth hour.

(Continued)

LISTENING GUIDE (*Continued*)

0:30	Next the narrator becomes more animated, his voice gets higher and louder. Und um die neunte Stunde schriee Jesus laut und sprach:	And about the ninth hour, Jesus cried in a loud voice, saying:
0:41	JESUS: Eli, Eli, lama asabthani? This phrase ends on an unresolved chord and there is a pause, letting the question sink in.	Eli, Eli, lama sabachthani?
1:01	Notice how the narrator sings at a higher pitch the second time he says, "my God." EVANGELIST: Das ist, "Mein Gott, mein Gott, warum hast du mich verlassen?"	That is to say, "My God, my God, why have you forsaken me?"
1:27	Now the narrator describes the crowd: Etliche aber, die da stunden, da sie das höreten, sprachen sie:	Some of them that stood there, when they heard that, said:
1:34	The chorus, accompanied by orchestra, comments on the action. The fast tempo, melodic leaps, and short interjections reveal the crowd's agitation. CHORUS: Der rufet dem Elias!	He calls for Elias!
1:37	Back to recitative while the narrator tells the story. EVANGELIST: Und bald lief einer unter ihnen nahm einen Schwamm und füllete ihn mit Essig und steckete ihn auf ein Rohr und tränkete ihn Die andern aber sprachen	And immediately one of them ran, and took a sponge, and filled it with vinegar, and put it on a reed, and gave it to him to drink. The rest said:
1:54	CHORUS: Halt! Laß sehen, ob Elias komme und ihm helfe?	Stop, let us see whether Elias will come to save him.
2:02	EVANGELIST: Aber Jesus schriee abermal laut und verschied. The singer ends this phrase inconclusively . . . in a ghostlike way. The organ provides the final resolution.	Jesus, when he had cried again with loud voice, yielded up his Spirit.
2:27	Finally, the last appearance in the *Passion* of the famous chorale tune. The words have been changed to suit Jesus's thoughts in the last moments of his life. Notice how Bach changes his harmonization in the second verse to fit the sentiments of the text. This is especially noticeable on the words "allerbangsten" (languish), "Angsten" (anguish), and "Pien" (woe). CHORUS: Wenn ich einmal soll scheiden, So scheide nicht von mir Wenn ich den Tod soll leiden, So tritt du denn herfür!	Be near me, Lord when dying. O part not Thou from me! And to my succor flying, Come, Lord, and set me free!
3:01	Wenn mir am allerbängsten Wird um das Herze sein, So reiß mich aus den Angsten Kraft deiner Angst und Pein!	And when my heart must languish In death's last awful throe, Release me from mine anguish, By Thine own pain and woe.

QUESTIONS FOR THOUGHT

- What constitutes a "good" or "beautiful" voice? Are the criteria different in religious music than in commercial music? Why might this be so?
- Are there any similarities between Tibetan and Western chanting?
- How does the function of chant differ from that of a hymn, such as "Amazing Grace," or the chorale, "O Sacred Head, Now Wounded"?
- What were the advantages and disadvantages of using plainchant for so many years in the Catholic church?
- Why do you think composers only set the Ordinary of the Mass polyphonically?
- Some traditions do not use music in their services. Why might this be?

The Yoruba of Nigeria

We journey now in both time and place to the modern day **Yoruba,** a large and influential ethnic group that resides in the central and coastal areas of Nigeria. The Yoruba (and related ethnic groups) practice a complex religion that, because of the slave trade, has had considerable impact not just in Nigeria but also on religions in the Americas, including Brazilian Candomblé, Trinidadian Shango, Cuban **Santería,** and Haitian Vodún.

The Yoruba have a complex and rich belief system. At the top of the Yoruba cosmology is Olodumare (God Almighty), a being too great to be comprehended by the human mind. Stationed just below are the **òrìṣà** (literally, "sacred heads"), powerful entities who embody specific aspects of Olodumare. It is the òrìṣà, rather than Olodumare, whom the Yoruba worship.

Like the gods of classical Greece and Rome, the òrìṣà have distinct humanlike personalities. They are generally associated with forces of nature. For example, there is the virile thunder god (Ṣàngó), the sensual river goddess (Ochún), the quick-to-anger god of smallpox (Obalúayé), and literally hundreds more. Some, like those previously mentioned, are worshiped all across Yorubaland. Others are recognized and worshiped only in specific regions.

The òrìṣà like to involve themselves directly in the affairs of humans. Thus, a believer might pray or offer sacrifices to an òrìṣà in exchange for assistance in life's daily events. The most dramatic contact is accomplished through possession trance, an event in which an òrìṣà "mounts" and takes control of the mind and body of a human medium. While mounted on its human "horse," an òrìṣà will actually speak, giving advice both mundane and profound to anyone who dares approach.

For a number of reasons, music—especially drummed music—holds a central

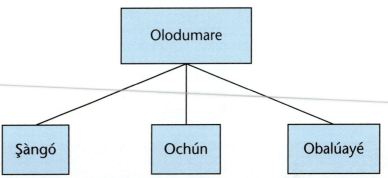

A small subset of the Yoruba religious hierarchy. Each of the hundreds of òrìṣà embodies aspects of God Almighty. Each òrìṣà is associated with specific praise poetry, called oríkì.

place in Yoruba worship. First of all, good music attracts the attention of the gods. Second, drum rhythms support worship through song and dance. Third, because Yoruba drums are capable of "speaking," drummers can praise the òrìṣà through drummed words. Such praise ensures the deities' beneficence.

The drums speak by imitating the inflections of the Yoruba language. Yoruba is tonal—the same sound combination will take on different meanings according to its inflected pitch. Thus, in Yoruba the same syllabic combination might signify something completely different when spoken with a high tone versus a rising tone, low tone, or falling tone. By imitating the rhythmic and melodic patterns of speech, drums "talk."

The most important texts that drums communicate are traditional *oríkì* (praise poems). An òrìṣà might be associated with hundreds of oríkì, each of which describes a particular aspect of the deity's personality. Drumming or singing an oríkì not only honors an òrìṣà but is also believed to attract him or her to a ceremonial event. Once the òrìṣà is in the vicinity, possession trance can occur. The likelihood of trance is further enhanced through dance, an activity the òrìṣà enjoy.

The Yoruba use two types of drums to create speech melody. The most versatile talking drum is the two-headed hourglass-shaped *dùndún*. Leather strings run along the length of the drum from one head to the other. When the strings are squeezed, the drum's pitch rises.

Less adaptable to speech are **bàtá** drums. Also double-headed, the bàtá's pitch cannot be changed. So instead, drummers build high and low tones by interlocking their rhythms one drum with another. Bàtá drums come in sets of three or four and are said to be owned by Şàngó. The instruments' shape resembles the head of Şàngó's thunder axe; the crack of the drum beat is said to represent a thunder clap.

Ritually blessed bàtá drums are rich in symbolism. They are constructed with only organic materials (wood, rope, animal skin) and are treated as living objects. Drums are sometimes adorned with brass bells, which symbolize the goddess Ochún, Şàngó's most

important lover. There is a wealth of gendered symbolism. For example, the largest instrument is the *iyá ilú* (mother drum) and the instrument's interior is said to be a womb from which sonic/spiritual energy is born. Drummers are sometimes said to impregnate the drums with their strikes.

Yoruba religious beliefs traveled to the New World with the slave trade. In Cuba, the Yoruba belief system merged with other African systems as well as Catholicism. The latter mix eventually formed Santería, a syncretic religion combining Catholic and Yoruba beliefs. For a practitioner of Santería, a statue of Saint Barbara also represents Şàngó; a statue of St. Lazarus also represents Obalúayé. Santería is increasingly practiced in the United States, particularly in Miami and New York City. Some practitioners, however, are looking to "purify" the religion by extricating the Catholic influences and focusing exclusively on Yoruba principles.

LISTENING GUIDE

CD II/Track 8
Download track 30
mysearchlab 6.7

ELEGGUA

Eleggua (or Èsù) is the first òrìşà honored at any religious ceremony. He guards the crossroads and is said to open or close all pathways. Because crossroads are places where new possibilities exist and where one must make decisions (for example, whether to turn left or right, to go forward or back), by extension, all human decisions fall under Eleggua's purview. The bàtá drums begin this excerpt by playing the following brief oríkì: Èsù látopa, Èsù gongo.

0:00	The iyá ilú, the lowest-pitched drum, calls the rhythm.
0:03	The middle-pitched drum enters with the tones "gongo."
0:04	The drums combine to play the first line: Èsù látopa [Èsù waves a stick].
0:06	The drums combine to play the second line: Èsù gongo Èsù gongo [gongo refers to an elongated head shape].
0:08	The phrase repeats with minor variations.
0:34	Fade out.

DID YOU KNOW?

TRANCE

What is possession trance like? Mediums—that is, those who actually become possessed—admit that even they do not know. This is because once the possession occurs, the individual's personality is displaced. Thus, the possessed person has no memory of the experience. People do remember the onset of possession, however. The following description comes from anthropologist and filmmaker Maya Deren. The event happened in Haiti, where she was making a documentary film about Vodún rituals. Deren was not a believer but attended ceremonies as her work required. She was not seeking to go into trance.

"The white darkness moves up the veins of my leg like a swift tide rising, rising; it is a great force which I cannot sustain or contain, which, surely, will burst my skin. It is too much, too bright, too white for me; this is its darkness. . . . The bright darkness floods up through my body, reaches my head, engulfs me. I am sucked down and exploded upward at once. That is all." (*Divine Horsemen: The Living Gods of Haiti*. McPherson & Company, 1953, p. 260.)

QUESTIONS FOR THOUGHT

- Yoruba religious practice and thought thrive in many parts of the Americas. Yet, there is considerable variation from one location to another. What factors might account for these differences?
- Might one version of Yoruba religious practice be more authentic than another? Is religious practice in Nigeria more authentic than religious practice in Havana or Miami? Consider arguments on both sides.
- Yoruba drums speak by imitating speech inflection. Western music also creates a strong connection between pitch and words. Try the following experiment. Hum a well-known song to a friend. Then, ask her if she hears the song's words in her mind. The answer is almost certainly yes. How does this additive process affect understanding?
- Are there clear boundaries between sacred and secular musics? If Bach's *St. Matthew Passion* is performed in a concert hall, does it remain sacred music by virtue of its subject matter? What about a batá rhythm? What if the performers themselves are agnostic?

The Mevlevi Sufi Order

The art of music may never have had a more enthusiastic supporter than the Persian poet, philosopher, and mystic Mevlana Celaleddin Rumi (1207–1273), who wrote that melody animates the soul and that rhythm once stirred the universe into existence. After Rumi's death in Konya, Turkey, his followers honored him by founding the **Mevlevi** order, known today in the West as the Whirling Dervishes.

The Mevlevi are a suborder of **Sufism**, the mystical branch of Islam. There are numerous Sufi orders, each with its own particular rites. But all the orders share a belief in a universal God with whom it is possible to experience direct spiritual union. The Sufi use a variety of techniques to achieve this, particularly meditation and contemplation. The Mevlevi place a strong emphasis on music, which sends the practitioner's physical body into a slow dance, a graceful and ecstatic turning.

Mevlevi worship unfolds in a highly formalized and many-sectioned ceremony known as **Samā'** (or *Sema*, "listening" or "presence"). The ceremony, which is highly symbolic, enacts a soul's passage to God. This metaphorical journey begins with the first flowering of the soul's awareness of divinity, which precipitates a gradual loss of self that ultimately leads to a mystical ascent to God's side.

Symbolism is pervasive in the Samā'. A *samazan*'s (Samā' practitioner) attire and actions reflect the ideal of surrendering one's individual identity to the all-encompassing

Samazans in motion.

"Hearken to the reed flute, how it complains, Lamenting banishment from its home."

Prologue from Rumi's nearly 25,000-verse poem *Mathnavi*

universalism of God. For example, a sama-zan will wear tall headgear that represents a tombstone for the ego; his white skirt represents the ego's shroud. The samazan's body is treated symbolically as well. The samazan enters the performance space slowly, with arms crossed and hands on shoulders, a posture meant to represent the oneness of God. As the counterclockwise *ayin-i şerif* or *mukabele* (spinning dance) begins, the samazan's arms are opened outward. The right palm is turned heavenward to receive God's blessings; the left palm is turned downward to transmit that power into the earth. Thus, the spinning dervish, like the reed flute in the Rumi verse discussed previously, becomes a conduit through which the divine is made manifest in the world.

The Samā' ceremony unfolds through a series of distinct sections:

- *Naat-i Sherif:* A eulogy in praise of the prophet Muhammad and those that preceded him.
- *Kun:* As the paired *kundüm* kettle drums are beaten, they sound the word "kun" (to be). The drum represents the divine voice whose rhythmic vitality is said to have brought all matter into existence.
- *Taksim:* A **taksim** is a nonmetric instrumental improvisation. In the Samā' ceremony it is performed on the *ney,* an end-blown reed flute, chosen because of the instrument's symbolic importance in the previously stated opening lines of the *Mathnavi.*
- *Devr-i Veled walk: Samazen* (pl.) perform salutations as they move three times around the performance circle accompanied by *peşrev* ("that which precedes"), an instrumental precomposed piece with roots in the Ottoman court.
- *The four-part Ayin section:* Each section has a distinct rhythm. (The third section contains three different cycles.) At the beginning and end of each section the *samazen* perform specific salutes.
  1. The birth of one's awareness of God's existence.
  2. Rapture at the majesty of creation.
  3. Submission to God. This is accompanied by an ecstatic state called *Fenafillah.*
  4. A return to material existence to live a life of service in God's name.
- *A reading from the Qu'ran, often Sura Bakara 2, Verse 115:* "Onto God belong the East and the West, and wherever you turn, there is God's countenance. He is All-Embracing. All-Knowing."
- *A prayer for all prophets and believers.* At this point, the samazen return to their chambers for *tefekkür* (meditation).

Additional instruments that might be heard in a Samā' ceremony include the bowed **kemençe** (often replaced by the Western violin); the plucked lutes **ud** and **tanbur;** the **kanun,** a plucked or hammered zither; and percussion instruments. The human voice is also central. Verses are drawn from the *Mathnavi.*

Except for some music that is specifically designed for ritual use, the development of Mevlevi practice went hand-in-hand with that of classical Ottoman-Turkish music. Such has been the case since the sixteenth century. As with traditional music throughout the Middle East, the style is monophonic or heterophonic. There is neither harmony nor polyphony. That does not mean that Mevlevi music is simple, however. In fact, Mevlevi melodies tend to be lengthy and rhythmically complex.

Melody and rhythm are governed by intricate theoretical schemes called *makam* and *usul,* respectively. Makam provides the blueprint for Turkish melody. **mysearchlab 2.3** In addition to designating a set of usable pitches (as does a Western scale), makam employs rules governing how those pitches are to be combined in performance. Thus, a specific makam might be identified not only by the pitches being used, but also by the characteristic ways in which a musician moves between them. Another difference between makam and Western scale is found in the distance between pitches. Makam uses intervals that are both smaller and larger than the rigidly constructed half and whole steps of the Western system. Thus, makam pitches might be said to "fall between the cracks" of the Western keyboard.

Governing rhythm is the usul system. Cyclical patterns from two to ten beats are common, though ones as long as 28 beats are occasionally heard. In theory, usul patterns could be much longer still.

In order to aid memory and provide a sonic map of rhythmic progress through the cycle, usul patterns are subdivided into short groupings of two or three beats that are further distinguished by low (*dum*) and high (*tek* & *ka*) drum tones.

Examples of two-beat patterns include:

1	2		1	2 +
Dum	tek	*and*	dum	tek-ka.

Examples of three-beat patterns include:

1	2	3		1	2 + 3 +
Dum	tek	tek	*and*	dum	tek ka tek ka.

These basic patterns can be highly embellished and developed through improvisation. The following example consists of a simple development of the two-beat subdivision across an eight-beat cycle:

1	2	3	4	+	5	6	+	7	8	+
1	2	1	2	+	1	2	+	1	2	+
dum	tek	dum	tek	ka	dum	tek	ka	dum	tek	ka

DID YOU KNOW?

MUSIC AND ORTHODOX ISLAM

Contrary to common belief in the West, the **Qur'an** (Koran) does not explicitly condemn music. In fact, evidence suggests that Muhammad himself enjoyed music. Even so, music's sensual power has long been a cause of concern in Islam (a tension we have already seen in Christianity and will encounter again in our discussion of Judaism).

Beginning shortly after Muhammad's death, music was disallowed in certain religious contexts. Concerns were further heightened in the ninth century with the introduction of music and dance into the Sufi's ecstatic ceremonies. Today, Qur'anic recitation is taught in formalized schools that are open to men and often women. Interestingly, many secular singers get their training by learning diction and makam in the religious schools. **mysearchlab 6.8**

LISTENING GUIDE

CD II/Track 9
Download track 31
mysearchlab 6.9

NAAT-I SHERIF (EXCERPT) TAKSIM AND PEŞREV

Instrumentation: ney, tanburs (bowed and plucked), kanun, kudüm, cymbals

TAKSIM

The seven-pitched *makam bayati* is built on two **tetrachords**. The lower one, known as the bayati tetrachord and including pitches 1–4, is characterized by a low (to the Western ear) second scale degree. The pitches of the upper tetrachord, known as *nahawand* and including pitches 4–7, sound like the first tones of a Western minor scale. Notice that pitch 4 ends the bayati tetrachord and begins the *nahawand* tetrachord. This important overlapping pitch is called the *güçlü* (dominant).

0:00	Phrase one begins with an upward step from the initial tone (*giriş*) to the home pitch or tonic (*karar*). From here the melody jumps up to the güçlü, then drifts down to the karar while establishing the powerful sound of the lowered second-scale degree.
0:17	Phrase two begins with a leap to the upper karar. Then the melody drifts downward an octave.
0:34	The lower karar is the starting point, then the melody moves upward to resolve on the güçlü.
1:00	The nahawand tetrachord is emphasized.
1:19	New pitches suggest that the performer has momentarily modulated to a different makam, but he quickly returns to bayati.
1:26	An ascending step-wise pattern begins on the lower karar. We will hear the same gesture in the ensemble *peşrev* that follows.
1:39	A leap to the upper güçlü. After a brief descent, the range expands upward.

(Continued)

LISTENING GUIDE (*Continued*)

1:56	Karar is strongly stated. Then again the ascending pattern to the taksim's highest point at (2:16).
2:31	A phrase begins on güçlü, which leads to final resolution on the karar.

PEŞREV

A *peşrev* consists of four main sections (*hane* or house) with identical interludes (*teslim*) following. Each hane will explore different aspects of the makam, or temporarily modulate to another makam. This peşrev, written by Neyaen Emin Dede (1883–1945) is in the 28-beat usul *devr-i kebîr*. If you count the beats, you will discover that each hane and the teslim lasts for exactly two 28-beat cycles.

3:08	First hane. The hane is in two nearly identical halves. The second half, as well the second usul cycle, begins at 3:32.
3:55	Teslim. The second usul cycle begins at 4:18.
4:40	The second hane covers two usul cycles but is not split into identical halves. The first half expands the upper melodic range and introduces new tones, perhaps suggesting a different makam.
5:25	Second teslim.
6:10	The third hane again expands the melodic range and introduces tone combinations.
6:54	The third hane again expands the melodic range and introduces tone combinations.
7:34	The fourth hane stays in a lower melodic range and explores the melodic implications of a lowered güçlü.
8:18	Fourth teslim.
9:00	Return to first hane (first half only)

QUESTIONS FOR THOUGHT

- Mevlevi ritual practice is rich with symbolism. This is true of religious music in general. What other religious symbolism have we encountered in this chapter? Are there commonalities? Important differences?
- Like Yoruba religion, dance is a central ingredient of Mevlevi practice. How are these traditions similar? Different?

Yom Kippur, The Jewish Day of Atonement: "Kol Nidre"

Every fall, on a date specified by the lunar calendar, Jews gather to commemorate the most sacred of High Holy Days, Yom Kippur, The Day of Atonement. During the holiday's 24-hour period, which spans sunset to sunset and focuses on repentance, there are several prayer services. The first takes place in the synagogue, just before sundown, as the holiday begins. Symbolism is pervasive. White is worn as a sign of purity. Men often wear prayer shawls called *tallit*, the fringe of which symbolizes the 613 *mitzvot* (commandments). Opening the service is a prayer called "**Kol Nidre**" ("All Vows"), which is sung three times by the **cantor**—first very softly, then louder with each repetition. The final Yom Kippur service ends with a single blast of the **shofar** (ram's horn) with the congregation exclaiming, "Next year in Jerusalem!"

MUSICAL THEMES
SHOFAR

The shofar is an ancient wind instrument made from a ram's horn. In biblical times, the shofar was also used as a signaling device. Today, the shofar is blown at various times of the religious year, including the Hebrew month of Elul, Rosh Hashanah (the Jewish New Year), and Yom Kippur. There are four different sounds of the shofar: (1) *Tekiah*—one long, straight blast; (2) *Shevarim*—three medium notes rising in tone; (3) *Teruah*—nine quick staccato blasts in short succession; and (4) *Tekiah gedolah*—a single blast held as long as possible that sounds after a combination of Tekiah, Shevarim, and Teruah. The different sounds are meant to awaken the soul, inspire self-reflection, and spark a closer relationship with God. **mysearchlab 6.10**

A Jewish musician plays a shofar, c. 1935.

The "Kol Nidre" asks that all individual vows made by petition to God or to the individual's own conscience be annulled. The recitation is a request for the forgiveness of sins and for renewal. The text is sung to an austere yet sorrowful melody that, though not notated until the eighteenth century, probably originated several hundred years earlier. There are many local variants to the tune, but the melody's opening phrase is common to many traditions.

LISTENING GUIDE

CD II/Track 10
Download track 32
mysearchlab 6.11

"KOL NIDRE"

Kol Nidre: Ve'esarei, Ush'vuei, Vacharamei, Vekonamei, Vekinusei, Vechinuyei.
D'indarna, Ud'ishtabana, Ud'acharimna, Ud'assarna Al nafshatana
Miyom Kippurim zeh, ad Yom Kippurim haba aleinu letovah
Bechulhon Icharatna vehon, Kulhon yehon sharan
Sh'vikin sh'vitin, betelin umevutalin, lo sheririn v'lo kayamin
Nidrana lo nidrei, V'essarana lo essarei
Ush'vuatana lo shevuot.

Translation:
All vows: prohibitions, obligations, oaths, and anathemas which we may vow, or swear, or pledge, or whereby we may be bound, from this Day of Atonement until the next (whose happy coming we await), we do repent. May they be deemed absolved, forgiven, annulled, and void, and made of no effect; they shall not bind us nor have power over us. The vows shall not be reckoned vows; the obligations shall not be obligatory; nor the oaths be oaths. (JewishEncyclopedia.com)

The "Kol Nidre" has been used by composers as the basis for new compositions. The best known of these is German composer Max Bruch's (1838–1920) *Kol Nidrei (Adagio on Hebrew Melodies)*, op. 47 for cello and orchestra (1881). Though Bruch was a Protestant, his love for this beautiful music transcended religious divides. We turn now to a setting of the prayer by the Austrian and naturalized American Arnold Schoenberg (1874–1951).

MUSICAL LIVES
ARNOLD SCHOENBERG (1874–1951)

One of the most influential composers of the twentieth century, Schoenberg is associated with Expressionism, an artistic movement that focused on portraying the dark turbulence of the human psyche. Schoenberg was the leader of the Second Viennese School of composition, which included his students Alton Webern (1883–1945) and Alban Berg (1885–1935). Mostly self-taught, early in his career Schoenberg wrote in the Romantic music style of the late nineteenth century. His music became increasingly chromatic and dissonant as the twentieth century unfolded.

Schoenberg was central to the development of modern music, particularly in the area of **atonality**, that is, music that lacks a tonal foundation, or key center. The remarkable *Pierrot Lunaire* (1912), Schoenberg's setting for vocalists and small ensemble of verses written by Belgian Symbolist poet Albert Giraud (1860–1929), remains the canonic example of atonal Expressionism. After World War I, Schoenberg and his students developed the **12-tone system**, a theoretical formula that, in principle at least, requires the composer to use all 12 pitches of the Western octave before repeating any. The 12-tone method (and its variations) virtually guaranteed extreme dissonance. It became the bedrock for many of the most innovative and experimental Western art music compositions of the first half of the twentieth century.

Schoenberg's life was one of transitions. Though raised Jewish, he converted to Lutheranism in 1898. In 1933 Schoenberg was forced to flee Nazi Germany. He emigrated first to Paris (where he returned to the Jewish faith), then to the United States, eventually moving to Los Angeles where he taught at the University of Southern California and UCLA.

| Arnold Schoenberg, c. 1941.

Arnold Schoenberg, "Kol Nidre" in G Minor, Op. 39 for Chorus, Speaker, and Orchestra

In the summer of 1938, the Los Angeles-based Rabbi Jakob Sonderling asked Schoenberg to arrange the "Kol Nidre" for Yom Kippur services. Schoenberg accepted and completed his work in less than two months. Because Schoenberg's piece departed too much from the traditional setting, however, the composition was deemed inappropriate for use in the synagogue. Instead, it was premiered in Los Angeles's Ambassador Hotel. Rabbi Sonderling performed the recitation; the orchestra and chorus consisted of hired film studio musicians that Schoenberg conducted. **mysearchlab 6.12**

Schoenberg's musical language can be dissonant and intense. Upon first hearing, his music may sound disorganized or disturbing, but in reality it is highly structured.

CD II/Track 11
Download track 33
mysearchlab 6.13

LISTENING GUIDE

"KOL NIDRE" OP. 39 (EXCERPT)

by Arnold Schoenberg (1938)

After an introduction, the narrator begins the "Kol Nidre" text.

0:00	At the beginning of our excerpt, we seem to be listening to two contrasting sonic worlds. The woodwinds sound the "Kol Nidre" melody softly but deliberately. Their rhythm is strict, the tone austere. Psychologically, these voices seem to imply the throne of a stern but just God. Opposing this feeling are the strings, which play a series of rapid chromatic figures. The narrator speaks: All vows, oaths, promises, and plights of any kind, Wherewith we pledged ourselves counter to our inherited faith in God. A pizzicato chord breaks the musical phrase. After a moment of repose, the entire orchestra becomes more active. The basic "Kol Nidre" melody has disappeared. The instruments play embellishments around important scale degrees, much like a cantor might have done. Gradually, but relentlessly, the music becomes increasingly militant. Notice the emphasized chord on the word "null."
0:23	Who is One, Everlasting, Unseen, Unfathomable, We declare these null and void. Next, the chorus, orchestra, and narrator engage in a dialogue about repentance, the main message of the prayer. The passage begins quietly, with a reduced orchestral texture emphasizing the woodwinds. With each utterance of "we repent," the orchestra's size increases along with dynamics. Notice that Schoenberg's lyrics have departed from the original text. Some of this might be attributed to differences in translation, but most of the changes were deliberate and reflect Schoenberg's interest in adding a stronger notion of personal responsibility. The "we repent" phrases, for example, are not found in the original prayer.
0:51	We repent that these obligations have estranged us from the sacred task we were chosen for. We repent. We repent, We repent, We repent. We shall strive from this Day of Atonement until the next to avoid such and similar obligations, So that the Yom Kippur to follow may come to us for good. The orchestra takes over, briefly sounding as if it will come to a loud and intense ending. Instead, we realize that it is a bridge to the next section of the piece. The chorus now sings its version of the *"Kol Nidre."* Some of the text is repeated, other portions are new.
2:05	We close our analysis here, but note that the piece ends with a return of the "Kol Nidre" melody, on top of which, the choir sings *"we repent."*

ACTIVITIES AND ASSIGNMENTS

- Search out additional recordings of "Kol Nidre." Here are some compositions that use at least a portion of the famous melody. **mysearchlab 6.14**
  - Ludwig van Beethoven's (1770–1827) *String Quartet in C# minor* op. 131 (opening bars of Adagio quasi un poco andante).
  - Max Bruch's (1838–1920) *Kol Nidrei (Adagio on Hebrew Melodies)*, op. 47.
  - David Axelrod's *Release of an Oath: Kol Nidre* (Electric Prunes, 1968).
  - Nicolas Jolliet's *Kol Nidre Goes East* (2006).
  - John Zorn's string quartet version of "Kol Nidre" (1999).
- The film *The Jazz Singer* (1927) uses the "Kol Nidre" in its final scene (see chapter 10: Music and Film).

CONCLUSION

We have looked at a variety of ways in which religious cultures use music to enhance spiritual experience. The differences are vast. Some practitioners use music to focus the mind and body, whereas others use it for its ability to attract benevolent spirits. Some practitioners favor nonmetric chant to quiet the body; others strive to excite the body with music that pulses with rhythm.

The boundaries between sacred and secular are not fixed, and are often permeable. Music originally conceived for performance in a temple, church, or synagogue often makes its way into concert settings. With Schoenberg's "Kol Nidre," we encountered an example of spiritual music that was rejected altogether for performance within a religious institution.

Individual belief or focus may or may not be relevant to our understandings of spiritual music. Tibetan monks regard mental focus as an essential part of their chanting. But consider the experience of film ethnographer Maya Deren. She did not practice Haitian vodún, nor did she strive to experience trance, but she fell into trance nonetheless. Presumably, a Mevlevi dervish could perform ayin-i şerif while thinking about the mundane matters of everyday life. How would those of us watching on ever know the difference?

Might certain sounds be inherently spiritual? One might be tempted to think so. Such a scenario would help explain Deren's trance experience, for example. But if so, how does one explain J. S. Bach's use of a secular love song in the *St. Matthew Passion*?

We began this chapter by asking what kind of music you consider to be spiritual. Perhaps working through this chapter has helped to clarify your answer. Perhaps, however, it has only made your response more tentative. Do not be dismayed if this is the case. The musical experience of spirituality is enormously complex. Every discovery seems to open new perspectives for understanding the human condition.

Music and Politics

CHAPTER GOALS

- To explore overt and hidden political meanings in music.
- To see how music has been used for political aims.
- To examine how music helps form, reflect, and alter national identity.

"All I did was play it. I'm American, so I played it."

—Jimi Hendrix (1942–1970)

QUESTIONS FOR THOUGHT

- What kinds of music might be considered political?
- Does music need words to be political?
- How might music move us to embrace or reject political ideas?
- Music performance involves more than just sound. What other aspects of a performance might be used to invoke political ideologies?

As the wave of distortion faded away, a melody emerged with bell-tone clarity. It was a relaxed falling gesture followed by an upward sweep:

```
                              do——
sol—              sol—
     mi–     mi—
     do—
```

Every American recognizes the opening tones to "The Star-Spangled Banner." But who would have expected to hear it then and there—as the sun rose on Max Yasgur's New York farm on an overcast August morning in 1969? The Woodstock Music and Art Fair was officially over, but rain, mud, and the swell of 500,000 people had delayed the performances through the night. Jimi Hendrix, icon of 1960s psychedelica, was finally playing his set. The audience could easily have sung along, "Oh, say can you see, by the dawn's early light. . . ."

mysearchlab 7.1

Hendrix took liberties with rhythm and pitch, but the tune was clear enough. Or at least it was initially. Soon, however, the song's melodic flow and formal structure disintegrated under a barrage of high-frequency and high-decibel distortion. Increasingly improvisatory, Hendrix's performance opened up the anthem to audacious interpretations, ones that brought the song's most fundamental meanings and values into question. Following the line, "the rocket's red glare," Hendrix digressed into a 30-second improvisation of percussive disruptions and Banshee-like screams. The tone painting of the next line—"The bombs bursting in air"—was half again as long and twice as startling—replete with the sounds of incoming missiles, explosions, and screams. The postscript for the next line—"That our flag was still there"—was "Taps," the army bugle call to end the day and honor the dead. When "Banner" finally ended (after several more sonic excursions), Hendrix slipped into one of his signature hits, "Purple Haze."

What should one make of such a performance in such an unlikely setting? Consider the time and place. Following the Tet Offensive of 1968, the Vietnam War had spun out of control. The same year had also seen the assassinations of Dr. Martin Luther King Jr. and Senator Robert F. Kennedy. The streets shook with anti-war and civil rights protests. The nation seemed at war both at home and abroad.

Was Hendrix protesting as well? Not consciously, at least. "I thought it was beautiful," he later told late-night television talk-show host Dick Cavett when asked about the performance. Many Americans disagreed and were deeply offended.

In this chapter, we study the ways in which music is used as a vehicle for politics and a symbol for nation. We begin by comparing and contrasting anthems and other political music from various nation-states. Next, we study how "folk" music was used to promote national solidarity in nineteenth-century Russia and twentieth-century China and Bulgaria. From there we step farther back in time and study how the German composer Ludwig van Beethoven (1770–1827) envisioned universal brotherhood in his Symphony No. 9 in D minor. We close the chapter with a look at the use of music in the ongoing Zapatista revolutionary movement in Chiapas, Mexico.

Music and National Identity

Like flags, songs of nation invoke powerful emotions. Director Michael Curtiz (1886–1962) understood this when he shot the remarkable "La Marseillaise" scene in the classic film *Casablanca* (1942), starring Humphrey Bogart (1899–1957) and Ingrid Bergman (1915–1982). Set against the backdrop of World War II, the film mostly unfolds in the relative peace of Rick's Café, a bar frequented by German soldiers and French expatriates. Generally speaking, the French are cowed by the Germans. That changes, however, when a flurry of national pride and courage is unleashed in a battle of songs. **mysearchlab 7.2**

MUSICAL LIVES
HYMN AND ANTHEM

Who could have imagined that a Christian hymn would become a song of African resistance and then, later, be incorporated into not one, but three African national anthems? It happened, though.

The song "Nkosi Sikelel' iAfrika" ("Lord, Bless Africa") was written in 1897 by Johannesburg-based South African Methodist choirmaster Enoch Mankayi Sontonga (1873–1905). It is simultaneously a song of petition and pride. In 1912, it was sung at the first meeting of the South African Native National Congress, the forerunner of the African National Congress (ANC), the political organization that struggled to gain civil rights for blacks in apartheid South Africa. The song soon became the anthem used to close ANC meetings. Today the melody is heard in the national anthems of Tanzania, Zambia, and South Africa. The current South African anthem, adopted in 1997, strives for ethnic inclusion. It is set in five different languages: Xhosa, Zulu, Sesotho, English, and Afrikaans. The anthem combines two melodies: "Nkosi Sikelel' iAfrika" and "Die Stem van Suid-Afrika," South Africa's anthem from the apartheid era.

In one corner of the bar, German soldiers assemble around a piano. An officer pounds his fist on the instrument as the men sing in German "The Watch on the Rhine," a song dating from the 1870 Franco-Prussian War (and a war that Prussia won). On other nights, the French would have listened silently and miserably. Not this night, however. Encouraged by resistance leader Victor Laszlo (played by Paul Henreid, 1905–1992), they stand as one and sing "La Marseillaise," the French national anthem.

Allons enfants de la Patrie,	Arise children of the fatherland,
Le jour de gloire est arrive.	The day of glory has arrived.
Contre nous de la tyrannie,	Against us tyranny's,
L'étendard sanglant est levé.	Bloody standard is raised.
Entendez-vous dans nos campagnes	Do you hear in the fields
Mugir ces féroces soldats?	The screams of the fierce soldiers?
Ils viennent jusques dans vos bras	They are coming into our midst
Egorger vos fils, vos compagnes.	To slaughter your sons, your countrymen.

CHORUS

Aux armes citoyens!	To arms citizens!
Formez vos bataillons.	Form your battalions.
Marchons, marchons!	March, march!
Qu'un sang impur	Until the impure blood
Abreuve nos sillons.	Waters our fields.

The scene concludes in tears of joy and pride, and cries of "Vive la France!" Enraged, a German officer orders the café to close. It is an incredible scene, one that stirs the blood still today. Imagine its power in 1942 with the world at war and France on its knees.

Originally titled "War Song for the Army of the Rhine," "La Marseillaise" was written in 1792 by French army officer Claude Joseph Rouget de Lisle (1760–1836) as his country braced for a Prussian invasion. The song quickly became associated with the French Revolution, and was designated the national anthem in 1879.

Contrast the lyrics of "La Marseillaise" with Francis Scott Key's (1779–1843) text for "The Star-Spangled Banner" (1814), written after Key watched the American defense of Fort McHenry from Baltimore Harbor during the War of 1812:

Oh, say can you see, by the dawn's early light,
What so proudly we hailed at the twilight's last gleaming?
Whose broad stripes and bright stars, through the perilous fight,
O'er the ramparts we watched, were so gallantly streaming?
And the rockets' red glare, the bombs bursting in air,
Gave proof through the night that our flag was still there.
O say, does that star-spangled banner yet wave
O'er the land of the free and the home of the brave?

There are no notions of a fatherland, no impurities of blood, as in "La Marseillaise." Instead, the lyrics present a quieter notion of fortitude and hope throughout a long night of resistance. Absent altogether are Hendrix's Woodstock-era images of death and suffering.

Francis Scott Key did not set out to write a national anthem, just a poem in response to his pride upon witnessing the battle. In fact, "The Star-Spangled Banner" was not officially proclaimed the national anthem until 1931. As for the melody, Englishman John Stafford Smith (1750–1836) composed it for a men's social club to which he belonged. Smith's song was titled, "To Anacreon in Heaven."

Disparate though their origins were, Key's words and Smith's melody were soon linked. Already by the American Civil War (1861–1865), the song had achieved a prominent place in the American consciousness. The song was so politically charged that in March 1861, just one month prior to the outbreak of fighting at Fort Sumter, George Tucker (1828–1863), a Secessionist Virginian, set the melody to pro-Confederacy words. He titled the song, "The Southern Cross." Would we all know this version today had the South won the war?

Oh! Say can you see, through the gloom and the storm,
More bright for the darkness, that pure constellation!
Like the symbol of love and redemption its form,
As it points to the heaven of hope for the nation.
Now radiant each star, as the beacon afar,
Giving promise of peace, or assurance in war,
'Tis the Cross of the South, which shall ever remain
To light us to freedom and glory again!

Tucker was not the only one to borrow this symbolism-laden melody. Italian composer Giacomo Puccini (1858–1924) used it to symbolize American hubris in his opera *Madama Butterfly* (1904) (see chapter 9: Music and Love). Other European composers to set the melody, though in decidedly more pro-American versions, were the Russians Sergei Rachmaninoff (1873–1943) and Igor Stravinsky (1882–1971), and the German Kurt Weill (1900–1950). **mysearchlab 7.2**

MUSICAL THEMES

MUSIC AND THE AMERICAN PRESIDENCY

Imagine yourself in Baltimore, Maryland, on May 4, 1840. The Whigs (a once formidable American political party) are marching into town to nominate William Henry Harrison (1773–1841) as their presidential candidate. The parade, some 25,000 marchers strong, is led by a phalanx of vintage Revolutionary War-era artillery. Behind are a series of marching bands, a carriage housing the famous lawyer and wordsmith Daniel Webster (1782–1852), a number of log-cabin floats (one with a working chimney), and hundreds of banners. To make sure the mood stays bright, hard cider is both plentiful and free.

"Tippecanoe and Tyler too!" the people cry out. Raucous throughout the route, the multitudes reach fever pitch when they pass Music Hall singing, "And with them we'll beat little Van, Van, Van/Van is a used up man." Inside, the Democrats are quietly nominating their own candidate, the incumbent, and soon to be unseated, President Martin Van Buren (1782–1862). In the months that followed, William Henry Harrison would be virtually "sung into the Presidency," as Whig politician Philip Hone (1870–1851) later remarked. American politics would never be the same.

Beginning with the Harrison campaign and lasting for more than a century, music was an essential ingredient in presidential campaigns. The songs were utilitarian—easy to sing and easy to remember. Typically, words were attached to well-known preexisting melodies, such as "Yankee Doodle," "Dixie," or any number of now mostly forgotten tunes.

Of all presidential campaign songs, perhaps the one best remembered today is "Happy Days Are Here Again" (1929), which Franklin Delano Roosevelt (1882–1945) used in his 1932 campaign. The song has been associated with the Democratic Party ever since.

QUESTIONS FOR THOUGHT

- Does "The Star-Spangled Banner" mean the same thing when performed by Jimi Hendrix at Woodstock as it does when played by the United States Marine Band?
- Do national anthems reveal something about the national ideologies of Germans, French, South Africans, and Americans?
- Can you imagine the words to "La Marseillaise" being written today? Why or why not?
- Why might a nation decide to change its anthem?
- Sacha Baron Cohen reset "The Star-Spangled Banner" melody to new lyrics in his mockumentary *Borat* (2006). View the sequence. Do you find the scene offensive? Funny? Why or why not?
- Pretend that Congress decided to scrap "The Star-Spangled Banner" and designate a new national anthem. What elements would you like to see contained in the new anthem? Why?
- A national anthem is one musical device for promoting national identity and pride. What are some others?

ACTIVITIES AND ASSIGNMENTS

- There has been a movement among some in the United States to change the national anthem. Investigate the reasons for the proposed change and the musical alternatives that have been suggested.
- Listen to a selection of national anthems from other countries. What do they have in common? How do they differ?

Nineteenth-Century Nationalism in Europe

Nineteenth-century Europe was strongly influenced by the era's overriding ideals of Romanticism and Liberalism, which together led to the idea that a nation should represent the will of an entire people, rather than that of a dynastic elite. Across Europe, new political allegiances were formed. The Italian peninsula, which before 1861 was governed by a collection of city-states, united to form a constitutional monarchy in 1870. Germany was united the following year. These large countries (as well as the long-united England and France) dominated the era's international politics and artistic movements. Increasingly, however, less powerful ethnic groups and/or nation-states—such as the Czechs and Bohemians, Norwegians and Danes, Poles, Hungarians, and Russians—sought to expand their influence. The political movement associated with these ideas became known as **nationalism**.

All this made for complicated politics. After all, nationalism is a double-edged sword. On the one hand, it binds people together, celebrates common goals and heritage, and creates a sense of solidarity and social pride. On the other hand, nationalism is divisive. It reflects and fortifies an "us-against-them" mentality.

MUSICAL LIVES
THE NINETEENTH-CENTURY NATIONALIST COMPOSERS

Central Europe
Bedrich Smetana (1824–1884)
Antonin Dvorak (1841–1904)
Leos Janacek (1854–1928)

Scandinavia
Edvard Grieg (1843–1907)
Jean Sibelius (1865–1957)
Carl Nielsen (1865–1931)

Russia
Mikhail Glinka (1804–1857)
"The Five" (or "Mighty Handful")
Mily Balakirev (1837–1910)
Alexander Borodin (1833–1887)
Cesar Cui (1835–1918)
Modest Mussorgsky (1839–1881)
Nikolai Rimsky-Korsakov (1844–1908)

Spain
Isaac Albéniz (1860–1909)

Nationalist composers strove to write music that highlighted and represented their heritage. To achieve their goals, composers often used folk melodies (or newly composed "folk-like" melodies) and folk-dance rhythms. Sometimes composers sought to tell a story with their music. In the orchestral repertoire, this led to the development of the **symphonic poem** (or tone poem). Such pieces had colorful names. For example, the Bohemian Bedrich Smetana wrote *Ma Vlast* (*My Country*, 1874), Finnish composer Jean Sibelius wrote *The Swan of Tuonela* (1895), and the Russian Alexander Borodin wrote *In the Steppes of Central Asia* (1880). These are just a few of many such compositions.

Borodin, a chemist by profession, was an important member of The Five, a group of nineteenth-century Russian nationalist composers. Led by Mily Balakirev, The Five sought to create a repertory of art music with a sound that was characteristically Russian.

The question, of course, was "What does 'authentic' Russian music sound like?" Balakirev contended that it had to be drawn from the "folk," and that it should sound unstudied so as to accurately reflect the native culture that it sought to promote.

In the Steppes of Central Asia

Russia at the end of the nineteenth century was the largest country in the world, in both land mass and population. It was also the most ethnically diverse. While size translated into potential economic and military power, it also worked against the creation of a central identity. Ethnic groups far from Moscow might easily feel stronger ties to their own local cultural heritage than to the more abstract concept of a Russian nation-state.

Perhaps we feel that tension in *Steppes*. Where exactly in the Central Asian steppes Borodin places us, we do not know. The area is vast; its peoples are many. Our immediate experience is clear, however. A caravan makes its way across the landscape. Soon, another caravan appears on the horizon. As the groups

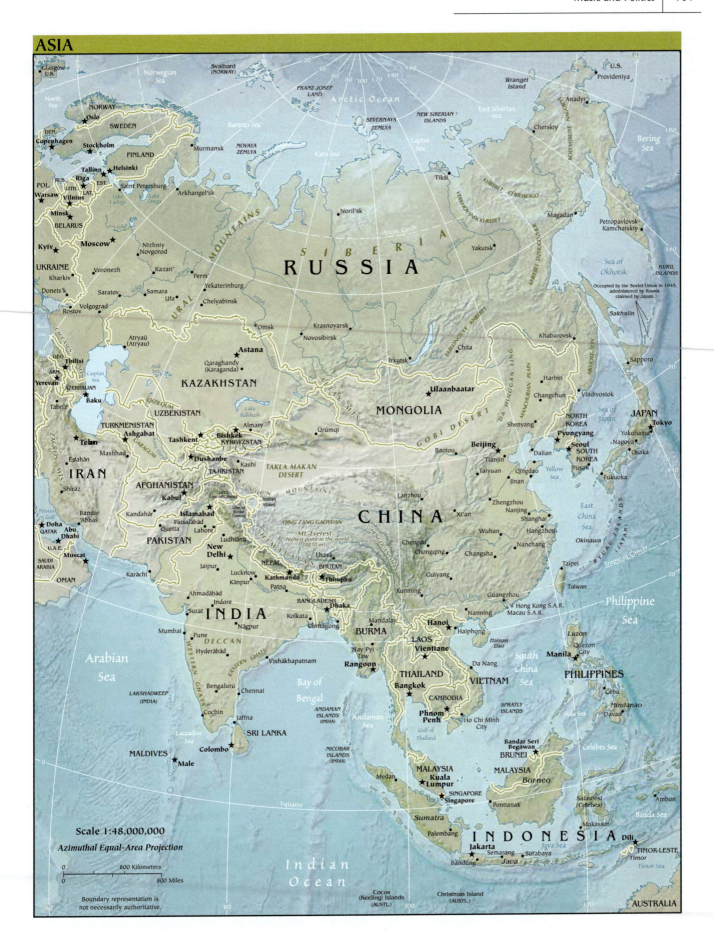

ASIA

Scale 1:48,000,000
Azimuthal Equal-Area Projection

0   800 Kilometers
0   800 Miles

Boundary representation is
not necessarily authoritative.

LISTENING GUIDE

CD II/Track 12
Download track 34
mysearchlab 7.3

IN THE STEPPES OF CENTRAL ASIA (1880)

by Alexander Borodin

0:00	Strings sound a single pitch that provides a tonal reference point for the music to follow. Naturally, we assume that this single pitch, so prominent and pervasive, is "do," the tonic of the musical scale. Presumably, this texture represents the steppes, unchanging and eternal. Woodwinds—clarinet, then oboe—fade in and out on the same pitch. The interjections strengthen the idea of timelessness, like seasons that come and go.
0:08	A clarinet reenters and plays a two-part melody consisting of a downward falling phrase followed by a longer phrase at a higher-pitch level. This is the "Russian" theme. Probably you are surprised by the melody's tonality, which tells us that our heretofore perceived tonic in the strings is actually "sol." Perhaps Borodin chose this deception to remind us that "home" is always relative, a matter of perception.
0:29	The horn enters with the same melody but at yet another pitch level. Our imagined "do" turned "sol" in the strings now becomes "mi" when heard against the horn melody. It's as if the landscape keeps shifting underfoot. It is hard to get a tonal footing.
0:48	Violas and cellos enter **pizzicato** (strings plucked, not bowed) with the "walking" theme. We move across the endless steppes, represented by sustained pitches in the woodwinds and brass. The music seems fragmented, without a clear personality. We seem to be suspended between worlds.
1:11	Arrival. The English horn enters with the lilting "Eastern" theme (ABA form). The range is narrow, and the progression is slowly downward. This is the first half of the theme, the A section.
1:26	The English horn continues with the B section of the melody.
1:40	The English horn returns to a slightly shortened version of the "Eastern" theme's A section.
1:54	Sustained tones are echoed across the orchestra. We now know this sound. It is transition music. The pizzicato texture appears again; energy is briefly increased.
2:21	The clarinet returns with our familiar friend, the "Russian" melody. Notice the countermelodies.
2:42	Brass instruments take up the "Russian" melody; again, with countermelodies.
3:06	With an abrupt jump in dynamics, the full orchestra takes up the "Russian" melody. This is the loudest point in the piece.
3:28	More traveling music. Transition.
3:53	Strings and English horn take up the "Eastern" theme. A section.
4:08	"Eastern" theme, B section.
4:22	"Eastern" theme, A section.
4:34	"Eastern" theme, A section. Sounds like a closing section (coda).
5:29	Dual themes continue, but the instruments shift. Violins now have the "Eastern" theme.
5:43	The "Eastern" theme fades away. The "Russian" is fragmented and spread across different instruments in the orchestra. Elongated cadence at 6:03.
6:48	Strings return to the opening texture representing the steppes.
6:51	Flute sounds the "Russian" theme one last time. Perhaps a memory left on the land? Sounds fade away.

cross paths, they trade stories, and maybe trade goods. Eventually, each continues on its journey. In the end, all that remains is the eternal landscape of Mother Russia.

Music that tells a story is programmatic (**program music**). Here the story is told through three main ideas: a "Russian" theme, an "Eastern" theme, and a "traveling" theme. The Russian theme has sweeping gestures; it is strong but gentle. The Eastern theme, played on an "exotic"-sounding double-reed instrument, is relatively narrow in contour and rhythmically anxious, as if it always wants to be on the move. The traveling theme is rhythmically steady and firm. Perhaps it represents the tread of powerful oxen teams moving across the seemingly endless landscape.

Composing for the State

Kings and czars, dukes and duchesses have all employed musicians. During the Renaissance and Baroque periods in particular, European courts vied for the best artists, whose very presence was sufficient to increase a sovereign's political clout. Composers sought the best positions as well. To get them, they often curried favor with important rulers. Frenchman Jean-Baptiste Lully (1632–1687), for example, wrote operas that used allegory to glorify the deeds of his patron, King Louis XIV. In the eighteenth century, George Frederick Handel (1685–1759) wrote rousing choruses, which, though mostly based on biblical topics, in reality were thinly veiled tributes to the power of the British Empire. Handel's coronation anthem *Zadok the Priest* was one of four anthems written in 1727 for King George II. It has been sung at every British coronation service since.

The line between patriotism and propaganda is often a matter of perception. In the following sections we examine works that were either written to support, or used as agents of, government policy.

Chinese Opera During the Cultural Revolution

A nation in crisis might be the best way to describe China from 1966 to 1976. The period, known as the Cultural Revolution, was a decade of terror. Loosely bound units of Red Guard youths roamed the streets seeking "closet capitalists," "bourgeois educators," and anyone else who dared think outside the Communist Party box. Hundreds of thousands

were murdered; millions more were sent to labor camps to be "re-educated." Books were burned, and artworks were destroyed. Homes were ransacked, and places of worship were razed. Children identified their own parents and teachers as traitors.

All this happened in the name of reform. Communist Party Chairman Mao Zedong (1893–1976) promised to rid China of what he called the "Four Olds"—old ideas, old culture, old customs, and old habits. In their place he would create a new society purged of capitalist and imperialist influences.

The new Chinese society would need appropriate art. Accordingly, Mao's wife, the former actress Jiang Qing, embarked on an initiative using art to build up China's proletarian culture. The result was the *Yang Ban Xi* ("The Eight Model Plays")—five operas, two ballets, and one symphony. Plots centered on loyalists who worked selflessly for Communist Party ideals. The main characters were brave, wise, and kind. And of course, they venerated Mao's vision for China. Future compositions were expected to take these original eight works as their models.

Chairman Mao Zedong casts his vote on December 8, 1953, in the elections for the people's congress of the Hsitan District, Beijing.

From 1967 to 1969, Jiang conducted a massive campaign to familiarize the population with the Yang Ban Xi. The works were performed frequently, played over the radio, and adapted to local dialects. Schoolchildren sang the tunes; all professional opera actors were required to learn the roles. Those who conformed exactly to Jiang's directions were paid handsomely and appointed to important political committees. Those who didn't were "re-educated" or eliminated.

The most popular of the model works was *Hong deng ji* (*The Red Lantern*). Though originally composed in the style of Shanghai opera, Jiang had the opera modified to fit better with revolutionary ideals and to reflect the more well-known **Beijing opera** style. The revised work premiered in March 1964 to a receptive audience. In 1967, shortly after the onset of the Cultural Revolution, *Hong deng ji* officially became one of the Eight Model Plays.

MUSICAL LIVES
BRIGHT SHENG

Composer and Shanghai native Bright Sheng (b. 1955) lived through the Cultural Revolution. Because of his musical gifts, Sheng avoided being sent to a labor camp. Instead, he was sent to work with a provincial band in Tibet. There he discovered a love for folk music and composition. Sheng currently lives in Ann Arbor, where he teaches at the University of Michigan. He has written four operas, most recently *Madame Mao* (2003), commissioned by the Santa Fe Opera.

"There is something unique about my generation of Chinese artists," says Sheng. "They are tough and stubborn, with an unbreakable spirit of perseverance."

Jingju (Beijing Opera)   Of the 50 or so operatic traditions in China, jingju emerged in the late nineteenth century as the dominant style. Its popularity was fueled by royal patronage and the 1909 declaration that Mandarin, Beijing's local dialect, would become the national language. Jingju includes singing, dialogue, acrobatics, and martial arts. Costumes are brightly colored and elaborate. The sparse staging relies heavily on symbolism to indicate time and place.

There are four main character types in jingju:

- *Sheng* is the main male role. This character type is cultivated and refined. There are many subtypes depending on the character's age or social status. Sheng usually have a nasal quality to their voices.
- *Dan* is the main female character type. Traditionally, only men played this role; makeup, costuming, and gestures signaled their femininity. During the Cultural Revolution, women took over these roles. Today, both men and women sing dan roles. Men sing in a stylized falsetto voice.
- *Jing* is a powerful, courageous, and action-oriented male character. He wears a long beard. His face is painted according to personality traits: red for greatness, white for slyness, and black for integrity and loyalty. Movements are exaggerated, and the voice is powerful.
- *Chou* is an affable male clown whose ugliness and laughter ward off evil. White paint around the nose may symbolize either wit or slyness. The singing style is shrill and laced with colloquial speech. Chou roles are associated with percussion instruments.

Beginning in childhood, these actors undergo years of intense training in acting, singing, dance, martial arts, makeup, and gesture. A performer will specialize in one character type for an entire career. *Farewell My Concubine* (1993), a film by Chinese director Chen Kaige (b. 1952), aptly chronicles the grueling preparation needed to become a jingju performer. It also displays the genre's magnificent costumes, painted faces, and vocal styles.

| Jingju opera performers on stage.

Jingju utilizes two distinct aria types, *xipi* and *erhuang*. Each has specific meters and melodic characteristics. Xipi is lively and cheerful, whereas erhuang is heroic. In both, percussion patterns punctuate speech and mark structural divisions. The *gu shi* (drum master) plays the *guban* (drum and clapper). He also serves as a conductor by signaling entrances and setting tempos. Other percussion instruments join in to accompany martial scenes. String instruments, especially the *jinghu* (bowed spike fiddle), accompany the melodies.

Reforms (Revolutionary Opera)

Jiang and Mao believed that jingju should serve "the workers, peasants, and soldiers." Furthermore, it should be used as propaganda for the state, as a means to convert the masses to Communist ideas. These goals necessitated numerous changes to traditional jingju.

Accordingly, revolutionary opera was presented in vernacular Mandarin rather than the heretofore-used dialect of the upper class. Because Mandarin is a tonal language, this required changes in melody types. Xipi and erhuang aria styles were merged. In proper Communist fashion, committees were put in charge of writing new arias and aria types.

The four traditional character types were dissolved, and new character types were divided into two categories: positive and negative. Elaborately painted faces that indicated personality and social class disappeared. Instead, positive characters were portrayed with warm, reddish makeup; negative characters, in contrast, wore colder, darker hues. Female characters were played by women. Costumes were simplified: peasants wore patched clothing, and police wore uniforms.

Staging became more elaborate with a focus on realism. Symbolic props and gestures mostly disappeared. Stylized dance movements were replaced by posed groups, which represented the struggles and rising power of the masses. As electrical grids became dependable, stage lighting became increasingly complex.

In addition to the traditional Chinese instruments used in Beijing opera, Jiang employed Western orchestral instruments. Why she did so is not clear. Some scholars contend that Jiang never liked traditional instruments; others suggest she was adhering to Mao's policy of "making foreign things serve China." In any case, Jiang clearly believed that the louder Western instruments sounded the revolutionary themes more forcefully. As in Western opera, a conductor led the instrumentalists from an orchestra pit, thus diminishing the function of the gu shi.

Other Westernizations were the addition of an overture and the use of leitmotives to unify the drama. Popular contemporary tunes, as well as "The Internationale" (an internationally recognized socialist anthem), were woven into several of the revamped operas. Performances were either free or available to the public at a low price.

Set during the Second Sino-Japanese War (1937–1945), *Hong deng ji* tells the stories of the railway worker Li Yu-he and his teenage daughter Tie-mei. The two struggle on behalf of China against the Japanese invaders. As a Communist Party member, Li is assigned to transfer a secret code to guerrillas holding out in the mountains. Betrayed by spies, Li is captured and tortured by the Japanese. When he refuses to give up the code, he is killed. The task of delivering the code then falls to Tie-mei, who, against all odds, succeeds. In remembrance of her family's sacrifices, and with red flags flying, she joins the revolutionary army.

Tie-mei's name, which means "iron-plum blossom," is symbolic. The hearty plum blossom blooms only in winter. Likewise, the iron-willed Tie-mei matures to full beauty only under the bitter circumstances of loss and sacrifice. Tie-mei served as a model of the youthful political devotion that Mao and Jiang cultivated during the Cultural Revolution.

MUSICAL THEMES

NIXON IN CHINA (1987)

American composer John Adams (b. 1947) and librettist Alice Goodman's (b. 1958) *Nixon in China* tells the story of President Richard Nixon's 1972 visit to China where he met with Mao Zedong and other government officials. Act II includes a performance of one of the Yang Ban Xi, although First Lady Pat Nixon, Jiang Qing, and Henry Kissinger repeatedly interrupt the "stage" action. The opera's libretto is written in rhymed, metered couplets similar to Chinese theatrical styles; the music is **minimalist** in style.

LISTENING GUIDE

mysearchlab 7.4

"MY HEART IS BURSTING WITH ANGER"

Scene 9, from **Hong deng ji**

Tie-mei has seen her family members killed. She herself has barely escaped capture by Japanese spies. In the piercing nasal voice characteristic of jingju, she sings of her resolve to deliver the code to her comrades. Orchestral interludes allow the audience time to digest the intensity of her passion. The melodic material is pentatonic. Rhythms are free.

0:00	Tíqǐ díkòu	When I think of my enemy. . .
0:14	Xǐn fèi zhà	My heart and lungs are bursting. . .

Tie-mei's fluttering hands reveal her nearly uncontrollable sadness. She quickly rallies, however, as percussion instruments—*guban* (drum and clapper), *dalau* (large gong), *xiaolou* (small gong), and *naobo* (cymbals)—sound her agitation.

0:44	Qiáng rěn chóuhén yǎosuí yá.	I keep the hatred inside me and in anger gnash my teeth
1:08	Zéi Jiūshān qiānfāngbǎi jì bīqǔ mìdiànmǎ,	Jiushan [the Japanese chief of police] tried every possible way to get the code. . .
1:25	Jiāng wǒ nǎinai diēdiē lái qiāngshā.	My grandmother and father he has killed.

Each line begins slowly and freely. The last syllable of every phrase extends in a long melisma that emphasizes the word's power—"enemy," "bursting," "teeth," "code," and "killed." As Tie-mei sings, the jinghu (spike fiddles) follow her lines heterophonically in traditional jingju style. Between the vocal lines, however, we hear a combination of Chinese and Western instruments—violins play in unison with jinghu; a guban punctuates the drama.

In traditional jingju, six-foot-long pheasant feathers extended from the hats of female warrior characters. Gesturing with the feathers would demonstrate anger or show frustration. Tie-mei gestures in a similar way, but with her long braid.

In the following section Tie-mei's rage is portrayed by the extremely high vocal range. A steady rhythm begins and the pace quickens. The *ban* (clapper) articulates each word. Sentence after sentence, Tie-mei's hatred grows as she gathers her strength. Only in the last line does the extended melisma characteristic of earlier lines return—now over her own name. Tie-mei will defy her enemies.

1:46	Yǎozhù chóu, yǎozhù hèn,	Harbor the rage, harbor the hatred.
	jiáosuì chóuhèn qiáng yànxià,	These were forced down my throat.
	chóuhèn rù xǐn yào fāyá,	Now they grow in my heart.
	bù kūqì, bù liúlèi,	No compromise! No hesitation!
	bùxǔ lèishuǐ sāibiān sǎ,	No tears on my cheeks.
	liúrù xǐntián kāi huǒhuā	Instead, they flow inside and burst in my heart.
	Wànzhàng núhuǒ ránshāoqǐ,	The blaze of rage burns
	Yào bǎ hěidì hūntiān lái shāotā	So hard that sky and earth collapse.
	Tiě-néi wǒ, yǒu zhǔnbèi,	I, Tie-mei, am prepared.
	bù pà zhuā, bù pà fang,	I don't fear capture! Don't fear exile!
	bù pà pí biān dǎ, bù pà jiānláo yā!	I don't fear lashing! Don't fear prison!
	Fěnshēnsuìgǔ bù jiāo mìdiànmǎ!	I won't turn in the code, even if my body is in pieces.
2:20	Zéi Jiūshān nǐ děngzhuó ba,	Jiushan, you wait,
	zhè jiùshì Tiě-méi gěi nǐdì hǎo huídá!	this is the answer of Tie-mei.

MUSICAL TERMS

FOLK MUSIC

The term "folksong" (*Volkslied*) dates back to late eighteenth-century Germany. As originally coined, the term was said to represent music of the common people. Folk music was thought to have been communally composed, passed down orally from one generation to the next, and organic in its general aesthetic quality.

Notions of "folk" music evolved alongside growing sentiments of nineteenth-century nationalism. Collectors and composers saw this music as representing links to a rustic and idealized past. Thus, these varied styles, which tended to change considerably from one region to the next, were seen as vital source material for creating national music styles. Hungarian composer Béla Bartók collected music both to preserve it and to borrow ideas for his own compositions. British collector Cecil Sharp (1859–1924) scoured England and Appalachia in search of traditional melodies that might come to constitute a national style.

Bulgarian Concert Folk Music

A lad asks the pretty Dilmano to teach him how to plant his peppers. Push them deep into the soil and they will blossom, she answers. The dialogue holds characteristics of **folksongs** found in many parts of the world—ordinary people striving to live in balance with both nature and their social world. "Dilmano, Dilbero" is not a folksong in the traditional sense, however. Most folksongs are handed down orally over generations. This one was composed in the 1950s by Bulgarian musician Philip (sometimes spelled "Filip") Koutev (1903–1982).

In times past, Bulgarian folk traditions often centered on love and courtship. Music and dance at traditional social events offered opportunities for introductions and close, but public, interaction. But that was then. The twentieth-century combination of technological innovation and modernization, of world wars and political totalitarianism, changed the social landscape. The village square no longer held the cultural currency it had in times past. Folk music in this Southeast European republic was dying.

Koutev sought to preserve the past by marrying it to the present. His idea was to rescue folk music by bringing it into the concert hall. The new style would be called "Concert Folk Music," and he would write it.

But while Koutev drew from the folk imagination, his music was actually something altogether new. His compositions were more sophisticated, regional differences of style were blurred, and the harsh vocal timbres of older times were softened. Singers from villages across the country were trained together and formed into professional choirs. The goal was to create a unified Bulgarian style. These so-called "authentic" folk ensembles would then sing their new songs in support of government policies.

From 1950 to 1951, Koutev established the National Folk Song and the Dance Ensemble Filip Koutev, an umbrella group that included a number of vocal and instrumental ensembles. In 1986, one of these groups, now

Dobarski Babi Folk Group singing in a garden in Dobarsko, Bulgaria.

working under a different director and known as Le Mystère des Voix Bulgares (The Mystery of the Bulgarian Voice), released to worldwide acclaim an album of the same name, *Le Mystère des Voix Bulgares*.

CD II/Track 13
Download track 35
mysearchlab 7.5

LISTENING GUIDE

"DILMANO, DILBERO"   *by Philip Koutev*

To the Western ear, perhaps the most striking aspect of this piece is its rhythm. Not only is the music fast, but the accented pulse seems to constantly shift. Although it certainly does shift, it does so in a highly ordered fashion consisting of two different patterns. The music opens with a rhythm consisting of eight quick pulses grouped in an accented pattern of 2-3-3 (heard twice). The second pattern, which begins with the line "Kazhi mi kak se sadi pipero," combines a group of 11 (combined into an accented pattern of 2-3-3-3) and the previous eight-pulse grouping.

We can hear both of these patterns articulated in the song's lyrics:

```
Dil   ma   no    Dil  be    ro

X x X x x X x x X x X x x X x x

Kazhi mi    kak se sa  di pi  pe    ro

X x X x x X x x X x x X x X x x X x x
```

Notice also the narrow vocal range and strident vocal style. The song's broad form is simple: Intro – A – A – B – Interlude – A – A – B. The A and B sections are further subdivided into individual phrases of aabb and ccdddd, respectively. Perhaps all of these factors—dance rhythms, rough timbre, and simple form—contribute to the folksong-like quality that Koutev sought.

0:00	Instrumental introduction	
0:06	Dilmano dilbero, Dilmano, dilbero. Kazhi mi kak se sadi pipero. (2x)	Lovely Dilmano Teach me how to plant the peppers.
0:16	Dilmano dilbero, Dilmano, dilbero. Kazhi mi kak se sadi pipero. (2x)	Lovely Dilmano Teach me how to plant the peppers.
0:27	Da ts'fti da v'rzhe. Da ts'fti da v'rzhe, Da beresh beresh beresh kak sakash. (4x)	So they blossom and give fruit That one can have whenever one wants.
0:42	Instrumental interlude	
0:47	Pomuni go pobutsni go Eta kak se sadi sadi pipero (2x)	Put it in the soil and push. That's how you plant the pepper.
0:57	Pomuni go pobutsni go Eta kak se sadi sadi pipero (2x)	Put it in the soil and push. That's how you plant the pepper.
1:07	Da ts'fti da v'rzhe. Da ts'fti da v'rzhe, Da beresh beresh beresh kak sakash (4x)	So they blossom and give fruit That you can have whenever you want.

MUSICAL LIVES

WOODY GUTHRIE (1912–1967) AND THE AMERICAN FOLK MUSIC REVIVAL

Rocked by the confluence of the Great Depression and the Great Dust Storm, 23-year-old Oklahoma native Woodrow Wilson (Woody) Guthrie left his wife and children and hopped a train for California. Like so many thousands of others, he went west seeking employment. What Guthrie found instead was music's power to affect social change. His songs championed the politically and economically disenfranchised, helped spur the labor movement, and served as a catalyst for the "American Folk Music Revival," which included Pete Seeger (b. 1919),

(Continued)

MUSICAL LIVES (Continued)

Folk singer/songwriter Woody Guthrie, c. 1943.

Odetta (1930–2008), Phil Ochs (1940–1976), Joan Baez (b. 1941), and Bob Dylan (b. 1941).
mysearchlab 7.6
Guthrie's most famous song is "This Land Is Your Land" (1940). Today we remember the song as an ode to the ideals of the American social contract. But as the following mostly forgotten verse demonstrates, the singer's tongue had a sharp edge:

In the shadow of the steeple I saw my people,
By the relief office I seen my people;
As they stood there hungry, I stood there asking
Is this land made for you and me?

> "Everything will pass, and the world will perish but the Ninth Symphony will remain."
>
> —Michael Bakunin, as quoted in Edmund Wilson's *To the Finland Station* (1940)

Beethoven's Ninth Symphony (1824): Politics and Beyond

On Christmas day 1989, Germany was aglow in newfound hope. The hated Berlin Wall, which had divided the city into East and West, had recently fallen. After 30 years of forced separation, families were reunited. To celebrate this remarkable event, American conductor Leonard Bernstein (1918–1990) led an international ensemble of musicians in a performance of the Symphony No. 9 in D minor by Ludwig van Beethoven (1770–1827).

The symphony is a monumental composition, nothing less than a musical telling of the soul's journey from darkness to light. Perhaps the work's most extraordinary feature is the final movement, a setting of Friedrich Schiller's poem "An die freude" ("Ode to Joy"). Think no more of sorrow, intones the baritone soloist as he introduces the poem:

Freunde, nicht diese Töne!
O friends, not these notes!

Sondern lasst uns angenehmere
Rather let us take up something more

Anstimmen, und freudenvollere.
Pleasant, and more joyful.

Freude!
Joy!

An exuberant chorus listens on, then almost shouts back:

Freude!   Joy!

For the Berlin celebration, Bernstein changed one word in Schiller's text—"Freude" became "Freiheit" (freedom). The concert was televised live in 20 countries to more than 100 million viewers. On that day, freedom sounded around the world.

Beethoven was German, of course, but no single nation or political movement can claim ownership of this great piece. Just months earlier, Chinese students had played the music during their fearless demonstrations in Beijing's Tiananmen Square. The symphony was also performed repeatedly in memorials held in the aftermath of 9/11.

Repressionist regimes have also claimed Beethoven. Soviet leadership praised the composer for having given voice to the ideals and aspirations of the proletariat. Birthday celebrations (1937 and 1942) for Adolf Hitler included a Berlin Philharmonic performance of the Ninth Symphony. In 1974, the white minority rulers of Rhodesia (now Zimbabwe) set new words to the "Ode" melody for their new national anthem, "Rise O Voices of Rhodesia."

The idea of individual freedom dominated Beethoven's intellectual life. These interests came to the musical forefront in two other major compositions from the early 1800s: his Symphony

No. 3 in Eb Major (1804) and the opera *Fidelio* (1805). Both made political statements, though arguably each focused most strongly on inner psychological victories. As for Symphony No. 3, Beethoven originally subtitled it "Bonaparte," after Napoleon Bonaparte, the French general and people's champion. When Napoleon proclaimed himself emperor and invaded Austria, Beethoven was infuriated. He took a knife to the original inscription and renamed the work *Sinfonia eroica* (*Heroic Symphony*). Beethoven's opera *Fidelio* was no less idealistic. It tells the story of the political prisoner Florestan and his wife Leonore, who is willing to sacrifice her own life to save his.

Universal brotherhood is the central theme of the Ninth Symphony. Setting this lofty ideal to music, however, proved no easy task. Beethoven made over 200 drafts of the "Ode to Joy" tune alone. The symphony took over eight years to complete.

MUSICAL LIVES

LUDWIG VAN BEETHOVEN (1770–1827)

Portrait bust of Ludwig van Beethoven by Hugo Hagen, based on life mask by Franz Klein from 1812.

German composer Ludwig van Beethoven lived by the principles of the Enlightenment, the late-eighteenth-century intellectual movement that produced the ideals of rationality, political freedom, and personal liberty. His philosophy was directly reflected in his music, which was grander yet more introspective, more heroic yet more abstract, than anything written previously in the Western tradition. Such was the originality of his work that it took generations for composers and audiences alike to digest its implications.

Little came easily for Beethoven, who often struggled to compose. His sketchbooks reveal years of working out even a single theme. While still a young man, Beethoven began to lose his hearing. So devastating was this realization that he contemplated suicide. Happily for posterity, he carried on and gave musical voice to the struggle within. Many of his compositions were written after he was completely deaf.

Beethoven was a prolific composer. He wrote one opera, five piano concertos, 16 string quartets, 32 piano sonatas, 10 violin sonatas, marches, songs, variations, and many other works. His nine symphonies are tours de force of the orchestral repertory. His stellar reputation as a symphonic writer weighed heavily on later composers. Fellow German composer Johannes Brahms (1833–1897) avoided the genre until his 40s for fear of falling short; others approached the completion of their own ninth symphonies as an omen of death.

Beethoven's compositional output has been divided into three creative stages. His first works (to 1802) are stylistically representative of the Classical period—clear tonalities, balanced phrases, and formal conformity. His second period (the "Heroic" period, 1803–1812) begins with the Third Symphony, a work twice as long and far more complex than any symphonies that preceded it. Here we see Beethoven departing from the traditions of the Classical style and ushering in a new era of extended forms and tonal expansion. The Third Symphony received mixed reviews. Some recognized its greatness, whereas others complained of its length. The middle period was also a time in Beethoven's life that was plagued with anxiety: over his impending deafness, over Napoleon's self-proclaimed emperorship, and over the French bombardment of his beloved Vienna (1809), as well as a failed love affair and poor health.

The beginning of the third stylistic period (1813–1827) was marked by months of depression and financial troubles. His compositions were uneven in quality with emotional foci ranging from intimate chamber works to the bombastic programmatic orchestral work *Wellington's Victory* (*The Battle Symphony*, 1813). While the work is perhaps Beethoven's weakest orchestral composition, it did much for his public appeal and led to financial stability.

The last three years of Beethoven's life saw the completion of his Ninth Symphony—a communal expression of optimism and Enlightenment ideals—and his last five string quartets, intensely personal testaments to a life of genius and disquietude.

CD II/Track 14
Download track 36
mysearchlab 7.7

LISTENING GUIDE

FOURTH MOVEMENT, SYMPHONY NO. 9 IN D MINOR, OP. 125 — *Ludwig van Beethoven*

0:00	Drum roll and agitated winds announce a short-lived "Fanfare of Terror."
0:08	As the sounds die away, the string basses enter with a sturdy speech-like melody, as if they were "singing" an operatic **recitative**. This reference to a vocal genre in a symphony would have sounded strange to Beethoven's audience but also prepared them for the true vocal section to come.
0:22	"Fanfare of Terror" interrupts.
0:30	Once again, the basses enter. Changing instruments and timbres seem to flip the emotional mood back and forth between darkness and light.
0:52	The bass recitative returns. It begins to feel as if the basses are taking us on a journey through life's tribulations.
1:12	Musical material from the second movement is introduced.
1:18	The bass recitative returns.
1:34	Musical material from the third movement is introduced.
1:44	The basses engage in dialogue with material from movement three.
2:05	A first brief sounding of the "Ode to Joy" in the winds appears. Bass interruptions continue. Cadence at (2:33).
2:37	Now the basses take up the "Ode." Beethoven writes three variations on the theme; the texture in each variation gets thicker as more instruments are added. Notice that the form of the "Ode" is ABB (subdivided as: aa' ba' ba').
3:20	Variation 1: theme in the viola section. Bassoon, cellos, and basses play a lovely countermelody.
4:03	Variation 2: theme in first violins. Second violins and basses provide a countermelody.
4:46	Variation 3: full orchestra. Theme is in the brass and woodwinds.
5:28	Transitional material is based on "Ode" theme.
6:10	The "Fanfare of Terror" returns. It feels as if the movement has begun anew. This time, however, the string bass recitative is replaced by the human voice.
6:18	Beethoven's words introduce the poem: Freunde, nicht diese Töne! / O friends, not these notes! Sondern lasst uns angenehmere / Rather let us take up something more Anstimmen, und freudenvollere. / Pleasant, and more joyful. Freude! / Joy!
7:06	The chorus echoes: Freude! / Joy!

7: 10	Baritone continues with the "Ode to Joy" theme: winds add countermelodies:	
	Freude, schöner Götterfunken Tochter aus Elysium Wir betreten feuertrunken, Himmlische, dein Heiligtum. Deine Zauber binden wieder, Was die Mode streng geteilt; Alle Menschen werden Brüder, Wo dein sanfter Flügel weilt.	Joy, lovely divine light, Daughter of Elysium We march, drunk with fire, Holy One, to thy holy kingdom. Thy magic binds together What tradition has strongly parted, All men will be brothers Dwelling under the safety of your wings.
7:37	The chorus repeats the last four lines of the stanza.	
7:57	Vocal quartet sings the "Ode" theme:	
	Wem der grosse Wurf gelungen, Eines Freundes Freund zu sein Wer ein holdes Weib errungen, Mische seinen Jubel ein! Ja – wer auch nur eine Seele Sein nennt auf' dem Erdenrund! Und wer's nie gekonnt, der stehle Weinend sich aus diesem Bund.	He who has had the great pleasure To be a true friend to a friend, He who has a noble wife Let him join our mighty song of rejoicing! Yes, if there is a solitary soul In the entire world which claims him If he rejects it, then let him steal away Weeping out of this comradeship.
8:22	Chorus repeats the last four lines.	
8:43	Quartet sings:	
	Freude trinken alle Wesen An den Brüsten der Natur; Alle Guten, alle Bösen Folgen ihrer Rosenspur. Küsse gab sie uns und Reben Einen Freund, geprüft im Tod; Wollust ward dem Wurm gegeben, Und der Cherub steht vor Gott. stand	All beings drink in joy From nature's breasts. All good and evil things Follow her rose-strewn path. She gives us kisses and grapes, A friend, tested unto death, Pleasure is given even to the worm And the cherubim before God.
9:10	Chorus repeats the last four lines of this section, emphasizing "vor Gott."	
9:40	Following a dramatic pause after the climax on the word "God," the bassoon plays single notes, then is joined by other woodwinds in yet another version of the "Ode." This section is known as the Turkish march, so called because of the addition of triangle, cymbals, and bass drum. Beethoven was familiar with the Janissary bands of the Turkish military from his early adulthood when Austria was at war with the Ottoman Empire. To composers of the Classical and early Romantic periods, these sounds represented the East. The sounds gave the work an exotic feel, which was perhaps Beethoven's way of broadening the cultural palate of his musical testament of brotherly love.	
10:11	Fade out.	

MUSICAL LIVES

THE ENIGMA OF SHOSTAKOVICH (1906–1975)

Dimtri Shostakovich (left) working on a score.

Russian-born composer Dmitri Shostakovich (1906–1975) was recognized as a "true son of the Communist Party." His second symphony commemorates the tenth anniversary of the October 1917 Bolshevik Revolution; his eleventh (subtitled "The Year 1905") commemorates the Russian Revolution of that year. He wrote music for propaganda films and served on various Soviet committees. For his pro-Communist speeches, the Communist Party gave him a summer home.

But his relationship with the Soviet authorities was often troubled. He was variously denounced as an ideologically unsuitable composer. The Soviet newspaper *Pravda* condemned his 1934 opera *Lady Macbeth of the Mtsensk District* as being immoral; it was withdrawn from the repertory. Other works were censored as well. Political problems also cost Shostakovich his teaching position at the Leningrad Conservatory.

So who was this man, a loyal Soviet or political dissident? The answer may be "both." While some aspects of Soviet ideology appealed to Shostakovich, others did not.

QUESTIONS FOR THOUGHT

- How is it that Beethoven's Symphony No. 9 can appeal to such diverse political agendas? Might this pose a problem for listeners with different national allegiances?
- Some think that Beethoven's "Ode to Joy" theme sounds like a folksong. Why might this be so?

ACTIVITIES AND ASSIGNMENTS

- Investigate how film director Stanley Kubrick (1928–1999) uses Beethoven's Ninth Symphony during the "aversion therapy" scene in *A Clockwork Orange* (1971). How does the particular performance that Kubrick chose affect the drama?
- Find other political or cultural references to Beethoven's Ninth Symphony.

The Zapatista Movement

On January 1, 1994, the same day that the North American Free Trade Agreement (NAFTA) went into effect, the revolutionary Zapatista Army of National Liberation (EZLN) mobilized in Chiapas, one of Mexico's poorest states. NAFTA would take from the poor and give to the rich, claimed the EZLN. The agreement was little more than a "death certificate" to Mexico's indigenous peoples, they contended.

In protest, EZLN militia took over towns and produced demands for dialogue with government leaders. They sought neither power nor independence, but equality in representation. Also, they sought payment to the indigenous peoples for the natural resources that NAFTA would take from the land.

The armed revolution was quickly subdued by the Mexican army. Politically, however, the EZLN remains strong. The movement is led by Subcomandante Marcos, an articulate and cagey politician who has used the media

LISTENING GUIDE

"EL HIMNO ZAPATISTA"

"El Himno Zapatista" is a *corrido*, a Mexican **ballad** form usually in triple meter. The corrido has deep roots. It arrived from Spain at least as early at the sixteenth century.

Corridos are designed to tell stories of identity and struggle. Thus, they have always been a favored song form in times of political upheaval. Many were written during the Emiliano Zapata-led Mexican Revolution; more are being written today in Chiapas in honor of the Zapatista movement.

"El Himno Zapatista" neatly bridges the gap between the Mexican Revolution and the struggle in Chiapas. The song borrows its tune from "Con Mi 30 30," a corrido that inspired revolutionary soldiers in 1910. The lyrics, which vary from one performance to the next, are new.

and Internet to take EZLN's philosophy to the world. In Chiapas, Marcos works for the needs of the Mayan underclass. His broader goal moves beyond ethnicity or national boundaries, however. Speaking as a voice for all oppressed peoples, he once told a journalist:

> Marcos is gay in San Francisco, black in South Africa, an Asian in Europe, a Chicano in San Ysidro, an anarchist in Spain, a Palestinian in Israel, a Mayan in the streets of San Cristóbal, a Jew in Germany, a Gypsy in Poland, a Mohawk in Quebec, a pacifist in Bosnia, a single woman on the Metro at 10 p.m., a peasant without land, a gang member in the slums, an unemployed worker, an unhappy student, and, of course, a Zapatista in the mountains.

For the Maya, the articles of everyday life have become associated with their political resistance. Traditional clothing, food, and language serve as markers of identity and political solidarity.

So too is the case with music. Songbooks, not unlike those once used by political parties in the United States, have been distributed. One-hundred-year-old songs about Emiliano Zapata (1879–1919), hero of the 1910 Mexican Revolution, have returned to the **mariachi** repertoire. The Mayan sound has become symbolic of the struggle to maintain ethnic tradition in a globalizing world.

The EZLN has also inspired musical responses abroad. In France, the political singer Renaud recorded the song "Adios Zapata," which remembers the deeds of Zapata, Pancho Villa (1878–1923), and Che Guevara (1928–1967). In Los Angeles, the punk rock band Rage Against the Machine recorded "Zapata's Blood" (1997) and "People of the Sun" (1996), which was also released as a music video. In

Emiliano Zapata Salazar (1879–1919; seated, at left), leader of the Mexican Revolution (1910–1920), with other revolutionary leaders.

fact, Rage Against the Machine did not have the politics right. Subcomandante Marcos is fighting his revolution with ideas, not blood. It is a revolution that begins with Mayans and welcomes others. Marcos finds unity in diversity:

> . . . there are young people, men and women, who name their own identities: "punk," "ska," "goth," "metal," "trasher," "rapper," "hip-hopper" and "etceteras." If we look at what they all have in common, we will see that they have nothing in common, that they are all "different." They are "others." And that is exactly what we have in common, that we are "other," and "different." Not only that, we also have in common that we are fighting in order to continue being "other" and "different."

ACTIVITIES AND ASSIGNMENTS

- Investigate how music is currently used as a tool in political campaigns, social movements, and expressions of nationality.
- Research the music of various twentieth-century North American political movements, such as suffrage, the labor movement, and the civil rights movement.
- Take a few minutes to reflect on the idea of nation. What would the ideal nation be like? How would its music sound?

CONCLUSION

"Man is by nature a political animal."
–Aristotle

We have focused in this chapter on music in relation to the modern nation-state. One can define politics more broadly, however. Political action includes any competition for social power between distinct interest groups or individuals. Seen from this perspective, we can speak of ethnic politics, gender politics, religious politics, and so on. Often these categories are interwoven one with the other.

To the extent that musicians strive to engage and influence, their art is political by nature. Ultimately, however, music's meaning resides in the mind of the listener. The same sounds that bind and empower one group might work to alienate and disenfranchise another. Hendrix's performance of "The Star-Spangled Banner" can alternately be interpreted as unpatriotic or a quintessential expression of civil liberty. Beethoven intended his Ninth Symphony to help usher in an era of universal brotherhood, but it has been successfully appropriated to forward the agendas of oppressive regimes around the world.

Whenever you listen, think about music's power to persuade. Musicians and audiences, the record industry and governments, indeed all individuals and institutions are motivated by ever-shifting combinations of self and social interest. Listen carefully and you are sure to hear the political nuances.

Cause this is live from Iraq
Home of too many soldiers' graves.
Where for our country
We gamble with our lives everyday.
And there are no blue skies here.
Every color's gray.
This is the blood of soldiers
Of which the streets are now paved.
And there is no reimbursement
For the price that we pay

Live from Iraq by 4th25 [pronounced Fourth Quarter]

Released in 2005 by 4th25 Music Group LLC, the album *Live from Iraq* reveals war from the soldiers' standpoint. The songs on the album are about survival and fear, sacrifice and loss. The group's music videos are muscle hard. Absent is the glossy sexuality and tough-guy posing of videos produced stateside. An early video shows images of war, real war— actual combat footage with trucks exploding and people dying. Production is primitive; in-the-trenches authenticity trumps packaging.

An entire body of music has sprung up in response to the war in Iraq. During the buildup and early months of the 2003 invasion, song-writers dug in their heels with hard and generally unnuanced positions either in support of, or in opposition to, the conflict. Country music star Toby Keith's (b. 1961) "Courtesy of the Red, White and Blue (The Angry American)" spoke for a short-tempered public lashing out for revenge in the aftermath of the September 11, 2001 attacks on the World Trade Center. A voice from the opposite end of the spectrum was that of British punk-rocker-turned-folk-singer Billy Bragg (b. 1957). In "The Price of Oil," Bragg saw the opportunistic hand of global economics as the real incentive for war.

Music and War

For thousands of years, music and war have gone hand in hand. A reference in the Old Testament of the Bible (Judges 7) cites Gideon's men blowing 300 *shofarot* (rams' horns) as they marched into battle. Roman legions employed similar instruments. Centuries later, European armies would add drums and **natural trumpets** to their musical arsenal.

Military music has always flowed back and forth between fields of combat and general culture. Beginning in 1095 and lasting for over 300 years, European Christians undertook a series of crusades into the Middle East. The early ventures were designed to recapture the Holy Land from Muslim rule; later projects sought to halt the Ottoman (Turkish) Empire's encroachment into Europe. The wars inspired entire repertories of music, including pilgrims' songs, planctus (laments), and rallying cries. One military-inspired melody from the fifteenth century, "L'homme armé" ("The Armed Man"), was embedded into more than 40 Catholic masses.

mysearchlab 8.1

In the sixteenth century, composers cultivated a programmatic genre of vocal and instrumental battle works. These compositions typically included military fanfares. Singers were given onomatopoeic figures such as ta-ri-ra-ri-ra-ri-ra-ri or pa-ti-pa-toc-pa-ti-pa-toc to represent the chaos of combat.

The best known of these battle pieces was the four-part **chanson** "La guerre" ("The War") (1528) by French composer Clement Janequin (ca. 1485–after 1558). This piece was so popular that it inspired not only a series of instrumental battle compositions but also **battle masses**.

"La guerre" was most likely written to celebrate the French victory over the Swiss-controlled Duchy of Milan (Italy) at the Battle of Marignano (1515). The battle marked a victory for modern warfare (artillery and cannons) over Swiss pike (long spear) and sword. Casualties were high: 28 hours of combat left over 16,000 dead.

Francois I (1494–1547) at the Battle of Marignano, 14th September 1515, depicted on a vellum manuscript by an anonymous French artist of the sixteenth century.

MUSICAL THEMES
JANISSARY BANDS

Turkish military bands (*Mehterân*, known in the West as Janissary Bands) were known for their colorful uniforms and shrill, penetrating sound. They made their mark in Europe during the seventeenth and eighteenth centuries in the Wars of the Ottoman Empire. Western art music composers such as Franz Joseph Haydn (1732–1809), Mozart, and Beethoven invoked the "exotic" by using Turkish-sounding instruments (large drums, bells, cymbals) in their compositions. European military bands greatly increased their ranks by adding Turkish percussion instruments. By the late eighteenth century Western military bands were employing Moorish or black percussionists, dressed in "Eastern" style clothing and using extravagant drumming gestures. The modern-day marching band, with its military style uniforms and precision drills, traces its origins directly to these Turkish-influenced military bands.

"La guerre" includes the earliest known musical examples of military battle calls (trumpet and drum signals that instructed soldiers to advance, retreat, or perform maneuvers). Interspersed and sung within Janequin's text and melody are five calls. **mysearchlab 8.2**

- *Alarm:* short-long, short-long (either a single pitch or "mi-sol, mi-sol")
- *To the Standard:* short-short-short-short-long ("fa-do-do-do-do")
- *Advance:* long--short-long--short-long (a single pitch)
- *Boots and Saddles:* even notes ("do-sol-sol-sol")
- *To the Horse:* short-short-long (a single pitch)

LISTENING GUIDE

CD III/Track 1
Download track 38
mysearchlab 8.3

"LA GUERRE"
by Clement Janequin

Janequin calls his fellow Frenchmen to listen to the story of Marignano. As was typical of the period's style, most of the words are lost in the dense polyphonic tangle of voices. Nevertheless, one can clearly hear the initial exhortation, "Escoutez" (Listen). Quickly repeating tones and syllables mimic the beating of drums and the chaos of combat. (The sung battle calls are indicated in bold type.)

PRIMA PARS (FIRST PART)

0:00	Escoutez tous, gentilz Galloys, La victoire du noble Roy Françoys	Listen, all gentlemen of France To the victory of the great King of France.

(Continued)

LISTENING GUIDE (*Continued*)

0:31	Et orrez, si bien escoutez, des coups ruèz de touts costés. Phifres soufflez. Frappez tambours, Tournez, virez. Faittes vos tours, Phifres soufflez battez tousjours	You will hear, if you listen, Blows thudding on all sides. Fifes resound. Beat the drums, Turn and wheel. Perform your maneuvers, Fifes resound, continue to battle.

Here the meter changes from duple to triple meter to provide contrast. Composers of the time often employed metric and textural changes as a way to give their music shape. In the following century, composers would develop this device by writing distinct stand-alone sections called movements.

1:03	Avanturiers, bons compagnons, Ensemble croisez vos bastons. Bendez soudain, gentils Gascons, Haquebusjers, faittes vos sons. Nobles, sautez dans les arçons, Armes bouclez, frisques et mignons.	Adventurers, good country men, Together cross your staves Bend the bow, noble Gascons Riflemen make your sound Noblemen leap into your saddles, Don your arms, gentlemen and servants.
1:24	La lance au poing hardis et promptz Donnez dedans, grincez les dents Soyez hardiz, en joye mis,	Lance in hand and ready Strike them, grit your teeth Be bold and joyful,
1:36	Alarme, alarme	Alarm, alarm.

The chanson then returns to duple meter. The texture thins and we hear clearly "let each urge himself on" set to a gently descending motive that repeats several times.

1:40	Chascun s'assaisonne, La fleur de lys. Fleur de haut pris, Y est en personne.	Let each urge himself on, The fleurs de lys. The noble prize, Is there in person (i.e., the King of France).

Here both duple and triple meter sound against one another in different voices.

2:09	Poulsez faucons et gros canons Pour faire bresche aux compagnons Et mettre à mort ces Bourguignons, Sonnez trompettes et clairons.	Let small and great cannons thunder To make of the Brescians And put to death these Burgundians (Burgundian territory was part of the Old Swiss Confederacy) Sound trumpets and bugles.

The prima pars ends in triple meter on a strong cadence at 2:30.

SECUNDA PARS (SECOND PART)

Onomatopoeic battle sounds, using both nonsense syllables and actual words, dominate the second part. Battle sounds come and go, covering up actual phrases. The resulting musical chaos pictures the melee of battle.

Janequin initially writes a fanfare using articulation syllables (used when learning to play the trumpet), then four military calls. Due to the thick polyphonic texture, however, the calls are nearly impossible to hear. Perhaps Janequin is duplicating the confusion of battle; perhaps he simply preferred to obscure his clever references. Interestingly, these same calls appear 100 years later in trumpet instruction manuals. That Janequin incorporates them indicates the existence of remarkably similar calls long before extant written documentation. Perhaps he found the calls in military manuals long since lost or still languishing in unexamined archives. Equally plausible is that Janequin heard them—on the battlefield or from colleagues.

2:37	Fan fan Frere le le lan fan	(Trumpet articulation syllables)
	Boutez selle.	Mount your horses
	A l'estandart	To the standard
	Tost avant	Everyone advance
	Gens de'armes **á cheval**	Men of the cavalry
	Farirarirariron	(battle sounds)
	Tost **à l'estandart**	Everyone to the standard
	Frere le le lan fan	(battle sounds)

The meter changes from duple to triple; pairs of voices answer each other for "fire and thunder."

| 3:40 | Bruyez, tonnez | Fire, thunder |
| | Bruyez bombardes et faucons | Fire the bombards and cannons |

The meter then slips back to duple.

3:55	Pour entrer sur ces Bourguignons.	To destroy these Burgundians.
4:01	Teu teu teu pedou pedou . . .	(battle sounds)
4:13	Rendes-vous Bourguignons	Rendezvous Burgundians
	Sortez du lieu, sortez, vuidez.	Leave, get out and be gone.
	Ne vous faittes plus canonner,	No longer use the cannon,
4:21	La place fault abandonner	Abandon the place.
	Tarirarira . . . la la la . . . Pon pon pon . . .	(battle sounds)
4:59	Courage, France. Donnez des horions	Courage, France. Strike your blows
	Chippe choppe, torche lorgne!	Chip, chop, well done, look!
	Zin zin patipatac . . .	
5:10	A mort à mort . . .	To the death, to the death
	Frappez, batez, ruez, tuez	Strike, beat, lash out, kill
	Serre, France, tarirarira . . .	Close ranks, France
5:26	Courage.	Courage.
	Donnez dedans, grincez les dents	Strike them, grit your teeth
	Fers esmolus, choquez dessus,	Sharpened swords, strike [them] down
	France, courage, ils sont en fuyte,	Courage France, they are in flight
	Ils montrent les talons, courage compagnons	They show their heels, courage companion
	Donnez des horions,	Give blows,
	tuez ces Bourguignons.	Kill these Burgundians.
	Ils sont confus, ils sont perdus,	They are confused, they are lost
	Prenez courage, après, après suyvez de près,	Take courage, after them, after them, follow them
	Donnez sur le bagiage, ne leur laissez nul.	closely.
6:07	Victoire au grand roy des Françoys.	Victory to the great King of the French.

In this last section the words are nearly unintelligible. The actual text is sung by the two lower voices, taking turns. Other voices sound the battle sounds. Occasionally one can hear "alarm" sounding through the confusion. It is not until the very end that one can make out each voice individually announcing the "Victory."

Three centuries later, German composer Ludwig van Beethoven (1770–1827) also incorporated military sounds into his Symphony No. 9 in D minor (1824), which includes a march that made use of cymbals and triangles. These instruments had been introduced to Western Europe by the stylish Janissary bands of invading Turkish armies. Russian composer Pyotr Ilyich Tchaikovsky used real cannons in his rousing *1812 Overture* (1880).

America's most famous "military" composer was John Philip Sousa (1854–1932). "The March King" wrote over 100 marches and directed the U.S. Marine Band from 1880 to 1892. Upon leaving the Marines, Sousa formed a civilian band, which toured the nation and the world for 39 years. The Sousa band became an American institution.

The composer's most popular work is "The Stars and Stripes Forever," written on Christmas Day, 1896. From that day forward, Sousa's band performed the piece at nearly every concert until the composer's death. A 1987 act of Congress made "The Stars and Stripes Forever" the National March of the United States.

In the pages that follow, we will study relationships between music and war in a variety of settings. We begin with the Vietnam War (1959–1975), then backtrack in time to the 1800s to study the American Civil War (1861–1865) and the Native American **Ghost Dance**. After the Ghost Dance, we investigate Eastern European Jewish society struggling to survive under the shadow of the Holocaust. Finally, we turn to the remembrance of war by studying

| John Philip Sousa.

a trio of twentieth-century concert pieces that commemorate valor, honor the dead, and represent war's inestimable horrors.

The Vietnam War, 1959–1975

America in the 1960s was a time of great turbulence. The Berlin Wall, the most visible sign of the Cold War in Europe, was built in 1961; the following year, the United States was brought to the brink of nuclear war during the Cuban Missile Crisis. The civil rights movement was in full swing at home while, on the far side of the world, war was heating up in Vietnam.

DID YOU KNOW?
MUSIC AS A WEAPON

"Acoustic bombardment" is the term military officials now use for the practice of using music to disorient, traumatize, and potentially break enemy combatants. The principle is simple—just like the horns at the gates of ancient Jericho, only a lot louder. In Iraq, prior to the 2004 invasion of Fallujah, soldiers strapped giant speakers to the roofs of their Humvees, then blasted heavy metal music into the city. The practice has been used time and again.

"Almost anything you do that demonstrates your omnipotence or lack of fear helps break the enemy down," Lt. Col. Dan Kuehl told reporter Lane DeGregory of the *St. Petersburg (FL) Times* back in 2004. "Soldiers play the stuff they like, of course. Music that gets them pumped up, songs like AC/DC's 'Hell's Bells.'"

The battlefield is not the only place where music is used as a weapon. The BBC, *Time* magazine, the *New York Times,* and other sources reported instances of blaring music being used to "soften" prisoners in Iraq and Guantanamo Bay. Often the music, which ranged from Metallica's "Enter Sandman" to Barney the Purple Dinosaur's "I Love You," was accompanied by sleep deprivation, solitary confinement, extremes of heat and cold, and other tactics.

Musicians expressed a variety of opinions about all of these events. Through their songs, they hoped to heighten awareness and influence others. The prominent folk singer Joan Baez took an active role in both the civil rights movement and the anti-war movement. Bob Dylan, who never wanted to be associated with any "movement," nevertheless recorded a number of anti-war songs in 1963/64, including "Blowin' in the Wind," "Masters of War," "A Hard Rain's A-Gonna Fall," "Talking World War III Blues," and "The Times They Are a-Changin'."

released "Dawn of Correction." The song borrowed McGuire's melody, added a bouncy country-and-western-style countermelody played on the Jew's harp, and tightened the song's formal structure. The lyrics of "Dawn of Correction" advanced the Domino Theory, which hypothesized that should South Vietnam fall to Communism, so would the rest of Asia and then the world, just like a neat line of tumbling dominoes.

"Dawn of Correction" was not commercially successful. Nor did it manage to engage the national consciousness. That, however, did not mean that pro-military music was out of step with the nation. Indeed, the most formally disciplined and commercially successful of all the Vietnam War songs was Staff Sergeant Barry Sadler's 1966 "Ballad of the Green Berets." This pro-military song featured a crisp drum cadence and taut orchestration. Sadler's voice had the simultaneously confident and humble tone of a man accustomed to giving and following orders. The crisp-sounding male chorus suggested the strict code of military comradeship.

Adding to the song's appeal was Sadler's personal history. Not only was he himself a Green Beret, but he had served as a medic in Vietnam where he received a purple heart. The song sold two million copies in just five weeks, and nine million copies overall. It was the best-selling single of 1966 and was subsequently featured in the 1968 movie *The Green Berets* starring John Wayne (1907–1979).

It was not until 1965, a year of dramatic American troop escalation, that rock 'n' roll musicians began to write about the Vietnam War. The first important endeavor was "Eve of Destruction" by the gravelly voiced Barry McGuire. The biblically nuanced folk-rock anthem blasted social injustice from Selma, Alabama, to the jungles of Vietnam. So controversial was the song's political message that ABC-affiliate radio stations refused to play it. Even so, "Eve of Destruction," with its awkward five-line verse and clumsy rhyme schemes, went to number one on the *Billboard* pop charts.

Despite his commercial success, McGuire did not speak for the majority of Americans, at least not in 1965. A musical firefight of sorts ensued when a trio named The Spokesmen

Students burning their draft cards to protest the Vietnam War.

LISTENING GUIDE

CD II/Track 15
Download track 37
mysearchlab 8.4

"BALLAD OF THE GREEN BERETS"   *by Robin Moore and Staff Sgt. Barry Sadler*

Few ballads tell grander stories than this one of service, death, and figurative rebirth. At the song's opening we are introduced to the "brave men of The Green Beret." Soon, a wife receives the news that her husband has died in combat. His last request? That the tradition continue. She must make sure that son follows father and becomes a Green Beret.

The song is technically unsophisticated but highly effective, a model of musical economy. A simple snare drum rhythm, suitable for marching, highlights the soldierly ideals of austerity and resolve. Utilitarian harmonies sound in the background. The lyrics are set strophically in simple aabb rhymes and follow (with minor variations) the same rhythmic scheme: short, short, long . . . , short, short, short, long. Each stanza is eight measures in duration. The textual form of the stanzas, though the actual melody never changes, is ABCBDE. Images are strong and direct: "fighting soldiers," "fearless men," "men who mean just what they say," "brave men," and, of course, men who die serving their country.

0:00	Drum rhythm and simple harmonies are present.
0:06	Sadler enters with the first stanza. The range is an octave and one-half, but there is a sense that Sadler is talking more than singing.
0:27	Now, and with each stanza that follows, the orchestration gets thicker and louder as the music moves toward a final climax. Listen to the bass as it enters to provide a strong foundation.
0:52	A men's choir enters with the next stanza singing a wordless countermelody. Perhaps they symbolize the anonymity of common soldiers supporting one another.
1:14	In another act of solidarity, the choir joins Sadler by singing stanza B in harmony.
1:37	Sadler continues his story. The choir returns to its wordless countermelody. An organ, symbolizing church and community, enters to support the harmony. Short trumpet fanfares punctuate the tale.
1:59	The choir joins Sadler with the lyrics. The fanfares become more prominent.

Contrast Sadler's neatly polished work with a piece by singer/songwriter Joe McDonald, leader of the San Francisco-based band Country Joe and the Fish. The group's most memorable song was also the decade's most sardonic anti-war contribution, a taunting jug-band parody titled "I-Feel-Like-I'm-Fixin'-to-Die Rag" (1967). The cheery apocalyptic lyrics, which invited young men to "put down your books and pick up a gun," are supported by a tooting kazoo and a grab-bag of musical clichés.

Despite young people's obvious stake in the war's progress, mainstream popular musicians produced comparatively little protest music.

The darkest release was "The End" (1967), a nihilistic **dirge** by The Doors (also featured in Francis Ford Coppola's 1979 film *Apocalypse Now*). By the 1970s, nearly every major sector of the pop music business had recorded at least a couple anti-Vietnam War songs, though most are best thought of as pop songs designed to sell records, not influence minds. The Temptations, for example, recorded "Ball of Confusion" (1970) and Edwin Starr recorded "War" (1970), both for Motown Records. Jamaican reggae star Jimmy Cliff recorded "Viet Nam" (1971). That same year the Beach Boys squeezed "Student Demonstration Time" onto the album *Surf's Up* (1971).

QUESTIONS FOR THOUGHT

- We studied the text, military drum rhythm cadence, and chorus in "Ballad of the Green Berets." What are some of the song's other musical attributes? How do they support Sadler's aesthetic and political intent?
- Some listeners find the "I-Feel-Like-I'm-Fixin'-to-Die Rag" to be deeply offensive. Others find it ironic. Where do you sit on this issue? Why?
- Music is often used as a marketing device. Do you think war and peace can be marketed through music? Can you think of examples?

ACTIVITIES AND ASSIGNMENTS

- View the helicopter gunship attack in Francis Ford Coppola's *Apocalypse Now* (1979). What music is playing and what does it symbolize? Is this an example of music as a weapon?
- Compare and contrast songs from the war in Iraq with those from the Vietnam War. Are there common themes? How has the musical language changed?
- Investigate how popular songs reflected war sentiment during World War I and World War II. Were the songs hawkish or dovish, interventionist or isolationist? Did the music impact popular thought or government policy?

The American Civil War, 1861–1865

"I don't believe we can have an army without music," remarked Confederate General Robert E. Lee. It must have seemed that way to his soldiers as well. Music was ubiquitous in camp and on the battlefield. As the armies mobilized, so did the bands. By the end of 1861, just eight months after the attack on Fort Sumter, the Union military supported 618 bands and nearly 28,000 instrumentalists.

In combat, field musicians—fifers, buglers, and drummers—were often stationed near commanding officers where they conveyed signals to the troops. Many musicians were just boys. The minimum enlistment age for musicians was officially 12, but the rule was often ignored.

Many boy soldiers were killed, and their sacrifices were memorialized in a variety of songs. The most famous of these, "The Drummer Boy of Shiloh," was tearfully sung in family parlors and military camps on both sides of the Mason-Dixon Line.

Union soldiers and military band march through a city street on their way to join the war.

MUSICAL THEMES
EMOTION IN MUSIC

Strange as it may seem to us today, sentimental songs of the era were expected to bring listeners of either sex to tears. Men were expected not to show "feminine" emotions in response to their own trying circumstances, but they were free to do so in response to a moving song. A tearful response was acceptable because the feelings were experienced communally as human universals. Seen in this light, tears confirmed one's depth of humanity. President Lincoln was typical of his time. Although firm enough to push America's bloodiest war to its conclusion, he wept freely when moved by song.

Music was used to bolster soldiers' spirits. Bands entertained in camp at night, helped men stay in line during long marches, and even lent moral support during combat. Union and Confederate bands were plentiful during the 1863 bloodbath at Gettysburg, for example. On the climactic third day of that battle a Confederate band played "Nearer, My God, to Thee" as the decimated Confederate ranks struggled back to their lines after General George Pickett's failed advance. The hymn's composer was Lowell Mason, a Northerner.

MUSICAL LIVES

LOWELL MASON (1792–1872)

In addition to being a well-known hymnodist, Lowell Mason was responsible for introducing music education into the public schools. Always an advocate for good music and correct singing, Mason wrote music instruction books and offered teacher training at his Boston Academy of Music. Though he saw himself primarily as a banker, Mason wrote over 1,600 hymns, was a choir director and organist, and helped his Presbyterian church create the first Sunday school for black children in the United States. Mason also wrote the melody for "Mary Had a Little Lamb."

More than any other American armed conflict, the Civil War caught the public's musical imagination. Thousands of war-related songs were published as sheet music. Sometimes, songs attempted to sway public sentiment; more often, however, they reflected concerns of the moment. Upbeat songs of 1861 and 1862 roused civilians and soldiers alike to "rally 'round the flag" (as in George Root's "Battle Cry of Freedom," 1862). But as the war continued unabated and casualties soared, topics took a darker tone. So pathos-drenched were some songs that the military banned their performance. Officers feared the songs would weaken their men's fighting resolve and perhaps even contribute to desertion.

Popular in both the North and South was John Hewitt's (1801–1890) strophic setting of the poem "All Quiet Along the Potomac To-night." Set for solo voice with a sparse piano accompaniment, the song is fragile and eerily moving. Part of the emotional effect derives from the meter. How discomforting it must have been to listen to this lonely song of death presented in the feel of a slow waltz, a genre normally associated with social dancing and romance.

LISTENING GUIDE

CD III/Track 2
Download track 39
mysearchlab 8.5

"ALL QUIET ALONG THE POTOMAC TONIGHT"   *by John Hewitt*

Although the song sold briskly in its original setting for voice and piano, in army camps it would often have been accompanied by guitar, as we hear in this arrangement. The song's vocal range is narrow; the style is unadorned and direct. This makes sense. After all, this story about the lives and deaths of common soldiers was designed to be singable and appreciated by untutored musicians and listeners. Of course, simplicity of delivery also enhances the lyrics, which is where the emotional power resides.

Verse 1:

All quiet along the Potomac, they say,
Except here and there a stray picket
Is shot, as he walks on his beat, to and fro,
By a rifleman hid in the thicket.
'Tis nothing, a private or two now and then
Will not count in the news of the battle;
Not an officer lost, only one of the men
Moaning out all alone the death rattle.

Music and Resistance

How can one stand firm when physical resistance is hopeless? The question has no answer, of course, but societies have often turned to music when all else has failed. We now study two examples of songs of resistance. First we look at the Ghost Dance, a millennial movement that sprang up in the American West in 1889. Then we look at the important role that music played during the Holocaust.

Ghost Dance

The Civil War briefly slowed down the nation's ongoing westward expansion. But with the war's end, the focus again turned to white settlement of the Great Plains, where Native American groups were forced to surrender their lands and traditional culture. By the mid-1880s, life for Plains Indians had become nearly unsustainable. Continued resistance through combat was impossible. Most Native Americans were confined to reservations where food was scarce and shelter inadequate. Those still free were on the run or had sought safe harbor in Canada.

The future looked worse still. It was in this period of desperation that the Plains Indians experienced a brief resurgence of hope. The source was Wovoka, a Nevada Territory-based Paiute medicine man. In 1889, Wovoka had a mystical vision. He foresaw an apocalypse in which the world would be devastated by natural disasters. As the event unfolded, the white man would be destroyed. Native Americans would regain their traditional lands and social ways. Even the dead would return to life.

In order to speed the great day's coming, Wovoka told the people that they needed to stop fighting the white man. Instead, they should turn their attention to song, dance, and prayer. Adherence would be rewarded. Those who internalized the philosophy with sufficient power would become invulnerable to the soldiers' bullets.

In effect, Wovoka's vision inaugurated the endgame in the battle for control of the Great Plains. His belief was that the spiritual power of song and dance would overcome the physical power of guns. Wovoka's philosophy developed into the Ghost Dance, a religion that quickly spread outward from Nevada's Great Basin. Soon, believers were

A print from c. 1891 depicting Sioux Indians performing the Ghost Dance Ceremony.

found all across the Plains, and from Arizona to Canada.

The religion's tenets were transmitted by word of mouth, though many followers made pilgrimages to the Great Basin so that they might receive the teaching directly from Wovoka. Songs, which were obtained through visions, were believed to hold great power. Only self-sacrifice, however, could bring about a true vision. Accordingly, believers prayed and subjected themselves to a variety of physical deprivations. Every song was individualized, providing a talisman that empowered the receiver and prepared the planet so that the apocalypse might come sooner.

Ghost Dance celebrations attracted practitioners by the thousands. Gatherings were peaceful. Even so, white officials fretted and feared the possibility of a new rebellion. Soon, the United States government banned both the religion and the singing of Ghost Dance songs. Gatherings were forcefully dispersed.

The short-lived Ghost Dance religion effectively ended on December 29, 1890, when 150 Lakota Sioux, mostly women and children, were shot down on a frozen plain in South Dakota by American soldiers during what has become known as the Battle of Wounded Knee. Many of the Lakota had been Ghost Dance practitioners. Some accounts suggest that the Ghost Dance itself might have helped raise tensions.

LISTENING GUIDE

CD III/Tracks 3 and 4
Download tracks 40 and 41
mysearchlab 8.6

ARAPAHO AND COMANCHE GHOST DANCE SONGS: "FATHER HAVE PITY ON ME" AND "LIGHT FROM SUN IS FLOWING"

Recorded in 1894 by James Mooney (chronicler and illustrator of the 1890 Ghost Dance)

Ghost Dance songs are sung in a chant-like fashion with a small melodic range and steady metrical flow. Texts focus on deprivation or revelation. Song forms were modeled on the Great Basin format of short, paired phrases (AA BB CC, etc.), often with slight variations. The Arapaho song, for example, ends with a final repeat of the AA section. The Comanche song has a brief vocable ("Hey yo") tag at the beginning:

Arapaho Ghost Dance song (AA BB CC):

	TRANSLATION:
0:03	Father, have pity on me Father, have pity on me
0:12	I am crying for thirst I am crying for thirst
0:20	All is gone, I have nothing to eat All is gone, I have nothing to eat Repeat form plus AA

Each phrase ends on the tonic, which is also the lowest tone in the piece. Thus, every phrase falls to its completion, which adds to the dirge-like feel. The range is narrow, just a perfect fifth from "do" to "sol." This range is attainable by any voice. The Ghost Dance used a slow walking step, which can easily be imagined in the song's tempo. Notice that the texture is monophonic and the song is performed by a single voice. Though sometimes thousands danced together, they sang their own individual songs and heard their own inner music.

Comanche Ghost Dance song (AA BB B'B'):

	TRANSLATION:
1:02	Light from sun is flowing Light from sun is flowing
1:09	Yellow light from sun is streaming Yellow light from sun is streaming
1:17	Yellow light from sun is streaming (sung at lower pitch level) Yellow light from sun is streaming (sung at lower pitch level)

MUSICAL LIVES
ANITA LASKER-WALLFISCH (b. 1925)

Anita Lasker-Wallfisch was just 17 years old when she was sent to Auschwitz, the most notorious of the Nazi death camps. Upon arrival she was stripped naked. Her head was shaved and her arm tattooed. When interrogated about her background, Wallfisch said that she played the cello. That answer saved her life. Wallfisch was told to wait in a corner while the camp's orchestra director was summoned.

"So I stood there. Instead of being led to the gas chamber, I had a conversation about cello playing and music," Wallfisch recalled during a 1999 BBC World Service radio broadcast.

The orchestra director was Alma Boset, niece of famed composer and conductor Gustav Mahler. Like her uncle, Boset ran her orchestra to exacting standards. Such was the pressure to play well, said Wallfisch, that it helped her forget the horrors all around.

"If you looked out of the window, you saw the chimneys and the smoke of burning people. And we, in an almost crazy way, concentrated on playing music, [on playing] the right notes," she said.

Every day the orchestra played as the men marched to and from the factories. As the Russians advanced through Poland in 1944, the camp's orchestra was disbanded. The musicians assumed they would be sent to the gas chambers. Instead, they were transported to Bergen-Belsen. Somehow, Wallfisch survived. After the war, she moved to England where she performed as a member of the English Chamber Orchestra.

Music of the Holocaust

The Nazi-driven genocide known as the Holocaust (1938–1945) resulted in the death of six million Jewish people, along with other oppressed minorities. Though mostly confined to urban ghettos or concentration camps, Jews occasionally were able to fight back. But without guns or mobility, uprisings were most likely to result in even greater death tolls, particularly because of vicious German reprisals on the populace at large. Tens of thousands were forced to dig their own graves, then shot. Millions were sent to death camps.

Even when facing a hopeless future, life in the newly created ghettos stumbled forward. Schools met and children studied. That sort of resistance could not be stopped. Neither could music. Street singers sang of hunger and corruption, of freedom and rebellion. Inside their homes families sang the songs of the Jewish faith: the "Kol Nidre" on Yom Kippur; songs from the Haggadah on Passover; and every Friday evening, songs of the Sabbath.

Songs of partisan resistance were heard in the countryside where armed guerrillas fought throughout the war. The most famous of the resistance songs was "Zog Nit Keyn Mol" ("Never Say"). Set to a Russian melody, the song was sung in at least seven languages and known throughout Eastern Europe.

Even the death camps had music. At one point, Auschwitz-Birkenau supported six orchestras, the largest featuring over 100 musicians. Mozart symphonies were performed as men, women, and children were sent to the gas chambers. Over one million people died at Auschwitz.

The strangest of the ghettos was Theresienstadt, Czechoslovakia. The town had not supported a Jewish population before the war, but Germans used the idyllic location to create a "model" ghetto filled with Jewish intellectuals. The site was opened for a June 23, 1944, visit by the Red Cross, which toured the town and attended a performance of *Brundibár* (1938) a children's opera written by Hans Krása (1899–1944), then a prisoner in Theresienstadt but later transferred to Auschwitz where he was exterminated. Hidden behind the tour's gloss, and not noticed by the Red Cross, were the horrendous living conditions and food shortages. To alleviate overcrowding, many had been sent to Auschwitz in the days before the Red Cross's arrival. In reality, Theresienstadt was a concentration camp. Of the 140,000 Jews brought there, fewer than 20,000 survived.

A Song from Vilna   Between July 4 and July 20, 1941, over 5,000 Jews were slaughtered by the German army and local volunteers at Ponar, a forest recreation center a few miles south of Vilna, Lithuania. A second wave of killings took place on August 31. Both massacres were in preparation for the opening of the two Vilna ghettos on September 6. By the end of October, another 10,000 Jews had been murdered, enough to close one of the ghettos. It was during this time that 18-year-old Rilke Glezer, herself imprisoned in the Vilna ghetto, wrote the poem "Es iz geven a zumer-tog" ("It Was a Summer's Day").

Glezer's Yiddish words gave voice to the horrors of the Ponar massacre and subsequent life in the Vilna ghetto. She emphasized shared experience—"We are tortured . . . cut off from the world"—and drew on biblical language of sacrifice. Perhaps her words provided some small comfort to those who struggled to survive.

"Looking at us, a stone would have burst out crying. Old people and children went like cattle to be sacrificed."

—Rilke Glezer

Shortly after writing this song, Glezer was deported to a death camp, presumably to be exterminated. Instead, she managed to escape and join a resistance group in the forests of Lithuania. Glezer survived the war and eventually settled in Israel.

LISTENING GUIDE

CD III/Track 5
Download track 42
mysearchlab 8.7

"ES IZ GEVEN A ZUMER-TOG"

The lyrics of this strophic song are set to the tune "Papirosn" ("Cigarettes"), a popular Yiddish theater song. This recording uses an accordion and mandolin as accompaniment. The melody uses both the natural and harmonic (**mysearchlab 2.3**) minor scales, with "ti" sometimes lowered to "te." The text is set syllabically. The arching melodic contour repeatedly reaches into the singer's upper range. He tells the story directly and from the heart.

The strophe is divided into two melodically similar parts, each with four phrases. The first phrase begins on the low tonic, moves up the octave, and extends to "me" in the next octave (the highest note in the piece). Then comes a quick descent to "sol."

0:00	Instrumental introduction	
0:27	Es iz geven a zumer-tog, Vi shtendik zunik-sheyn,	It was a summer's day, Sunny and lovely as always,

The second phrase begins where the last left off and leaps back up to "me." Then comes a slow descent to "fa."

	Un di nature hot dan gehat In zukh azoyfil kyeyn,	And nature then Had so much charm,

The third phrase is a symmetrical arch moving from "fa" up to the next octave's "re" and back down to "fa."

	Es hobn feygelekh gezungen, Freylekh zukh arumgeshpringen,	Birds sang, Hopped around cheerfully,

The last phrase, shorter than the others, resolves to the tonic.

	In geto hot men undz geheysn geyn.	We were ordered to go into the ghetto.

The second half of the strophe proceeds in much the same way, though melodic changes here and there accommodate the different text. The general curve of each phrase remains the same.

0:53	Akh shtelt zikh for vos s'iz fun undz! Gevorn! Farshtanen hobn mir: s'iz alts farloyrn. S'hot nit geholfn undzer betn, Az s'zol emitser undz retn– Farlozn hobn mir dokh undzer heym	Oh, just imagine what happened to us! We understood: everything was lost. Of no use were our pleas That someone should save us– We still left our home.

QUESTIONS FOR THOUGHT

- If you had a story like this to tell, what kind of music would you use? How might using a popular tune add to or take away from the story?
- Does "Es iz geven a zumer-tog" share commonalities with the Ghost Dance songs?

ACTIVITIES AND ASSIGNMENTS

■ The Library of Congress offers an online video of Ghost Dancing by members of Buffalo Bill's Wild West Show (1894). The film is silent so we cannot know the music to which they were dancing. Perhaps these were Ghost Dance movements, perhaps not. **mysearchlab 8.8**

■ What kind of music was used to support Hitler's regime? Does this taint the music today? Investigate the reception of Richard Wagner's music in Israel.

Music and Remembrance: Three Responses to World War II

"We laughed, knowing that better men would come,
And greater wars; when each proud fighter brags
He wars on Death—for Life; not men—for flags."

—*Wilfred Owen*

Finally, we move to the concert hall and look at a trio of contrasting compositions written in response to, or in remembrance of, World War II. French composer Olivier Messiaen's *Quatuor pour la fin du Temps* (1941) is an intimate and complex chamber music work written in a German prisoner of war camp. British composer Benjamin Britten's *War Requiem* commemorates the 1962 re-consecration of St. Michael's Cathedral in Coventry, England. Polish composer Krzysztof Penderecki's *Threnody for the Victims of Hiroshima* (1960) experiments with unusual sound textures while remembering the most destructive seconds in human history.

Olivier Messiaen (1908–1992): *Quatuor pour la fin du Temps*

World War II began in Europe on September 1, 1939, with Germany's *blitzkrieg* invasion of Poland. Although a series of treaties were supposed to compel France, Great Britain, and other countries to protect Poland and declare war on Germany, none came to its defense. Despite fierce resistance, Poland fell in just 34 days. A period of calm followed as Germany rested and repositioned its armies. Through the winter, the world anxiously waited. The inevitable came on May 10, 1940, when Germany sidestepped France's imposing Maginot Line and invaded through the Ardennes Forest. France surrendered in just six weeks.

Among the French army prisoners of war was composer Olivier Messiaen, who was shipped east to Stalag VIIIA in Silesia, Poland. It was there, on a snowy January evening in 1941, that Messiaen premiered his *Quatuor pour la fin du Temps* (*Quartet for the End of Time*). The music was inspired by the biblical description of the Apocalypse in The Book of Revelation.

Messiaen's audience consisted of fellow POWs and German guards. Many prisoners were sick; most were undernourished. The only musical instruments apparently available—clarinet, violin, cello, and piano—were barely functional.

Despite the conditions, Messiaen's music transcended time and space. For a short time at least, these hardened men—prisoners and guards thrown together by the horrors of war—found inner shelter and shared common bonds. "Never before have I been listened to with such attention and understanding," Messiaen remembered years later.

I Olivier Messiaen.

For Messiaen, a devout Catholic, the music was a response to the suffering brought on by war. It was also a musical testament of spiritual faith. Across some 40 minutes of "clock" time and eight individual movements, Messiaen's quartet portrays the end of the physical universe and suggests humankind's path to spiritual salvation.

LISTENING GUIDE

CD III/Track 6
Download track 43
mysearchlab 8.9

"LITURGIE DE CRISTAL" FROM *QUATUOR POUR LA FIN DU TEMPS*   *by Olivier Messiaen*

The four instruments are sorted into two groups, which are then juxtaposed one against the other. The clarinet and violin, representing the voices of the blackbird and nightingale, respectively, symbolize nature. The cello and piano symbolize the impersonal eternal, what Messiaen calls "the harmonious silence of Heaven."

The songbirds' characters could hardly be more different. The blackbird sings out rambling melodies that float across octaves and metered time. Against this, the sprightly nightingale interjects high-pitched chirps. Each creature seems to live in its own world, each self-absorbed and blithely unaware of the other.

The vibrant life of birdsong is silhouetted against the screen of a cool and dispassionate musical eternity. How does one create such an effect? Messiaen does so by juxtaposing mathematically derived cycles of melody, harmony, and rhythm. The piano part, for example, juxtaposes a repeating 29-chord sequence against a repeating 17-event rhythmic pattern. As the following diagram maps out, the rhythmic sequence repeats nearly twice before the chords complete a single cycle. Because of the two large prime numbers involved (29 and 17), it takes 493 events for the two patterns to realign to their original positions. The movement ends long before that happens.

Event #:	1 2 3... 17 18 19... 28 29 30 31 32... 492 493 494
Rhythmic sequence #:	1 2 3... 17 1 2... 11 12 13 14 15... 16 17 1
Chordal sequence #:	1 2 3... 17 18 19... 28 29 1 2 3... 28 29 1

The cello part is also built on asymmetrical cycles. Most striking, however, is the pentatonic melody featuring **glissandos** and **harmonics**, which create eerie tones atypical of the instruments' characteristic sound.

"Liturgie de cristal" is perhaps the most impenetrable of the quartet's eight movements. Its complexity derives from Messiaen's desire to represent and integrate the impersonal austerity of eternity with the freedom of nature.

How might one listen to this complicated piece? Instead of following along with a timed listening guide, we suggest you listen to the work several times in its entirety, focusing your attention differently on each listening.

- On first listening, take in the entirety. Get a feel for the timbres and tempo at which events unfold.
- On second listening, follow the clarinet/blackbird, where the majority of the melodic material resides. Get a feel for the shape of the music and the creature's personality. You will probably notice how the other instruments occasionally intrude and interrupt your focus.
- On subsequent listenings, gradually expand your focus.

MUSICAL THEMES
CYCLES AND MUSIC

To help understand the cyclical concept underlying the piano part of *Quatour pour la fin du Temps*, visualize the orbital duration of planets in our solar system. To begin, choose a spot in the zodiac: say, 1° Aries. Viewed outward from the Sun, Earth is in that position one time per year; Venus (because its solar orbit is smaller) returns after just 225 Earth days. Mars (because its solar orbit is larger) returns after 687 Earth days. Occasionally, two of the planets align at 1° Aries. Venus and Earth will do so every 82,125 Earth days. Earth and Mars will do so every 250,755 Earth days. All three planets align just once in every 56,419,875 Earth days. Then, of course, the cycle starts all over again.

MUSICAL THEMES
ST. MICHAEL'S CATHEDRAL (ALSO CALLED COVENTRY CATHEDRAL)

Ruins of the Coventry Cathedral which was bombed during World War II.

Situated in the city of Coventry (95 miles northwest of London), the skeletal ruins of St. Michael's Cathedral stand today as a daily reminder of the horrors of war. The late fourteenth-century Gothic church (elevated to cathedral status in 1918) was bombed by the German Luftwaffe on the night of November 14, 1940. The attack lasted for over 10 hours, destroying over 4,000 of the city's homes and three-quarters of its factories.

The people of Coventry rallied and the very next day agreed that the cathedral would be rebuilt. Ten years later, architect Basil Spence (1907–1976) was chosen from over 200 candidates to design the new cathedral, which he adjoined to the ruins. The new building was consecrated in May 1962.

Coventry is also known for its famous Christmas tune, the "Coventry Carol." The sixteenth-century song comes from a sacred play—likely mounted by the city's textile guilds—that portrays the Christmas story, including the Slaughter of the Innocents. The carol itself depicts a mother quieting her soon-to-be-murdered infant.

Benjamin Britten (1913–1976): War Requiem

When commissioned to write a piece to mark the 1962 reopening of St. Michael's Cathedral, British composer and committed pacifist Benjamin Britten decided to write a **Requiem Mass**. The 85-minute work requires army-sized forces: two orchestras, organ, adult chorus, boy choir, and three vocal soloists. Verses drawn from the Catholic Mass for the Dead (the Requiem) are sung in Latin. The remaining text comes from the poetry of World War I infantryman Wilfred Owen.

The character of the music ranges from anguish to joy, the dynamics from whisper soft to cannon loud. Sometimes bells toll and martial trumpets sound. Other times, a single fragile voice entreats for peace. The text juxtaposes images of violence and suffering with pleas for redemption. There are searing indictments of the political leaders who led the various nations into war. Always, however, Britten's message is one of peace.

Britten divided his musical forces into three symbolism-rich groups:

- The soprano soloist, adult chorus, and full orchestra represent tradition. They perform the Catholic Mass for the Dead and stand for the impersonal and universal ritual that the Mass signifies. The text is in Latin.
- The two male soloists represent British and German soldiers. They are supported by a small orchestra. The men sing of war's brutality and senselessness. The text is drawn from Owens's poetry.
- The delicate sounds of the boy choir and organ represent innocence and hope. The text is Latin.

The juxtapositions of the three groups can be horrifying, yet darkly exhilarating. Time and again, glorious passages for trumpets and rattling drums portray the terrible grandeur of war, which the boy choir seems to notice not at all.

The music is set in six movements, each named after sections of the Requiem Mass: (1) Requiem aeternum, (2) Dies Irae, (3) Offertorium, (4) Sanctus, (5) Agnus Dei, and (6) Libera me. Each movement is unique in character; each also combines Latin text with Owen's poetry. The "Offertorium," for example, draws on the biblical story of Abraham and his son, Isaac (Genesis 22:1–24). In Owen's version, however, Abraham (who represents Europe's political leaders) ignores the angel's instruction. He slays the boy, "and half the seed of Europe, one by one." As the tenor and baritone soloists repeat this text, the celestial voices of the boy choir, which are apparently unaware of the horror that is unfolding in the bloody trenches below, sing of the rejuvenating power of sacrifice:

Hostias et preced tibi Domine	Lord, in praise we offer to Thee
laudis offerimus; tu suscipe pro	sacrifices and prayers, do Thou receive them
animabus illis, quarum hodie	for the souls of those whom we remember
memoriam facimus: fac eas, Domine,	this day: Lord, make them pass
de morte transire ad vitam.	from death to life,
Quam olim Abrahae promisisti	as Thou didst promise Abraham
en semini ejus.	and his seed.

Closing the Requiem is the paralyzing "Libera me" (Free me), which takes place in the darkened land of the dead. There, the souls of soldiers, once enemies and now comrades in death, remember how they killed one another. The boy choir, still oblivious to earthly suffering, sings of life everlasting. Then the baritone sings:

I am the enemy you killed, my friend.
I knew you in this dark; for so you frowned
Yesterday through me as you jabbed and killed.
I parried; but my hands were loath and cold.
Let us sleep now.

LISTENING GUIDE

CD III/Track 7
Download track 44
mysearchlab 8.10

AGNUS DEI FROM *WAR REQUIEM* (1962)

by Benjamin Britten

The Agnus Dei juxtaposes the tenor soloist against the boy choir. The tenor darkly intones Owen's "At a Calvary Near the Ancre." The poem symbolically combines the story of Christ's crucifixion with fighting along the Ancre River, which was part of the massive World War I Battle of the Somme. At Golgotha, says the Bible, soldiers guarded the crucifixion while Christ's disciples hid in fear and the scribes displayed their scorn. In the trenches near the Ancre, says Owen, the priests prayed in relative safety while soldiers bore the cross of death. The Beast of the poem is both the Devil and war itself. Owen's priests, with their renunciation of brotherly love in the interest of petty nationalism ("bawl allegiance to the state"), are in league with the Devil.

The scalar motion in the strings that opens the Agnus Dei runs like a string of pearls throughout the movement. Notice that the chorus intones this exact opening melody in each of its entrances.

0:00	The tenor enters with a descending melody that, like a series of sighs, seems to rise only so that it might fall once again. *Tenor:* One ever hangs where shelled roads part. In this war He too lost a limb, But His disciples hide apart; And now the Soldiers bear with Him.
0:54	*Chorus:* Agnus Dei, qui tollis peccata mundi, dona eis requiem (Lamb of God, that takest away the sins of the world, grant them rest)
1:13	*Tenor:* Near Golgotha strolls many a priest, And in their faces there is pride That they were flesh-marked by the Beast By whom the gentle Christ's denied.

| 1:35 | *Chorus:* Agnus Dei, qui tollis peccata mundi, dona eis requiem |

Britten now quickens the pace of the entrances. With the line "The scribes on all the people shove," the statements are cut in half so the soloist and chorus interact more frequently.

| 1:52 | *Tenor:* The scribes on all the people shove and bawl allegiance to the state, |

| 2:03 | *Chorus:* Agnus Dei, qui tollis peccata mundi . . . |

The tenor returns to the opening gesture.

| 2:10 | *Tenor:* But they who love the greater love Lay down their life; they do not hate. |

| 2:31 | *Chorus:* Dona eis requiem |

The text shifts from anguish to hope. Listen to the tenor's fragile upper range, as he shifts to Latin and intones his transcendent final plea, "Give us peace."

| 3:10 | *Tenor:* Dona nobis pacem (Give us peace) |

Krzysztof Penderecki (b. 1933): *Threnody for the Victims of Hiroshima*

All of music's customary elements—melody, harmony, and meter—are eliminated in Penderecki's jarring *Threnody*. Instead, walls of discordant tones grate one against another. *Threnody* offers no tune and no beat, just searing, brutal dissonance. Who would have imagined that such sounds could come from the same string ensemble of violins, violas, and cellos that composers from Bach to Britten used to create such beauty? As in a nightmare, the familiar has become alien and foreboding, even darkly hallucinogenic.

Penderecki achieved his effects by using clusters of pitches that are packed so closely together—sometimes just ¼-**tone** apart—that individual pitches are lost in the wash of sound. The result is that instead of hearing melodic lines, one hears broad bands of texture that slide upward and downward in murky and dissonant rivers of sound.

Other techniques employed by Penderecki include "extended" techniques, such as playing the instruments' unspecified highest possible note, tapping on the instruments with fingers, and drawing the bow in unusual places (such as across the **bridge** and between the violin's bridge and **tailpiece**).

Threnody lacks rhythm in the usual sense. There is no beat or meter to follow with the tap of a foot or nod of the head. That does not mean that sonic events occur randomly, however. Penderecki mapped out his score according to clock time. Certain effects last for 10 seconds, others for much longer. It is as if human time—as defined physically by heartbeat, bodily movement, and breath—has been replaced by the impersonal time of machines, or perhaps nuclear physics.

LISTENING GUIDE

CD III/Track 8
Download track 45
mysearchlab 8.11

THRENODY FOR THE VICTIMS OF HIROSHIMA (1960)

Composer Krzysztof Penderecki

Careful listening reveals that the piece is organized into a simple ABA form, each section marked by a change in musical texture.

0:00	**SECTION A** The first section is the longest. Here the thick tones slide against one another. Sometimes they expand outward. Other times they seem to collapse in upon themselves.
6:25	**SECTION B** The B section is in a **pointalistic** style, that is, the sounds appear as many separate, even disconnected, events, almost like a universe of slowly blinking stars existing in three-dimensional space. This section has a rhythmic quality to it, but it is one of bubbling activity rather than toe-tapping metric consistency.
7:25	**SECTION A** The sustained sounds of the A section return and intermingle with those of section B.

What do all these sounds have to do with nuclear holocaust? That's for the listener to decide. In fact, when Penderecki wrote the piece, Hiroshima was not on his mind. Instead, he was using experimental sound textures, perhaps in an expressionistic fashion that attempted to explore the dark emotional reaches of the human mind. The music's original title was simply the descriptive *8'37"*, reflecting the music's length. It was only later that Penderecki connected the music to Hiroshima and changed the title.

QUESTIONS FOR THOUGHT

- What do you think of *Threnody*? Does it fit your definition of music?
- What was your emotional response to *Threnody*? Try to understand why you felt the way you did.
- What does war sound like in music?
- Imagine you have just received a commission to write a piece commemorating a war. Describe what it might sound like. What instruments would you use and why? Would it be solemn? Religious? A rousing march? Would the melody be singable? The harmonies discordant?
- Messiaen combined sounds of nature with sounds of eternity. Britten contrasted sacred and secular understandings. Penderecki took the familiar (a stringed orchestra) and turned it into something forbidding and alien. What other sorts of juxtapositions might make for powerful listening experiences?

DID YOU KNOW?

THE SHINING

Music by Penderecki was prominently featured in director William Friedkin's (b. 1935) *The Exorcist* (1973) and director Stanley Kubrick's (1928–1999) 1980 film adaptation of the Stephen King (b. 1947) novel *The Shining*. *Threnody* was also used in the 2008 Oscar-winning war film, *The Hurt Locker*, directed by Kathryn Bigelow.

Epilogue: Darfur

"What happened to you, Sudan? We mourn the deaths. We long for an end to war."

—Hakamma singer Zaida Hamad Jabro (Marc Lacey, *The New York Times*. July 12, 2004)

Among the *Baggara*, an Arab people of western Sudan, the **hakamma** bards hold a revered place. Since at least the sixteenth century these women have improvised poems and songs that monitor the social pulse of their ethnic group. The hakamma's job is to extol and censure. Individuals who live up to tribal values are praised; those who break the codes are publicly reviled. When the hakamma sing, the Baggara listen.

In 2003, the hakamma were singing songs of war. They sang for Baggara men fighting with the *Janjaweed* militia in battle-torn Darfur. They sang to brace resolve and inflame ethnic pride. On occasion they even accompanied their men into battle.

There was plenty of that. The Darfur conflict claimed up to 500,000 lives, mostly civilian. In addition, millions were displaced to squalid refugee camps.

Boundaries of the Darfur conflict unfolded along ethnic lines. On one side were government-supported nomadic Arabs (Janjaweed) who sought new territory for their livestock. On the other side were non-Arabs who wanted to hold the land for agrarian use.

Always, the hakamma have played a role. In the war's first year, hakamma songs were often vicious. During a 2003 Janjaweed attack on the civilian village of Disa, the Baggara warriors killed and raped. The hakamma were

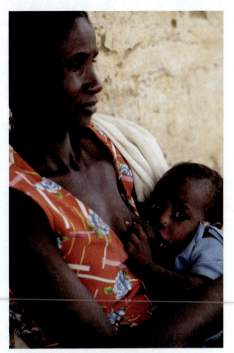

Darfur mother and child in a refugee camp, displaced by the long-running Civil War.

there too, looting and unleashing songs of derision against the defeated. The women's attitudes were changed in 2004, however. In the summer of that year the hakamma were invited to Sudan's University of Nyala to participate in a two-day workshop sponsored by the university's Peace Studies Center. Officials gave the hakamma a broader understanding of the conflict. They also convinced them to sing for peace, not war.

As of June 2011 an uneasy ceasefire exists in the region, though sporadic violence continues.

CONCLUSION

In the preceding pages we have examined the different ways in which music portrays, supports, and protests war. We have seen how civilians and soldiers alike have used music to endure suffering and memorialize war's victims, even turn the tide of battle. Unfortunately, the war music repertoire continues to grow unabated.

Music and Love

CHAPTER GOALS

- To examine the expression of love in musical settings from various time periods and genres.
- To hear how different aspects of love can be portrayed musically.

QUESTIONS FOR THOUGHT

- Ask your parents what love songs were popular when they met. Do they have any special feelings for those songs?
- What are your favorite love songs? Has your taste changed since you were in high school? Junior high? What aspects of love do the songs portray?
- Is there a typical love song "sound"?
- Investigate how courtship rituals differ across cultures. How do love songs in these cultures reflect different social norms?

Love is infinitely varied. On occasion, its realization inspires bold leaps of faith. Other times, it brings on inner struggle and self-sacrifice. Sometimes, love just plain hurts. You might feel love for family or friends, for God or country, or for the beauty of nature. The ancient Greeks grouped love into four categories: philia (friendship), xenia (social hospitality), agape (idealized love), and eros (sensual love). Perhaps you can identify other groupings that better reflect our own times.

Love has always been a favorite topic for musicians. This chapter focuses on the many sides of romantic love. We begin with the blossoming of young love, then journey into the dark corners of unrequited love and infidelity. We close with sounds as blissful as those with which we began, with French chanteuse Edith Piaf's classic love song "La Vie en Rose."

The Dawn of Love

Since the 1937 release of *Snow White and the Seven Dwarfs*, the world's first full-length animated musical, the Walt Disney Company has been introducing children to the thrill of love's first blush. That film's classic love song, "Some Day My Prince Will Come," became a jazz standard and one of the most performed songs of all time.

Think back to your own childhood. Perhaps you watched Disney's *Beauty and the Beast* (1991), winner of Academy Awards for

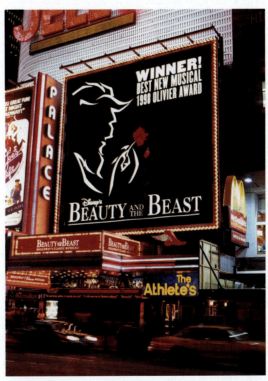

Billboard for *Beauty and the Beast* in New York's Times Square.

"If music be the food of love, play on, give me excess of it."

—William Shakespeare (1564–1616) *Twelfth Night*, Act 1, scene 1

Best Music/Original Score and Best Music/Song. The story, based on a French folk tale, tells of a young woman at the threshold of adulthood. A cursed prince turned ugly beast holds her captive. To break the spell, the prince must win the girl's love. After a series of misunderstandings, he succeeds. The moral is clear: true beauty is more than skin deep.

Let's listen to "Something There" from the film's soundtrack. **mysearchlab 9.1** Notice how melody and lyrics combine to portray unfolding love. Belle sings, "There's something . . ." She pauses; then sings ". . . almost kind." Pause again. She is hesitant, and we hear it in the fragmentation of the tune. In the next line, Belle blurts out—in shorter note values—the reason for her uncertainty, that "he was mean . . . and unrefined." No hesitancy here. Her mind is clear when it comes to the unpleasant stuff.

But the story is not yet over. We know this from the melody, which pauses on an unresolved harmony. Belle's music starts over, "And now he's dear. . . ." Belle says she is sure, but is she really? If so, why does she continue to hesitate? Why didn't she see all these nice things before, she wonders. Still, the phrase ends on the tonic. Belle's thoughts are complete, even if the relationship remains unresolved.

Now it is the Beast's turn. Using the same melody, rhyme scheme, and phrase structure (all telling signs that the two are on the same wavelength), the Beast reveals his own unsure steps toward loving Belle by singing "And when we touched. . . ." Whatever his feelings, however, he must wait. Belle is in charge. She is the one who will decide the fate of their deepening relationship.

Resolution arrives with the third stanza, when Belle changes the melody. Listen carefully with heart and mind. Is there any doubt, from her very first word and tone, that she has fallen in love? She moves into a higher vocal range, sustains and embraces the tone, and enjoys its luminous freedom.

The discovery of love is always fresh, of course. But this love—for an ugly beast—is truly remarkable. As Belle drinks in its splendor, so do we. After all, neither she nor we anticipated that such a love could be so wonderful.

So lovely was the "new and a bit alarming" phrase that the composer repeats the melody for us with "true . . . he's no Prince Charming." "New" and "True"—the words are raised in melody for our approval, like glasses held high in a wedding toast.

One cannot stay suspended in midair forever, though. So, the melody continues, gradually winding downward into familiar territory with "there's something in him that I simply didn't see." Resolution has been achieved in the music, and—if the melody can be believed—in Belle's heart.

Unattainable Love

For Belle and the Beast, things worked out just fine. More often, however, the would-be lover does not even get to first base. For most of us, affection spurned leads to lonely nights and inner hurt. Long ago, songwriters learned to turn love's pain into artistic gain. Such was the case in medieval France, where poet/musicians called **troubadours** (female: trobairitz) and **trouvères** (female: trouveresses) developed an entire tradition of song and poetry cataloging love's many sides. In particular, they were fascinated with the unattainable romance of

MUSICAL THEMES
THE MIDDLE AGES

Life in the Middle Ages (ca. 400–ca. 1430) was not easy. Common people lived in thatched or stone cottages near or on their Lord's estate. Sharing the living quarters with livestock provided much-needed warmth in the winter. The church and the nobility controlled wealth and power. The social order of these two institutions was highly regulated. Almost every aspect of upper class and religious life unfolded according to strict formulas of behavior. Rituals and ceremonies provided welcome routine in an age when nature's capriciousness, rulers' whims, and wandering armies could wreak havoc at any time.

Since commoners were not literate, the only extant music from the Middle Ages was notated by the clergy or nobility. Sacred monophonic chant constitutes the largest repertory from this period, but by the thirteenth and fourteenth centuries polyphonic genres such as the **motet** and chanson had been established. See **mysearchlab 1.3**

courtly love, also called *fin amours*. According to the idealized rules of the time, a knight pledges his love and obedience to the lady of the court. His love inspires great deeds and he strives always to be worthy of her affection. But because of her higher social status (not to mention that she is married to his Sire), their love can never be consummated.

Luckily, there is a bright side to all this. Through his suffering, the knight is ennobled. And like the era's belief in alchemy, which sought to turn lead into gold, his erotic desires are reborn on a higher plane. He develops firm character and honorable bearing.

In an age when marriage was based on merging property rather than compatibility, the troubadours and trouvères did much to legitimize the notion of romantic attraction. In their vision we see the roots of our own society's ideals of romantic love.

Antoine Busnoys (ca. 1430–1492)

The creative era of the troubadours and trouvères came to an end around the time of the Black Death (1348), but the idea of unrequited love lingered on. Here we look at an example from the fifteenth century, a chanson (French for "song") by Antoine Busnoys (Boon **wah**, or Boon **way**). Little is known of Busnoys' professional life. Presumably, like other composers of the time, he moved from church to court as opportunities became available. One thing we know for certain is that he worked as a singer at the powerful Burgundian Court of Charles

the Bold (1433–1477). We also know that Busnoys had a scandalous side. On five occasions he arranged to have "a certain priest" beaten. One consequence of those acts was excommunication (though he was later reprieved), no small penalty in those times.

Like most composers of the fifteenth century, Busnoys wrote polyphonic chansons, usually for three voices and usually in one of three *formes fixes* (fixed forms). These works were mostly love songs intended for the entertainment of the court. As with the medieval tradition of courtly love, the topics often dealt with unrequited love, forced separation of lovers, or excessive praise and devotion toward a noble Lady. Quite often, the male in the song suffered extreme anguish over a lost or unattainable lover.

Busnoys was known for putting secret messages in his music. Sometimes he hid his name in the text; sometimes, instead of musical notation, he wrote cryptic poems to indicate the exact notes and rhythms of a line. The chanson we examine contains an acrostic that spells out the name Jaqueljne D'Aqvevjle (j = i and v = u). (See the first letter of each line.) Only those few who looked at the manuscript would have noticed the reference. This is one of four Busnoys chansons that, in one way or another, refer to the mysterious Jacqueline.

There were two women named Jacqueline de Hacqueville whom we can identify during Busnoys' life. Either might be the chanson's subject. One was the wife of Jean Bouchart, a Parisian nobleman. There is some evidence that Busnoys had an affair with this Jacqueline in the 1460s. The other candidate was a lady-in-waiting, first for Princess Margaret Stuart (of Scotland) and later for Marie d'Anjou, wife of France's Charles VII. In either case, neither woman would have been openly available to Busnoys, a cleric bound to celibacy in the Catholic church. Perhaps this is why Busnoys uses the formulaic voice of courtly love to further hide his real lover's identity.

"Je ne puis vivre" is in the form of a *bergerette* (one of the era's formes fixes). At the beginning and end of a bergerette there is a refrain, where the text and music are the same (notated as "A"). Following the first "A" is a pair of two-line stanzas sung to the same music (notated as "b, b"—lowercase because the stanzas have different texts). Next comes a new seven-line verse sung to the same music as the "A" refrain (notated as "a"). Finally, the opening "A" section is repeated. Thus, the form of the bergerette is AbbaA (7 lines-2 lines-2 lines-7 lines-7 lines).

Two more of the song's characteristics exemplify the era's aesthetic values. First, the rhythmic quality of the melody is ambiguous, alternating between duple and triple groupings. Second, Busnoys alternates between syllabic and melismatic text settings. In "Je ne puis vivre," each section of the form opens syllabically, with every tone given one syllable of text. The end of nearly every phrase ends melismatically, with a flurry of notes for each syllable.

Notice, too, the relationship between the three voices. Using a technique called imitation, they sing almost the same melody, but each voice enters a bit later than the other (much like a round). As the piece develops, Busnoys changes the distance between the imitating voices. He also varies the order in which the voices enter. Composers in the later half of the fifteenth century were just beginning to experiment with an imitative texture. Busnoys was among the first.

For early Renaissance composers, experimenting with texture, the interweaving of individual lines, and the subtleties of rhythmic play trumped the logical and neatly ordered expression of text. Emotional tone painting of the sort we previously explored with Belle was not part of the fifteenth-century aesthetic. That said, today's listeners might easily interpret the imitating (or "chasing") voices as mirroring the pursuit of unattainable love that occasioned the narrator's teary misery.

MUSICAL THEMES
PERFORMING CHANSONS

Composers in the fifteenth century rarely specified performing forces. Most chansons were written for three voices, but as far as scholars can tell, they could have been performed by vocalists (male or female), instrumentalists, or a combination of singers and instruments.

LISTENING GUIDE

CD III/Track 9
Download track 46
mysearchlab 9.2

"JE NE PUIS VIVRE AINSY TOUJOURS"   *Composer Antoine Busnoys*

0:00 SECTION A
The first voice to sing is the soprano, imitated quickly by the tenor (0:03). At 0:15 the alto enters and the tenor drops out. All three voices cadence at 0:28. Notice that some words are pronounced differently from modern French.

0:00	Je ne puis vivre ainsy toujours	I cannot live like this forever
	Au mains que j'aye en mes dolours	unless I have, in my misery

In this section, the tenor and soprano begin together, imitated by the alto at 0:32.

| 0:30 | Quelque confort
Une seulle heure ou mains ou fort;
Et tous les jours
Léaument serviray Amours
Jusqu'a la mort. | some comfort;
only an hour—or less or more,
and every day
I will serve you loyally, Love,
until death. |

SECTION b *(words and music are different from above, meter changes from triple to duple).* Each b section begins homophonically for the first three words.

| 1:09 | Noble femme de nom et d'armes,
Escript vous ay ce dittier cy. | Lady, noble in name and arms,
I have written this song for you. |

SECTION b *(music is the same as "b" above, but with new words).*

| 1:40 | Des ieux plourant a chauldes larmes
Affin qu'ayés de moy merchy. | Weeping warm tears from my eyes
In order that you have mercy upon me. |

SECTION a *(music is the same as "A" above, but with new words).*

| 2:15 | Quant a moi, je me meurs bon cours, | As for me, I die slowly but surely, |

| 2:43 | Vellant les nuytz, faisant cent tours,
En criant fort,
"Vengeance!" a Dieu, car a grant tort
Je noye en plours
Lorsqu'au besoing me fault secours,
Et Pitié dort. | Awake at night, walking back and forth a hundred times
Crying loudly,
"Vengeance," to God, because most unfairly,
I'm drowning in tears
Just when I need help, I get none,
And Pity Sleeps. |

SECTION A *(words and music are the same as "A" above).*

| 3:19 | Je ne puis vivre ainsy toujours (etc.) | I cannot live like this forever (etc.). |

Obsessive Love

Franz Schubert's "Gretchen am Spinnrade" ("Gretchen at the Spinning Wheel")

Austrian composer Franz Schubert (1797–1828) composed approximately 600 **Lieder** (songs). Love in all its varieties was a regular theme. The Lied "Der Erlkönig" (1815) describes a desperate father riding for help as his beloved son is dying in his arms. *Die Winterreise* (*The Winter's Journey*, 1827) is a massive 24-song cycle telling the story of a spurned lover wandering through the dead of winter. We will study "Gretchen am Spinnrade" (1814), which Schubert composed for solo voice and piano when he was only 17 years old.

The text for "Gretchen" is from Johann Wolfgang von Goethe's (1749–1832) play *Faust* (1806), the story of the lonely intellectual who makes a pact with Mephistopheles (the devil). Theirs was the usual one-sided bargain: a few years of earthly pleasure in exchange for eternal damnation.

Faust's pleasure quickly results in other people's misery. As the play unfolds, he meets the innocent Gretchen, whom he is determined to seduce. With the devil's help, he succeeds—but not without complications. Along the way, Faust poisons Gretchen's mother, then murders her brother. When Gretchen becomes pregnant, Faust deserts her. Forsaken, the despairing Gretchen murders her newborn child and is condemned to death.

MUSICAL LIVES
FRANZ SCHUBERT (1797–1828)

Statue of Franz Schubert.

Franz Schubert showed extraordinary musical talent as a child, but he never became a great performer—a skill essential to making a decent living as a nineteenth-century musician. As a teenager, Schubert studied composition with Antonio Salieri (1750–1825), who was wrongly immortalized as Mozart's arch rival in the 1984 movie *Amadeus*. By the age of 16, Schubert had already composed numerous piano pieces, string quartets, and his first symphony. Though he died at age 31, Schubert had time to write over 600 songs, nine symphonies, and a wealth of chamber music.

LISTENING GUIDE

CD III/Track 10
Download track 47
mysearchlab 9.3

"GRETCHEN AM SPINNRADE"

Composer Franz Schubert

Gretchen turns her spinning wheel and obsesses over Faust, who has deserted her. Emotional balance destroyed, her mind runs in circles like the wheel upon which she works. All this we infer before Gretchen sings even a word. The piano tells us with the relentless melodic pattern that opens the composition.

Except for the first verse, which Schubert uses as a refrain, each stanza is given new music, a technique that helps to portray Gretchen's restless mind. The refrain, in contrast, provides an anchor of familiarity and reinforces the theme of circularity. Try as she might, life is going nowhere for Gretchen, just round-and-round. Schubert changes the harmonies throughout the piece, which, by shifting the floor upon which the melody stands, further contributes to the feeling of uneasiness.

The song's climax arrives on the words "sein Kuß!" ("his kiss"). As the moment approaches, the melody rises and harmonies intensify. The text becomes shorter, more breathless as Gretchen lists Faust's traits, each one fortifying the others—he is lofty, noble, kind, and strong. But his touch and kiss . . . beyond description. She is overwhelmed. The spinning stops. All is silent.

Then the obsession starts all over again. Round and round she goes. Escape is impossible.

0:00	Refrain		
	Meine Ruh' ist hin,	My peace is gone,	
	Mein Herz ist schwer,	My heart is heavy,	
	Ich finde sie nimmer	I'll never find peace,	
	Und nimmermehr.	Never again.	
0:24	Wo ist ihn nich hab'	When he is not with me	
	Ist mir das Grab,	It's like a tomb,	
	Die ganze Welt	The whole world	
	Ist mir vergällt.	Is bitter.	
0:38	Mien armer Kopf	My poor head	
	Ist mir verrückt,	is turned around,	
	Mein armer Sinn	My poor senses	
	Ist mir zerstückt.	Are torn apart.	

0:57	Refrain Meine Ruh' ist hin, . . .	My peace is gone, . . .
1:15	Nach ihm nur s chau' ich Zum Fenster hinaus, Nach ihm nur geh' ich Aus dem Haus.	I look only for him Out the window, For him only do I go Out of the house.
1:39	Sein hoher Gang, Sein' edle Gestalt, Seines Mundes Lächeln, Seiner Augen Gewalt,	His lofty bearing, His noble form, The smile on his lips, The power of his gaze,
1:43	Und seiner Rede Zauberfluß, Seine Händedruck, Und ach, sein Kuß!	His speech's Magical flow, The touch of his hand, And then, his kiss!
2:16	Refrain Meine Ruh' ist hin, . . .	My peace is gone, . . .
2:36	Mein Busen drängt sich Sich nach ihm hin. Ach, dürft' ich fassen Und halten ihn	My heart pines For him. Ah, if I could just touch him And hold him
2:49	Und küssen ihn, So wie ich wollt'. An seinen Küssen Vergehen sollt'!	And kiss him As much as I want. Beneath his kisses I would melt away!
3:03	O konnt ich ihn kuessen So wie ich wollt. An seinen Kuessen Vergehen sollt! An seinen Kuessen Vergehen sollt!	If I could just kiss him As much as I want. Beneath his kisses I would melt away! Beneath his kisses I would melt away!
3:27	Meine Ruh' ist hin.	My peace is gone.

MUSICAL THEMES

THE ROMANTIC PERIOD IN MUSIC HISTORY (1820–1900)

Romanticism as a historical label refers to a time when artists, writers, and philosophers reacted against the tidy rationality of the Enlightenment. Romantics acknowledged and emphasized the importance of individual expression and inner feelings, the power of nature and history. Composers became free agents unattached to courtly or clerical patrons. They wrote music that moved them without worrying about the wishes of a benefactor.

(Continued)

MUSICAL THEMES (Continued)

Expressive range expanded. Harmonies became increasingly unstable as composers sought new colors to create subtle shades of emotional nuance. As the belief in music's power rose, so did the public's fascination with those who performed it. The greatest virtuosos—performers like Italian violinist Niccolò Paganini (1782–1849) (see chapter 13: Music and Concert) and Hungarian pianist Franz Liszt (1811–1886)—had cult followings similar to those of today's elite rock stars. See **mysearchlab** I.3

QUESTIONS FOR THOUGHT

- How do tempo and dynamics affect the emotional content of "Gretchen am Spinnrade"?
- How would you describe the texture of "Je ne puis vivre" compared to that of "Gretchen am Spinnrade"?
- We discussed the idea of obsession's circularity in "Gretchen am Spinnrade." Do you see any notion of circularity in the form of "Je ne puis vivre"?
- How does form affect the meaning of each song?
- In Schubert's work, how does the spacing of the stanzas affect the drama?
- In the three pieces we have discussed so far, which composer do you think was most concerned with creating music that mirrored the meaning of the text? How was this accomplished?

Love's Betrayals

Part of what makes Schubert's "Gretchen" so powerful is the fact that she is so unaware of her true relationship with Faust, a liaison that we on the outside understand all too well. Could any real person be as foolish as poor Gretchen? Of course, it happens all the time.

In this section we meet a pair of spurned lovers—one innocent, the other quite worldly. On the one hand, the teenaged geisha Cio-Cio-San sings of rapturous love that she believes crosses cultural boundaries and will endure time and distance. She soon learns that her husband has long deserted her. On the other hand, country-and-western star Hank Williams has no such illusions. In song after song he looks betrayal straight in the eyes.

American opera star Geraldine Farrar (1882–1967) in the role of *Madama Butterfly*, c. 1908.

Madama Butterfly

Gazing seaward from the balcony of a small house in the hills above Japan's Nagasaki harbor, Cio-Cio-San waits for the return of Lieutenant Pinkerton, her American husband. Three years have passed since the dashing American naval officer set out to sea. There has been no contact. Pinkerton does not even know that he is a father. Even so, Cio-Cio-San sings of her husband's fidelity. She sings of love's unshakeable power to bridge time and space, to navigate the abyss between cultures East and West.

Alas, Cio-Cio-San lives a fantasy. Pinkerton has not been faithful. In fact, apparently he hardly even thinks of her. He will soon return, however. When that happens, Cio-Cio-San's world will come crashing down.

Italian composer Giacomo Puccini's (1858–1924) *Madama Butterfly* (1904) is one of the most beloved of all operas. The music is gorgeous; the plot is heartbreaking. The story—a tale of American hubris and a Japanese girl's innocence—reflects the ways in which Europeans perceived America and Japan at the dawn of the twentieth century. The broader theme of love betrayed is timeless and universal.

As for the plot, not much happens externally. The important events are internal, played out in the players' hearts and minds. Here is a synopsis of the story:

ACT I: Nagasaki, Japan U.S. Navy Lieutenant B. F. Pinkerton inspects a house he has just leased from a marriage broker. Included in the deal is Cio-Cio-San (Madama Butterfly), a ready-made geisha wife. For the foot-loose Pinkerton, the marriage is just a lark. Not for Cio-Cio-San. The 16-year-old girl plans to devote her life to her new husband. In renouncing her Buddhist faith to become Christian, she turns her back on both family and culture.

ACT II: Three years have passed. Cio-Cio-San awaits her husband's return. The money is almost gone; other suitors are asking for her hand. Cio-Cio-San insists that she has not been deserted. And even if she has, the point is moot. Pride will not allow her to return to her former life. A cannon blast in the harbor announces the return of Pinkerton's ship. As dusk falls, Cio-Cio-San prepares for her husband's arrival.

ACT III: It is dawn and Cio-Cio-San has fallen asleep waiting. Pinkerton enters with Kate, his American wife. Cio-Cio-San awakens and finally realizes the terrible truth. She agrees to surrender her son to the couple but only if Pinkerton himself returns to fetch him. Alone again, Cio-Cio-San bows before a statue of Buddha, then takes a dagger and prepares to commit *seppuku*, ritual suicide. As she dies, Pinkerton's voice can be heard calling to her from the distance.

LISTENING GUIDE

CD III/Track 11
Download track 48
mysearchlab 9.4

"UN BEL DÌ, VEDREMO"
from the opera, Madama Butterfly (1904)

In this Act II aria Cio-Cio-San sings of her lover's return. She tells her servant, Suzuki, how she will hide at his approach, both to tease him and so not to die from the excitement of reunion.

She will die, of course, but not from love's ecstasy. We in the audience already know all this. But we are powerless observers and Cio-Cio-San cannot be saved. As Puccini understood, this makes listening to the aria all the more devastating.

The music begins with a soaring melody in the soprano's upper range. Gradually the melody relaxes its way downward. Notice the characteristic sound of the highly trained operatic vocal style: the smooth diction, the pure tone nuanced by the use of vibrato. Cio-Cio-San seems to pause and savor each word of the opening line—"One fine, clear day, we will see. . . ."

Anticipation, which kept her suspended in that lovely hopeful upper range, is eased as she describes the smoke of the ship entering the harbor. Think about the imagery. Is love strong like a great ship plowing the seas? Or is love fleeting, like smoke in the wind?

0:00	Un bel dì, vedremo	One fine, clear day, we shall see
	Levarsi un fil di fumo	A thin trail of smoke arising
	Sull'estremo confin del mare.	On the distant horizon, far out to sea.
	E poi la nave appare.	And then the ship appears.

(Continued)

LISTENING GUIDE (*Continued*)

0:37	Puccini moves the lyrics forward as he paints a sensuous picture of the ship—brave and powerful against the blue sea. Once again, he slows the action. "En . . . tra . . . nel porto," she sings, pausing on the word "enter," as if the ship will never arrive. An upward melody paints the stalwart power of the ship's cannons. And again, the words slow as Cio-Cio-San savors Pinkerton's arrival.

Poi la nave bianca	Then the white ship
Entra nel porto,	Enters into the harbor,
Romba il suo saluto.	And thunders out its greeting.
Vedi? È venuto!	You see? He has arrived!

1:08	Now we learn about the inner life of this child/woman. Despite the years of waiting, she will continue to play love's seductive games. She will be coy. He must come to her.

Io non gli scendo incontro. Io no.	I'll not go down to meet him. Not I.
Mi metto là sul ciglio del colle e aspetto,	I shall stay on the hillside and wait,
E aspetto gran tempo	And wait for a long time,
E non mi pesa	And I'll not grow weary
La lunga attesa.	Of the long wait.

1:46	E uscito dalla folla cittadina,	Emerging from the city crowds,
	un uomo, un picciol punto	A man is coming, a tiny speck
	s'avvia per la collina.	Starts to climb the hill.

2:17	Chi sarà? chi sarà?	Who is he? Who?
	E come sarà giunto	And when he arrives
	Che dirà? che dirà?	What will he say? What will he say?
	Chiamerà Butterfly dalla lontana.	He will call "Butterfly" from the distance.
	Io senza dar risposta	I, without answering
	Me ne starò nascosta	Will remain hidden
	Un po' per celia.	A little to tease him.

2:47	The opening melody reappears, giving balance and a sense of closing to the aria. The familiar melody is briefly interrupted by an almost frantic assertion to Suzuki that Pinkerton will return. The aria ends in an emotional frenzy, literally on a high note as Cio-Cio-San sings "l'aspetto" ("I will wait for him"). The orchestra sounds the last trace of the hopeful, poignant theme.

E un po' per non morire	And a little so as not to die
Al primo incontro;	At our first meeting;
Ed egli alquanto in pena	And then rather worried
Chiamerà, chiamerà:	He will call, he will call:
"Piccina mogliettina,	"My little one, my tiny wife
Olezzo di verbena"	Perfumed Verbena"
I nomi che mi dava al suo venire.	The names he gave me when he came last.
[a Suzuki]	[to Suzuki]

3:30	Tutto questo avverrà,	All this will happen,
	Te lo prometto.	I promise you.
	Tienti la tua paura,	Keep your fears to yourself,
	Io con sicura fede l'aspetto.	I, with faithful trust will wait for him.

Libretto by Luigi Illica and Giuseppa Giacosa

Hank Williams (1923–1953)

Puccini built his story on a matrix of innocence, deception, and revelation. Country-and-western love songs rarely bother with such complexity. Instead, the genre cuts right to the chase. Infidelity may hurt, but it is rarely a surprise.

Few figures in American popular life have inspired the public imagination as much as singer/songwriter Hank Williams. In a few short years, the once dirt-poor Alabama country boy helped transform country-and-western music from regional curiosity to national voice. Along the way, Williams brought new depth to the genre's principal song topic: love gone wrong.

Authenticity and hard living were the Williams trademarks. He grew up tough and fast, learned to smoke and drink before his teens, and was soon addicted to painkillers and women. His music drew from bitter personal experience—from the hurt of poverty, the hurt of a hapless father, the hurt of both a domineering mother and wife, and from the dull pain of too many one-night stands.

Mostly hidden from the public was the rage. Williams was insecure, self-destructive, and often violent. He commonly engaged in fistfights and carried a handgun. Williams burned his candle quickly and brightly. He would be a national star by age 25 but dead from drink and drugs at age 29.

Williams never learned to read music. He learned to play guitar mostly by watching others. His only teacher, and perhaps his strongest adult role model, was Rufus Payne, a black street singer. Payne taught Williams how to drink, how to survive on the streets, and how to play some guitar. Most importantly, he taught Williams how to entertain an audience.

By the seventh grade, the boy was featured twice weekly in 15-minute slots on Montgomery,

Audrey (third from left) and Hank (fourth from left) Williams singing together on WSM radio with the Drifting Cowboys.

Alabama's WSFA radio station. The airplay led to regional performances. Some were in schoolhouses, but most were in roadhouses where Williams performed on stages protected by chicken wire to keep flying bottles at bay. Williams dropped out of school at age 19 while still in the ninth grade.

The following summer Williams met Audrey Mae Sheppard Guy. She became his first wife and hoped to become his onstage partner as well. Utterly lacking in musical talent, Guy never succeeded on stage. She does deserve some credit for her husband's career, however. She was the inspiration for some of his loneliest songs.

By 1946, Williams was a rising star. He headed to Nashville to audition for the publisher Acuff-Rose. A songwriting contract followed, then recordings. Even the early titles—such as "Wealth Won't Save Your Soul," and "Never Again (Will I Knock on Your Door)"—suggest the dark abyss that was the singer's private life. More upbeat in mood but firmly within the country-and-western love genre was the songwriter's first big hit, "Honky Tonkin," a classic party song for the down and out.

Hank and Audrey lived the stories about which he sang. They fought often and violently. Infidelity was rampant on both sides. Audrey filed for divorce in early 1948, but the couple stayed together a while longer. (That fall they conceived Randall Hank Williams, country-and-western superstar Hank Williams Jr.)

Later that year Williams's career bumped upward when he was booked onto Shreveport's *Louisiana Hayride*, which was broadcast over the 50,000-watt radio station, KWKH. A contract at Nashville's Grand Ole Opry soon followed. The slump-shouldered 6'1", 140-pound singer/songwriter was on his way to becoming the genre's biggest star.

In 1948 he also recorded "The Lovesick Blues," Williams's first *Billboard* number one country-and-western hit. The song, quaintly upbeat despite the desperation in the lyrics, is a study in contradictions. One moment Williams's voice cracks, as if overcome by emotion. The next moment the hurt transforms into a playful yodel suggesting perhaps an "easy come/easy go" approach to relationships. Overall, Williams does not seem particularly upset at his loss. Williams had found his mature compositional voice, which generally combined at least two perspectives on love. At the center was heartbreak. But the narratives were also aloof, as if one partner or the other was determined to keep love at a distance.

A series of hits followed this pattern, including in 1950 "Why Don't You Love Me" and "Long Gone Lonesome Blues," and in 1951 "Hey Good Lookin'" and "Cold, Cold Heart." Invariably, the songs' lyrics rang with autobiographical truths and the guilty hurt of infidelity. Most successful of all was "Your Cheatin' Heart," one of Williams's last compositions. A popular belief is that the song draws directly from his real-life marriage to Audrey. That may be so, but Williams never lacked for relationships capable of fulfilling this song's narrative.

As his reputation grew, Williams found himself imitated in musical areas far outside country-and-western music. Italian-American crooner Tony Bennett (b. 1926) covered "Cold, Cold Heart." Others who recorded his music included pop singers Rosemary Clooney (1928–2002) (actor George Clooney's aunt) and the versatile singer/comedienne Jo Stafford (1917–2008). Almost single-handedly, Williams was giving country-and-western music a national profile.

It is a curious reality that while country-and-western performers often project a hard-drinking and fast-loving persona, things tend to fall apart when that image is actually lived. This is especially true in the upper echelons of the entertainment industry where the financial consequences of canceled or compromised performances can be catastrophic. For Williams, fame and fortune did nothing to slow his self-destructive behavior. The drinking binges worsened and sometimes lasted for weeks. His career quickly disintegrated.

Yet even as his life descended into chaos, Williams's songs remained fragile studies in contradiction. He lived a life of too much alcohol and too many women, of failed promises and broken hopes. Yet he never wrote as if any of these attributes were desirable. The songs throb with hurt.

Williams was inside all of his best songs. The personality that emerges from the music is of a sensitive, fractured, and easily wounded mercurial loner. Often he is aloof and sometimes just beaten down. But—in stark contrast to his real life—the Williams of song is never heartless, never hurtful.

LISTENING GUIDE

CD III/Track 12
Download track 49
mysearchlab 9.5

"COLD, COLD HEART"

by Hank Williams

Form: Strophic (AAAA)

The melody and lyrics have a natural and untutored feel, as well as a relentless rhythmic flow to the downbeat. These aspects combine to give the song the quality of inevitability. The lyrics tell us about a conversation that has been had too many times, always with the same unhappy result. He is giving his all, but she, hurt by an earlier doomed love affair, cannot respond. Ultimately, her bad luck becomes their bad luck. Resolution, if the line that completes each stanza is to be believed, is impossible.

Notice the arrangement as well. While Williams plays guitar chords, instrumentally the melodic interest comes from the pedal steel guitar and the violin. The violin provides a constant countermelody to Williams's singing. The steel guitar, which was still a relatively new sound to country music in the early 1950s, is used sparingly but forcefully "to comment" at the end of vocal phrases.

MUSICAL THEMES

THE PEDAL STEEL GUITAR

Though perhaps the most iconic of all country-and-western music sounds, the steel guitar has its roots not in Nashville or Memphis, but in Hawaii. The term "steel" comes not from the instrument itself, which originally was an ordinary guitar, but from the metal slide the performer would use with his left hand. A similar technique, known as bottleneck guitar, was developed in early blues styles. The biggest

A pedal steel guitar.

difference between the two styles was that steel guitars were played horizontally, with the strings facing upward. Perhaps because the instrument traveled quickly with sailors, Hawaiian steel guitars soon became popular worldwide, from Nigeria (where they were heard in the pop music style *juju*) to Nashville. In the United States, innovators quickly dropped the acoustic body, which was replaced by electric pick-ups, a development that also helped to spur innovations in the electric guitar.

QUESTIONS FOR THOUGHT

- Think about the orchestral accompaniment of "Un bel di vedremo." What instruments are used? How does the accompaniment contribute to the overall feeling of the aria?
- A Puccini trait is to double the vocalist's melody in the orchestra. Notice when he does this. Does he always double with the same instruments?
- Look at the lyrics to Williams's "Honky Tonkin'." The singer invites "Miss Sad and Lonely" over to party but expects her to pay. And when is she to come over? When she is down and out. Some party this will be. Notice also how he repeats "honky tonkin'." Why might he do this?
- How do the vocal qualities of Belle versus Cio-Cio-San versus Hank Williams affect the emotional content of each piece?
- Belle, Gretchen, and Cio-Cio-San are all in their teens. Do their vocal styles reflect their youth? How so or why not?

ACTIVITIES AND ASSIGNMENTS

- Compare the plots of *Madama Butterfly* and the musical *Miss Saigon*.
- Find additional songs about betrayal. How do the composers/performers communicate meaning?
- Compare Hank Williams's performance of "The Lovesick Blues" with other performers such as Patsy Cline, Charley Pride, or LeAnn Rimes. How do they differ, both musically and emotionally?

Love's Remorse

Deception and infidelity are common themes in songs of love. Only rarely does a protagonist admit personal failure for a relationship gone wrong. This is the situation we now take up.

In chapter 2, "Listening to Music," we encountered the Hindu epic *The Ramayana* as part of our study of Balinese kecak. Now we return to Indonesia, to Hindu mythology, and to *The Ramayana*'s chief villain Ravana, the nearly invincible demon king who kidnapped Sita, King Rama's wife. In that tale there is little to recommend about Ravana, who is arrogant and cruel. Other Hindu myths, however, present him in a more positive light, sometimes even as a heroic figure of great intelligence and moral fortitude. In all myths, however, Ravana is tagged with the fatal flaw of hubris.

A repentant Ravana is featured in the Sundanese love song "Ceurik Rahwana" ("The Tears of Ravana," pronounced "**Cheu**-rik Ra-**wa**-na"). The demon lies dying, Rama's spear driven through his heart. With his last breaths Ravana finally realizes the folly of his pride. He seeks not revenge against Rama but forgiveness from Banondari, the still-beloved wife he has betrayed.

DID YOU KNOW?

SUNDA

Centered on the island of Java, the Sundanese ethnic group consists of some 35 million people. Nearly all Sundanese practice Islam, though remnants of earlier religious traditions are still found. Hinduism, which arrived from India centuries before Islam, constitutes one such layer. While Hindu religious practice has been displaced, the Hindu epics retain an important place within the culture.

"Ceurik Rahwana" is drawn from the vocal music genre **tembang Sunda**, which developed in the nineteenth-century Sundanese court of Cianjur (Chi-**an**-jur). Though little known even in greater Indonesia, the music remains prized among upper-class urban Sundanese who value the way the genre subtly mines the emotions of melancholy and loneliness. When performed in traditional fashion, songs feature a vocal soloist accompanied by three instruments: the *kacapi indung* (a large plucked zither), the *suling* (a bamboo flute), and the *kacapi rincik* (a small plucked zither).

LISTENING GUIDE

CD III/Track 13
Download track 50
mysearchlab 9.6

"CEURIK RAHWANA"

"Ceurik Rahwana" is in the *rarancagan* style, which is characterized by its emotional texts and impassioned delivery style, particularly by *cacagan* (a pulsing and jagged vocal vibrato). This particular song consists of a five-verse dialogue between Rahwana (Ravana) and Banondari. The lyrics are supported by a motoric ostinato produced by the kacapi indung. The singers deliver the lyrics within a narrow melodic range in syllabic chant-like phrases reminiscent of *pantun*, an epic Sundanese narrative style dating back to the sixteenth century. Vocal lines are accompanied heterophonically by the suling. Singers use subtle pitch inflections to enhance the sense of extreme emotion.

0:00	Running scalar patterns in the kacapi indung introduce the tones that identify *sorog* as the song's pentatonic tuning system. Because the Sundanese conceive of scale as building downward from high to low, we too will organize the tones in that fashion. In this recording, the Sundanese solfege syllables da-mi-na-ti-la (high to low) correspond to the Western syllables fa-mi-re-te-la. At 0:11 Kacapi indung sounds a central motive (mi—na-mi . . . . . . la—ti—na—da-mi—la—da-la-da-mi).
0:12	Suling enters.
0:16	Verse 1. Banondari anu lucu, boho kakang anu geulis (geuning, duh anu geulis) *Banondari who is beautiful. My lovely wife. (Oh, who is lovely.)* kadieu sakeudeung geuwat, akang rek mere pepeling (aduh geulis, mere pepeling) *Here, just a second. I wish to give a message (Oh lovely one, I give a message.)* geura sambat indung bapa, samemeh akang pinasti *Go summon mother and father before I perish.* As the verse begins, the vocalist focuses the phrase on "mi," which forms the melodic center for the entire first line. With the second line, the vocalist begins higher (on "la") but gradually drifts back down to "mi." The third line shifts to "da," then relaxes down a half step to "mi" before a downward resolution on "la." Each succeeding verse follows the same melodic framework.
1:04	Verse 2. Aduh engkang buah kalabu sembaheun lahir jeung batin (geuning, lahir jeung batin) *Oh beloved fruit of my heart, dedicated body and soul. (Oh, body and soul.)* Aya naon pengeresa tara-tara ti sasari (aduh geuning, ti sasari) *How should one feel from now on? (Oh, from now on.)* nyauran ragrag cisoca, abdi mah saredih teuing *Calling, streaming down tears, I am devastated.* The shape of the melody at the word "cisoca" (tears) symbolizes the tears streaming down Banondari's face.

1:54	**Verse 3.** Aduh Enung anu ayu nu geulis pupujan ati (geulis, pupujan ati) *Oh Darling who is so delicate, who is so lovely, praiseworthy heart.* Akang tangtu ngababatang, samemeh akang pinasti (aduh geulis, akang pinasti) *I am fated to die, but before I perish. (Oh my lovely, I perish.)* Arek menta dihampura, lahir tumeka ing batin. *Let it be that I ask to be forgiven, body as well as soul.*
2:42	**Verse 4.** Duh engkang panutan kalbu, teu kiat abdi wawarti (geuning, abdi wawarti) *Oh object of my heart. I am not strong, I warn you. (I warn you.)* Ulah sok ngumbar amarah antukna kaluli-luli (aduh, geuning, kaluli-luli) *Don't so follow anger, resulting in forgetting. (Oh, forgetting all.)* Nu matak mawa cilaka, kaduhung ngajadi bukti. *Which apparently leads to catastrophe, regret becomes proof.*
3:31	**Verse 5.** Kaduhung kakang kaduhung, kataji nu lain-lain (geulis, nu lain-lain) *Regret, I regret, I was drawn by an extraordinary other. (Yes, Lovely, by an extraordinary other.)* Kaiwat goda rancana, kagembang ku Sintawati (aduh geulis, ku Sintawati) *Ensnared and seduced by temptation, enchanted by Sita. (Oh Lovely, by Sita.)* Geuning kieu karasan, malindes malik ka diri. *This is how it feels when the suffering (that one inflicts on others) returns to oneself.*

QUESTIONS FOR THOUGHT

- Why is music so often used to express love?
- What makes a love song convincing?

ACTIVITIES AND ASSIGNMENTS

- The Internet abounds with lists of love songs: "Top 100 Love Songs of All Time," "Best Love Songs," and so on. Click on some of these songs. Compare several from past decades.
- Plan out a love song. What kind of poem would you use? What form? What instruments? How would your music portray meaning?

The Last Word: "La Vie en Rose"

Having surveyed new love, unobtainable love, obsessive, unfaithful, and remorseful love, we close the chapter with enduring love as portrayed in French chanteuse Edith Piaf's "La Vie en Rose" (1945). The song presents a gentle, poignant vision of soft touches and knowing looks. Piaf, whose own life was filled with the hurt of love defiled, performs the song with an edge that convinces even the most hardened cynic that love is sweet.

MUSICAL LIVES
EDITH PIAF (1915–1963)

| Edith Piaf.

Edith Piaf remains one of France's most celebrated cultural icons. Her rags-to-riches story began with a broken family. Her parents abandoned her so she stayed with her grandmother, who ran a brothel. Prostitutes helped raise her. Weaned by trouble, Piaf had a child of her own by age 17. Her love life went from bad to worse when she took up with a pimp. He forced her to hand over singing wages—either that or be forced to sell her body as a prostitute.

At age 20, Piaf was discovered by Louis Leplée, a successful nightclub owner. With Leplée's help, Piaf received her first recording contracts. The good luck did not hold, however. Leplée was murdered the following year. Piaf was initially a suspect.

Despite a string of lovers, failed marriages, and scandals, Piaf's career continued to grow. She would perform eight times on American television's Sunday night variety-show staple *The Ed Sullivan Show* (broadcast 1948–1971), sing twice in Carnegie Hall, and appear in 10 films. Her discography fills 10 CDs. Piaf's last years were riddled with tragedy, including the death of a lover in a plane crash, a series of car accidents, alcohol abuse, and drug dependence. She died of liver cancer at age 47.

LISTENING GUIDE

mysearchlab 9.7

"LA VIE EN ROSE" (1945)

music by Louise Gugliemi, lyrics by Edith Piaf

0:00	Orchestral introduction presents the song's main tune.
0:14	Piaf begins with a short recitative-like introduction.
0:28	Phrase A. The melody begins at the top of the scale and relaxes gently downward, with the ease of the embrace that it describes. "When my lover holds me in his arms, I see the world through rose-colored glasses," she sings. The tune ends on the inconclusive dominant harmony, telling us that there is more to come. Brass instruments seem to respond to her sentiments.
0:40	Phrase A[1]. Not only is there more to come, but better things as well. We move from a remembered embrace to words of love. As emotions move a notch higher, so does the lovely melody, which begins on "re" instead of "do" and then follows a similar downward trajectory.
0:51	Phrase A[2]. Piaf returns to the opening pitch of phrase A, then sings a variation on the opening melody. Graceful and fresh, the melody, like love itself, seems to hold infinite possibilities for change and development.
1:03	Phrase B. Here comes the confident—"we are destined for each other"—conclusion to all those A variations. On the song's highest pitches, Piaf sings that she and lover are bound together "pour la vie," for life.
1:18	Phrase A[3]. This is very similar to the first A phrase but ends conclusively on the tonic.
1:32	This is another recitative commentary.
1:56	(Repeat from above.)

Piaf's American legacy is rich. Since 1990 over 57 CDs of her music have been reissued. "La Vie en Rose" has been featured in 24 movies, including *Bull Durham* (1988), *Saving Private Ryan* (1998), and *Something's Gotta Give* (2003). Performers who have recently covered the song include Grace Jones (b. 1948), Cyndi Lauper (b. 1953), and Celine Dion (b. 1968).

CONCLUSION

In the movie *La Vie en Rose* (2008), an American journalist asks Piaf, "If you were to give advice to a woman, what would it be?" Piaf answers, "LOVE." To a young girl? "LOVE." To a child? "LOVE." Piaf understood that lives are shaped by love's peaks and valleys. Such is the human condition. Busnois may have expressed his love in the musical language of the distant past, but the emotional experiences to which he gave voice may well be ours. So too, might we share the distress of Schubert's Gretchen and Puccini's Cio-Cio San, or the remorse of Sunda's Ravanna. Though separated by time and place, perhaps we are not so different after all.

CHAPTER GOALS

- To demonstrate how social issues are reflected in musical theater.
- To provide an overview of twentieth-century American musical theater.
- To understand three groundbreaking twentieth-century musicals.

QUESTIONS FOR THOUGHT

- Do you have a favorite musical? Why does it appeal to you? Is it the music? The plot? The message? A combination of all of these?
- What are the characteristics of musicals you have seen or know about?

The lights are bright on Broadway—especially around Times Square, the heart of New York City's theater district. Today's tourists look skyward to gawk at giant computerized billboards; earlier generations, however, were dazzled by the millions of electric lights that illuminated theater marquees. It was not for nothing that in 1902, just 20 years after the building of New York City's first electric power plant, the district earned the moniker "The Great White Way."

For actors, the theater district is a land where dreams are sometimes realized but more often crushed. Generations of the nation's most talented thespians have flocked to New York in hopes of seeing their names on a theater marquee. Few succeed.

For audiences, the spotlighted stages of darkened theaters are sites where imagination becomes reality. Days are lived in minutes; lives are lived in hours. Love is often right around the corner, perhaps as close as a well-crafted song.

This chapter provides an overview of American musical theater. We discuss and study examples from a variety of shows but focus on three seminal productions covering roughly a 50-year period: *Show Boat* (1927), *West Side Story* (1957), and *Sweeney Todd: The Demon Barber of Fleet Street* (1979). The three share five specific characteristics:

- All are "book musicals," that is, music and dance are integrated into the story.
- All are based on earlier literary sources.
- Each was subsequently made into a movie.
- All feature romantic love while highlighting vexing issues regarding social class or ethnicity.

- Each brought important innovations to Broadway.

The works are connected by "creative" heritage as well. Oscar Hammerstein II (1895–1960), who wrote the book and lyrics for *Show Boat*, was a mentor to Stephen Sondheim (b. 1930). Sondheim's first Broadway assignment was as lyricist for *West Side Story*. Twenty-two years later, Sondheim wrote both the music and lyrics for *Sweeney Todd*, the work we consider first.
mysearchlab 10.1

Sweeney Todd: The Demon Barber of Fleet Street (1979)

How does one turn a story about mass murder into a musical? That was the task Stephen Sondheim tackled in writing *Sweeney Todd*. Throats are slit; victims' flesh is served up on dinner plates. In Broadway's goriest thriller, characters sing their way through pools of blood, carnal depravity, and insanity. Obsession is the order of the day.

The tale is set among the festering streets of nineteenth-century London. As the story opens Todd has just returned from 15 years in an Australian penal colony. His "crime"? Only that his wife, Lucy, was beautiful. Coveting her, the lascivious Judge Turpin had Todd arrested and convicted of "a trumped-up charge."

Todd hopes to reunite with Lucy and their daughter (Johanna), but that will not happen. Soon he will be told that Lucy took arsenic after being raped by Turpin. Johanna, now 16, is the judge's ward. He has locked her away.

DID YOU KNOW?

MORE ON *SWEENEY TODD*

Sondheim's *Sweeney Todd* is drawn from a serial story titled "The String of Pearls: A Romance" (1846), published in London in *The People's Periodical*. The original story, probably by Thomas Prest, presents Todd as thoroughly depraved. The story was twice adapted for the theatrical stage, first by George Dibdin-Pitt as *The Fiend of Fleet Street* (1847) and later by Christopher Bond as *Sweeney Todd, The Demon Barber of Fleet Street* (1973). The story was also made into films (1936 and 2007) and choreographed as a ballet (1959). There is no evidence that Todd is based on historical fact.

LISTENING GUIDE

CD III/Track 14
Download track 51
mysearchlab 10.2

SWEENEY TODD, ACT 1, SCENE 1: "NO PLACE LIKE LONDON"

0:00	Orchestra sounds the melodic theme "No place like London."
0:05	Orchestra echoes the theme.
0:10	A fog horn sets the scene at a London wharf. Todd is accompanied by Anthony Hope, the young sailor who rescued him from a shipwreck. The two men sing about London. Anthony describes a city of wonder; Todd sees nothing but misery. Despite their differences, the two men are inextricably bound. Todd was once a youthful optimist; Anthony will soon discover the world's cruelty. Anthony will soon fall in love with Johanna. Both men find a common enemy in Judge Turpin.
0:13	Oboe introduces an extended melody of the song "No Place like London."
0:30	Anthony takes up the song. I have sailed the world, beheld its wonders. . . .
0:49	Anthony begins a second verse. I could hear the city bells, ring whatever I would do. . . .
0:55	Todd interrupts and, changing the key from major to minor, moves from light to dark, joy to pain. The music becomes more agitated, the metric pulse shifts unpredictably. Todd's obsession for revenge is heard in the clarinets' sparring countermelodies.
1:10	As Todd concludes his warning, "You will learn," a recurring theme—let's call it "hope turned to sorrow"—sounds in the orchestra. The theme consists of two notes rising (hope) followed by two notes falling (sorrow).
1:20	In the background, the flute introduces the melody of the song "There Was a Barber and His Wife." Todd will sing this soon enough, but for now the melody works as a leitmotive that serves to introduce a beggar woman.
1:35	The beggar woman pleads for alms. She is accompanied by a dreary downward-tumbling and chromatically inflected melody that lacks tonal footing. Strings reinforce the vocal line. Alms, alms, for a miserable woman . . .

1:54	Anthony gives the woman some change and her mood flips to sexual aggression. Her song is accompanied by piercing, violent gestures from the brass instruments. (We hear similar sounds later in the show, when the story of Lucy's rape is told.) How'd you like a little squiff dear, a little jig jig. . . .
2:04	The beggar woman asks Todd for money. Notice the falling melody as she asks, "Don't I know you?" Alms, alms, for a pitiful woman. . . .
2:21	Todd should, but does not. He shoos her away. She responds with another verbal explosion.
2:23	Beggar woman returns to asking for alms as she leaves the stage. How'd you like to fish me squiff . . .
2:34	Strings continue "Alms" theme while Anthony calms Todd. Alms, alms, for a desperate woman . . .
2:54	"Hope to sorrow" theme reappears in the orchestra.
2:59	Todd raps out "There's a hole in the world like a great black pit" while the "hope to sorrow" theme continues underneath. Todd's outburst serves as the introduction to his version of the song "There's No Place Like London," which begins at 3:15.
3:39	Todd sings, "There was a barber and his wife. . . ."
4:24	Todd sings the song's second verse, "There was another man who saw. . . ." Notice how Sondheim has slowed the pacing to add emotional power to this story of lost love.
5:38	Obsession motive sounds in the woodwinds (see 0:55).
5:46	Reduced to primal emotions that seem to steal his capacity for melody, Todd spits out his exit words, "There's a hole in the world. . . ."

The scene ends.

QUESTIONS FOR THOUGHT

- Why does Sondheim place the beggar woman in the opening scene? How might the social issues of Victorian England be relevant to audiences today?
- How is *Sweeney Todd* different from or similar to other musicals you know?

ACTIVITIES AND ASSIGNMENTS

- Compare the filmed theatrical version of *Sweeney Todd* (1982, directed by Terry Hughes and Harold Prince, RKO Pictures) to the 2007 movie starring Johnny Depp and directed by Tim Burton. Which expresses the subtleties of the plot more effectively? Which is more musically expressive?

American Musical Theater: The Early Years

Historians tend to mark the beginning of American musical theater with the 1866 premiere of *The Black Crook*, a five-and-one-half-hour extravaganza that featured an inane plot and forgettable music. No matter. Audiences flocked to see the remarkable stage sets and especially the scantily clad 100-woman

"Amazon" chorus. (Then, as now, sex sold.) The show ran for over a year at Niblo's Garden, a 3,200-seat auditorium located at the corner of Broadway and Prince Street in Lower Manhattan. *Crook* set the bar for a series of similarly grandiose extravaganzas that followed.

Also popular at the time were two other musical genres, **burlesque** and **blackface minstrelsy**. The former were not girlie shows as the word would imply today but comic musical parodies of serious plays, operas, or dance. A number of works by William Shakespeare (1564–1616) were reconceived as burlesques.

Minstrel shows featured skits, songs, and dance in which white entertainers—their faces blackened with burnt cork—lampooned African American culture. The genre's origin is attributed to New York City comedian Thomas Dartmouth Rice (1808–1860), who created the character Jim Crow. Rice's song "Jump Jim Crow" (we know the melody today as "Turkey in the Straw") achieved popularity nationwide. Imitators developed a series of "black" characters, including the urban dandy Zip Coon and the exuberant musician

A mid-nineteenth-century depiction of "Jim Crow," the stereotyped rural slave depicted in minstrel shows.

Mr. Tambo. The song "Dixie's Land," probably written in 1859 by Ohio native Daniel Decatur Emmett (1815–1904), was popular on the New York City minstrel stage before it became associated with the Confederacy. Minstrelsy remained popular into the twentieth century. Jack Robin, the protagonist in *The Jazz Singer* (1927), cinema's first "talkie," performed in blackface (see chapter 11: Music and Film).

European **operettas**, which were popular in the United States throughout the nineteenth century, also helped shape the earliest Broadway productions. Operettas were lighthearted, comic, and contained catchy tunes and spoken dialogue. Hugely popular was the British team of W. S. Gilbert (1836–1911) and Arthur Sullivan (1842–1900), whose operettas include *H.M.S. Pinafore* (1878), *The Pirates of Penzance* (1879), and *The Mikado* (1885). A generation later, immigrant composers such as Irishman Victor Herbert (1859–1924) (*Babes in Toyland*, 1903 and *Naughty Marietta*, 1910) and the Czech Rudolf Friml (1879–1972) (*Rose Marie*, 1924 and *Vagabond King*, 1925) would write for both Broadway and film.

George M. Cohan (1878–1942) gets credit for "inventing" American musical theater as we know it today. The child of traveling **vaudeville** performers, Cohan grew up on stage. He wrote and performed his own material before reaching his teens. Cohen's shows were feel-good celebrations of Americana. Storylines featured ordinary people experiencing extraordinary moments in their everyday lives. His characters spoke in the vernacular language of the time; music and dance numbers drew from the latest fads in popular culture. Classic Cohan songs include "Give My Regards to Broadway" and "Yankee Doodle Boy," both from his 1904 musical *Little Johnny Jones.*

Variety was central to the approach of the great impresario Florenz Ziegfeld (1867–1932), whose annual *Follies* were a Broadway fixture from 1907 until 1932. Ziegfeld himself had no training in any of the theatrical arts, but he knew how to deliver what people liked. Regular stars of the *Follies* included W. C. Fields, Will Rogers, Anna Held, Fanny Brice (portrayed later by Barbra Streisand, b. 1942) in the Jule Styne (1905–1994) musical *Funny Girl* (1964), and many others. Always, Ziegfeld featured bevies of beautiful women in various states of undress. Productions were a mishmash of stand-up comedy, skits, and song and dance. Teams of composers supplied the music.

There were many fine composers on Broadway in those years, but three dominated: Irving Berlin, Cole Porter, and George Gershwin. The men could hardly have been more different. Berlin and Gershwin both grew up poor in New York City; both were also the children of Russian Jewish immigrants. But while Gershwin was a trained musician and a piano virtuoso, Berlin could barely plunk out a tune. Poverty meant that both had jobs before their teens. Porter, by contrast, grew up wealthy in the Midwest. He graduated from Yale (where he wrote the university's fight song). Berlin and Porter wrote both music and lyrics; Gershwin only wrote music, which his

older brother Ira (1896–1983) set to words. All possessed an uncanny ability to write music that seemed prototypically American.

Their creative range was remarkable. Berlin, who wrote at least a song a day for his entire professional life, composed "God Bless America" and "White Christmas." His first hit, "Alexander's Ragtime Band" (1911), helped bring the broken syncopations of early jazz into popular song. "There's No Business Like Show Business," from his last hit Broadway show, *Annie Get Your Gun* (1946), would become Broadway's unofficial anthem.

Porter was the most elegant, and occasionally most eloquent, of the Tin Pan Alley composers. What was the gay Episcopalian millionaire Indiana farm boy's secret to songwriting success? "I'll write Jewish tunes," he told Richard Rodgers in 1926. Around that time Porter's melodies grew longer and more chromatic; he began to favor the brooding minor keys.

Porter frequently wrote of love, but usually from a cool, detached perspective. His lyrics for songs like "Let's Do It" knowingly wink at the distinction between having sex and being in love. Adolescents learn about the birds and bees, but who, besides perhaps a biologist, ever thinks about the bees "doing it"? *Fleas* rhymes fine with *bees*, but why are they educated? Porter's juxtapositions become even more absurd as the song unfolds, bringing

Gene Buck, Victor Herbert, John Philip Sousa, Harry B. Smith, Jerome Kern, Irving Berlin, George W. Meyer, Irving Bibo, and Otto Harbach, c. 1920.

Cole Porter.

in sponges, oysters, clams, and jellyfish to the catalog of amorous creatures.

Porter—educated and worldly, gay in a still-closeted world—knew a thing or two about incongruous juxtapositions. He excelled in making the distinguished appear mundane, the mundane appear distinguished. Often juxtapositions of high and low culture are presented side-by-side in comedic production-line style, as in "You're the Top" (1934), where Porter pairs a Shakespeare sonnet with Mickey Mouse.

Perhaps Porter's most charming juxtaposition came in his 1948 musical *Kiss Me Kate*, based on Shakespeare's *The Taming of the Shrew*. Both Shakespeare's and Porter's plots are too involved to detail here. Suffice to say, Baltimore replaces Shakespeare's Padua setting and *Kate* involves "real-life" lovers fighting as they play parallel roles in a production of *Shrew*. Porter's finest comic moment comes when two thuggish gangsters give a lesson on how to win a girl in the song "Brush Up Your Shakespeare."

The most versatile of our three composers was George Gershwin. While groomed in Tin Pan Alley, Gershwin also had ambitions in the world of classical music. His jazz-inflected scores *Rhapsody in Blue* (1924) and *An American in Paris* (1928) both have secure positions in the orchestral repertoire.

Gershwin's first hit song was the minstrel-styled "Swanee" (1919), which became a vehicle for a blackfaced Al Jolson (1886–1950) (see chapter 11: Music and Film). Gershwin and lyricist brother Ira had their first Broadway hit with *Lady Be Good* (1924), which featured the songs "Fascinating Rhythm" and "The Man I Love," which are both jazz standards today. A string of shows followed, including *Funny Face* (1927); *Strike Up the Band* (1927); *Of Thee I Sing* (1931), which won a Pulitzer Prize; and the "American folk opera" *Porgy and Bess* (1935) (see "Summertime," chapter 2: Listening to Music).

Show Boat (1927)

American musical theater came of age in New York City on the evening of December 27, 1927. The occasion was the Broadway premiere of *Show Boat*, a wide-ranging story of life on a Mississippi riverboat. Written by composer Jerome Kern (1885–1945) with a book and lyrics by Oscar Hammerstein II, the musical went to the heart of the American social experience. The ingredients that had traditionally dominated American musical theater—plot-free revues, light romantic comedy, blackface minstrelsy, and young women in titillating costumes—were pushed to the background. Brought forward were moral confrontations over social class and race. The lives portrayed on *Show Boat*'s stage were beaten down, and sometimes broken, by social injustice, alcoholism, and marital infidelity.

The musical is based on a story by Pulitzer Prize-winning novelist Edna Ferber (1885–1968). Action unfolds along America's geographic spine, the Mississippi River. There, along the mighty waterway that divides East and West and connects North and South—the social artery that provided passage south for early explorers and passage north for the blues and jazz—Kern and Hammerstein tell their American tale of racial prejudice and social oppression. It is also the story of ordinary individuals working out their daily lives in relatively insignificant ways as they attempt to navigate life's eddies and shoals. Along the way, some of these people do great things.

Kern and Hammerstein sought to write a new sort of American musical, one in which music and drama were richly integrated. But they also worried about moving too far away from audience expectations. Thus, *Show Boat* unfolds at two levels. First and foremost, *Show Boat* is a powerful drama about the best and worst of American culture. Characters are richly developed, both by dialogue and the adept use of music. Second, *Show Boat*'s plot—which conveniently takes place on a "show" boat, after all—allows for the insertion of conventional theatrical entertainments. Thus positioned, Kern and Hammerstein were

DID YOU KNOW?
MISCEGENATION

Miscegenation refers to the mixing of races (from the Latin *miscere* "to mix" and *genus* "type"). Though a term of science, it was used in the United States as early as the pre-Civil War era to stir up fears of interracial marriage should slavery be abolished. Sixteen states still had antimiscegenation laws in 1967, the year that the United States Supreme Court, in the case of *Loving v. Virginia*, ruled them unconstitutional.

able to satisfy their audience's hunger for lighthearted music and dance while infusing an unprecedented level of social realism.

Show Boat is a lumbering giant, running nearly four hours in its uncut form. Musical styles are drawn from an eclectic mix of American sounds, including spirituals, blues, and jazz; popular musical theater; and even the long and soaring melodies of late nineteenth-century European opera.

Show Boat's storylines are labyrinthine. First and foremost, *Show Boat* tells the story of Magnolia Hawks, daughter of the show-boat's captain. We first meet her as an innocent 17-year-old girl on the cusp of first love. By show's end, Magnolia has suffered a broken marriage and raised a daughter on her own. A self-made woman, she has also become worldly wise.

A secondary storyline revolves around Miss Julie Laverne, the showboat's leading lady, who is also Magnolia's childhood mentor. Miss Julie is black but is so fair-skinned as to pass for white. Only a few people know her secret. One of these is her white husband Steve, the showboat's leading man. Because of miscegenation laws, their interracial marriage is illegal. Midway through the first act their secret is disclosed. To save Julie from arrest, Steve cuts her finger and swallows some of her blood. Steve proclaims his "blackness." He too has "more than a drop of Negro blood" in him, he tells the sheriff (and his stunned 1927 audience).

Show Boat offers a gold mine of wonderful songs, including the operatic "Make Believe," during which Magnolia falls in love with the riverboat gambler Gaylord Ravenol; "Can't Help Loving That Man of Mine" and "Bill" (both of which became jazz standards); and "Old Man River."

The Curtain Rises

In musical theater, first impressions are everything. So getting the opening scene right is essential. It is there we meet the characters, learn the issues, and get a feel for the musical language.

As we did with *Sweeney Todd*, we will study *Show Boat*'s opening minutes, undoubtedly the most provocative minutes in the history of American musical theater. In order to set the mood, turn back the clock 80-some years. Imagine that you—along with many of New York's social luminaries—are in the Ziegfeld Theatre for opening night. The musical's title suggests a lighthearted evening of song and dance, all situated on a Mississippi riverboat. The idea sounds delightfully quaint to you and your fellow urban sophisticates.

MUSICAL LIVES

PAUL ROBESON (1898–1976)

Paul Robseon, 1942. Photographed by Gordon Parks.

"To be free to walk the good American earth as equal citizens, to live without fear, to enjoy the fruits of our toil, to give our children every opportunity in life—that dream which we have held so long in our hearts is today the destiny that we hold in our hands."

—Paul Robeson

Paul Robeson, the son of a minister and former slave, was born in Princeton, New Jersey. In 1915, he matriculated at Rutgers University, only the third African American to do so. He earned letters in four sports, was twice elected to the All-American football team, and graduated as class valedictorian. Robeson studied law at Columbia University, but racial prejudice soured him to the profession. He eventually returned to his boyhood loves of singing and acting.

Robeson's most famous role was in *Show Boat* as Joe, who sings "Old Man River." Eventually, Robeson's sympathy for the Soviet Union, a place he considered less racially prejudiced than the United States, led to a 1947 indictment by the House Committee on Un-American Activities. The State Department denied Robeson a passport until 1958.

LISTENING GUIDE

CD IV/Track 1
Download track 52
mysearchlab 10.3

SHOW BOAT, OPENING SCENE

0:00	The orchestra's low brass sounds represent Sheriff Vallon. It is a foreboding chromatic minor-keyed motive. Although you cannot possibly know this yet, the phrase will come to represent the brutal fist of the law. The curtain rises on a group of African American stevedores singing as they load cotton at a dock in Natchez, Mississippi. The year is 1880. Though slavery is 15 years abolished, life for these men has hardly changed. Bales across their shoulders, they sing in a ragged jazz-inflected rhythm. Are you outraged by the lyrics? *Show Boat* brought to Broadway the bitter taste of American social realism. The words were calculated to shock, embarrass, and anger. Almost immediately, productions found alternatives to "Niggers." Substitutions included "colored folks," "darkies," and even the color-blind "Here we all." For historical reasons and to preserve the shock that Kern and Hammerstein intended, conductor John McGlinn insisted on using "Nigger" for the definitive 1988 EMI *Show Boat* recording. Rather than sing the word, baritone Willard White and an all-black British chorus resigned from the project. They were replaced by baritone Bruce Hubbard (who is black) and London's Ambrosian Chorus. Hubbard agreed only after seeking counsel with colleagues and friends. Said Mr. Hubbard, "The way the word was once used is not fiction but fact. Blacks today may want to forget the past and build on the future, but we should never lose our sense of history" (*New York Times,* September 25, 1988).
0:44	The stevedores move to a supporting role as a chorus of African American women takes up singing a song of their own. Underneath the women's melody, the men sing a bass riff.
0:56	The women join the men in a final repetition of the opening verse. Then comes new material.
1:09	"Cotton blossom" they sing. There is a lot going on here. Cotton Blossom is the name of the showboat, but here the words are tied to the land, to hard labor, and to the industry that once made slavery so lucrative. See how Hammerstein's lyrics are setting up connections. Kern is busy making musical connections as well. Here is how: ■ Sing the words "Cotton blossom." ■ Now hum just the melody. ■ Now slow it down and hum it backward with the same rhythm (long-long-short-short) and singing the first pitch twice. Do you recognize the melody and hear the implied words? It is *Show Boat*'s most famous song, "Old Man River." The chorus ends as the clarinet, then oboe introduce a lovely new melody, a snippet from the song "Can't Help Lovin' That Man of Mine." A brief dramatic interlude unfolds. Queenie the cook and Steve greet each other. Queenie is then confronted by Pete, a ship hand who wants to know where she got the broach she is wearing. Queenie answers that Miss Julie gave it to her. That means trouble. Pete, who is white, had given the broach as a present to Miss Julie, who he knows is black.
2:24	The interracial confrontation over, attention again focuses on the stevedores who reprise the show's opening lines. Tension is high and we are still only halfway through the scene.
2:53	Now the focus shifts from black to white America. The music becomes less syncopated and more playful, even a bit juvenile. Groups of well-dressed socialites come on stage. ("Mincing Minces" and "Beaux" are how Hammerstein identifies them.) Two young women look at a poster of Miss Julie and comment on her beauty.
3:13	The men break into song. They sing, "What a pretty bevy . . ." to a new melody, but the harmonic background is essentially the same as that of the original black chorus.
3:24	The Minces flirt back.

3:35	Beaux and Minces sing together.
3:47	Beaux sing, "See the show boat. . . ."
4:17	Finally, the music returns to the "Cotton blossom" melody first introduced by the stevedores.

Kern and Hammerstein have used the show's opening minutes to set up sharply contrasted social worlds: one of hard labor, the other of frivolous indulgence. In real life, the Deep South worlds of nineteenth-century black and white culture were just as divided. But they were also symbiotically connected by generations of social interaction and acculturation. In theatrical life, Kern and Hammerstein show these connections metaphorically by putting blacks and whites on the same stage (in itself a remarkable occurrence in 1927). They even sing together (though the words are wildly different).

This brings us to an axiom of well-written dramatic musical theater. When people sing together it is to show their connections, perhaps even to reveal relationships that the characters themselves do not understand. Seen from this perspective, the implication of this opening scene is that the fate of black and white Americans (and by extension all Americans) is intertwined.

Show Boat mines the best and worst of the American social experience. In 1927, it provided an uncompromising mirror by which Americans might gaze at the national soul. It continues to do so today.

QUESTIONS FOR THOUGHT

- Race is a central focus in *Show Boat*. It also casts its lens on gender. The two leading characters, Magnolia and Miss Julie, must make their way through life on their own. What other marginalized groups existed in 1920s America? What about today? Have other composers addressed these issues?
- Kern and Hammerstein have romanticized African American culture. We see, for example, Joe's nature-informed wisdom when he sings "Old Man River." What do you think of this perspective?
- In the first act, Queenie, the ship's African American cook, says that she is surprised that Miss Julie knows "Can't Help Lovin' That Man" because it's a "colored person's song." Might that have been a reasonable inference in 1880? What about today?
- If you were staging *Show Boat*, would you include the original opening lines or change them? Why or why not?

Moving On

Oscar Hammerstein, along with composer Richard Rodgers (1902–1979), would complete the integration of music and story begun in *Show Boat*. Theirs would become the most influential musical theater lyricist/composer team of the twentieth century.

Before teaming with Hammerstein, Rodgers worked with lyricist Lorenz Hart (1895–1943). The team wrote wonderful songs, including "Blue Moon" (1934) and, for the 1937 Broadway show *Babes in Arms,* "The Lady Is a Tramp" and "My Funny Valentine."

Both songs from *Babes in Arms* became jazz standards. But for Hart's failed struggle with alcoholism, the partnership might have produced much more.

Hart was a master lyricist, as we can see in the song "Bewitched, Bothered and Bewildered" (from the 1940 musical *Pal Joey).* **mysearchlab 10.4** Notice the multiple-syllable rhymes ("wild again," "beguiled again," and "child again), the inner rhymes of line three ("simpering" and "whimpering"), the alliteration of line four ("bewitched, bothered and bewildered"), and the inversion of the stanza's opening "I'm" with the closing "am I."

And what about the breakdown of resistance in the stanza that follows? Have the inner conflicts of seduction ever been told in song with more clarity? The narrator's emotional anchor, such as it is, seems to be no more than the confused consistency of the final line.

The Rodgers and Hart team produced jewel-like songs, but the team never found the dramatic formula to fully integrate words and music into the unified narrative style begun in *Show Boat*. That would be achieved in 1943 with *Oklahoma!*, the first of numerous Rodgers and Hammerstein collaborations that also produced *Carousel* (1945), *South Pacific* (1949), *The King and I* (1951), and *The Sound of Music* (1959), among others.

In many ways, all of these shows borrowed and expanded on the ideas brought forth in *Show Boat*. Central to most of them was a concern with the American experience, either at home or abroad. Also depicted—and subsumed under a larger heading we might call "doing the right thing"—were the tensions related to social class and freedom, women's rights and sexual autonomy, racial prejudice, and violence. In these musicals people make mistakes and suffer for them. Sometimes they die violently. Always there is a moral.

Think of music as a sonic photograph that allows us to step out of normal time and reflect upon the emotional consequences of the moment. In theater, characters break into song at emotional pressure points, instances of decision and resolution, of change and unfolding insight. These are the times when the passions are such that mere words are not enough. Nobody, for example, would remember *Show Boat*'s Joe if he had simply told Magnolia that love's course can be as muddy as the Mississippi. Heck, we all know that. Instead, Joe sang. He took the moment of a teenager's first magical romance and universalized it.

Let's briefly compare *Show Boat* with *Oklahoma!* Both were drawn from earlier sources, a book and play, respectively. Both engage American themes and conflicts. Both sought to achieve a sense of authenticity by featuring natural folk-like settings.

Then there is the naturalness of the language. We saw previously the sophisticated word play of Lorenz Hart. One can hardly listen to his lyrics and not consciously admire their grace and flow. Such is the case with almost all of the best Broadway lyricists, but not with Hammerstein. His lyrics seem to spring straight from the souls of the ordinary people who sing them. Just as with "Old Man River," Hammerstein took the particular and made it stand for the universal. Oklahoma, with its wind-swept plains and sweet-smelling wheat, suddenly becomes more than a place. It is an American state of mind, a wide-open sanctuary where dreams become reality. In 1943, as World War II raged and Americans fought in Europe, North Africa, and Asia, the image of this unspoiled landscape must have seemed as agreeable as heaven itself.

Rodgers and Hammerstein shows were invariably life embracing, even as they fearlessly explored their era's most difficult social issues. Race was once again at center in *South Pacific* when both U.S. Navy nurse Nellie Forbush and U.S. Marine Corps Lieutenant Joe Cable fall in love. Both are stymied by their prejudice ("You Have to Be Carefully Taught").

Broadway, the primary theatrical voice of a nation of immigrants, has mostly concerned itself with the American experience, with issues of ethnicity, religion, social class, and assimilation. Rodgers and Hammerstein may have set shows in the South Pacific and Siam (*The King and I*, 1956), but we see those faraway places through American eyes. Even the ostensibly Austrian-themed *The Sound of Music* has a real-life American ending with the von Trapp family immigrating to the United States in 1942.

A rare exception to this formula was *Threepenny Opera* (premiered in Berlin as *Die Dreigroschenoper* in 1928) by composer Kurt Weill (1900–1950) and Marxist playwright Bertolt Brecht (1898–1956), both German. The show has seen many revivals since its 1933 Broadway premiere, most recently in 2006 with Allan Cumming and Cyndi Lauper.

Dreigroschenoper is a scathing portrayal of social corruption. Brecht depicts a vicious world of thieves and beggars, pimps and prostitutes. Weill's music is dissonant and coarse, and sometimes lurches as if performed by an intoxicated Salvation Army band.

The show's most famous song is "Mack the Knife," which became a jazz standard as well as a vehicle for gravel-voiced trumpeter Louis Armstrong (1901–1971). Most of the music has a brutal edge. In the song "Pirate Jenny," newlywed Polly rattles off a fantasy-revenge song cruel enough to shock even the hardened criminals for whom she sings. "Pimp's Ballad" is a mesmerizing duet featuring Macheath and his prostitute girlfriend Jenny.

MUSICAL THEMES
THE BEGGAR'S OPERA, (1728)

An 1807 print depicting two of the leading stars of *The Beggar's Opera* serenading John Bull, a figure representing Great Britain.

Two hundred years before *Dreigroschenoper*, John Gay's *The Beggar's Opera* was a mainstay on the London stage. Although titled an opera, the work is actually a spoken play augmented with **pastiche** songs, that is, well-known melodies set to new words. Characters came from the underbelly of society: thieves, convicts, whores. The plot satirized Italian opera and ridiculed the city's politicians and public figures. *The Beggar's Opera* spawned a new genre (the ballad opera) and paved the way for English operetta. Weill and Brecht used a darker version of Gay's plot for their *Threepenny Opera*.

QUESTIONS FOR THOUGHT

■ Select a song by Berlin, Porter, or Gershwin and investigate its history. Who recorded it? In what genres? Does the song appear in any movies? On stage? Is the song still performed today? Why or why not?

West Side Story (1957)

Moving to the rhythmic inflections of jazz and Latin America, members of two rival gangs prowl the reaches of Manhattan's West Side. They keep their center of gravity low, as if drawing in sustenance from the earth. Occasionally, frustrations seem to boil over as figures leap upward in liberating, gravity-defying balletic movements. Sometimes the gangs' paths intersect. The foes posture and threaten; violence seems imminent. But then, like wind-blown leaves, they disperse.

West Side Story begins not with a song or clarifying dialogue. The voice of reason is silent. Instead, we are confronted by the angular and feral muscularity of movement.

The gangs—one Anglo, the other Latino—are strangely bound. They hate each other but move to the same music. They also share the same mean streets and derelict playgrounds. Lost in parallel cycles of poverty and hopelessness, it seems as if these street toughs hate for no better reason than the invigorating power of hate itself.

The Russian playwright Anton Chekhov (1860–1904) once noted that if you hang a shotgun on the wall at the beginning of a story, someone has to get shot. Applying Chekhov's axiom to the opening scene of *West Side Story*, we know this for certain: blood will flow; people will die. This being Broadway, some will also fall in love.

Perhaps the storyline sounds familiar. *West Side Story* is an updating of Shakespeare's *Romeo and Juliet*. Gangs of Jets and Sharks

Leonard Bernstein, working on a score in his apartment, c. 1946.

West Side Story	Romeo and Juliet
• The street	• A public place
• Officer Krupke intercedes.	• The Duke intercedes.
• Backyard—Tony sings "Something's Coming."	• Party preparation at the Capulet home; Juliet meets Paris.
• Bridal shop; Maria and Anita	• Capulet home
• Dance at the gym	• Capulet's party
• Balcony scene	• Balcony scene
• The drugstore	• Friar Lawrence's cell
• Bernardo, Maria's brother, kills Tony's buddy Riff.	• Tybalt, Juliet's cousin, kills Romeo's friend Mercutio.
• Tony kills Bernardo.	• Romeo kills Tybalt.
• Tony sleeps with Maria.	• Romeo sleeps with Juliet.
• Tony is told that Maria is dead. But that is not true.	• Juliet takes sleeping potion to feign death.
• Tony roams the streets hoping to be gunned down. Just as he finds Maria alive, Chino shoots him.	• Romeo arrives at Juliet's grave. Thinking her dead, he poisons himself.
• Maria chooses life.	• Juliet stabs herself.

replace families of Montagues and Capulets. Tony is our Romeo; Maria is our Juliet. When they meet at a gym dance, love is instantaneous.

As originally conceived in 1949 by playwright Arthur Laurents (b. 1918) and director/choreographer Jerome Robbins (1918–1998), the show was to be set in Manhattan's Lower East Side. The love interest paired an Irish Catholic with a Jew, a classic Broadway formula of socially unacceptable interaction.

But while religion provided the explosive chemistry of earlier American times, its power to alienate had lessened by the mid-twentieth century. It was decided to move the setting across town and north where social tensions were on the rise as a result of the recent influx of Puerto Rican immigrants. Not only did the stereotype of hot-blooded Latinos seem to offer a more compelling storyline, but it also invited a musical score filled with the rhythmic inflections of Latin jazz. Leonard Bernstein composed the music; Sondheim wrote the lyrics.

Dramatically, the show is tightly knit. In this sense, it is perhaps even more dramatically effective than Shakespeare's original. Here is how:

- It's more concise. The entire story—first love to death—unfolds in less than 24 hours.

- At story's opening, Tony has broken free of the Jets, his old gang. He is on the way to becoming his own man. Tony is drawn back in as a favor to old comrades, and just for a night. Fidelity to a false ideal leads to his destruction.
- The Jets are responsible for the confusion that leads to Tony's death.
- Unlike Juliet, Maria rises above the hatred that surrounds her. She chooses to live.

We will study the great Quintet that forms the second section of the three-part ensemble finale to Act I. Part one of the finale begins intimately. Tony and Maria are alone together and make wedding vows during which they sing "One Hand, One Heart." Part three is all action. A rumble unfolds during which Bernardo kills Tony's friend Riff and Tony kills Bernardo, Maria's brother.

Sandwiched in between is the Quintet, which pits Sharks against Jets, allows Tony and Maria to sing of their unfolding love, and spotlights the icy Anita anticipating a hot-love rendezvous that will never happen. All sing about what they most desire. The Sharks and Jets sing of revenge. Tony and Maria sing of their love. Anita sings of carnal bliss. Tying the various actors together is the element of immediacy. All want their satisfaction "tonight."

MUSICAL THEMES

THE ENSEMBLE FINALE

Bernstein borrowed the ensemble finale from a convention that developed in early eighteenth-century comic opera and which was exploited with great success by Wolfgang Amadeus Mozart. Librettists would devise scenarios that required all the main characters to be on stage together. The composer would then take the opportunity to (1) show his skill in manipulating multiple sets of music simultaneously, and (2) provide a rousing conclusion to the act.

LISTENING GUIDE

CD IV/Track 2
Download track 53
mysearchlab 10.5

QUINTET, FINALE TO ACT I FROM *WEST SIDE STORY*

0:00	SECTION A: The Quintet opens with the instrumental sounds of a world in disorder. Brass and percussion riffs explode in flashes of dissonance and belligerence. Aggression rules. In the bass line we hear a three-note ostinato. These triple groupings jar against a duple feel in the brass and percussion. Adding to the tension, the brass instruments and bass play in different keys.
0:06	*Jets* "The Jets are gonna have. . . ." Notice the alliteration with the growling "r" repetitions.
0:22	*Sharks* ". . . gonna hand' em a surprise. . . ." New ostinato rhythm. The Sharks's "Tonight" both closes the first section and opens the door for the Jets to begin a new section that is shorter (three lines instead of eight/nine) and more exuberant. Notice Sondheim's word play: the Jets "rock it" and the hungry Sharks "get it."
0:39	*Jets* (one verse); *Sharks* (one verse)
0:51	The interaction builds as the two gangs shout accusations, oblivious that the other gang (through the musical form) is "listening." Finally, they shout in unison.
0:58	SECTION A¹: The musical texture is similar to the opening, but the orchestration is lighter and sounds less aggressive. Tones slide sensually up and down. Whereas the opening was gang tough, this section sounds more like tough love. Now we hear Anita, who is going to "get her kicks tonight." She maintains the Sharks's nine-line format. Presumably, she does so for two reasons. First, Anita is Bernardo's lover, so she follows the Sharks's verse pattern. Second, the end of her lines acts as a transition. As before, the refrain "Tonight!" serves as a hand-off, this time to Tony and Maria. Now, however, the baton-pass is more graceful. For brief moments, Anita and Tony have hold of "tonight."
1:19	SECTION B: Tony and Maria reprise their song from earlier in the act. Now "tonight" reveals the possibilities of first love, first passion. Yet there is trouble hidden in the words. The morning star they sing of is Venus, the planet of love. But Tony will not live to see the dawn. Sondheim plays with concepts of time. Tony longs for a night in which time might stop; Maria begs the endless day to hurry up and finish. Contrast Tony's melody line with Maria's. His is grounded in strong scale degrees; the melodic intervals are relatively wide. Perhaps this is indicative of his masculinity.

(Continued)

LISTENING GUIDE (*Continued*)

2:10	SECTION A: Following Maria's verse, Bernstein writes an orchestral climax of brass and pounding timpani. The romantic reverie is interrupted by the return of the Quintet's percussive opening. Perhaps this material felt exciting on first hearing. Now, however, juxtaposed against Maria's dreams, it has explosive nastiness.
2:27	SECTIONS B, A, AND A¹ TOGETHER: Maria sings of love as the Jets posture in the background. Bernstein is starting to lay contrasting sections on top of each other. We can enjoy this layering in two ways. First, we see it from "inside" the play. Bernstein is showing us important relationships within the story, reminding us how everything is interwoven. Second, we can enjoy it from "outside" the play, that is, from a technical point of view. Bernstein is about to show off his compositional skill. He adds lines and complexities like a juggler who, although already having an impossible number of balls in the air, keeps adding more. Earlier the Jets were "gonna rock it" and "jazz it." The Sharks and Anita were "gonna get it." Sondheim is intertwining lyrics as well.

MUSICAL THEMES

LINCOLN CENTER: ANOTHER WEST SIDE STORY

New York's Lincoln Center for the Performing Arts.

Bernstein's Sharks and Jets are fictional, but the rough West Side neighborhood they inhabited was real. Once a working-class African American community, by the 1950s Manhattan's "San Juan Hill/Lincoln Square area," as it was known, was comprised of crowded, run-down tenements. Its residents dealt with ever-present racial and ethnic tensions. When NYC officials declared the neighborhood a slum, extensive urban renewal ensued. Now situated on more than 16 acres of old San Juan Hill is The Lincoln Center for the Performing Arts, one of the world's most important performance complexes. Theaters, concert halls, opera houses, and lecture halls provide performance space for resident groups such as the New York Philharmonic, the Metropolitan Opera, and the New York City Ballet, as well as theater groups, chamber ensembles, jazz groups, cinema, and students of The Juilliard School and the School of American Ballet. Ground was broken in 1959. The last concert hall was completed 10 years later. Construction halted briefly to accommodate the filming of *West Side Story*.

QUESTIONS FOR THOUGHT

■ Gang violence is far more prevalent today than in 1957. It is also far more deadly. How would a musical about today's gangs differ from *West Side Story*? What kind of music might be used?

Stephen Sondheim

Following *West Side Story*, Sondheim received an appointment as lyricist for composer Jule Styne's *Gypsy*, which featured Ethel Merman

(1908–1984) portraying Mama Rose, show business's most fanatical stage mother and arguably American musical theater's greatest female role. Perhaps Sondheim drew from his own dysfunctional childhood when writing for Rose—his father abandoned the family when Stephen was just 10 years old; his mother was emotionally abusive. At any rate, Rose was the first of many overbearing females to populate Sondheim musicals. Consider the lyrics from "Everything's Coming Up Roses," the rousing finale of *Gypsy*'s first act. Mama Rose may want her daughter to succeed, but even more (as the final line suggests), she seeks vindication for herself.

With *A Funny Thing Happened on the Way to the Forum* (1962) Sondheim made his debut as both lyricist and composer. Thus began a string of more than a dozen musicals, each of which broke new ground in terms of style and content. The theme of love—most often quick trysts and infidelities—runs through Sondheim's work. Lacking a story-line altogether (perhaps Sondheim's theatrical metaphor for the one-night stand) is *Company* (1970, revived in 2006). *Company* explores the superficial love life of the confirmed bachelor Bobby, as witnessed through the eyes of his not very helpful married friends. Marriage has rarely looked so uninviting.

A Little Night Music (1973) is a modern take on nineteenth-century European operetta. It is written almost completely in the triple meter of the waltz and features an entire cast involved in tangled and misguided love affairs across generations and social classes. Only the innocent prepubescents and wise aged are spared love's foibles.

Into the Woods (1987) draws from a catalog of children's fairy tales. Two characters could be drawn from Sondheim's own biography: a spell-casting witch of a mother and a young man trying to reconcile himself with the father who abandoned him. Also included in the cast are unfaithful princes, a libidinous wolf, a confused Cinderella, and a slightly loony Rapunzel.

The 1960s and Forward: Broadway Searches for a New Voice

As it turned out, *West Side Story*'s Maria and *Gypsy*'s Mama Rose were just the first of a decade's worth of strong women to populate the Broadway stage. Soon to follow were the entrepreneurial Dolly Levy (*Hello Dolly!*, 1964), the willful Fanny Brice (*Funny Girl*), Tevye's strong-minded daughters (*Fiddler on the Roof*, 1964), and the flamboyant Mame (*Mame*, 1966).

In addition to the theatrical rise of women (which paralleled the emerging women's movement in real life) the social upheavals of the 1960s also had their effect on Broadway. As the turbulent decade unfolded, producers wondered what kinds of music and stories would bring the next generation of patrons into the theaters. Some thought the answer might be hippies and rock 'n' roll. *Hair: The American Tribal Love-Rock Musical*, in which the show's characters let their hair hang down while searching for their identities, opened in 1968. The off-Broadway nude musical show *Oh, Calcutta* (1969) focused primarily on letting it *all* hang out. Skits were provided by The Beatles's John Lennon (1940–1980) and other pop music icons.

All in all, however, rock musicals have been pretty tame affairs. Andrew Lloyd Webber (b. 1948) would have his first hit with *Jesus Christ Superstar* (1971), which helped usher rock music into the Christian church. Webber followed the success of *Superstar* with another biblical rock musical, *Joseph and the Amazing Technicolor Dreamcoat* (1973). Opening around the same time were *Grease* (1972) and *The Wiz* (1975), a retelling of *The Wizard of Oz*.

The 1980s were powered by a pair of blockbuster productions: Claude-Michel Schönberg's (b. 1944) *Les Misérables* (1980, adapted from a novel by Victor Hugo, 1802–1885) and Andrew Lloyd Webber's *The Phantom of the Opera* (1986, adapted from a novel by Gaston Leroux, 1868–1927). These shows continue to fill theaters worldwide.

A trio of rock musicals were major successes in the late 1990s—*Rent* (1996), *Hedwig and the Angry Inch* (1998), and *Mamma Mia!* (1999), which featured music by the Swedish group ABBA. *Rent* drew inspiration from *La bohème*, an 1896 opera by Italian composer Giacomo Puccini. Set in Paris, *La bohème* told the story of young Bohemian artists living hand-to-mouth as they struggled to find their way in a world decimated by tuberculosis. *Rent* picks up the same themes but sets the story in New York City's East Village, where lives are destroyed by AIDS. Composer Jonathan Larson (1960–1996), who lived in Greenwich Village and wrote *Rent* while earning his living as a waiter, drew his inspiration from a world he knew well. He died of an aortic aneurysm while the show was still in previews.

CONCLUSION

What will be Broadway's future? Because the expense of mounting a show is so great, the recent trend has been to go with proven winners, either revivals of past hits or adaptations of successful movies, such as *The Lion King* (1997); *The Little Mermaid* (2007); *Legally Blonde the Musical* (2007); and *Shrek the Musical* (2008).

There are exceptions, of course. A recently premiered original production is composer/lyricist Lin-Manuel Miranda's (b. 1980) *In the Heights* (2008). The show presented a musical collage of ethnic life in New York City's Washington Heights neighborhood. In spirit, it is a return to New York's early theatrical days when shows' narratives often featured the vibrant and diverse lives of the city's own.

And Broadway will always surprise. Consider the music and dance review *FELA!* (2009).

One has to assume that never in his wildest spliff-inspired dreams did Nigerian pop superstar Fela Anikulapo Kuti (1938–1997) expect his life and art to be the stuff of Broadway theater. The iconoclast creator of the funk-inflected Afro-beat style, gadfly to Nigeria's corrupt politicians, and polygamist (he married 27 women in a single ceremony) spent his life rebelling against the constricting bonds of social norms).

FELA! is set in the Afrika Shrine, the Lagos-based nightclub in which the musician and his band, Africa 70, held residency for much of the 1970s. Fela's audiences included all types—drug dealers and prostitutes, college students, foreign dignitaries, and rock stars. Nigerian officials, who persecuted Fela from the halls of government by day, arrived by limousine to listen by night.

All of the show's music is Fela's own. The sound of his band has been meticulously duplicated, although song lengths are abbreviated to fit American tastes. While lyrics are almost invariably political, their bite is softened by hearing them in a context far removed from the hard realities of Nigerian life. Perhaps two decades of hip-hop invective has also anesthetized Americans to Fela's pointed language.

Fela cast his barbs in many directions. When they hit their mark reactions were sometimes violent. Consider the song "Zombie" (1976), a scathing dance-groove protest against Nigerian soldiers, and by extension Nigeria's then military dictatorship. The song may have in part inspired a 1977 government raid on Fela's compound, his self-declared independent Kalakuta [Rascal] Republic. The men were beaten; many of the women were raped, and the compound was burned. "Zombie" becomes a major dance number in the Broadway production.

Perhaps featuring the African political revolutionary Fela Kuti helped prepare Broadway for a musical revolution of its own: punk rock. Until now rock 'n' roll on Broadway has mostly kept its shirt tucked in and its hair combed, albeit greased. Not with *American Idiot* (2010), a driving punk-rock opera about suburban teen angst. Music is drawn from the raucous music of the punk band Green Day. Bored and restless, the show's teenaged characters embark on an elusive search for meaning in New York City.

Do these shows represent new directions for Broadway or more nostalgia, albeit in racy packaging? Time will tell. At any rate, both *FELA!* and *American Idiot* are drawing younger and more diverse audiences into the theaters. That is good news for the art form.

श्री जगन्नाथ फिल्मस प्रा लि कृत

सईंया से सोलह सिंगार

CHAPTER GOALS

- To explore ways that music communicates cinematic characters, action, mood, and emotion.

- To provide a brief overview of the history of music in film.

QUESTIONS FOR THOUGHT

- Think of a favorite movie. Can you remember the musical score? Why or why not?
- Watch a movie scene with the sound turned off. Now watch it again with sound. How is the experience different?
- What kind of music would you use in a movie about your life? Would you use any specific styles or songs?
- You are a film composer assigned to write a score for a love scene. What style of music will you compose? What instruments will you use? What type of music would you compose for a car chase?
- Choose two friends and assign them theme songs. What influenced your choices?

> "I've always tried to subordinate myself to the picture. A lot of composers make the mistake of thinking that the film is a platform for showing how clever they are. This is not the place for it."
>
> —Max Steiner
> (1888–1971)

Come summertime, the Hatch Shell on the Boston Esplanade is a busy place for music. With fair weather, the annual Fourth of July celebration with the Boston Pops can attract 400,000 people. Millions more watch the event on television. Along the shell's stone façade are inscribed the names of the luminaries of Western art music: Bach and Beethoven, Mozart and Haydn, Copland and Williams. For Bostonians, film composer extraordinaire John Williams (b. 1932) has earned a place among music's immortals.

Most film composers live their creative lives in relative anonymity. Their music is widely heard, but few theatergoers know their names. In this chapter, we move cinema music from background to foreground and explore the complex relationships between music and film. In particular, we study the ways in which film music is specifically designed to represent, enhance, and clarify the social experience unfolding on screen. We begin by studying the flying scene from Williams's *E.T.: The Extra-Terrestrial* (1982), then gradually weave our way forward chronologically from film's origins to the recent past. Along the way we investigate musical scenes from select iconic films, including *Metropolis* (1927), *Cabin in the Sky* (1943), *The Day the Earth Stood Still* (1951), *The Hidden Fortress* (1957), and *The Lord of the Rings* (2001–2003) trilogy. Each film offers rich insights into the social times in which it was created.

MUSICAL LIVES

JOHN WILLIAMS (b. 1932)

Born in New York City, Williams spent his youth in Los Angeles where he eventually attended UCLA. After serving in the Air Force, Williams returned to New York to attend The Juilliard School. In the 1950s Williams began writing music for television, earning four Emmy Awards. His film scores include, among many others, music for *The Poseidon Adventure* (1972), *The Towering Inferno* (1974), *Jaws* (1975), the *Star Wars* series (1977–2005), the *Indiana Jones* series (1981–2008), the first three *Harry Potter* movies (2001–2004), and many others. Williams has composed music for over 100 films. He has won five Academy Awards, 20 Grammy Awards, and four Golden Globe Awards. His commissions include themes for four Olympic Games as well as the *NBC Nightly News*. Williams served as music director of the Boston Pops Orchestra from 1980 to 1993. He holds honorary degrees from 21 American universities.

Narrative Film: The Sounds of Science Fiction and the Modern World

E.T.: The Extra-Terrestrial (1982)

Police vehicles block the road; the chase is over. E.T.'s capture appears certain. Suddenly the bicyclists lift into the sky. E.T. is going home after all.

In one of cinema's most inspired moments we are reminded that kids can be right, and grownups can be wrong. Maybe we even learn that magic can be real. Credit the visual conjuring to film director Steven Spielberg (b. 1946). But if you watch with ears wide open, it feels as if the power of flight is provided by the swirling, leaping string melodies of John Williams. Such is music's command.

Music is an essential part of the cinematic experience. Soundtracks intensify emotion, provide structure, and help viewers make connections. But soundtracks do this work furtively. Often, we are only dimly conscious of music's presence.

The E.T. chase pits boys on bikes against men in cars. Outgunned and out-horse powered, the kids furiously pedal up neighborhood streets and barrel down hills. Their getaway is accompanied by the sounds of squealing tires, racing engines, clattering bikes, and choppy dialogue. These are the film's **diegetic** sounds, that is, the sounds of the world inhabited by the film's characters.

Inaudible to those characters is the non-diegetic music of Williams's orchestral score. The music is irregular and peripatetic, like the chase scene it enhances. Short brass fanfares echo the children's noble desire to save E.T.; propulsive rhythms keep the tension high. As events become more desperate, Elliott and his friends split up. Musical ideas seem to break apart as well. They crystallize and disintegrate with virtually every camera change.

Midway through the chase, E.T.'s face momentarily fills the screen. Williams's music follows the visual. Sounds seem to slow down, then expand. The shift provides a momentary reduction in musical tension, a chance to catch our breath. But it also foreshadows the escape to come. The melody, with its opening octave leap upward, tells us a secret the desperate boys cannot fathom: E.T. has a plan.

The chase continues. Momentarily, the boys have dodged the police. They think they have escaped. Suddenly, however, the road is blocked, and capture is imminent. Once again, the camera presents a close-up of E.T.; the music holds a drawn-out chord. Action is suspended. Have the boys been caught? Is E.T. doomed?

As the "flying" theme sounds, the bikes lift skyward. Tension is replaced with wonder, restraint with freedom. The film's diegetic world is mostly silent. Even the boys seem to live in the magic of Williams's soundscape. We watch and listen and marvel.

LISTENING GUIDE

E.T.: THE EXTRA-TERRESTRIAL, FLYING SCENE

You can find this scene on the DVD or on the Internet; excerpt begins at 1:43:08 in the DVD.

1:43:08	The boys begin their escape. In the score, rhythmic string figures are punctuated by a series of repeated fanfare-like motives in the brass instruments. (Notice how neatly the police siren fits in between the brass themes.)
1:43:46	The boys go off-road and glide downhill. Choppy figures occur in the brass. Musical ideas shift even more quickly.
1:44:20	Rhythmic ostinati appear in the high strings and shortly after the brass fanfares return.
1:44:33	The camera focuses on E.T.'s face. The "flying" theme is heard.

(Continued)

LISTENING GUIDE (Continued)

1:44:42	More chasing. We hear new brass figures, which will later form a secondary thematic idea in the flying section.
1:45:30	A drawn-out chord occurs. E.T.'s future hangs in the balance.
1:45:34	The boys and bicycles lift off. Strings move to the foreground as the flying theme sounds.
1:46:24	The boys return to Earth. Listen as Williams "lands" the children with his descending major scale—do-ti-la-sol-fa-mi-re-do.

QUESTIONS FOR THOUGHT

- Does listening to the flying theme trigger any other emotional cues for you?
- Think about the following musical sounds: a harp, a marching band, a jazz solo. What might each of these sounds represent in our culture? How might a film composer use them to communicate characters, moods, or settings?
- What does the *E.T.* story suggest about our social order and values? How does Williams's music for the chase scene reflect the movie's moral stand?

ASSIGNMENTS AND ACTIVITIES

- Once music and flight are connected, the link is super-glue inseparable. Think of other film music that inspires strong imagery.
- Have someone play short clips of well-known movie scores or television theme songs. Can you identify the movie or show? Even a specific scene? How does music reflect, even enhance, the movie's or show's social character? Can you identify the music's composer?
- Recall the opening octave upward leap in Arlen's "Over the Rainbow" (chapter 3: Three Listening Examples). Compare and contrast that song's melodic shape and emotional imagery with Williams's "flying" theme.
- Listen to the orchestral suite *The Planets* (1916) by British composer Gustav Holst (1874–1934). Compare Holst's early twentieth-century symphonic portrayal of outer space with Williams's score for *E.T.* Keep Holst and Williams in mind when later in the chapter we discuss Bernard Herrmann's (1911–1975) iconic score for *The Day the Earth Stood Still*.

Early Film

The first publicly screened motion pictures appeared at the end of the nineteenth century. Silent and short, the films were novelties offered as part of bigger theatrical entertainment packages featuring live comedy routines, music, and dance. Theater managers soon discovered they could use music to mask the distracting noise made by primitive projection systems. Music also seemed to add emotional warmth to the ghostly black-and-white on-screen images. Curiously, music seemed to make film more "real," perhaps through the medium's power to engage emotions.

Of course, it was also helpful if the musical emotions fit the film's narrative. Accordingly, silent films were soon released with musical cue sheets. These earliest "soundtracks" drew freely from a standard repertory of melodies that audiences were sure to recognize. Sometimes the score was written out, but usually it was improvised on organ or piano. The first major American movie to be fitted with a full orchestral score was director D. W. Griffith's racially incendiary saga *The Birth of a Nation* (1916). Much of the music, composed by Joseph Carl Breil (1870–1926), was original.

The Jazz Singer (1927)

Music itself was the focus of *The Jazz Singer*, cinema's first feature-length "talkie." The film was adapted from a successful Broadway stage show and starred the popular **blackface** entertainer Al Jolson. The score was a musical grab bag that included popular songs, traditional Jewish sacred melodies, and classical music.

The film's protagonist is Jack Robin. Born and raised on New York City's Lower East Side, Jack is the son of a Jewish cantor. His father wants him to follow the family tradition and sing in temple. But Jack dreams of a life on Broadway. The two argue and Jack, still a boy, runs away. Over the succeeding years, Jack breaks from his ethnic and cultural heritage and experiments with new ones. He changes his name (from Jakie Rabinowitz to Jack Robin), falls in love with a gentile woman, and becomes a jazz singer. In spite of all, father and son ultimately reconcile. The movie concludes with Jack forsaking his Broadway debut to sing "Kol Nidre" in his father's place for Yom Kippur, the most sacred of the Jewish high holidays (see chapter 6: Music and Spirituality).

Similar stories portraying the complex issues surrounding ethnic identity and the pressures to culturally assimilate had long

| Poster for the film *The Jazz Singer*, 1927.

been popular on the American stage. *The Jazz Singer*, however, struck a pressure point. The film was remade three times. A 1952 version starred Danny Thomas (1912–1991); a 1959 made-for-television version featured Jerry Lewis (b. 1926); a 1980 version cast Neil Diamond (b. 1941). Other movies that follow a similar storyline of a musician from an ethnic minority assimilating into mainstream American culture include *The Benny Goodman Story* (1955) and *La Bamba* (1987), the story of pop star Ritchie Valens (1941–1959).

MUSICAL THEMES

COMPOSING A FILM SCORE: STEP BY STEP

The composer's job is to serve and enhance the film's narrative. After initially "screening" the film, the composer, along with the director and perhaps others, begins the **"spotting"** process in which initial decisions are made about where music should sound. Each such musical insertion is called a "cue." A cue might last just seconds, or even minutes. Generally, the composer and director will work together to develop a general concept for the entire score. Often stylistically appropriate models, called "temp tracks," are borrowed from preexisting music and used as musical placeholders to establish a temporary feeling for the scene. As the composing gets underway, particular ideas, actions, or characters are often linked with specific melodies, rhythms, or instrumental textures. These leitmotives, or leading motives, as they are called (see chapter 5: Music and Gender), are used to tie the film's narrative together.

Composers today often write only the piano score, then rely on a team of "orchestrators" to arrange the music for additional instruments. Because musical timings must be exact, recording is typically done with a conductor leading the instrumentalists while watching the actual film footage. In a process called ADR (automated dialogue replacement), basic dialogue is often dubbed in after the filming is completed. This process is particularly common when singing is involved.

The director and composer work closely together, often forming strong relationships that continue beyond the initial film project. Long-term director-composer teams include Alfred Hitchcock (1899–1980) and Bernard Herrmann, Steven Spielberg and John Williams, and Tim Burton (b. 1958) and Danny Elfman (b. 1953).

Metropolis (1927)

German director Fritz Lang's silent-film classic *Metropolis* presents a dystopian urban future that pits poor against rich, humanity against machine.

The story takes place in 2026. Deep beneath the city's skyscrapers live the numbed laborers who endlessly maintain the giant engines that run the city. Living high above in their pleasure gardens are the elite few who benefit from the work below. Added to the mix is a maniacal *Machinenmensch* (human machine). Human in appearance, the robot wreaks destruction across all levels of society.

DID YOU KNOW?

ANOTHER VERSION

In 1984, Italian record producer Giorgio Moroder created an 80-minute version of *Metropolis* using music by Pat Benatar, Adam Ant, Freddy Mercury, and others. The Internet features a number of *Metropolis* clips refitted with contemporary soundtracks.

The mostly original score was conceived by German composer Gottfried Huppertz (1887–1937), who conducted a live orchestra at the Berlin premiere. Huppertz called for thick sound textures heavy with brass instruments. Rhythms drive; harmonies grate. We examine the first few minutes of the score, which begins near the conclusion of the film's opening credits.

LISTENING GUIDE

mysearchlab 11.1

METROPOLIS, OPENING

1:40	The music commences in grandiose style, with the ascending brass tones of a gigantic fanfare. Timpani pound as the music begins a long cadence coinciding with the geometric on-screen presentation of the film's title. As the title dissolves into a vast city skyline, humanity's glorious technological future is implied in both sight and sound.
2:29	Then we see the gears and wheels, driving pistons and billowing steam of the enormous machines that allow the city to run. Wheels spin and pistons pump. Their visual power is seductive, a seeming testament to humankind's ingenuity. What to make of all this mechanical muscle? The music tells us. Contrasting rhythms and textures agitate one against the other, like bullies restlessly pushing their way down a sidewalk. Each melody is displaced by another as the camera pans across the mechanical images.
2:52	Listen to the ominous pulsing of clarinet and bell. The sound is tied to the seconds ticking away on a 10-hour clock, the duration of the workers' shifts. This is a world tied to labor, not the natural cycles of nature. The rhythmic energy gradually breaks apart. As the whistle blows, we see rows of deflated workers changing shifts.
3:18	Brutalized by the machines they serve, the workers stand zombie-like. Heads down, they trudge to and from the elevators that connect their underground quarters to the machines above. Now we hear a group of themes, all of which signify the dull misery of the laborers' underground existence. Theme 1 3:26: A dreary string melody Theme 2 3:45: A pair of descending scales Theme 3 4:10: A simple melody sounded in the brass and echoed in the strings

Time and again these various leitmotives reappear in the movie. Each repetition intensifies the film's emotional content while helping to connect scenes separated by time and place.

Huppertz also used previously composed music, carefully chosen to stir strong emotions. "La Marseillaise," the French national anthem (see chapter 7: Music and Politics), was used during the workers' revolt. The Catholic funeral chant "Dies Irae" is heard when Death dances with the statues of the Seven Deadly Sins.

MUSICAL THEMES
MUSIC AND MACHINE

Composers have long been fascinated by the possibilities of representing machines through music. In the early twentieth century, some attempted to wed music to the sounds of industrialization. Music of the future would be "the music of noise," claimed Italian composer Luigi Russolo (1885–1947). Russolo and other Futurists encouraged colleagues to fill their scores with sounds of pots and pans, rattling sheets of metal, typewriters, and car horns. In the 1950s and 1960s, composers experimented with electronically produced sounds to portray futuristic worlds. The soundtrack for the sci-fi classic *Forbidden Planet* (1956), composed by Louis (1920–1989) and Bebe Barron (1925–2008), features a score filled with bleeps, whirs, and a variety of other-worldly sounds.

Hollywood's Golden Era

Many thought "talkies" would mark the end of music for film. After all, what need would there be for musical filler now that pictures spoke? For a brief period, music was mostly abandoned. The exceptions were opening credits (where music functioned like an overture) and when musicians were performing diegetically within the film's narrative. Between 1927 and 1930, over 22,000 theater musicians across the country lost their jobs.

It soon became clear, however, that audiences wanted music in their entertainment mix. Academy Award winner *The Broadway Melody* (1929) was the first feature-length movie to fully integrate music, dance, and plot. It also heralded an exodus of artists from the stages of New York City to more lucrative opportunities in Hollywood. Thus began the "Golden Age" of movie musicals, which lasted from the 1930s to the early 1950s. Its stars were many and included the ever-boyish Mickey Rooney (b. 1920), the hipster Frank Sinatra (1915–1998), the sexy comedienne Marilyn Monroe (1926–1962), and Olympic swimmer Esther Williams (b. 1921), who performed many of her "dance" routines underwater.

MUSICAL LIVES
NEW YORK TO HOLLYWOOD

Three of the greatest Golden Age film composers were Max Steiner, Dimitri Tiomkin (1894–1979), and Alfred Newman (1900–1970). All three left New York City for Hollywood.

Steiner, an Austrian who studied piano with German composer Johannes Brahms (1833–1897), came to the United States in 1914 and worked on Broadway as an arranger and conductor. He moved to Hollywood in 1929 and worked primarily for Warner Brothers. A gifted melodist, Steiner pioneered the use of original music in film. He scored over 300 films, including *King Kong* (1933) and *Gone with the Wind* (1939). Steiner received 26 Academy Award nominations and won three Oscars.

Tiomkin began his career in St. Petersburg, Russia, as a silent-film pianist. He came to New York City in 1925 and four years later moved to Hollywood, where he wrote music for about 125 films. Tiomkin

(Continued)

MUSICAL LIVES (Continued)

is remembered for his scores to *Lost Horizon* (1937) and his long association with Frank Capra, which included the films *Mr. Smith Goes to Washington* (1939) and *It's a Wonderful Life* (1946). Tiomkin won four Academy Awards.

Newman, an American from Connecticut, began his performing career in vaudeville at the age of 13. Five years later he was conducting Broadway shows. In 1930 Newman moved to Hollywood where for 21 years he served as general music director at 20th Century Fox. Newman scored over 200 films and won nine Academy Awards. He also wrote the theme music for the popular television show *Rawhide* (1959–1966).

Then as now, audiences loved spectacle. The choreography of Busby Berkeley (1895–1976) added titillation to the cinematic mix. His dance routines featured phalanxes of scantily clad women moving with drill-team precision. Berkeley's film *Whoopee!* (1930) helped launch the dance musical. Hard-pressed Depression-era patrons flocked to the choreographer's upbeat films, including *42nd Street*, *Footlight Parade*, and *Gold Diggers of 1933*, all released with domino inevitability in a single year.

Equally well received was the work of dance legend Fred Astaire (1899–1987). Astaire teamed up with Ginger Rogers (1911–1995) in 10 films, including *The Gay Divorcee* (1934) and *Top Hat* (1935). The duo attracted the period's finest songwriters, including Irving Berlin, Cole Porter, and George Gershwin.

mysearchlab 11.2

The end of the decade saw the release of *The Wizard of Oz* (1939), one of Hollywood's most enduring movie musicals.

QUESTIONS FOR THOUGHT

- Are there musical movie stars today whose careers might compare to Fred Astaire, Marilyn Monroe, or Judy Garland?
- Are there movies today that incorporate music, dance, plot, and spectacle in the same way as those of Hollywood's Golden Age?

Cabin in the Sky (1943)

Up through World War II, American film had parallel industries. One was marketed to whites, the other to African Americans. The latter were known as "race films." A great many race films featured African American musicians in leading roles.

One such film was *Cabin in the Sky*, a Broadway musical made into a movie directed

Poster for the original release of *Cabin in the Sky*, 1943.

by Vincente Minnelli (1903–1986). Along with comedian Eddie Anderson (1905–1977), *Cabin* featured some of the era's greatest musical entertainers, including vocalists Ethel Waters (1896–1977) and Lena Horne (1917–2010), trumpeter Louis Armstrong (1901–1971), band leader Duke Ellington, and dancers John "Bubbles" Sublett (1902–1986) and Bill Bailey (1912–1978).

Cabin tells the story of "Little Joe" Jackson (Anderson), a gentle-spirited backslider who, having strayed one time too many from the straight and narrow, is mortally wounded during a fight. Though slated for an afterlife in hell, the prayers of his loving wife Petunia (Waters) reach the gates of heaven. Joe is given a second chance at life and redemption.

Cabin was filmed during World War II (1939–1945), an important time in American race relations. Overseas, African American regiments in the segregated American armed forces were distinguishing themselves in combat. Here at home, both the Roosevelt Administration and the NAACP were pressuring Hollywood to create more substantial roles for black actors. *Cabin in the Sky* was supposed to help break black/white barriers.

That was the idea, anyhow. In fact, the film was a stew of the usual racial stereotypes. The story was set within a hodge-podge of clumsy oppositions: rural versus urban, virtue versus vice, fidelity versus infidelity, folk music versus jazz. Heaven's forces wear white, Satan's minions wear black. Scenes alternated between plantation-style "darkie" locations on the one hand and highly sexualized nightclub life on the other. Presumably, sticking to the former gets one to heaven; the latter earns a ticket to hell.

The film's many musical numbers generally accentuate these stereotypes, such as when dancers strut and swing to the Ellington orchestra's pulsing rendition of "Things Ain't What They Used to Be." But when the band switches to the strikingly named tune "Goin' Up," stereotypes briefly falter. The mood feels like a religious revival. Dancers stand transfixed as trombonist Lawrence Brown (1907–1988) plays like the angel Gabriel himself. When the dancing continues, the mood combines secular frenzy with quasi-religious ecstasy.

We study an earlier moment in the film, when Waters is featured in the song "Taking a Chance on Love." **mysearchlab 11.3** Little Joe has just given Petunia a washing machine for her birthday. When Petunia starts to cry from joy, Little Joe picks up a guitar, whistles an introduction, and Petunia starts to sing. The nondiegetic sounds of a jazz big band mysteriously appear in the background.

The song is set in a straightforward 32-bar song form. Neatly symmetrical, the performance goes through the 32-bar cycle four times. Waters is featured in the first two cycles. Her lyrics are clever, full of inner rhymes and one-line refrains. In the next 32 bars, Bailey adds physicality as he dances and moonwalks his way through the cycle. In the final 32 bars, Anderson calms things down with a comedic soft-shoe routine that includes accidentally

sitting on the stove and then jumping into the sink to cool off.

Throughout Anderson's routine, Waters vocalizes a lovely countermelody. At first, her tone is sweet and gentle. Then it becomes rough, sensual, and jazz inflected. It is a sound well within Waters's stylistic range, but not the churchy Petunia's. Little Joe is shocked, and maybe even a little intimidated, by his wife's sudden display. He gets her to stop singing. The song ends.

QUESTIONS FOR THOUGHT

- How does film create and maintain the distinction between character and actor? What role does music play in this?
- What conditions are necessary for an actor to reside invisibly with his character? Does Elvis Presley or Eddie Murphy ever disappear completely within his character? What about Madonna?
- Does music in film still portray race in such stark contrasts? Give examples for or against.

Post World War II

War's end brought America a new worldliness and confidence. This can be seen in a variety of post-war films. *On the Town* (1949), with music by Leonard Bernstein (1918–1990) and Roger Edens (1905–1970), combined Frank Sinatra, Gene Kelly (1912–1996), and Jules Munshin (1915–1975) as three irrepressible sailors on shore leave in New York City.

Kelly went on to star in two more dance musical classics: *An American in Paris* (1951) and the invariably sunny *Singin' in the Rain* (1952). In the first of these Kelly plays a young artist abroad. In the second he is a silent-movie star trying to make the transition to "talkies."

MUSICAL THEMES

PLAYBACK SINGERS: WHO'S REALLY SINGING?

In some films, playback singers are used to pre-record the songs for on-screen personalities who then lip-synch in front of the camera. For example, the American soprano Marni Nixon (b. 1930) sang for Deborah Kerr (1921–2007) in *The King and I*, Audrey Hepburn (1929–1993) in *My Fair Lady*, and Natalie Wood (1938–1981) in *West Side Story*. She dubbed for so many famous actresses she was nicknamed "The Ghostess with the Mostess."

(Continued)

MUSICAL THEMES (Continued)

One of the most convoluted uses of playback singers occurs in *Singin' in the Rain*, whose plot revolves around the very idea of vocal dubbing in the early days of sound films. Here we watch the film's ingénue, Kathy Sheldon (played by Debbie Reynolds, b. 1932), dubbing on screen the unfortunately shrill voice of Lina Lamont (played by Jean Hagen, 1923–1977), a silent movie star trying to make the transition to "talkies." But in reality, it is Reynolds herself who is being dubbed by Hagen's real-life voice in their scenes together. Furthermore, in the songs "Would You?" and "You Are My Lucky Star," the never-credited Betty Noyes (1912–1987) sings in place of Reynolds. Such substitutions, though studios did their best to keep their secrets, were quite common.

The Day the Earth Stood Still (1951)

Despite the initial post-World War II exuberance, the emerging Cold War with the Soviet Union stirred considerable anxiety. In 1947, the House Un-American Activities Committee (HUAC) singled out Hollywood as a source of Communist propaganda. Subsequent hearings led to the blacklisting of many within the industry, including composer Aaron Copland, singer Paul Robeson, and E. Y. "Yip" Harburg (1896–1981), whose contributions included song lyrics to both *The Wizard of Oz* and *Cabin in the Sky*. The Korean War (1950–1953), the first of two American wars fought to contain Communism, would claim some 54,000 American lives. It was in this climate of fear that author Harry Bates's (1900–1981) short story "Farewell to the Master" (1940) was adapted into the film *The Day the Earth Stood Still*.

Directed by Robert Wise (1914–2005) with a musical score by Bernard Herrmann, *The Day the Earth Stood Still* presents Klaatu, the interplanetary traveler who lands a flying saucer in Washington, DC. Klaatu's mission is to warn Earth's governments that they must mend their warlike ways before venturing into space. Disobeying this command will result in humankind's annihilation. To emphasize the point, Klaatu travels with Gort, an invincible robocop.

DID YOU KNOW?

THEREMIN

A musician playing a theremin. Photographed by Arnold Genthe.

Imagine making music just by waving your arms. You can if you have a theremin, an electronic instrument invented in 1919 by the Russian physicist Leon Theremin (1896–1993). The theremin is a favorite in science fiction, but is also used in popular music. The Beach Boys' "Good Vibrations" (1966) features an electro-theremin. Led Zeppelin, Mötley Crüe, and Phish used theremin design variations as well.

The original theremin works by sensing electromagnetic waves in the body. The instrument has two antennae. One controls pitch; the other controls amplitude. The performer performs by adjusting the distance between her hands and the antennae, thereby manipulating pitch and volume. **mysearchlab 11.4**

How does one capture the sounds of outer space? Herrmann created new tone palettes. His orchestra used a combination of 30 brass instruments, groups of pianos and harps, as well as a vibraphone, an electric violin, and two theremins (see sidebar). In order to add to the otherworldliness, some of the music was inserted into the soundtrack backward.

We will analyze the film's opening sequence, which unfolds as the title captions are rolling. The music sounds strange to our ears, but the overall form is straightforward (Intro/A/B/A/B/A/B). The credits begin traditionally, with a picture of the 20th Century Fox marquee accompanied by the company's drum-roll-to-brass fanfare. Then the screen goes dark.

LISTENING GUIDE

mysearchlab 11.5

THE DAY THE EARTH STOOD STILL, OPENING SEQUENCE   *from the soundtrack recording*

INTRODUCTION

| 0:00 | The movie begins with Herrmann's score sounding over a black screen. An eerie downward-moving glissando sounds like a missile falling from the sky. There is a cymbal roll crescendo. As the screen lights up, stars race toward the viewer. We are traveling through outer space. Out of the starry void, the film's title appears in plain block letters. |

SECTION A

| 0:07 | The full musical ensemble makes its appearance. Low brass tones tumble downward in four gestures. Scored in the background, the more brilliant and high-pitched sounds of the theremins move in slow countermelody. The harps add rhythmic punctuation at each phrase ending. The effect of all this is an uncomfortable but nevertheless weirdly seductive stretching and seething. The movie, the score tells us, will be serious and thought provoking. It will also be far outside our everyday experience. |

SECTION B

| 0:24 | Now we hear the high brass instruments play a fanfare, which is echoed in the low brass. Geiger counter-like, harps and pianos pluck and hammer. It seems that outer space is not only vast but endlessly active. |

SECTION A

| 0:41 | As these heroic tones fade, the music seems to open up, like the deep space that fills the screen. Listen to the theremins, which have been brought to the melodic forefront. Tubas provide the countermelody. Do the theremins, which are now sounding an octave lower, remind you of singing? Perhaps Herrmann is presenting us with the irresistible Siren sounds of space. |

SECTION B

| 1:00 | Brass fanfare and low echo are heard again. |

SECTION A

| 1:16 | The original "stretching" gesture returns as we see two planets on screen. Is one Earth? Is the other Klaatu's? Do the planets move in tandem? Do they resist each other like the accompanying tones in the brass section? |

SECTION B

1:33	There is time for one last brass fanfare as the clouds of Earth appear on screen. We seem to have moved through space to our destination; perhaps we see through the eyes of Klaatu. Have you also noticed how the music has forced you to slow down emotionally, as if you really were traveling through the vastness of space? How different that feeling is from the frantic activity we are about to witness on the planet below.
1:42	There is a cadence of sorts and a view of water. This signals the end of the credits section and the beginning of the movie proper.
1:46	Pulsing ostinati are heard from the pianos as the water fades into radar screens revealing the presence of a UFO.

QUESTIONS FOR THOUGHT

- Do you think the music for *The Day the Earth Stood Still* sounds as strange today as it did to audiences in the 1950s? Why or why not?
- Search the Internet for music associated with Gort. What does the music tell us about the robot?

MUSICAL LIVES
BERNARD HERRMANN (1911–1975)

Born in New York City, Herrmann's early musical career was centered at the Columbia Broadcast System (CBS). He was hired to compose and conduct for educational radio programs but eventually became the staff conductor of the CBS Orchestra. It was at CBS that Herrmann met Orson Welles (1915–1985) and provided music for Welles's infamous 1938 *War of the Worlds* radio broadcast. Three years later, Herrmann wrote the soundtrack to Welles's cinematic masterpiece *Citizen Kane* (1941). In 1955, Herrmann began an eight-film and ten-year collaboration with the director Alfred Hitchcock. Herrmann died in his sleep after a long recording session of his score for Martin Scorsese's (b. 1942) *Taxi Driver* (1976). It is said that the composer, who had been in poor health, exhausted himself to death.

Films in which Herrmann collaborated with Alfred Hitchcock are:

1955: *The Trouble with Harry*
1956: *The Man Who Knew Too Much*
1956: *The Wrong Man*
1958: *Vertigo*
1959: *North by Northwest*
1960: *Psycho*
1963: *The Birds*
1964: *Marnie*

Beyond Hollywood: *The Hidden Fortress (Kakushi-toride no san-akunin)* (1958)

While the West looked fearfully into the future, the great Japanese film director Akira Kurosawa (1910–1998) explored the social values developed during his country's feudal past. Prominent in Kurosawa films are themes of honor and duty, self-control, and loyalty. Kurosawa was a master of spectacle who generally reserved his biggest set pieces for battles. But not always. His drama *The Hidden Fortress*, with music by Masaru Sato (1928–1999), offers instead a traditional dance that is seamlessly integrated into the overall narrative.

The action takes place in sixteenth-century Japan. As war rages, 16-year-old Princess Yuki (Misa Uehara, b. 1937) must cross enemy lines to reach the safety of her clan. Adding to her burden is the fact that she must bring with her 400 ingots of gold, money needed to ensure her clan's survival. Guarding Yuki is her general, Rokurota Makabe (Toshiro Mifune, 1920–1997). Tagging along are the hapless and hopelessly untrustworthy farmers Tahei and Matakishi.

All along the escape route, the company moves from one harrowing experience to another. The fugitives survive detection by Makabe's wits but time and again are nearly undone by the foolishness of Tahei and Matakishi. With each new adventure, the haughty princess has new experiences. Yuki moves toward wisdom as she gradually learns the ways of the world.

All of these notions come into play during the fire festival scene. Yuki and Makabe (with their ingots carefully hidden within sticks of wood) join a procession to the festival site. The event seems to be the perfect disguise. Since everyone is carrying wood, princess and company can simply evaporate into the crowd.

LISTENING GUIDE

THE HIDDEN FORTRESS, FIRE FESTIVAL SCENE

You can find this scene on the DVD or on the Internet; excerpt begins at 1:43:48 in the DVD. The scene opens with the fugitives' arrival at the festival. They push their cart to the edge of the fire circle. The princess, distant as always, looks on from the perimeter as the fervent peasants chant:

The life of a man
Burn it with the fire
The life of an insect
Throw it into the fire
Ponder and you'll see
The world is dark
And this floating world is a dream
Burn with abandon

The chanting is accompanied by a shakuhachi playing softly in the background. A drum punctuates the end of each line. An orgiastic dance ensues as the peasants throw burning brands into the fire; **taiko** drummers beat out pulsing rhythms.

mysearchlab 11.6

All goes smoothly until the revelers see the cart of sticks. To the horror of Tahei and Matakishi, the crowd attempts to push the entire cart into the flames. A struggle ensues and soldiers arrive. Fearing discovery, Makabe takes charge. He rolls the cart, gold and all, into the fire. Everyone dances.

It's a wonderful scene. Tahei and Matakishi stumble through the choreography, unable to take their eyes off the burning cart. Yuki and Makaba dance as well. Yuki, embracing the expectations of separate worlds, holds the hand of the peasant to her left. To her right is her general and protector. They do not touch.

MUSICAL THEMES
A FAMILIAR PAIR?

The bumbling peasants Tahei and Matakishi—one tall and one short—may seem familiar. They were George Lucas's (b. 1944) inspiration for the characters of C3PO and R2D2. The opening scene of *The Hidden Fortress*—with the battle-weary peasants stumbling across an open landscape—is echoed in the original *Star Wars* movie.

QUESTIONS FOR THOUGHT

- Yuki holds the hand of the peasant woman. Why not General Makaba's?
- Do you think the music of this scene communicates the same ideas to Western and Japanese audiences?

Diversification

As the 1950s progressed, production companies diversified their output. A series of successful Broadway stage musicals were adapted for film. The racially incisive 1927 musical *Show Boat* (see chapter 10: Music and Broadway) was adapted into a socially softened 1950 film. That same year featured the film release of composer Irving Berlin's 1946 Broadway hit *Annie Get Your Gun*.

"Bigger is better" marked the Hollywood approach. Stages were abandoned for grandiose outdoor sets; marquee film stars often replaced lesser-known stage actors. The 1955 film adaptation of Frank Loesser's (1910–1969) *Guys and Dolls* (1950), for example, featured superstars Frank Sinatra and Marlon Brando (1924–2004). The adaptation of *The Sound of Music* (1965), shot in Austria and Germany and starring Julie Andrews (b. 1935), remains the most financially successful film musical of all time.

The same period saw the rise of the pop music film. One of the genre's biggest stars was Elvis Presley, who between 1956 and 1970 starred in 31 movies. His first, *Love Me Tender*, pitted brother against brother in the post-Civil War South. Future movies cast Presley as a convict (*Jailhouse Rock*, 1957), boxer (*Kid Galahad*, 1962), soldier (*GI Blues*, 1960), and trapeze artist (*Fun in Acapulco*, 1963), among myriad other professions. In every movie, Elvis found reasons to sing and dance.

Pop music of all sorts lit up movie screens. Beginning in 1963, co-stars Annette Funicello (b. 1942) and Frankie Avalon (b. 1939) starred in a series of "beach party" movies. Innocence was the rule of thumb. Probably never before nor since have teens in love acted with such restraint. The Beatles made three movies in the 1960s: *A Hard Day's Night* (1964), *Help* (1965), and *Yellow Submarine* (1968). Rock documentaries included Bob Dylan's (b. 1941) *Don't Look Back* (1967), the concert film *Woodstock* (1970), and The Band's *The Last Waltz* (1978). Rock parodies included Rob Reiner's (b. 1947) *This Is Spinal Tap* (1984) and Jack Black's (b. 1969) *School of Rock* (2003).

Animated film musicals have had a long and successful run. Walt Disney's (1901–1966) *Snow White and the Seven Dwarfs* (1937) was the first full-length animated musical. The score featured a number of memorable pieces, including "Whistle While You Work" and "Someday My Prince Will Come," which became a jazz standard. Jiminy Cricket's "When You Wish Upon a Star" from *Pinocchio* (1940) became the Disney theme song. That same year Disney released *Fantasia* (1940), which featured cartoon animation set to music by J. S. Bach, Ludwig van Beethoven, Igor Stravinsky (1882–1971), and others. Disney has continued to produce animated musicals. Its most successful came in the early 1990s with *Beauty and the Beast* (see chapter 9: Music and Love), *Aladdin* (1992), and *The Lion King* (1994).

MUSICAL THEMES
BOLLYWOOD

The world's largest film industry resides in India. Bollywood is the nickname given to that portion of the industry that emanates from Mumbai (Bombay). Though the primary language is Hindi, films often incorporate two or three languages, including English. Bollywood films generally feature comedy, spectacle, formulaic characters, and actors and actresses whose star status rivals that of any Hollywood idol. Song and dance are essential. There are many Bollywood clips available on the Internet.

Poster for a typical Bollywood film.

New Explorations

Composer Philip Glass (b. 1937) has made a point of using contemporary musical styles to celebrate the cinematic past. He wrote scores to accompany two early film classics, director Tod Browning's (1880–1962) *Dracula* (1931/1999), featuring Bela Lugosi (1882–1956), and French director Jean Cocteau's (1889–1963) *La Belle et la Bête* (*Beauty and the Beast*, 1946/1995). The latter he transformed into a film/opera (vocalists sing from behind the screen).

Also important has been Glass's work with director Godfrey Reggio (b. 1940). Together they created the QATSI trilogy of *Koyaanisqatsi* (*Life Out of Balance*, 1982), **mysearchlab 11.7** *Powaqqatsi* (*Life in Transformation*, 1987), and *Nagoyqatsi* (*Life as War*, 2002). Think of these films as portraits in motion. Reggio says that he sought to "rip out all the foreground of a traditional film" (actors, plot, story) and bring background imagery forward. The subsequent emptiness is both thrilling and emotionally challenging. In *Koyaanisqatsi*, Glass supports the unfolding scenes with **minimalist** music of slowly fluctuating harmonic patterns. Insistent pulsating rhythms take charge as the visual imagery gradually shifts from natural to urbanized settings.

In *Decasia: The State of Decay* (2002), director Bill Morrison (b. 1965) draws material from deteriorated black-and-white nitrate film stock. Disembodied characters seem to move through a world coming apart. Images bubble with the destructive energy of decomposition. The effects are surreal; sometimes beautiful, other times horrifying. A boxer bobs and weaves as he punches into decayed oblivion. Machine gears spin toward their own destruction.

Composer Michael Gordon (b. 1956) scored the film. He says that his compositional idea was to make the music sound as broken as the images look, as if the music were "covered in cobwebs." The score opens with the grinding sounds of percussionists scraping metal sticks in circles around the rims of old automobile brake drums. The orchestra, which is "broken," is divided into two halves, each intentionally out of tune with the other. Rhythms pulse with feverish energy. Pitches grate and waver as if the musical machine is too decrepit to hold a solid center. Dissonance is constant and jarring.

ACTIVITIES AND ASSIGNMENTS

- Watch a clip from *Decasia: The State of Decay*. **mysearchlab 11.8** Can you discover thematic narratives or messages imbedded in the decay?
- Get together in a group and create your own short film using video clips or photos. Using the same visual materials, create two different soundtracks that portray contrasting moods, emotions, or plots.

Dissecting an Epic:
The Lord of the Rings

Since cinema's beginning, filmmakers have reveled in filling the screen with themes of epic proportion. Among the most famous attempts are *Gone with the Wind* (1939), *Ben Hur* (1959), *Doctor Zhivago* (1965), *Apocolypse Now* (1979), *Saving Private Ryan* (1998), and *Avatar* (2009), all of which portray struggling individuals caught within a broader clash of cultures.

Now we consider one of film's grandest of epic stories, director Peter Jackson's (b. 1961) trilogy *The Lord of the Rings* (2001, 2002, 2003), with musical score by Howard Shore (b. 1946). The films are based on fantasy novels written by British author J. R. R. Tolkien (1892–1973).

Although Tolkien denied any direct connection, it is significant that he wrote his tale over a 10-year span that encompassed World War II. There are many parallels between the world in which Tolkien lived and the world he created from his imagination. Tolkien's story presents the trial of Middle Earth, a land inhabited by elves and dwarves, wizards and sorcerers, men and gentle-spirited hobbits. It is a time of great trials. Long-dormant forces of evil have reemerged; the vitalizing power of the elves is fading.

The fate of all rests with a magical ring of power. Forged in ages past by the Dark Lord, Sauron, the ring was long lost to the world. But now it has been discovered in the most unlikely of places. It is possessed by Frodo Baggins, hobbit of the Shire. Should Sauron regain the ring, the free world will fall. Frodo's job is to destroy the ring. To accomplish this, he must travel to the heart of Sauron's realm and throw the ring into a volcanic fire. Eight colleagues—representing an alliance of the free world—volunteer to travel with him, thus creating "the fellowship of the ring."

For the film trilogy, Shore's biggest musical hurdle was to create a sense of continuity over time and space. He had to score more than

10 hours of footage to be released in three films over a three-year span. Shore's solution was pure economy. Since the films were tied together by story and ideas, he decided to link his musical themes to specific people, places, and things. Shore's leitmotives bind and connect the action. Shore created more than 25 nondiegetic leitmotives, including ones representing the ring, the fellowship, and the Shire. Shore uses a leitmotive when the object or idea that it represents is in sight or about to appear; sometimes just thinking about the object is sufficient.

Each theme is distinct in character, and is designed to embody the nature of the object or idea it represents. For example, the winding melody associated with the ring of power is filled with dark and uneasy longing; the joyful Shire themes, in contrast, have a spirited Celtic feel. Themes representing the elves are otherworldly in character, whereas those representing the forces of evil are percussive and militant. **mysearchlab 11.9**

Let's consider the fellowship theme, which, in various guises, is heard dozens of times throughout the trilogy. The theme first appears when Frodo and Sam leave the Shire. As Frodo recalls Bilbo's adage about the dangers of travel, the soundtrack quietly presents the first phrases of the fellowship theme. In tones soft but resolute, the march-like music foreshadows the creation of the nine-member fellowship. The hobbits cannot possibly understand the journey they are beginning, but the musical score does. So too will the careful listener.

The fellowship theme goes through a variety of transformations, always in accord with the on-screen action. When the theme is sounded in the elfin city of Rivendale, it has gained in stature. It is confident, even triumphant. The theme will not always carry such élan, for the fellowship will be strongly tested. Shore's score must reflect those struggles.

CONCLUSION

We began the chapter with a quote from Max Steiner, who throughout the 1930s and 1940s was arguably Hollywood's most important composer. Now we return to him. Steiner's music was ingenious, filled with leitmotives, innovative textures, and psychological depth. Quite simply, Steiner cut the path on which subsequent film composers would follow.

To demonstrate this, we examine a snippet of Steiner's work, the fog scene of the original *King Kong* (1933). Armed with our new understandings, we can easily detect the way in which Steiner guides, even coerces, us into the psychological drama.

KING KONG: FOG SCENE

Twenty minutes into the film we are aboard the ship at night cruising through a foggy veil toward Kong's island. **mysearchlab 11.10** Echoing the visual effect of the fog, the music soundtrack opens mysteriously, with disembodied tones set up by stagnant strings, plucking harp, and distant-sounding winds. Adding to the effect is the lack of rhythmic direction, which produces a suspended, timeless feeling. From this texture emerges an ominous three-tone downward-moving theme that is already familiar from the film's opening credits. In sight and sound we sit at the boundary between worlds as we drift blindly between the modern and the primitive, between the conscious and unconscious, and between the known and unknowable. We also come to understand that descending three-tone motive. It is Kong. And Kong, Steiner's music tells us, is no mere furry, girl-loving, building-climbing,

Poster for the original release of *King Kong*, 1933.

chest-thumping monster. He is a representation of our own primal nature, of the destructive and noble drives that make us human.

Steiner's score binds us to the action and disturbs our inner tranquility. Curiously, however, the musical themes themselves are not particularly memorable. One doesn't leave the theater singing the fog music, for example; Kong's doleful three-tone motive is too short to have much of an independent melodic life. That was the way Steiner wanted it. He preferred that audiences focus on the film's images, while he worked musical magic surreptitiously in the background.

Future composers, such as John Williams and Howard Shore, would take a different approach. For them, the central musical themes would often be placed in the foreground where they would become essential parts of the remembrance package that we take home from the film. Who can forget the jolly can-do march theme that binds the various *Indiana Jones* movies, or the booming drums of Saruman's Isengard from *Lord of the Rings*? How about the five-tone "Call of the Mother Ship" from *Close Encounters of the Third Kind* (1977).

Take a moment to hear in your mind E.T.'s flying theme. Did the scene's images and emotional quality come along in tandem? As the music unfolded in your head, did the weighty troubles of the world seem a bit lighter, if just for a moment? If so, you have witnessed—and inwardly manifested—music's power to spur the imagination, to deepen breadth of experience, and to sustain and enhance emotional worlds.

CHAPTER GOALS

- To examine dance genres in different cultures and times.

- To see how dance reflects regional/national histories and identities.

- To understand the relationship between music and movement.

QUESTIONS FOR THOUGHT

- Do you like to dance? Why or why not?
- What kind of music makes the best dance music?
- How many different kinds of dance cultures are there on your campus?

"I want you to be a dirty girl," complained Bruno Tonioli (b. 1955). The effusive choreographer and *Dancing with the Stars* judge had just watched a **tango** routine performed by Olympic figure skater Kristi Yamaguchi (b. 1971) and partner Mark Ballas (b. 1986). Justly or not, Tonioli was underwhelmed.

Throughout the competition, Yamaguchi easily adapted her athletic skills to the dance floor. She had occasionally struggled, however, in portraying the dance contest's over-the-top emotional demands. Particularly difficult for the emotionally reserved skater was the exhibition-style tango segment.

Dance is music embodied. It is found in all cultures, and, like music, it appears to be essential to the human condition. In this chapter we explore dance traditions from South America, West Africa, Europe, and the United States. We begin with the tango. Then we move to Brazil where we study the Afro-Brazilian dance/martial art *capoeira*. From capoeira we go to Ghana, West Africa, to study *baamaya*, a colorful dance of the Dagbamba ethnic group. Next we go back in time to learn about dance during the European Renaissance. Then we follow European dance forward for an overview of the development of classical ballet. The chapter closes in the United States with a brief discussion of modern and popular dance traditions.

Tango: Argentina

Now popular throughout the world, tango's roots lie in the smoky bars and dancehalls of 1890s Buenos Aires, Argentina. There, people of Iberian, Italian, and African heritage shared and merged bits and pieces of their respective music and dance traditions. They created a style that, though drawing from older practices, expressed contemporary identity. Tango soon became synonymous with Argentine culture.

The dance spread quickly, probably carried by sailors who took it across the Atlantic Ocean. The tango was a sensation in 1912 Paris and was quickly established as one of the world's most popular dances. It remains so today. **mysearchlab 12.1**

Tango is about the heat of romance. Song lyrics tell of loves gained and lost—of jealousies and rivalries, broken hearts and wounded pride. A tangoist's pain does not heal. Instead, it becomes a source of creative expression. These emotions are captured in countless tango songs. Pascual Contursi (1888–1932) used slang-inflected lyrics in his 1916 classic "Mi noche triste" ("My Sad Night") to describe his broken heart.

The earliest tango ensembles were small; their instrumental heritage was European. *Tercetos* (trios) usually consisted of violin, flute, and either guitar or accordion. By the early 1900s, the ensemble had grown in size and standardized into the *orquesta típica criolla*, which included violin, flute, guitar, and *bandoneón*, a small German-made button-style accordion. Later ensembles would grow to the size of small orchestras, with string bass, piano, cello, expanded string sections, and up to four bandoneóns.

The most important tango musician of the second half of the twentieth century was Argentine bandoneón player, composer, and

> "Dance is a song of the body."
>
> —Martha Graham (1894–1991)

bandleader Astor Piazzolla (1921–1992). Although born in Argentina, Piazzolla spent much of his childhood in New York City, where he heard both jazz and classical music. Piazzolla began playing the bandoneón at age 9, and was a virtuoso by age 13. When his family returned to Argentina in 1937, the 16-year-old Piazzolla left home. He rented an apartment in Buenos Aires and began his performing career.

Piazzolla's musical interests were broad. When not on the bandstand, he studied classical composition and later orchestral conducting. After travels in Europe, Piazzolla returned to Buenos Aires, where in 1955 he formed his own tango orchestra. Piazzolla's approach drew from the full breadth of his musical experience. He revolutionized the tango sound.

Tango is a dance for couples. It is led by the man, who holds his partner in the *abrazo* (embrace) position. Dancers move in strong, broad steps. The body is erect, though slightly forward. Except for flourishes, feet generally stay close to the floor.

Improvisation is the key to great tango dancing, but improvisation is built on standard movements. These include the *caminata* (walking step), its reverse direction (*el retroceso*), the *salida* (the "exit," actually the step that often begins the dance), and *giros* (turns and rotations). More complex movements include *el lapis* ("the pencil," in which a dancer seems to draw figures on the floor with his or her foot), *ochos* (steps and pivots that outline figure eights), *ganchos* (in which the dancer hooks his or her leg around a partner's leg), and whip-like leg movements called *boleos*.

Tango has been featured in many films. Heartthrob Rudolf Valentino (1895–1926) danced to "La Cumparsita" (1917, composed by Gerardo Matos Rodríguez, 1897–1948) in *The Four Horsemen of the Apocalypse* (1921). Half a century later, Marlon Brando (1924–2004) and Maria Schneider (b. 1952) lay drunken waste to a tango contest in *Last Tango in Paris* (1972). Two films of the 1990s—*Scent of a Woman* (1992), with Al Pacino (b. 1940); and *Evita* (1996), with Madonna (b. 1958) and Antonio Banderas (b. 1960)—featured the classic song "Por una Cabeza" ("By a Head," 1935), written by Carlos Gardel (1890–1935) and Alfredo la Pera' (c. 1900–1935).

Real-life experience inspired director Sally Potter's film *The Tango Lesson* (1997). The story, which unfolds in Paris and Buenos Aires,

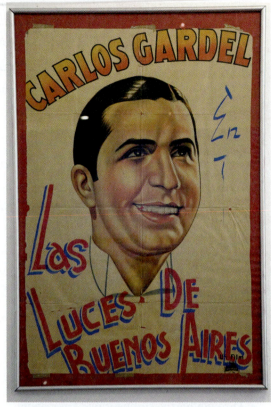

A poster depicting Carlos Gardel from the Museo Casa Carlos Gardel, Buenos Aires, Argentina.

is quasi-autobiographical. Potter, playing herself, is having trouble writing a screenplay. To relax, she decides to take tango lessons with Argentine tango master Pablo Veron. The two strike a deal. If he can teach her to dance like a professional, she will give him the leading role in her next film. Both events come to pass. The romantic rub is that Veron the dancer expects to lead. But when it comes to making the film, he must follow.

The dance scenes are inspirational. We will study just one, a quartet with Potter, Veron, and two additional men. The scene is shot in an empty loft—the space is ample, but stark, like tango itself. The choreography is set to Piazzolla's "Libertango" (1974).

"Libertango" is simple in form—a 16-bar sequence repeated again and again with ever changing orchestration. After four repetitions the form is shortened to eight bars, a device that has the effect of quickening dramatic pace and intensifying the emotional impact. Notice how the choreography follows the form, how Potter uses the loft's architecture—first the doorway leading into the hall, then the pillars—as markers to signify the breaks between musical sections and dance partners.

LISTENING GUIDE

"LIBERTANGO" FROM *THE TANGO LESSON* *(soundtrack recording)*

The scene opens with a male dancer moving alone. He bursts through the double doors (literally la salida) into the open space of the loft. As he does so, the music's 16-bar form begins.

0:00	Potter and her partner move quickly across the loft in caminata steps. As their motion slows, Potter seems to draw lines across the floor with her toes (el lapiz). The bandoneón is prominent, playing a lively rhythmic and melodic ostinato.
0:27	Potter takes a new partner as another 16-bar section begins. In the film, notice the boleos and ganchos. On the soundtrack recording, the cello enters with a languishing drawn out melody while the bandoneón ostinato moves to the background.
0:55	In this 16-bar section, Potter again changes partners. The dance flow changes as well.
1:23	Potter picks up the visual pacing by having the entire quartet appear as the 16-bar section begins. One woman; three men. All three men act simultaneously as partners to Potter. The orchestration becomes thicker and the bandoneón briefly abandons its ostinato role to take up a new melody.
1:51	The musical pacing quickens as the form shifts to eight-bar cycles. As the form shortens, so do the dance partnerships. Potter changes partners every few bars. Strings and bandoneón return to the ostinato.
2:04	Quick partner changes continue.
2:17	Quick partner changes continue. The camera pans away. The men start to emphasize lifts as the dance contour becomes increasingly vertical.
2:31	Lifts continue to be emphasized. At the end of the dance, Potter settles with Veron, who began the dance as a soloist.
2:44	Veron spins Potter as the scene fades out.

MUSICAL LIVES

ASTOR PIAZZOLLA (1921–1992)

Astor Piazzolla playing the bandoneón on stage in 1987.

Piazzolla recalls his composition lesson with Parisian pedagogue Nadia Boulanger (1887–1979): "When I met her, I showed her my kilos of symphonies and sonatas. She started to read them and suddenly came out with a horrible sentence: 'It's very well written.' And stopped, with a big period, round like a soccer ball. After a long while, she said: 'Here you are like Stravinsky, like Bartók, like Ravel, but you know what happens? I can't find Piazzolla in this.' And she began to investigate my private life: what I did, what I did and did not play, if I was single, married, or living with someone, she was like an FBI agent! And I was very ashamed to tell her that I was a tango musician. Finally I said, 'I play in a night club.' I didn't want to say cabaret. And she answered, 'Night club, *mais oui*, but that is a cabaret, isn't it?' 'Yes,' I answered. . . . It wasn't easy to lie to her. She kept asking: 'You say that you are not a pianist. What instrument do you play, then?' And I didn't want to tell her that I was a bandoneón player. . . . Finally, I confessed and she asked me to play some bars of a tango of my own. She suddenly opened her eyes, took my hand and told me: 'You idiot, that's Piazzolla!' And I took all the music I composed, ten years of my life, and sent it to hell in two seconds."

Capoeira: Brazil

In tango, men and women play a game of seduction. Perhaps the dance takes place in a steamy nightclub where seduction is truly the objective. More likely, however—as with *Dancing with the Stars*, and every choreographed and staged performance—the seduction is simply a façade, play acting designed to project the aesthetics of the dance. In this sense, dance is closely related to theater. Performers take on new personae, which are acted out for themselves, their partners, and those looking on.

Traveling north from Argentina to Brazil, one encounters a different sort of dance theater. Tangoists play at seduction; Brazil's practitioners of capoeira play with the idea of combat. And just as tango's seduction can be real, the kicks and spins of capoeira also offer its practitioners real-life skills that can be used on the street.

Two capoeiristas eye each other warily as they "dance" the **ginga**, a back-and-forth-step pattern designed to facilitate quick movements and sudden changes in direction. Suddenly, one opponent breaks the pattern. He spins and kicks in the other's direction. The strike falls short as the would-be victim cartwheels out of range, then initiates a counterstrike.

The combatants move to the percussive rhythms of the *berimbau*, a one-stringed musical bow. They are surrounded by a *roda* (ring) of fellow capoeiristas singing songs, playing percussion instruments, and clapping. Each awaits his or her own opportunity to step inside the roda and play the *jogo* ("game") of capoeira. The jogo is exhausting. When the players tire, they are quickly replaced. And so it goes. Competition and camaraderie mix and mingle as the afternoon wears on.

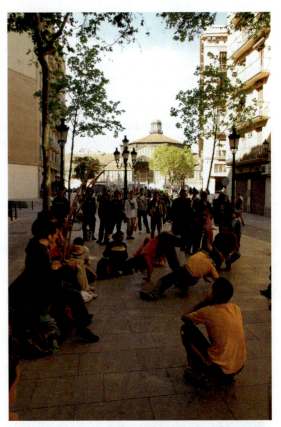

An impromptu capoeira performance on the streets of Barcelona, Spain.

Capoeira is lightning quick and exciting to watch. It can also be deadly. A century ago, capoeiristas who had honed their skills within the roda fought for real on the streets of Rio de Janeiro. They fought barefoot, sometimes holding straight-edged razors between their toes. Legs, you see, reach farther than arms.

Capoeira's roots are unclear. Folklore holds that capoeira originated during Brazil's slavery era and that African slaves used it as a vehicle for resistance and escape. The fight, according to folklore, was hidden within dance. Thus, slaves were able to hone their fighting skills on the master's plantation, right under the noses of their oppressors.

While there is no hard evidence to back up these ideas, it is certainly true that slaves did escape frequently enough to found a number of free communities in the Brazilian forests. These *quilombos*, as they were known, varied in size and permanence. The largest was the multi-settlement area of Palmares, with a population perhaps as large as 20,000 and a government system based on African political conventions. Palmares survived as an independent community for over six decades until its destruction in 1695.

At the very least, Brazilian slavery and capoeira are intertwined. Slavery was abolished in 1888. In 1890, legislation was enacted that made it illegal to practice capoeira. The practice continued nonetheless.

Whatever role capoeira may have had in Brazil's early history, it is clear that the ideas embodied in the previous stories are central to the dance/sport's affective power. The jogo is about learning to stand strong for one's rights, about showing tenacity in times of adversity. Capoeira is also about building a community of support, about finding people who will stand with you in times of need.

The father of modern capoeira was Mestre Bimba (Manuel dos Reis Machado, 1900–1974). Bimba added new techniques to the jogo, thereby making it a more efficient fighting art. Perhaps more importantly, he advocated for capoeira's cultural value as a marker of Afro-Brazilian heritage. Due in large part to Bimba's efforts, capoeira was legalized in the early 1930s. Under Bimba's guidance, capoeira, which had previously been confined to the lower social classes, became a national sport. No longer simply a fight against oppression, it also became part of a cooperative initiative for racial understanding and national identity.

Music is central to the jogo. Players must move in accordance with the musical tempo as provided by the berimbau, the instrument that leads the ensemble. Percussion instruments—which might include the *pandeiro* (tambourine), *agogo* (iron bell), *atabaque* (hand drum), *reco-reco* (rasp), and hand clapping—add rhythmic support.

Songs are sung in Portuguese in a call-and-response style typical of African communal singing. The melodies are short and easy to sing; response sections are usually just a few words long. As a sign of solidarity, everyone in the roda sings. Texts may have to do with everyday life, but generally concern some aspect of capoeira.

"My woman will tell you that capoeira conquered me," says the song "Paranà ê." "The capoeirista may stumble, but does not fall," says another. Frequently heard is the song "Nao nego voce nao da" ("Don't give him a thing"), which exhorts the players to fight their hardest. As the song progresses, the solo leader may create an endless variety of lyrics, so long as they fit the theme and music structure. Always, however, the choral response will be "Da, da, da no nego."("Go get him.")

MUSICAL THEMES

THE BERIMBAU

The berimbau is a musical bow, probably of African origin. A hollowed-out gourd is attached to the bow and serves as a resonating chamber. To play, the bow string is struck with a stick. Different sounds can be achieved by pressing against the string with a coin or flat stone. In the stick hand, the player also holds a small rattle (*caxixi*), which thickens the music's texture and provides a rhythmic counterpoint. In capoeira, some berimbau rhythms have names and are associated with specific movements.

| Musician playing a berimbau.

ASSIGNMENTS AND ACTIVITIES

- Search among the many videos of capoeira on the Internet. Compare and contrast two styles: Angola and Regional.
- Compare capoeira to other martial arts traditions. What are the similarities and differences?

Baamaya: Ghana, West Africa

Dressed in monkey-skin hats and pom-pon-adorned waist belts, the baamaya dancers move in a counterclockwise circle. Their hips swivel back and forth in a tight shimmy, a double time variation of a dance movement made famous in America by rhythm-and-blues icon Chubby Checker (b. 1941) with his Top 40 hit, "The Twist" (1960).

In Africa, where there is music, there is dance. In traditional contexts, adolescents dance to signify their coming to adulthood; adults dance to honor their ancestors, celebrate the dead, and honor the gods. In urban nightclubs, lithe dancers move to the seamless grooves of Congolese *soukous*, Nigerian *jùjú*, Zimbabwean *chimurenga*, and other popular music styles.

Baamaya is a traditional dance style popular among the Dagbamba, an ethnic group residing in Ghana's Northern Region. The dance's roots are unclear. Elders in the community often refer to the dance as *tubankpele*, which recalls the custom of dancers performing with corn husks stuffed into their belts. There are conflicting stories about tubankpele's origin. One account says it was danced at night because the movements kept mosquitoes away. Another account says the dance, with its twisting hip motions, was done to tease women. Yet another account says that tubankpele refers to *tubani*, a popular dish made of beans wrapped in leaves.

A separate origin tale is attached to the name "baamaya," which translates to English as "the fields are wet." In this account, recorded in the Center for National Culture in Tamale, the Northern Region's largest city, it is told that many years ago there was a drought in the region, causing widespread famine. The village priests blamed the drought on a crime committed by a man against a woman. To appease the gods, the men were told to wear women's clothing and to dance until the rain began to fall. The dancing did the trick, but to be certain that the entire region had relief, they sent out a young boy to check. The boy returned, calling out the words "*baa maya*" ("the fields are wet"). Whatever the story's factual truth, its moral imperative is plain enough: the entire community is responsible for the actions of the individual. A bad deed by one results in suffering for all.

Baamaya is performed for many occasions but is most closely associated with funerals, which are often grand affairs that take months to prepare and days to perform. At large funerals, it is common to have performances by numerous music and dance ensembles (each specializing in a particular genre). Baamaya generally takes place in the pre-dawn hours, beginning sometime around the first cockcrow and continuing until dawn.

A baamaya performance has multiple sections, each associated with a specific rhythm, dance step, and section of the baamaya myth. The first section is called baamaya *sochendi*, or baamaya "procession." This is the music that the dancers move to as they walk from the place in which they prepared for the performance (the "backstage dressing room," if you will) to the actual performance location. Some musicians say the drum rhythm (a repeated pattern of short-short-short-long) speaks the word *tu-ban-kpe-le*. Others attach to the rhythm the words *naa daa wariba* (Naa Daa dancers [are coming]). Baamaya sochendi is associated with the section of the story when the men, after having been instructed by the priests, made their way to the dance grounds.

A baamaya performance's main section is called baamaya *mangli*, or "principal" baamaya. This section reenacts the way the men danced to appease the gods and bring the rain. Baamaya mangli may continue for a number of hours. Several shorter sections follow, each related to subsequent parts of the mythology.

The dancers' costumes are designed to make men look like women. Essential to the costume is the belt in which the original corn husks of the tubankpele dance have been replaced with beads, cowries, and colorful yarn pom-pon balls. Under the belt is a skirt, though far shorter than a woman would ever wear. More elaborate costumes include a monkey-skin hat. Dancers generally carry a goat-tail switch in their right hands. On their ankles they wear metal jingles, which add an additional rhythmic layer to the music.

Besides the jingles, the instrumental ensemble consists of drum, *sayalsa* (rattle), and *calamboo* (wooden flute). Some performances also include praise singers.

Two types of drums are played—the hourglass-shaped variable-pitched *luŋa* and the *guŋgoŋ*, which has a single snare on each drumhead. Dagbamba musicians are renowned for the *luŋa* drums, which, like the *dùndún* drums of the Yoruba, speak by imitating the pitch and rhythmic inflections of speech (see chapter 6: Music and Spirituality, The Yoruba of Nigeria).

Throughout a baamaya performance, the *luŋa* drummer beats out proverbs that comment on community events, recall family histories, and encourage the dancers to "give their all" to the performance. The proverbs are often aimed at social pressure points. Many appeal to notions of individual virtue or the importance of community. Proverbs aimed at social wrongs can be highly confrontational. Consider the lessons embodied in the following *luŋa* phrases: "*Nubliyini nubliyini kupi kogli*" ("One finger can never pick up a stone"); "*Dakoli kutoiko*" ("The bachelor cannot be a good farmer").

Language unfolds from other sources as well. The calamboo player performs melodies of well-known songs that everyone will recognize. Praise singers address the dancers, or perhaps onlookers. Thus, baamaya can have a counterpoint of three language sources unfolding simultaneously—drum language, flute melody, and praise poetry.

DID YOU KNOW?
DANGEROUS MOVES

Dancing skill is highly valued in Dagbamba culture. But because dance tends to focus attention on highly skilled individuals, it can also be a source of social tension. It is common practice for baamaya dancers to protect themselves from psychic attacks (especially from rival dancers) by wearing protective amulets sewn into their belts or armbands, hung from necklaces, or attached to their goat-tail switches.

LISTENING GUIDE

mysearchlab 12.3

BAAMAYA

This video is from a May 2002 folkloric performance by the Suglo N'mali Dang Ensemble (Patience Maintains Family Ensemble). The performance is informal. Notice that many of the traditional accoutrements are missing from the costumes. Notice also that a woman is dancing with the men.

The dancers process into the performance space with baamaya sochendi. Once inside the dance ring, drummers switch to the faster rhythm of baamaya mangli. Dancers move in a counterclockwise rotation performing a movement that looks like "the twist." This is an unusual movement for the Dagbamba, one found only in baamaya. While the general style of the motion is set, each dancer performs the movements in his or her own fashion. Individuality is encouraged; there is much improvisation.

In this performance there are no praise singers. Even so, the event is language rich. The following drum language is performed within the first two minutes alone:

> *Jarigu ziem bin barigu*
> *Ka bin barigu gbago.*
> [A foolish person underestimates
> a trap and becomes caught himself.]
>
> *Yam ni yam kutoi kpe.*
> *Jarigu mini yam dan be.*
> [Two wise people cannot live together.
> One must be foolish, the other wise.]
>
> *Jerigu ziem peto.*
> *So di bori lala o daa bi nya.*
> [A foolish person refuses pants.
> Another wants them and cannot have them.]
>
> *Biegu ni n'sa nya chugu.*
> *Kadi sagm ka nubi nimdi.*
> [Tomorrow is Chugu (a festival day).
> We will eat lots of cornmeal and meat.]

QUESTIONS FOR THOUGHT

- Baamaya developed in Dagbamba villages. Today it is performed by folkloric ensembles across Ghana and throughout the world. Imagine ways in which outsiders might experience baamaya as compared to the Dagbamba themselves. What is lost? What might be gained?
- Some Dagbamba believe that the dance's twist-like motion was brought to Dagbon from the country of Gabon in Central Africa. If this is true, does this fact make the dance less authentic? What might it suggest about traditional dance?
- Imagine that you can understand the drum language and recognize the song melodies. Suddenly the musical texture becomes relatively transparent; the rhythmic complexity gives way to language. How does this change your listening experience?
- Read the following drum phrase. How do you interpret it?

Jankuno makpeme cheng kuliga ka jangbarisi ya tori tora. (Literally: Cat/matrilineal aunt travels to draw water, mice dance tora.)

European Dance

From the West African present, we now travel back in time to the European Renaissance (ca. 1430–1600). The term (from "re-naissance" or "rebirth") refers to a time in European history when artists, writers, and musicians looked back to ancient Greece and Rome for intellectual and artistic inspiration. **mysearchlab 1.3** It was a time of extraordinary development in the arts and sciences, when scholars used their growing understanding of the past as a springboard into the future. Those centuries produced some of Western civilization's greatest thinkers and artists, including Brunelleschi (1377–1446), Leonardo da Vinci (1452–1519), Machiavelli (1469–1527), Copernicus (1473–1543), Michelangelo (1475–1564), Raphael (1483–1520), and William Shakespeare (1564–1616). The technological and scientific advances of the Renaissance—among them the printing press in 1439—changed the course of history.

Renaissance Dance

Well-bred ladies and gentlemen of the sixteenth century were required to master certain skills. For the woman, sewing and embroidery were essential. Men had more vigorous obligations such as jousting, falconry, or archery. Both sexes were taught to dance—social standing and the ability to catch a mate depended on it. Witness the following account from a 1589 dance manual:

CAPRIOL (the student): I much enjoyed fencing and tennis, and this placed me upon friendly terms with young men. But, without knowledge of dancing, I could not please the damsels, upon whom, it seems to me, the entire reputation of an eligible young man depends.

ARBEAU (the teacher): You are quite right, as naturally the male and female seek one another and nothing does more to stimulate a man to acts of courtesy, honor, and generosity than love. And if you desire to marry you must realize that a mistress is won by the good temper and grace displayed while dancing. . . . And there is more to it than this, for dancing is practiced to reveal whether lovers are in good health and sound of limb, after which they are permitted to kiss their mistresses in order that they may touch and savor one another thus to ascertain if they are shapely or emit an unpleasant odor as of bad meat. Therefore, from this standpoint, quite apart from the many other advantages to be derived from dancing, it becomes an essential in a well-ordered society.

The author, Thoinot Arbeau (1519–1595), was a French cleric and dancing master. His *Orchesography* is the best-known and most detailed dance treatise of the Renaissance period. From this work we learn much about the role of dance in the sixteenth century. Perhaps most important for posterity, Arbeau devised a method for notating dance steps in coordination with the music. Without this system, many period dances would have been forever lost.

A master of contemporary etiquette, Arbeau also suggested how to behave in polite society. A gentleman must "spit and blow [his] nose sparingly" and if such actions prove unavoidable, he should turn his head away and "use a fair white handkerchief." Good advice even now.

So what did Renaissance dance look like? First and foremost, proper posture was essential. The torso was erect, but relaxed; the head held high. As for movement, the emphasis was on fancy footwork. This was especially true for the male, who was unconstrained by the long skirts and heavy undergarments worn by women. Men's movements included skips, leaps, and turns. All these movements were designed to demonstrate virility, to allow the man the opportunity to exhibit his athletic prowess before the fairer sex.

Some dances resembled modern-day circle or line dances. Any number of dancers could participate. One such dance was the *branle* (pronounced "brawl")—a relatively simple dance with peasant origins. Dancers held hands and moved from side to side in a circle or line. Arbeau mentions many kinds of branles but perhaps the most fun are those he calls "mimed" branles—ones that mimic sounds or actions of animals or people at work or play. We will look at an old favorite, the "Branle des Lavandieres," or "Washerwomen's Branle." The dance was so named because the clapping of the dancers sounded like the noise of women beating clothes as they did laundry along the banks of Paris's Seine River.

Let's examine the piece as presented in Arbeau's treatise. First, notice the musical notation is read top to bottom. Do not be confused—this is not the norm for Renaissance notation, which, like today, was read horizontally left to right. Arbeau uses this format so that the notes line up one-to-one with the dance

A page from Arbeau's *Orchesographie*.

steps (*piedi*), which are written in the middle column. Typical of dance music notation of the time, Arbeau notates only a melody. Renaissance musicians, like today's jazz musicians, would have improvised accompanying harmonies on the instruments they had available.

LISTENING GUIDE

mysearchlab 12.4

"BRANLE DES LAVANDIERS"

First you will hear the soprano recorder play the unaccompanied melody as notated in Arbeau. The phrase structure is: AABBCC. Next a bass recorder and lute harmonize the melody as the dancers begin the steps. Eventually the entire ensemble joins in.

The dance is done in a circle with dancers facing in toward the center (in this case, three couples). Men and women alternate places. The basic movements are simple:

Phrase A
  Step to the left, right foot closes.
  Repeat.
  Step to the right, left foot closes.
  Repeat.
Repeat phrase A

Phrase B (Now the pattern shortens. Dancers face each other.)
  Step left, right foot closes.
  Step right, left foot closes.
Repeat phrase B

(Continued)

LISTENING GUIDE (*Continued*)

Phrase C (Notice that the directional symmetry is broken.)
  Step left, right foot closes.
  Repeat.
  Repeat phrase C

The more complicated choreography, as listed in Arbeau's far right column, has the women putting their hands on their hips in phrase B as the men scold them with a menacing finger. On the repetition, the movements are reversed—the women scold. In the last section, Arbeau instructs the dancers to clap their hands. The choreography can change according to the number of repetitions of the various melodic lines. Rather than the basic steps to the left to close the movement, dancers might choose to turn in a circle and hop, as shown here.

ASSIGNMENTS AND ACTIVITIES

- The steps to the "Branle des Lavandieres" are quite simple. Form a circle with your classmates and give the dance a try.
- For another version of the dance, see **mysearchlab 12.4**.

QUESTIONS FOR THOUGHT

- Arbeau connects dance with good etiquette and courtship. Are there any vestiges of this today?
- How do the social functions of the four dance traditions described so far (tango, capoeira, baamaya, and Renaissance dance) differ? How are they the same?

Classical Ballet

Not all of Europe's dance traditions are as easy as the "Branle des Lavandieres," of course. Classical ballet, which also has its roots in the Renaissance, is one of the world's most technically difficult styles.

Historians generally cite the year 1661 as the beginning of Europe's formally schooled theatrical dance tradition. That was the year the Académie Royale de Danse was founded in Paris. Housed inside what is now the Louvre museum, the school was sponsored by Louis XIV (1638–1715) who hoped to "reestablish the dance in its true perfection." The "Sun King" (he earned the moniker as a boy when he danced the role of the Greek god Apollo) was a great lover of music, dance, and theater. In ballet, the three art forms would be combined.

At first, ballet was presented in between movements of plays. Over the next century, ballet would also be incorporated into opera. Sometimes ballet would forward the storyline,

while other times it was simply to be enjoyed in its own right. By the mid-eighteenth century, three principal ballet character types had developed:

- The noble, or *sérieux* character (gods and kings)
- The *demi-caractère* (noblemen, fauns, and other lesser gods)
- The *comique*, or *grotesque* character (woodsmen, buffoons, and other colorful commoners)

By the mid-nineteenth century, ballet had developed into its own full-blown entertainment genre, the **story ballet**.

Strongly influenced by the era's Romanticist bent, story ballets tell tales of love and deceit, magic and mayhem. Typical of the genre is Adolphe Adam's (1803–1856) *Giselle* (1841), a tale thickly wrapped in nineteenth-century Romantic symbolism. Here, the innocent peasant girl Giselle is wooed by Albrecht, a nobleman whose father is forcing him to marry a noblewoman he does not love. When Giselle discovers Albrecht's deceit, she dies of a broken heart. The distraught Albrecht then wanders off into the forest. As darkness descends, he is attacked by the vampire-like *wilis* (the ghosts of girls who died after their lovers betrayed them). The *wilis* dance about Albrecht as they slowly steal away his life essence. Luckily for Albrecht, Giselle's spirit comes to his aid. She protects him until the rising sun dispels the spirits. As the final curtain falls, the lovers separate for eternity.

By the mid-nineteenth century, ballet's creative center had moved from Paris to Russia. There, French émigré ballet-master Marius Petipa (1818–1910) would expand ballet's technical and expressive range. Revered for his artistry and feared for his obsessive and controlling personality, Petipa choreographed over 50 different ballets. Petipa's choreography is still remembered and duplicated today. Nineteenth-century Russia also produced the century's greatest ballet composer, Pyotr Ilyich Tchaikovsky, who wrote *Swan Lake* (1877), *The Sleeping Beauty* (1890), and the perennial holiday favorite *The Nutcracker* (1892).

MUSICAL THEMES
BASIC BALLET TERMS TO TAKE TO THE THEATER

Arabesque (in Arabic fashion): The dancer places weight on a single leg while the other is extended behind.

Ballerina: A female dancer.

Corps de ballet: The full dance ensemble, minus soloists.

Danseur: A male dancer.

Fouetté: A whipping motion of the leg used to change direction or propel the body in circles.

Grand pas (grand step): A suite of dances within the story of the ballet. The dances are to display artistry and do not contribute to the storyline.

Pas de deux (step of two): A duet, usually performed by female and male leads.

Pirouette: A spinning turn on one leg.

Plié: A bending of the knees outward. The back remains straight.

The Twentieth Century, Modern Dance, and Beyond

The Russians revolutionized twentieth-century ballet in Paris where, in 1909, impresario Sergei Diaghilev (1872–1929) formed the *Ballet Russes* (Russian Ballet). The company featured two of Russia's greatest dance artists, ballerina Anna Pavlova (1881–1931) and danseur/choreographer Vaslav Nijinsky (1890–1950). Over the next four years, Diaghilev commissioned and premiered ballets by Europe's finest composers, including Maurice Ravel's

Pyotr Ilyich Tchaikovsky, c. 1880s.

The Ballets Russes in rehearsal.

(1875–1937) *Daphnis et Chloé* (1912), Claude Debussy's (1862–1918) *Jeux* (1913), and three ballets by the young Russian Igor Stravinsky (1882–1971): *L'Oiseau de feu* (*The Firebird*) (1910), *Petrushka* (1911), and *Le sacre du printemps* (*The Rite of Spring*) (1913).

Musically, the most important of Stravinsky's ballets was *Le sacre du printemps*. *Le sacre* tells of the arrival of spring in pagan Russia. In order to ensure the season's benevolence, a virgin girl is forced to dance herself to death. The ballet is divided into two parts, "The Adoration of the Earth" and "The Sacrifice."

It is fair to say that the world had never heard sounds like those conceived by Stravinsky for this ballet. Likewise, ballet had never before employed movements like those choreographed by Nijinsky. Stravinsky's harmonies were intensely dissonant, his rhythms brutal and unbalanced. Nijinsky's choreography mirrored the music.

Whereas classical ballet emphasized graceful leaps and vertical lift, Nijinsky's choreography for *Le sacre* kept dancers close to the earth. Whereas classical ballet emphasized the beauty of the human torso, Nijinsky buried his dancers under heavy costumes. Movements often had a brutal quality. There was no place for the Romanticism of earlier times. Nijinsky's poor virgin quivered with fear.

At the premiere, the audience probably did not know what to make of the production. They were opinionated nonetheless. Fist fights broke out between supporters and detractors; items were thrown on stage and into the orchestra pit. A near riot ensued. Despite the opening night chaos, Stravinsky's score would go on to become one of the most influential orchestral compositions of the century.

Nijinsky's choreography had a less auspicious fate. The ballet had only eight performances in Paris. Shortly after the premiere, composer and choreographer quarreled. When Nijinsky later developed a mental illness, the choreography was lost.

In the 1980s, dance scholars recreated the Nijinsky choreography by piecing together scraps of information taken from reviews, dancers' recollections, and instructions written into the rehearsal score. The Joffrey Ballet "premiered" the reconstruction in 1987. Appraising the reconstructed "original," dance historians now see Nijinsky's choreography as a groundbreaking attempt to break free of the strict regimen of movement and expression that had both guided and confined classical dance.

LISTENING GUIDE

CD IV/Track 3
Download track 54
mysearchlab 12.5

"THE AUGERS OF SPRING" ("DANCES OF THE YOUNG GIRLS")

from Le sacre du printemps (The Rite of Spring)

Le sacre is scored for an unusually large orchestra—quintuple winds—meaning five of each woodwind instrument, eight horns, five trumpets, three trombones, two tubas, nine timpani, plus numerous other percussion instruments and a larger-than-normal string section. Stravinsky also has the instruments playing in atypical and sometimes difficult registers. The result is an orchestral timbre that was as shocking as the choreography.

The entire ballet lasts about 30 minutes. We listen to the second scene, where the dancers first appear. They celebrate the advent of spring.

0:00	Strings play a loud, dissonant chord with irregular accents, punctuated by horns.
0:09	English horn and bassoon interrupt with an ostinato.
0:14	Strings and horns enter again, as above, now with piccolos, trumpets, and oboes commenting.
0:29	Trumpet interjections and piccolo twittering appear.
0:39	Strings and horns repeat the opening figure.

0:48	Bassoons join in with melody fragments. At 0:59 other instruments begin to participate with the bassoon.
1:19	Pizzicato string chord is followed by a long note in the horn and bass, and a percussion crash interrupts the constant motion.
1:23	The break is short; descending trumpet call dissolves into the bassoon ostinato with English horn trill.
1:30	Violins enter with glissando chords. At 1:38 strings play with the wooden part of the bow (*col legno*, with wood) producing a clicking sound.
1:43	The horn, then flute, plays a soaring legato melody. Other instruments comment percussively at 1:45.
2:04	While winds and strings continue playing ostinati, the low-pitched alto flute plays a quiet, lyrical melody in the background, answered by flute.
2:15	The orchestra gets louder as more instruments are added. Timpani plays a broken-chord ostinato. The clarinet adds shrill comments.
2:36	Strings play ostinati with syncopated pizzicato chords. As more instruments join in, the texture gets increasingly dense. Instruments sound melodic fragments above the ostinati. Tension builds to the end.

MUSICAL LIVES
IGOR STRAVINSKY (1882–1971)

Stravinsky composed in nearly every compositional style of the twentieth century. His early works reflect Russian nationalism. This was followed by a period of Neoclassicism in which the composer embraced the styles and forms of the eighteenth century—though with a modern compositional language. In the 1950s, Stravinsky experimented with the 12-tone system formulated by Arnold Schoenberg (see chapter 6: Music and Spirituality). Stravinsky was born in Russia. He lived in Switzerland and France before immigrating to the United States in 1939.

Igor Stravinsky posing with a score, c. 1930s.

Modern Dance

The incentive for new, more natural movements was in the air before *Le sacre*. American dancer Isadora Duncan (1877–1927), who had moved to Paris in 1900, had already abandoned ballet's restrictions. Dancing barefoot while dressed in flowing robes reminiscent of ancient Greece, Duncan moved in an improvisatory style that sought new freedoms in movement and new ways to liberate the female body from the restrictive confines of Western social norms. Thus, even as Duncan looked backward to Greek models she was creating a springboard for the emerging ideas and ideals of artistic modernism. In this sense, Duncan is the founder of the modern dance movement.

But while Duncan initiated the modern dance movement, it was American Martha

Isadora Duncan and dance partner, photographed by Arnold Genthe, c. 1915–1923.

Graham (1894–1991) who most profoundly developed and shaped it. Consider Graham's *Lamentation* (1930), music by Zoltan Kodaly, a sparse and emotionally unsettling work created as America fell deep into the hurt of the Great Depression. There is little dance movement in the traditional sense. Instead, the performer—who is confined within a tube of stretchy fabric that, like skin, extends from feet to head—seems to struggle for freedom. She grieves, begs, even writhes, but solace is denied. There is no catharsis, no resolution.

Graham choreographed nearly 100 works. Perhaps best known outside dance circles is the vibrant *Appalachian Spring* (1944), set to music by Aaron Copland. Important choreographers who spent formative years in Graham's company include Erick Hawkins (1909–1994) and Merce Cunningham (1919–2009). Graham's students included a variety of actors as well as pop star Madonna.

ASSIGNMENTS AND ACTIVITIES

- Watch the dance clips on **mysearchlab 12.6** and compare the different kinds of music and dance styles.
- Investigate the Joffrey Ballet's 1987 reconstruction of *Le sacre du printemps*. How accurate do you think the performance was? On what do you base your judgement?

A World of Popular Dance

While American choreographers were exploring the abstractions of modern dance, new popular styles were evolving in the dance halls. Swing dance—known in various times and styles as Lindy Hop, Jitterbug, and other names—drew from African American dance movements and soon gained popularity across all strata of American society. In the 1930s and 1940s, dance styles developed alongside the rise of jazz, particularly with the swing bands of the 1930s and 1940s. The style was fast, athletic, and designed for partner dancing.

With the rise of rock 'n' roll, swing gave way to new dance styles, including the twist, the Latin-inflected boogaloo, and a variety of short-lived dances with names like "the swim," "the monkey," and "the mashed potato." An important resource in disseminating the new dances was the popular Philadelphia-based television show *American Bandstand* (1952–1989), hosted by the ever-youthful Dick Clark (b. 1929). Virtually every popular music star and ensemble from rockabilly idol Jerry Lee Lewis (b. 1935) to Run-D.M.C. appeared on the show. Teens danced the latest steps as the celebrities performed.

Memphis dancers doing the jitterbug.

QUESTIONS FOR THOUGHT

- How does dance function in our society? How different are the dance experiences of North Americans from those of Ghanaians or South Americans?
- Who dances in our culture? Is dance associated with any gender, sexual orientation, age, or ethnic background? How so?
- How does one explain the popularity of television shows such as *American Bandstand* and now, *Dancing with the Stars*? Would North Americans rather watch dance or dance themselves?

CONCLUSION

We have seen that dance is about much more than physicality. Dance is a vehicle for personal expression and a corporeal repository for social values. Baamaya, for example, combines dance, music, and theater to give voice to cultural ideas about justice and social balance. Capoeira's mock fight keeps alive memories of those who fought for real in a centuries-long battle against slavery and racial oppression.

Bruno Tonioli may or may not have correctly assessed Kristi Yamaguchi's tango performance, but he was surely right about one thing. Athletic brilliance alone will never satisfy the rich expressive world of dance. The mind and heart must lead. Nijinsky's choreography in *Le sacre du printemps* may have been groundbreaking in terms of movement, but that in itself is not enough to make for a compelling performance. It is only when we see terror in the eyes of the innocent girl chosen to die that we in the audience are inescapably drawn in. It is at that moment that we begin to understand the power of society to order our lives, even decide who lives and who dies. By watching on we become unwitting accomplices to that horrifying act. Such is the richness and power of dance.

CHAPTER 13

Music and Concert

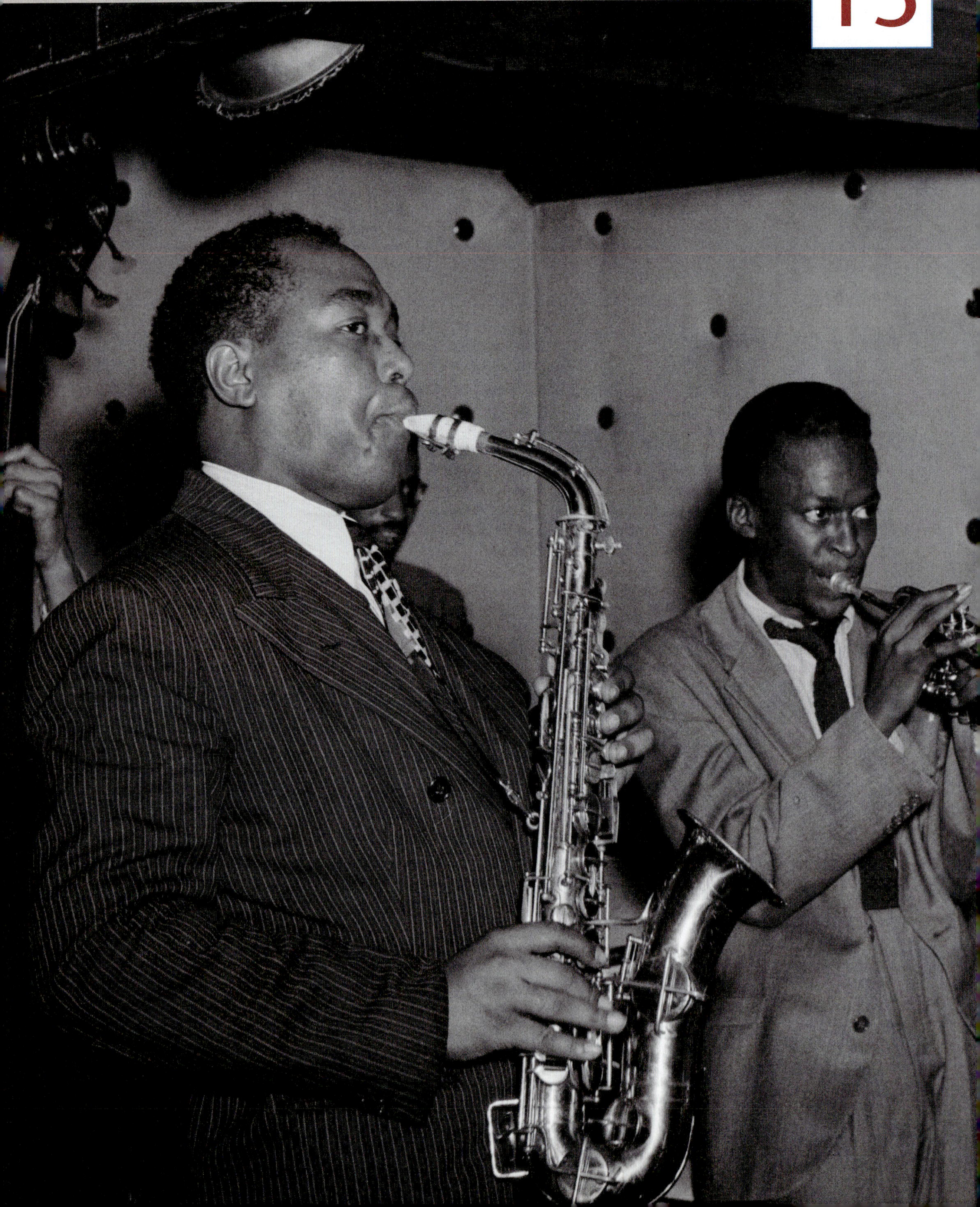

CHAPTER GOALS

- To examine concert traditions of different genres and cultures.
- To learn about different performing forces and styles of music.
- To examine significant works from three concert traditions.

ACTIVITIES AND ASSIGNMENTS

- Share your concert experiences with others in the class. What are the commonalities? The differences?
- Attend a variety of concerts and observe the customs and behaviors of performers and attendees. How does musical style relate to concert ritual?

Singer Ashlee Simpson (b. 1984) stood ready to perform as the *Saturday Night Live* cameras rolled. The band started—the audience heard Simpson's voice—but her lips didn't move. It was SNL without the L. Something had gone terribly wrong.

The idea had been for the band to play live along with a prerecorded rhythm track while Simpson sang or lip-synched along with a prerecorded vocal track. Because the band was live, the audience would never know that Simpson was not. Or that was the idea, anyhow. The prerecorded tracks started as planned, but it was the wrong song—the same one the band had played earlier in the show.

It was an unforgettable moment, one not unlike the little dog Toto pulling open the curtain to reveal the not-so-great-after-all Wizard of Oz. Simpson did not even pretend to sing. She bounced around for a few moments—she later called it a "hoe-down"—then got off stage. As the band played on, the show's director quickly cut to a commercial.

Live performance is not for the faint of heart. Consider the famous case of tenor Jerry Hadley (1952–2007), who in 1979 made his New York City Opera debut as a last-minute replacement. Not having had a chance to rehearse on stage, Hadley's first gaffe occurred when he caught his sword in the rungs of a chair. Moments later Hadley got too close to a candle that turned the plume of his hat into a torch. Every performer hopes to "catch fire," especially in a debut performance, but not like that.

While things do go horribly wrong—they can also go wondrously right, such as when a speaker captures the heart of a crowd or a band finds the perfect groove. When a great performer is "on," witnessing the event can be transformational. In this chapter, we focus on performance and present music as it might be heard in concert, that is, in musical events where the music itself is the focus and in which the audience sits and listens rather than actively participates. We begin with a mock program by a symphony orchestra. Next we downsize and look at chamber music, works written for small ensembles. From there we travel to South India to study an improvisatory musical form called **kriti**. The chapter closes with a selection from a mock jazz concert, a performance of trumpet master Miles Davis's (1926–1991) modal composition "So What."

As you work though this material, keep in mind the concepts you have learned in previous chapters. Issues of identity—whether seen through the lenses of ethnicity, nation, gender or spirituality—are invariably playing in the background. Remember, even events in the concert hall are about more than musical tones. Concerts reflect attitudes about the way people expect society to function. Paying close attention to these actions and attitudes can tell us important things about who we are.

> "What we play is life."
>
> —Louis Armstrong
> (1901–1971)

QUESTIONS FOR THOUGHT

- Rock bands rarely play "live" on television. Singers often lip-synch "live" performances, especially when their acts include dance routines. Does this information make a difference in your appreciation of the artist's performance?
- How does your familiarity with a band's recordings affect your live performance expectations?

(Continued)

QUESTIONS FOR THOUGHT (Continued)

- Why bother to see a band live? After all, the recordings will present a more polished sound. And they are error free.
- The band Milli Vanilli achieved infamy when it was revealed that Fab Morvan (b. 1966) and Rob Pilatus (1965–1998) did not actually sing on their recording. Their 1990 Grammy Award for Best New Artist was revoked and the band's popularity went into a tailspin. Were these consequences fair?
- Think back to a concert that you particularly enjoyed. What elements made the event so special? What elements impacted your feelings about a concert that you did not enjoy?

MUSICAL LIVES

PERFORMING THE AMERICAN DREAM

American Idol, which debuted on June 11, 2002, offers a piece of the American Dream. On *Idol*, even a girl from tiny Checotah, Oklahoma (2005 winner Carrie Underwood, b. 1983), or a former paint salesman (2010 winner Lee DeWyze, b. 1986) can become an international star.

Doors also open for those who don't win top honors, such as Clay Aiken (b. 1978), Chris Daughtry (b. 1979), or Adam Lambert (b. 1982). In 2010, the fantastically successful show was broadcast to 113 countries; the franchise included over 40 similar shows worldwide.

A Symphony Orchestra Concert

As the lights dim, the well-dressed audience in Chicago's Orchestra Hall becomes quiet. A disembodied voice requests that cell phones be turned off, and perhaps also tells patrons how to find the nearest exits. Moments later, the **concertmaster** walks on stage to polite applause. He bows, then looks at the oboist who sounds the pitch **A 440**. The orchestra tunes—first the woodwinds and brass, then the strings. This is followed by more silence and waiting.

Finally, the conductor enters. He bows to the audience, steps onto the podium, and raises his baton. Motion ceases and time seems to stop. With the wave of an arm the concert begins.

It is music from Aaron Copland's ballet *Rodeo* (1942). You probably recognize some of the melodies—perhaps from a movie soundtrack or a television commercial. Maybe you are wondering about the musical context. Why perform a ballet without dancers? **mysearchlab 13.1** What is "cowboy music" doing in a place so elegant?

There are no hard-and-fast rules about how an orchestral concert should be put together. There are, however, general models. Pops concerts, for example, usually open with a selection of light classical pieces. After intermission, the program is turned over to a well-known pop or jazz soloist.

"Serious" orchestral concerts also have standardized programming. The most common format features three works. The program opens with an overture or light "warm-up" piece. This is followed by a **concerto**, a composition featuring a solo instrumentalist with orchestra. Then comes intermission—a chance for the audience to stretch, make social and business connections, and, if the soloist was sufficiently inspiring, perhaps even order a subscription for the upcoming season. Following intermission, the orchestra offers its most serious and expansive composition of the evening, generally a **symphony**.

Our mock concert follows the standard model outlined previously. We feature three compositions, each from a different historical period. Aaron Copland's *Rodeo* is from the mid-twentieth century. Antonio Vivaldi's Concerto in E Major is from the Baroque era. Wolfgang Amadeus Mozart's Symphony No. 40 in g minor is from the Classical era. Our concert opener, the high-spirited *Rodeo*, would fit equally well in a pops or classical concert.

The Program

Four Episodes from *Rodeo* (1942) . . . . Aaron Copland (1900–1990)
Buckaroo Holiday—Corral Nocturne—Saturday Night Waltz—Hoe-Down

Concerto No. 1 in E Major (1725) . . . . Antonio Vivaldi (1678–1741)
("La Primavera")
        Allegro—Largo—Allegro

Intermission

Symphony No. 40 in g minor K. 550 (1788) . . . . . . W. A. Mozart (1756–1791)
      Molto allegro—Andante—Menuetto—Allegro assai

LISTENING GUIDE

CD IV/Track 4
Download track 55
mysearchlab 13.2

"HOE-DOWN" FROM *RODEO*

Composer Aaron Copland

Form: Introduction/A/B/A

	INTRODUCTION
0:00	A percussive cymbal crash and swirling string pattern open the music. It is easy to imagine spinning lariats, bucking broncos, and lots of dust.
0:04	Just moments into the music, the trumpets play an angular theme that is echoed in the woodwinds and strings. Notice how impatient those trumpets are—full of adolescent energy. They play and the strings echo. Before the echo is even completed, the trumpets jump in again.
0:19	Listen to the clippity-clop of the horses and how the rhythm jumps around. Are you beginning to wonder about these cowboys' riding skills? Or are they just teasing us tenderfoots, like clowns at a rodeo?
	SECTION A
0:40	Another cymbal crash and the strings (embellished with winds and xylophone) play a catchy country fiddle-like melody.
0:48	Dance groove appears.
0:56	The fiddle theme returns. Then it breaks into smaller fragments and expands throughout the orchestra.
1:20	Fiddles appear again.
1:35	A string flourish occurs, just like the opening measures of the introduction. This return to the opening music serves as both an exit from section A and an entrance into section B.
	SECTION B
1:39	A trumpet solo initiates section B. Notice the colorful sound made by a snare drum. Is that a gun? A whip? Some cowboy strutting his stuff?
1:48	Oboe, followed by clarinet and violin, takes up the trumpet melody. Notice how the instruments share the melody and play off each others' ideas. It sounds like these instrumentalists are great friends, just like the happy-go-lucky cowboys.
1:55	Return to the music that opened section B.
2:04	Here begins a syncopated figure in the winds and piano that alternates four times with the strings. After the fourth wind entrance, the strings can no longer be contained. They take off in real hoe-down style.
2:25	A flourish leads to this closing section. The horse clip-clops return, but everyone seems much too tired to care.
	SECTION A
2:50	Back to the fiddle melody for a couple go-rounds. Then a rousing finale occurs.

Aaron Copland

Brooklyn, New York-born Aaron Copland composed in many styles during his long career. He is best remembered for the earthy "everyman" style of music that he wrote during the years surrounding and including World War II. As titles of that era suggest—the ballets *Billy the Kid* (1938), *Rodeo* (1942), and *Appalachian Spring* (1944); the opera *The Tender Land* (1954); and orchestral works *El Salon Mexico* (1936), *An Outdoor Overture* (1938), *Fanfare for the Common Man* (1942), and *Lincoln Portrait* (1942)—these were years in which Copland (like many of his colleagues) celebrated the hopes and freedoms of American life. Copland's work occasionally drew from authentic folk music themes. More often, however, the melodies were original; they were just folk-like in character.

Copland's music is a part of American popular culture. The booming brass and drums of *Fanfare for the Common Man*, for example, were used to open the 1996 Atlanta Olympics. It has been heard in countless television commercials. "Hoe-Down" was featured in television advertisements sponsored by the American Beef Association. His music can also be heard throughout Spike Lee's film *He Got Game* (1998).

It might seem odd to take music from a ballet and turn it into a commercial, but such musical transformations across cultural and temporal boundaries happen all the time. In fact, Copland was borrowing as well. He took his "Hoe-Down" fiddle melody from *Our Singing Country*, a book he found in the New York Public Library. Contained within were folk songs collected in the 1930s by the father and son team of John (1867–1948) and Alan (1915–2002) Lomax. The melody, which has its roots in England, was also popular in the Appalachian fiddling repertoire where it was known by the title "Bonyparte" or "Bonyparte's Retreat." **mysearchlab 13.1**

As we read at chapter's opening, a typical symphony orchestra concert generally begins with a brief composition, usually less than 15 minutes. A short opening piece serves two main purposes. First, it allows audience members a chance to settle in and warm up their ears for the more complex music to follow. Second, it allows latecomers to be seated relatively early in the concert. In this latter point, there is a significant difference between classical music concerts and rock, pop, or jazz concerts. In classical music performances, late patrons are only allowed into the hall between pieces or at intermission. In these cases, it is best to be prompt.

MUSICAL LIVES
ALAN LOMAX (1915–2002)

Ethnomusicologist and folklorist Alan Lomax spent much of his life collecting music from around the world, particularly the American South. Among the musicians he and his father "discovered" and helped popularize was blues artist Huddie Ledbetter ("Lead Belly"). Lomax's complete recordings add up to some 150 hours of music and interviews.

QUESTIONS FOR THOUGHT

- Listen again to "Hoe-Down" and imagine a story. Create choreography. What might your dance look like?
- Copland wrote this music for dance. Yet, it is very successful when heard all by itself. Why?
- Do you think it was appropriate to use "Hoe-Down" in a beef commercial? Why or why not? Can you think of situations in which musical borrowing would not be appropriate?

| Aaron Copland, c. 1940s.

earned a central place in contemporary culture through commercials, film scores, and as background music in shopping malls. "Spring" is from a collection of four concertos called collectively *The Four Seasons*. Each three-movement concerto depicts a different season. Every movement musically depicts a poem apparently written by Vivaldi himself. The poem for the first movement of "Spring" is full of opportunities for musical descriptions of nature—birds, breezes, and thunderstorms:

Springtime is upon us.
The birds celebrate her return with festive
*   song,*
And murmuring streams are softly caressed
*   by the breezes.*
Thunderstorms, those heralds of spring, roar,
Casting their dark mantle over heaven,
Then they die away to silence,
And the birds take up their charming songs
*   once more.*

Alan Lomax performing on stage at the Mountain Music Festival, Asheville, N.C., c. 1940.

We continue our "virtual" concert with a concerto by Venetian composer Antonio Vivaldi.

Antonio Vivaldi

Venice, Italy, is situated in a saltwater lagoon at the edge of the Adriatic Sea. Today, just as 300 years ago during Vivaldi's lifetime, people travel the city's narrow pavements by foot and its canals by gondola or water taxi.

Besides its waterways, Vivaldi's Venice was known for its four *ospedale*, charitable institutions that cared for orphaned girls and young women. These institutions provided unusual and exceptional training—even professional opportunities—for those who showed talent in music. Among the faculty was Vivaldi, who wrote nearly half of his more than 500 concertos for the girls in his charge.

You have probably heard his Concerto in E Major, titled "La Primavera" ("Spring"). Like Copland's "Hoe-Down," this music has

MUSICAL THEMES
CONCERTO

A concerto is a large-scale work, usually in three movements (fast, slow, fast), that features an instrumental soloist (or a small group of instrumentalists) with orchestra. Vivaldi was highly influential in the genre's early development. Generally, a concerto alternates musical passages featuring a soloist with passages featuring the orchestra. Both soloist and orchestra share thematic material, but the soloist often has virtuosic sections that stretch the technical capabilities of the instrument. Important later composers of the concerto include Mozart, Beethoven, Johannes Brahms, and Pyotr Ilyich Tchaikovsky.

LISTENING GUIDE

CD IV/Track 5
Download track 56
mysearchlab 13.3

FIRST MOVEMENT (ALLEGRO), OP. 8, NO. 1, "LA PRIMAVERA" ("SPRING")

Composer Antonio Vivaldi

Ritornello form: orchestral refrain (ritornello) alternates with solo passages.

0:00	Orchestral introduction. The piece begins with a lively, bouncy violin theme played over a steady pulse in the cellos and basses.
0:10	The orchestra repeats the same phrase more softly.

(Continued)

LISTENING GUIDE (*Continued*)

0:18	Violins play a slightly different theme, in the same character as the introduction. This theme will be repeated many times throughout the movement and is called a ritornello. Low strings continue pulsing as before.
0:27	Repeat the ritornello more softly.
0:35	Now the solo violin enters, accompanied by the violins in the orchestra. Listen to the violin trills, as well as the short descending scales and repeated tones. What does this depict from the poem?
1:10	The orchestral ritornello is transformed into a new, smoother idea depicting murmuring streams and caressing breezes.
1:42	Orchestral ritornello occurs.
1:50	String tremolo (agitated, fast-repeated notes) depicts the impending thunderstorm.
1:57	Virtuoso solo passages and orchestral tremolo alternate.
2:19	Orchestral ritornello occurs.
2:27	Solo with repeated notes answered by orchestral violins.
2:47	Orchestra.
2:59	Solo.
3:15	Orchestral ritornello occurs.
3:21	Orchestra repeats ritornello more softly.

Now it is intermission. It is time to relax and refresh, perhaps to compare with friends your reactions to the concert's first half. So, take a break yourself. When you come back we will tackle the evening's most challenging work, Mozart's Symphony No. 40 in g minor, K. 550.

Wolfgang Amadeus Mozart

Mozart wrote over 600 works including symphonies, operas, concertos, sacred works, string quartets, and other chamber pieces. In 1862, Ludwig Ritter von Köchel (1800–1877) published a chronologically arranged catalog of Mozart's compositions. To this day, "K" numbers are used to identify this body of work.

The last three years of Mozart's life were difficult. Vienna was at war, and the opportunities for musicians waned. Accordingly, Mozart's performing opportunities decreased and his income dropped. He was forced to move his family to less expensive lodgings and borrow money from friends. Despite his troubles, this was a remarkably fertile period for composition. Mozart wrote his last three symphonies (no. 39, 40, 41) during the summer of 1788.

The four-movement structure of Symphony No. 40 is typical of the eighteenth-century symphony:

- Molto allegro. *First movements usually have a fast tempo and are in sonata form*
- Andante. *Slow or moderate tempo, usually lyrical*
- Menuetto. *Quick or moderate tempo; dance derived, in triple meter*
- Allegro assai. *Fast tempo (This one is in sonata form, although last movements can be in a number of different forms.)*

We shall focus on the first movement, Molto allegro. Like nearly all first movements written in the Classical period, this one is in sonata form. Sonata form has three main sections: exposition, development, and recapitulation (see the following diagram). In the exposition, two main key areas are presented, one following the other. This sets up harmonic unease. The two key areas, or sections, usually comprise contrasting themes that are memorable on first hearing. In the development section, the composer expands on the ideas presented in the exposition materials. He may break them apart, stretch them out, combine them, or explore new key areas, all techniques that will increase the sense of instability. In the recapitulation, the two sections presented in the exposition come back, except now the second key area sounds in the home key—and harmonic resolution is achieved.

Exposition		Development	Recapitulation
Key area 1 (transition)	Key area 2 (closing)	Composer plays with the materials from the exposition	Key area 1 (trans.) Key area 2 (closing)
Tonic key	Related key		Both areas now in tonic (home) key
Harmonically stable	Harmonic shift	Harmonically unstable	Harmonically stable--------------------
(section repeated)--------------------------------			

LISTENING GUIDE

CD IV/Track 6
Download track 57
mysearchlab 13.4

FIRST MOVEMENT FROM SYMPHONY NO. 40 IN G MINOR   *Composer W.A. Mozart*

EXPOSITION

0:00 FIRST KEY AREA: This is in the tonic (home) key of g minor. This first section is characterized by a rising and falling tune with a distinct rhythm: short-short-long; short-short-long; short-short-long-long. The melody is heard first in the violins. Violas play below in continuous short notes, providing momentum and a sense of agitation. The tune is repeated several times on different pitch levels. Sometimes the melody is slightly varied, making the phrases sound as if they are conversing with one another. Toward the end of the section (0:24) woodwinds enter with sustained notes.

0:30 TRANSITION: The violins now become more animated. The familiar short/short/long rhythm stops abruptly. Violins begin short, with clipped notes followed by a series of fast scales. We know something different is about to happen.

0:47 SECOND KEY AREA: This is in a new but closely related key (B-flat Major).
A rest in all voices (called a grand pause) precedes the beginning of the second key area. This section lacks the forward momentum of the first theme and parts of it sound like musical sighs because of the descending chromatic scale passages. Notice the conversation between the woodwinds and strings.

1:18 CLOSING MATERIAL: Mozart uses fragments of the opening melody as well as transition material to close out the exposition.

1:48 REPEAT EXPOSITION: In the Classical period sonata form the exposition is repeated. Musicians simply turn back to the beginning and start again.

DEVELOPMENT

3:39 The end of the exposition and beginning of the development is signaled by four decisive chords. Immediately following is a brief descending line in the woodwinds. Mozart changes keys throughout this section. You can hear the different harmonic colors accompanying the now unstable melody first heard at the beginning of the exposition. Soon, the texture thickens while the familiar melody is passed from section to section. The rest of the orchestra weaves independent countermelodies around the ever-moving tune. A pulsating rhythm underlies the section. The music sounds busy and slightly nervous. Finally the action winds down when the violins and flutes trade off fragments of the opening melody (4:36). A burst of energy inspires the rest of the orchestra to join in, but they quickly tire of the game and it is up to the violins and flutes to end the section.

(Continued)

LISTENING GUIDE (*Continued*)

RECAPITULATION

4:45	FIRST KEY AREA: This is in g minor.
5:52	SECOND KEY AREA: This is now in the home key, g minor. Notice how the minor key makes this theme sound darker than when it appeared in the exposition.
6:22	CLOSING MATERIAL: Mozart ends the piece with reminders of the opening melody and emphasizes the home key with a series of final chords.
6:50	CLOSING MATERIAL: Mozart ends the piece with reminders of the opening melody and emphasizes the home key with a series of final chords.

MUSICAL THEMES

SYMPHONY: A PIECE OR AN ENSEMBLE?

As we know from chapter 2: Listening to Music, the word "symphony" refers to a large performing ensemble that includes strings, winds, brass, and percussion instruments. But the term "symphony" also refers to a multi-movement composition performed by that ensemble. The genre developed in the mid-eighteenth century when Haydn, Mozart, and others established its importance in the concert repertory. Beethoven (see chapter 7: Music and Politics) greatly expanded the form in both length and complexity.

Symphony orchestras and symphonic compositions continue to spark the imagination. In 2009, American conductor Michael Tilson Thomas (b. 1944) led the YouTube Symphony Orchestra in the world premiere of Chinese composer Tan Dun's (b. 1957) "The Internet Symphony." The orchestra was made up of young musicians from around the world, all of whom auditioned by uploading their performances to YouTube. **mysearchlab 13.5**

Chamber Music

Far more intimate than orchestra concerts are recitals, which feature soloists or small chamber ensembles. During the eighteenth and nineteenth centuries, much of this music was written for the pleasure of amateur musicians who performed for one another and friends in the parlors of private homes. Today, because relatively few people are skilled performers, most chamber recitals are given by professionals in small concert halls.

The most popular chamber music combinations were, and still are, the string quartet (two violins, viola, and cello) and the piano trio (violin, cello, and piano). Piano recitals were enormously popular as well, especially during the nineteenth century when most middle class families owned a piano.

There is a large body of chamber music literature, far more than for the orchestra. We will look at an example of chamber music by Franz Joseph Haydn (1732–1809). Historians consider Haydn to be the "father" of both the string quartet and the symphony. Even though he did not invent either genre, he brought them to a high level of artistry and established their long-term importance.

After Haydn's quartet, we examine a solo violin piece by Niccolò Paganini (1782–1840), one of the most charismatic and accomplished virtuosos in the Western art music tradition. Performing his fiendishly difficult music represents a rite of passage for every serious violinist.

MUSICAL LIVES
FRANZ JOSEPH HAYDN (1732–1809)

Haydn's parents recognized his musical talents early. Because they could not afford to give him proper training, they sent the 6-year-old boy to live with a musical relative. When Haydn was 8 he became a choirboy at St. Stephen's Cathedral in Vienna.

Haydn spent most of his adult life working for the wealthy and prominent Esterházy family. As their employee, he was required to wear a servant's uniform and follow the family to their various estates. One of these was Esterháza, a mosquito-infested palace in rural Hungary. There Haydn was in charge of running the orchestra, playing chamber music for important guests, producing operas, and composing music. Although Haydn often felt isolated, the seclusion seems to have inspired him to creative heights.

In the last years of his life, Haydn became a free agent. He journeyed to London where his symphonies were performed at some of Europe's earliest public concerts. His music became wildly popular.

| Franz Joseph Haydn.

Franz Joseph Haydn, String Quartet in E-Flat Major, Op. 33, No. 2, "The Joke"

Franz Joseph Haydn had a keen wit. Often, his humor shone in his music. A prime example is the last movement of "The Joke" quartet. In order to "get" a joke, one has to understand its context. After all, humor functions by setting up, then breaking, expectations. Getting the humor in "The Joke" quartet requires that we understand the expectations of **rondo** form.

A classic rondo presents initial thematic material (A), which is followed by an "episode" of new material (B). The music then returns to the original A refrain before setting off in another episode (C). This process of alternating new and old continues throughout.

Thus, a rondo form with three episodes would be ABACADA.

The rondo in this quartet has just two episodes; thus, Haydn's audience would have expected the basic form to be ABACA, which it is, sort of. Once they knew what A sounded like, they would have felt confident in predicting how the movement would end. That's where Haydn decided to have a little fun. After the first phrase of the final A section, he inserts a **coda** (literally "tail")—an extra ending section. It begins as an adagio (slow section). Soon, we hear a bit of the A material—then a grand pause—then a little more of A. Another pause—more of A—pause—and finally the end of A. The movement has ended at last. Or so we think. . . .

LISTENING GUIDE

CD IV/Track 7
Download track 58
mysearchlab 13.6

PRESTO (LAST MOVEMENT) FROM STRING QUARTET OP. 33, NO. 2, "THE JOKE"

Composer Franz Joseph Haydn

0:00	A (REFRAIN): The A section has two ideas; a and b arranged as follows:
	a
0:06	a
0:12	b

(Continued)

LISTENING GUIDE (*Continued*)

0:28	a
0:34	b
0:50	a
0:57	B (EPISODE): This section modulates away from the home key.
1:25	A (REFRAIN): The refrain is back in the home key of E-flat. Notice that the "a and b" ideas do not repeat. a
1:31	b
1:48	a
1:54	C (EPISODE): This episode stays in the home key. Another joke—Haydn's audience would have expected it to change keys.
2:23	A (REFRAIN): This very short refrain uses only one iteration of "a."
2:31	CODA: The coda begins with a slow tempo—an adagio. Haydn then teases his audience by playing the "a" phrase again but interrupting it. Each interruption gets longer until the audience wonders when the piece will actually end. When he finally ends the phrase we are relieved. But stay tuned. The best joke is yet to come.

Niccolò Paganini, Caprice in A Minor, Op. 1, No. 24

Public concerts for a middle-class audience had only recently become the norm when violinist, guitarist, and composer Niccolò Paganini came of age. Music's first "box office hit," Paganini spent much of his life concertizing throughout Europe. One year alone he gave 151 concerts and traveled over 5,000 miles by carriage.

Tall, gaunt, and pale, with unruly shoulder-length black hair, the violinist gave a wraithlike appearance on stage. Women overcome with emotion wept when he played. Critics, perhaps jealous of the great performer's charisma, remarked on the demonic quality of his appearance and unprecedented technical facility.

Paganini's offstage life only added to his mystique. He earned a fortune performing but lost much of it gambling. A notorious womanizer of "hot Genovese blood" (a self portrayal), intrigues followed his every move. Unfounded rumors that a "crime of jealousy" had sent him to jail for 15 years (during which, conveniently enough, he learned to play the violin so well) both dogged and enhanced his reputation.

Paganini rarely published his own works, thus ensuring he would be their only performer. Indeed, he was probably one of only a few

Niccolò Paganini.

violinists at the time who *could* perform them. With long fingers and remarkable flexibility, Paganini's violin playing astounded audiences. Oftentimes he would dazzle them by playing entire works on only one string, fingers crawling up and down the violin's neck with spiderlike dexterity.

CD IV/Track 8
Download track 59
mysearchlab 13.7

LISTENING GUIDE

CAPRICE IN A MINOR, OP. 1, NO. 24

Composer Niccolò Paganini

Form: Theme and Variations

The 24 Caprices for Solo Violin—short, fanciful, and virtuosic—were perfect vehicles for Paganini. Though originally intended for his own performances, today they are standard recital pieces.

The work begins with a theme based on a snappy rhythmic motive: long—short-short-short-short-short. Eleven variations follow, each exploiting a different technical feat for the violinist. The work ends with a bravura finale.

0:00	THEME a
0:03	a
0:07	b: Notice the contrast between conjunct motion and the occasional octave leaps. As you listen to the variations, try to keep this theme in mind. Although the melodies change, the harmonic and formal structures remain the same.
0:15	Variation 1: Rhythms change to steady triplets with grace-note flourishes. The range expands up an octave.
0:30	Variation 2: The melodic material returns to the original range; the rhythmic density increases and much of the original melody is decorated with undulating chromatic passages.
0:48	Variation 3: A plaintive variation using "double stops" (playing on two strings at once) occurs at the interval of an octave. Notice that some of the melodic material is inverted and retrograde. The rhythm is augmented to half speed.
1:20	Variation 4: This is played one to two octaves above the original theme. Much of this variation consists of descending chromatic scales.
1:37	Variation 5: Notice the disjunct motion and wide range of this variation as the violinist plays the theme in broken octaves. The underlying harmonies are emphasized in the accented low notes.
1:58	Variation 6: Now we hear scales played in double stops, this time at the interval of a third in the A phrases and in tenths in the B phrase.
2:24	Variation 7: The rhythm returns to triplets that move at twice the speed of Variation 1.
2:45	Variation 8: The rhythm is simple, but the texture is suddenly homophonic. Chords are played by drawing the bow over three of the strings.
3:06	Variation 9: The technique used here is called "left-hand pizzicato"; instead of plucking with the right hand, as usual, the violinist must keep the bow in the right hand in order to play alternating bowed and plucked notes, executed by the left hand. This was one of Pagnini's signature techniques.
3:25	Variation 10: Played in the very top of the violin's range, this variation's delicacy and soft dynamics contrast with the more exuberant sections that surround it.
3:54	Variation 11: This variation uses double stops, sudden leaps from low to high, and melodically ascending flourishes.
4:18	Finale: Extends the last variation, now in a major key, for a flashy finish.

- How did Mozart and Haydn use musical form to create audience expectations? What happens to the musical experience if the audience does not understand the musical forms?
- Some people say that going to a Western art music concert is a passive experience. Would you say this is true? Why or why not?
- Imagine your favorite musician is performing in the living room of your home without the assistance of amplification. How would your experience of this "chamber" concert differ from an amplified event in an outdoor stadium? Which would you rather attend? Why?

ACTIVITIES AND ASSIGNMENTS

- Compare the forms of the compositions outlined previously. Can you find similar structures in art, literature, or architecture?
- Write a poem that parallels rondo or sonata form.
- Listen to the final movement of Mozart's Symphony No. 40 in g minor. Can you identify the form and its different sections?
- Does your town or university have a symphony orchestra? Investigate its history or document its repertory. How does this compare to other American orchestras? See the League of American Orchestras for comparative data (www.americanorchestras.org/).

South Indian Karnatic Music

India has ancient and esteemed performance art traditions, the theoretical foundations of which can be traced back to the *Natya Shastra*, written between 200 BCE and 200 CE. Even today, this text serves as a central authority in the production of traditional dance, theater, and music.

Like many aspects of Indian culture, musical traditions are split between north and south. Northern musicians perform in the Hindustani tradition. Southern musicians perform in the Karnatic (or Carnatic) tradition. Both traditions have roots in the *Natya Shastra*, but beginning with the thirteenth century influx of Persian influence in the north, they followed different lines of development. We focus on the Karnatic tradition.

MUSICAL LIVES

THE "TRINITY" OF SOUTH INDIAN COMPOSERS

Muthuswami Dikshitar (1776–1835), Syama Sastri (1762–1827), and Tyagaraja (1767?–1847) are venerated as Karnatic music's greatest composers. Tyagaraja is perhaps the most beloved of the three. He was a humble and devout man, believing that music was a way to experience god. He wrote over 600 kritis and two music dramas. Every January in Thiruvarur, Tyagaraja's birthplace, thousands gather to commemorate the composer in a music festival called the Tyagaraja Aaradhana. Tyagaraja festivals are also held in Cleveland (March), Salt Lake City (May), and Chicago (May).

Karnatic music uses a system of melodic modes called *ragas* (see chapter 2: Listening to Music). As with the Middle Eastern makam (see chapter 6: Music and Spirituality), ragas have specific defining characteristics:

- They are a collection of tones (*svaras*).
- Like a Western scale's "do-re-mi," each svara has a name: *sa-ri-ga-ma-pa-dha-ni-(sa)*.
- The distance between the tones, except for the foundational interval between "sa" and "pa," may be slightly larger or smaller from one raga to the next.
- There are rules governing the way the pitches are used. For example:
  - Ragas may be characterized by the vacillation between pairs of notes.
  - Raga melodic sequences may require that notes be skipped over, repeated, or left out.
  - The ascending form of a raga may be different from its descending form.

There are 72 **melakarta**, or parent scales, that include all seven tones. **Janya ragas**, which leave out one or more tones, are derived from these. Given the many different combinations of tones, ascending and descending versions, and pitch variations, it is mathematically possible to derive nearly 35,000 different ragas. Although only a fraction of these are used in common practice, the raga system provides an incredibly varied and colorful palette of melodic material.

Karnatic rhythmic structure is governed by the **tala** system. There are seven basic families of talas, each of which is subject to variation. Because of their length and complexity, tala cycles are broken up into smaller units of one, two, or more pulses. Listeners keep their place within the units by following along with specific hand motions as indicated in the following list:

- *Dhrutam:* two beats: palm down (hit against the thigh or other hand as in a clap) and palm up; notated by "O."
- *Anudhrutam:* one beat: palm down; notated by "U."
- *Laghu:* variable number of beats. Beat one is palm down, followed by counting beats with the fingers, starting with the little finger; notated by "I" followed by a number that indicates the total number of beats in the *laghu*.

The most common cycle is *Adi tala*, which consists of eight beats organized as laghu/dhrutam/dhrutam (notated I 4 O O). Here is how it works:

Beat 1	2	3	4	5	6	7	8
clap	5th finger	4th	3rd	clap	palm up	clap	palm up
laghu (I 4)				dhrutam (O)		dhrutam (O)	

Karnatic music concerts use a small group of musicians: one or more featured vocalists or instruments, with instrumental accompaniment. The performers sit barefooted on the floor, usually on a carpet. In India, concerts are sponsored by **Sabhas**, societies devoted to cultural and scholarly activities, and may take place in an auditorium or outdoors. In contrast to the very formal behavior expected at Western art music concerts, audiences at a South Indian concert may come and go while the musicians perform. Many listeners will "keep" the tala with their hands. They might even exclaim out loud at exciting points in the music. A typical concert will last two to three hours without intermission.

The musical texture can be divided into three parts: drone, melody, and rhythm. Usually, the **tambura**, a four-stringed long-necked chordophone, sounds a drone on the pitches "sa" and "pa." This provides a stable pitch center for the soloists. Today, however, an electric **śruti box** often replaces the tambura.

Even if the concert features a vocalist, a melodic instrument will often be used to provide a heterophonic texture as well as occasional improvisatory interludes. Melody instruments include the **venu** (a transverse bamboo flute), violin, and **veena**. The veena is a lute-family instrument with four melodic strings and three drone strings. It is about four feet long and played horizontally. On one end is a large round resonating chamber; on the other is a small gourd that helps a player balance the instrument. The veena player often sings while accompanying him/herself on the instrument.

The South Indian violin is the same instrument as the Western violin, though it is tuned and held differently. The venu has eight finger holes. By regulating the breath and adjusting the embouchure positions, a performer can achieve the pitch subtleties required to perform different ragas.

The **mridangam**—the main percussion instrument—is a double-headed drum made of a hollowed jackfruit tree trunk with goat-skin heads. The heads are connected by leather straps that can be adjusted to change the drum's pitch. The two heads are different sizes; one sounds low, the other high. On the higher head is a circle of black paste made of rice flour, ferric oxide, powder, and starch. The paste, which changes the way in which the drum head vibrates, allows the drummer to create a variety of tones and timbres.

Improvisation and precomposed works are both essential ingredients in a South Indian concert. Even when a work is composed, the musicians are expected to improvise certain sections. A traditional *kriti*, a sacred Hindu

| Tambura.

song, is the most common genre. It has three sections:

- *Pallavi:* the first verse, which can reappear throughout the piece
- *Anupallavi:* the second verse

- *Charana:* the last and longest verse, which can be repeated several times

Even when a singer is not present, the instrumentalists will maintain the kriti's text-based form.

LISTENING GUIDE

CD IV/Track 9
Download track 60
mysearchlab 13.8

"MANASU VISAYA"   *by Tyagaraja (Natakuranji Raga and Adi Tala)*

Tyagaraja's text asks whether the grace of Rama is attainable if the mind is thinking about worldly concerns. The kriti is loosely translated below:

Pallavi:
If the mind surrenders to the objects of senses, will the grace of Rama be attainable?

Anupallavi:
Chasing the objects of the senses can be compared to leaving your home open to the world so that the hounds of passion may enter and take control.

Charanam:
To follow the senses is like committing adultery to earn food. But that is no good for when you return home tainted, you will find that the cooking utensils have been stolen. Those who follow the senses are like the deaf. If instead of thinking of the Lord (who Tyagaraja praises with this poem), the mind surrenders to the objects of senses, will the grace of Rama be attainable?

The virtuous and venerated Rama is the focus of Tyagaraja's poem (see chapter 2: Listening to Music and chapter 9: Music and Love).

While the *Ramayana* is relatively unfamiliar in the West, it is universally known in the Hindu world. So too are Tyagaraja's poetry and songs. Thus, even in an instrumental performance of a kriti (as in our listening example), the instrumentalists will maintain the poem's text-based form. And because audience members also know the kriti, even in instrumental performances the words are heard in the listeners' minds. The musicians' improvisations take advantage of this relationship by emphasizing, and often repeating, melodic fragments associated with specific text.

This performance of "Manasu Visaya" includes the venu, violin, mridangam, and *ghatam* (a clay pot percussion instrument). The piece is in the eight-beat Adi tala. The raga is *Natakuranji*, which was probably introduced in the seventeenth century and uses a lowered svara ni: sa-ri-ga-ma-pa-dha-ni-(sa). The tendency of the raga's ascending direction is not a linear progression from low to high. It can be written as:

Sa ma ga ma ni dha ni pa dha ni sa

Descending as:

Sa ni dha ma pa ga ri sa

Notice that tones are skipped in this raga. "Pa" is rarely used. The most important tones are "sa," "ga," "ma," and "dha."

0:00	ALAPANA: We listened to this section of the performance in chapter 2: Listening to Music. We will not repeat the section's analysis but will include the music because the alapana plays an essential role in introducing the raga and its characteristics. Hear the drone outline "sa" and "pa," the raga's pillar tones over which the venu and violin outline the pitches of the raga.
2:34	KRITI: PALLAVI: When the violin stops improvising on the raga, the flute begins the first section of the kriti, the pallavi. The melody begins on the second beat of the tala cycle. With its repetition (2:38), the mridangam joins on the second half of the tala cycle (5, 6, 7, 8). Listen for the eight-beat cycles of Adi tala. (The beats go by at a walking tempo, approximately five seconds per cycle.) The section ends with a rhythmic cadence in the drums.
3:38	KRITI: ANUPALLAVI: The anupallavi explores the upper register of the raga. The upper "sa" is the usual destination, though the flute occasionally goes higher. Notice the heterophonic texture between flute and violin.

4:30	KRITI: CHARANAM: The flute returns to the lower register, before expanding upward again. The pallavi melody returns at 5:31. This signals the conclusion of the kriti. A series of soloistic improvisations follow, first for the melodic instruments, then for the percussion instruments. (fade out)
9:07	Mridangam solo: Here the mridangam player shows off his expertise by playing complex rhythmic patterns fitted skillfully against the tala.
9:58	Ghatam solo.
10:27	Mridangam solo.
10:54	Ghatam solo.
11:13	Kalpana Svaras: The interaction between the two percussionists increases and the solos become ever shorter. By 11:56 the two musicians have combined rhythmic forces. They continue this show of virtuosity until. . . .
12:57	Mridangam and ghatam solo ends with a **mora**, a thrice-repeated rhythmic cadential formula.
13:12	Flute and violin enter with the basic pallavi melody, which brings the performance to a close.

QUESTIONS FOR THOUGHT

- How do the concepts of rhythm and melody differ between Western art music and South Indian music? What concepts do they share?
- What do the concert traditions of Western Europe and South India have in common? What are the differences?
- Why do the performers return to the pallavi melody at the composition's close?

ACTIVITIES AND ASSIGNMENTS

- Investigate how South Indian musicians are trained. How does it differ from music students in the West?
- Listen to the fusion group Shakti, featuring British jazz guitarist John McLaughlin, Hindusani tabla virtuoso Zakir Hussain, Karnatic violinist L. Shankar, and others. Each musician represents a different heritage, yet their music seems to fit well together. Why is this so?

Jazz

From its roots in turn-of-the-twentieth-century New Orleans, the story of jazz has been one of synthesis, innovation, and adaptation. Jazz began when musicians from this culturally diverse city found ways to combine African and European traditions. Rhythms were freed up; scales were given new shapes and colors. As jazz spread, first up the Mississippi River, then east and west, and eventually across the oceans, new influences were assimilated. Jazz found worldwide appeal.

But what exactly is jazz? First of all, it is music that is improvised. Musicians are expected to create and develop new ideas in the moment, with the same ease as two people having a conversation. Second, jazz swings. The rhythmic groove is expected to flow and feel loose. Third, jazz performance is passed down from one musician to the next by oral tradition. Still today, and even in college settings, musicians primarily learn through a three-step process of listening, assimilating, and imitating (re-creating), in addition to coming up with original ideas.

Other characteristics also define jazz. Some argue that it is fundamentally an African American genre. As evidence, they cite the music's black and Creole roots in New Orleans dance halls and red-light district (a neighborhood called Storyville). Further proof comes in the fact that the majority of jazz's greatest exponents and innovators have been black.

Others argue that jazz is a state of mind. They say jazz is a way of thinking about and making music. In support of this idea they might point to the emphasis on musical individuality and creativity, or the emphasis on learning by ear rather than by musical notation. Or they might argue that jazz reflects a certain urban lifestyle, an attitude of social resistance to the status quo, and even resistance to authority in general.

Still others will say that jazz is about life, that it is a visceral in-the-moment response to the world in which we live. For them, performance is about the evolving and ever-deepening relationship between musician and music, among musical colleagues, and between musicians and their audiences. Communication is everything.

Early on, there was a strong connection between jazz and dance. The big bands of Fletcher Henderson (1897–1952), Duke Ellington, Count Basie (1904–1984), and many others powered the swing dance crazes of the 1920s through 1940s. In later years, with the advent of the rhythmically complex bebop style and the rise of rock 'n' roll, jazz moved away from dance and toward an aesthetic based on listening.

Filling concert halls was the next step. This first happened in 1938, when clarinetist Benny Goodman (1909–1986) and his racially integrated band sold out America's most prestigious venue, New York City's Carnegie Hall. Today, jazz festivals in Newport, Rhode Island; Monterey, California; New Orleans; and Detroit provide the genre some of its broadest visibility.

Dividing the jazz century more or less in half, we will study the 1959 recording of "So What." This modal composition is found on the landmark album *Kind of Blue*. Featured is bandleader and trumpeter Miles Davis along with alto saxophonist Julian "Cannonball" Adderley (1928–1975), tenor saxophonist John Coltrane (1926–1967), pianist Bill Evans (1929–1980), bassist Paul Chambers (1935–1969), and drummer Jimmy Cobb (b. 1929). While the tune's tonality might sound unusual to your ears, the form should sound familiar. It is AABA 32-bar song form (see "Over the Rainbow," chapter 3: Three Listening Examples).

MUSICAL THEMES
GETTING IN THE MODE

Try singing up and down a major scale: DO RE MI FA SOL LA TI DO—DO TI LA SOL FA MI RE DO. "Do" is the home tone, right? It is the place where our musical journey begins and ends. It is the place of ultimate relaxation. That relationship is the central characteristic of the major scale.

Now sing the scale tones again, but this time begin on "Re." Sing up one octave to the next "Re," then back down: RE MI FA SOL LA TI DO RE—RE DO TI LA SOL FA MI RE. This may take some mental gymnastics, but position "Re" in your mind so that it functions as the home tone instead of "Do." Voila! You have just entered the Dorian mode, the same mode that Davis used when writing "So What."

Successful musicianship comes with the ability to hear and understand relationships. Go back to the scale and shift the "home" tone once again. It can be anywhere, and each repositioning of the home tone changes the relationship between the rest of the tones. In music, as with most everything else in life, understanding comes with gaining the proper perspective.

MUSICAL LIVES
MILES DAVIS (1926–1991)

Left to right: Tommy Potter, Charlie Parker, Miles Davis, and Duke Jordan.

Miles Davis was a trumpeter, bandleader, and composer. He performed and wrote in nearly every jazz style from bebop on, but he is particularly known for his contributions to cool jazz, modal jazz, and fusion. In the 1950s and 1960s, Davis played and recorded with some of the greatest names in jazz history: Charlie Parker, John Coltrane, Bill Evans, and Thelonius Monk, among others. In the early 1970s he made the switch to amplified instruments and his recordings, such as *Bitch's Brew* (1970), used cutting-edge studio techniques, such as multi-tracking and tape loops. Toward the end of his life, Davis even experimented with hip-hop. Like many musicians who came of age in the be-bop era, Davis was plagued by drug addiction. He died at age 65 of a stroke. **mysearchlab 13.9**

LISTENING GUIDE

CD IV/Track 10
Download track 61
mysearchlab 13.10

"SO WHAT"

by Miles Davis

0:00	Introduction	The bass and piano introduction provides a contemplative opening that, like the alapana section of Karnatic music, involves a nonmetric exploration of the mode's melodic possibilities.
0:34	A SECTION, 8 bars	The melody is in the bass with punctuating chords in the piano joined later by the other instruments. Notice the conversation taking place. The bass makes a statement to which the piano answers, "So what?" Follow this conversation as it unfolds over AABA form. The second A section repeats the scenario. In the B section, the bass asks the same question but raises the pitch level, almost as if imploring the piano to listen. Still the response is, "So what?" Finally, the return to A. The bass returns to the original pitch level. Again, "So what?" This section of a jazz tune, where the basic melody is introduced, is called the "head." Generally it appears at both the beginning and conclusion of the performance.
0:49	A SECTION repeats, 8 bars	
1:03	B SECTION, 8 bars	The B section has the same melody as A. It just begins on a slightly higher pitch (1/2 step higher).
1:17	A SECTION, 8 bars	Trumpet solo. Listen with mind and body to Davis's solo. The playing is relaxed and full of meditative space. He takes his time, and is almost casual in expanding the possibilities of the melodic mode. There is no sense of urgency. Try to hold on to the regularity of the AABA form. Notice how Davis's phrasing meanders along the boundaries of 8-bar sections. Also notice how the musical role of bass and piano has changed. Before, their playing was in the foreground. Now their job is to support the soloist.
1:32	A SECTION	
1:48	A	
2:01	B	
2:15	A	The trumpet continues to improvise in the mode.
2:29	A	
2:43	A	
2:57	B	
3:12	A	
3:26	A A B	Tenor saxophone solo: John Coltrane. Coltrane picks up the mood from Davis, then proceeds to animate it. The playing is more syncopated, more rhythmically active, and has many more notes.
4:08	A (fade out)	

So far in this chapter we have looked at typical concert pieces from three different traditions: Western art music, South Indian art music, and jazz. We've seen variations in musical styles, performance space, and expectations of behavior. These variables only increase when you consider the many other concert traditions around the world.

What makes a concert? It is far more than the music. A concert is a social phenomenon that brings people together to experience and express shared values. Attending a musical event helps people feel like they are part of a group. It reaffirms their social history and legitimizes interests and beliefs. The kinds of concerts one enjoys can be just as clear a marker of identity as political, religious, ethnic, and gender identifications. In fact, all of these things contribute to, and reflect, the types of music we enjoy.

Just as our identities evolve and grow in accord with ever-broadening life experiences, so too do our musical tastes.

"You know what you like; you like what you know."
—Cornelius & Natvig

Coda

Three Performances
Consider the following scenarios.

1. On stage in Seattle a band of Mbuti pygmy hunters from Central Africa moves stealthily through the haze of dry-ice fog and the brownish hues of carefully designed stage lighting. They enact the successful hunt of imaginary game, then celebrate with song and dance. At intermission, the audience strolls past sale tables of CDs and African art.

2. In Darmstadt, Germany, a large metal box sits alone on stage. The audience waits. This being the city's international biennial new music festival, it is anyone's guess as to what will happen. The performance begins with taps and clanks coming from inside the box. Eventually—with the help of sledge hammers, metal sheers, and a blow torch—the performers bang, slice, and melt their way out. One of them, a saxophonist, blows for a couple minutes. Then the piece is over.

3. In Pengosekan, a village on the Indonesian island of Bali, American university students file nervously into a courtyard. They sit down among the gamelan instruments and adjust their traditional batik wraps. Just a few weeks ago few of them had ever even heard a gamelan. Today they will perform for the Balinese community.

What should one make of these performances? The first example, which might be termed folkloric, invites the audience to imagine a strange and primal world in which the lives of man and nature are interwoven, perhaps as they were at the dawn of humankind. The Darmstadt example also apparently focuses on humankind's relationship to the world. But there the focus seems to be on freeing oneself from the unfeeling metal of modern industrial life. Alternatively, perhaps the piece is a call to "tune in" to the sounds of our modern environment. The Bali example suggests a journey of initiation and integration—from musical ineptitude to understanding, from social alienation toward social acceptance.

Any performance can be read in an endless variety of ways. The previous interpretations focus on broad cultural ideas. In what other ways might we look at these performances? What might a focus on the performers and audience reveal? What might we learn by focusing on the musical sounds alone?

Wouldn't you like to know what was going through the Mbutis' minds as they "hunted" on that Seattle stage? When the performance was over, did they head backstage for a real meal . . . perhaps Chinese takeout? And what about the audience? Did they feel closer to the Mbuti or more alienated than ever? What was the difference between this performance and "human zoos" of the nineteenth and early twentieth centuries (see chapter 4: Music and Ethnicity)?

The college students performing in Bali (a mixed ensemble of women and men) might have felt as if they too were exhibits in a human zoo. Here, however, the centuries-old imbalance of power between cultures West and East was inverted. This time it was the "exotic" West on display as the East watched on.

As for the Darmstadt performance, what was it like inside of the box? Hot? Smoky? Were the musicians worried about fire from the blowtorch? Were they banging and cutting in a consciously "musical" way or just trying to get the heck out? We know something about the audience's response—they hooted and whistled (a particularly derisive act in Europe), and even threw coins at the stage. Might we consider these actions as part of the performance, even if they were spontaneous?

How else might we analyze these three performances? Do you see gendered scripts being played out? What about scripts demonstrating ethnicity or nation, politics or

spirituality? What about love or war? What was the relationship between Mbuti music and dance? Were the Darmstadt banging and cutting a kind of musical theater? What are the rules of performance when jungle meets stage, blow torch frees saxophonist, or when West travels East?

We have not talked about the musical sound in any of these performances. But those too are based on culture-bound codes of understanding. Certainly the Mbuti understood the music they were singing. They knew how the sounds should fit and when to start and stop. Presumably few, if any, in the audience possessed these skills. In contrast, the Balinese audience knew exactly what the music should sound like, though it is likely the students' technical shortcomings had little impact on their enjoyment of this novel performance. Harder to figure out is the Darmstadt concert. Clearly the audience did not think highly of the piece, but whose fault was that? The composer's? The performers'? To what was the audience reacting? To the sounds alone—perhaps as combinations of tones that failed to be meaningful? Or were listeners reacting to the absurdity of the performance itself? (And finally, in their noisy reaction, was the audience "performing" as well?)

What makes music (or any art form) good? How do we judge excellence? Why do we like the music we like? It is never as simple as appreciating sequences of well-constructed tones. Culture is central.

We began this book with the story of Mrs. Campbell, the 93-year-old Alzheimer's patient who upon hearing the music of her childhood threw off two years of silence and began to sing. Then, when the music stopped, she once again faded away.

What did Mrs. Campbell "hear" in those old tunes? Did she remember back 90 years to when, sitting atop her father's shoulders, she was the tallest kid in the room? Maybe she remembered smelling the sweetness of a homemade pie or sharing a secret with a childhood friend. Perhaps she even felt the tentative touch of love's first kiss. We cannot know, of course. But these sorts of memories seem more than possible. After all, musical experience connects us to the present and the past, and also prepares us for the future. Quite simply, music helps light the way as we live our lives.

A440 The musical pitch A above middle C. It has the frequency of 440 Hz, that is, a vibratory rate of 440 cycles per second. A440 is the standard tuning pitch in Western art music.

1/4 tone (Quarter tone) A pitch that splits the difference between two half steps, such as the pitch midway between F and F sharp or B flat and B.

12-bar blues A form of the blues that divides phrases into three equal sections of four measures (equaling 12 measures, or bars). The lyrics generally follow an AAB format. The harmonies proceed in a fixed pattern of tonic, subdominant, and dominant chords.

12-tone system (also called serialism or dodecaphony) A compositional method developed in the 1920s by Arnold Schoenberg.

Aerophones Instruments whose sound is produced by columns of vibrating air. Examples include the flute, oboe, trumpet, bagpipe, whistle, and so on.

American Song Book (or Great American Song Book) A conceptual collection of popular songs composed for the music industry primarily between 1920 and 1960. The collection draws from Broadway show tunes, Hollywood film, and popular culture in general. Many of these songs are known as "jazz standards."

Arabesque A ballet position in which the dancer places weight on one leg while the other is extended behind.

Aria A song for a vocal soloist in genres such as opera or oratorio. The aria contrasts with recitative, a speechlike style of singing that conveys the dialogue.

Atonality Refers to music that lacks a tonal foundation or key center. Atonal music was developed in the early twentieth century as an alternative to the lush harmonic structures of late Romanticism.

Baamaya A dance of the Dagbamba ethnic group of Ghana, West Africa.

Balafon A xylophone from West Africa.

Ballad A sung poem or verse that tells a story.

Ballerina A female ballet dancer. The term was once exclusively used to designate the principal female dancer in a professional dance company.

Bàtá Double-headed hourglass-shaped drum of the Yoruba ethnic group of West Africa.

Battle Mass A polyphonic setting of the Ordinary sections of the Catholic Mass. The music replicated battle sounds.

Beat A steady rhythmic pulse, usually organized into measures (or bars).

Beijing opera (Jīngjù) The most influential style of Chinese opera; includes singing, dialogue, acrobatics, and martial arts.

Big band A jazz ensemble of 10 to 15 instruments performing the music of the Swing Era, the period from the 1930s through World War II.

Binary form A common musical form consisting of two sections (AB). When a portion of the material from the beginning of the piece returns at the end, the form is known as rounded binary (ABa).

Birimintingo A soloistic style of kora playing that features melodic improvisation.

Blackface Theatrical makeup used by white performers to portray African Americans in minstrel shows and vaudeville.

Blackface minstrelsy see Minstrel show.

Blues A music genre that grew out of the African American experience in the Mississippi Delta.

Bocet (plural: bocete) A Transylvanian funeral lament.

Bolon An arched harp from West Africa.

Branle A Renaissance dance in which participants move from side-to-side in a circle or line.

Brass An instrumental section of the symphony orchestra, which generally includes trumpet, horn, trombone, and tuba.

Breeches role see Pants role.

Bridge On a stringed instrument, a small piece of wood that supports the strings and conducts their vibrations into the body of the instrument.

Burlesque Comic parodies of serious genres such as plays, operas, or dance.

Cadence The ending point of a musical phrase, which often consists of a formulaic harmonic pattern.

Cantor The person who sings liturgical music and leads the prayers in either Christian or Jewish religious traditions.

Capoeira Dance/martial art with roots in Afro-Brazilian slave communities.

Castrato (plural: castrati) An adult male vocalist castrated before puberty so as to prevent the change of voice. Castrati were used in church choirs and in opera. The practice was prevalent in the seventeenth and eighteenth centuries.

Chamber music In Western art music, music for a small ensemble of musicians with one performer per musical part.

Chanson The French word for song, which often pertains to French songs of the thirteenth to sixteenth centuries.

Chant Genre of vocal music used by the Catholic church from the Middle Ages to Vatican II. Chant is sung in Latin, is monophonic, and uses free, nonmetered rhythms. It is also known as plainchant.

Chest voice In singing, the sound that resonates in the chest (rather than the head, as in falsetto). The speaking voice is considered to resonate from the chest.

Chord Three or more pitches sounding at the same time.

Chordophones Instruments whose sound is produced by vibrating strings. Examples include the violin, guitar, piano, and kora.

Chromatic notes Notes other than those of the prescribed key.

Chromatic scale A scale of half-step (semitone) pitches that contains all 12 tones within the Western octave.

Church modes A melodic system consisting of eight "scales" or modes used in music of the Medieval

Period: dorian/hypodorian, phrygian/hypophrygian, lydian/hypolydian, mixolydian/hypomixolydian.

Cimbalom An Eastern European hammered dulcimer.

Coda An optional section added to the end of a musical composition (literally: tail).

Coloratura An intricate vocal melody in eighteenth- and nineteenth-century Western art music; it is also a soprano voice type characterized by the singer's ability to execute highly elaborate melodies.

Composition A musical work.

Concertmaster/concertmistress The principal violinist in an orchestra who tunes the orchestra, helps make decisions regarding bowings and fingerings, and leads the first violin section.

Concerto A three-movement (usually) work for a soloist(s) and orchestra (or band).

Conjunct motion The stepwise progression of pitches in a melody.

Consonance Sounds that please the ear. Notions of consonance are socially defined and vary according to time and place.

Corps de ballet The dancers in a ballet company not including the soloists.

Corrido A popular Mexican narrative ballad in triple meter. Lyrics often detail social ills and feature heroes or villains.

Countermelody A contrasting melody played with a main melody.

Countertenor A male singer with a well-developed falsetto who sings in the alto or soprano range.

Danseur A male ballet dancer. It generally refers to a company's principal male dancer.

Development The middle section of a sonata form where the musical materials from the exposition are manipulated rhythmically and harmonically.

Diatonic Tones contained within the key or tonality.

Didgeridoo An Australian aboriginal wind instrument that produces deep and varied drones.

Diegetic In film, music that is part of the narrative action; music that can be heard by the characters in the film.

Dirge A slow-paced mournful piece associated with death and/or funerals.

Disjunct motion Angular melodic motion that moves in leaps.

Dissonance Sounds that clash or harmonies that are not pleasing to the ear. Notions of dissonance are socially defined and vary according to time and place.

Dominant The fifth tone (or the chord built on the fifth tone) in a major or minor key.

Donkilo The basic tune of a jali's song.

Downbeat The first beat of a measure.

Drone A continuously sounding pitch; the instrument that sounds the drone pitch.

Electrophones Instruments whose sound is produced electronically.

Enlightenment The philosophical movement in the eighteenth century that emphasized reason and individualism.

Exposition The initial section of a sonata form where the musical themes are introduced, which usually consists of two distinct themes in contrasting keys.

Falsetto A method of vocal production that allows males to sing naturally in the alto or soprano ranges.

Fin amours French term meaning "chivalric" or "courtly love"; a formalized tradition of love between a knight and a married noblewoman. It is associated with troubadour and trouvére songs of the Medieval Period.

Folksongs Songs that are usually transmitted by oral tradition and associated with the ordinary "folk" in a particular country.

Form The overall shape or structure of a piece of music.

Formes fixes French term referring to the three "fixed forms" used in songs of the troubadours and trouvéres.

Fouetté In ballet, a quick turning motion of the leg used to change direction or propel the body in circles.

Fugue A polyphonic musical composition in which a short melody or phrase, called the subject, is used imitatively in alternation with new musical material.

Gamelan An instrumental ensemble of Indonesia; generally includes bronze xylophone-like instruments and gongs.

Genre A category, usually of artistic output. Genres may be classified according to styles, eras, forms, subject matter, and so on.

Ghost Dance A late nineteenth-century Native American religious movement initiated by Wovoka.

Ginga Back-and-forth-step pattern designed to facilitate quick movements and sudden changes in direction in Brazilian capoeira.

Glissando An ascending or descending slide between two tones.

Grace note A quick, nonmetered tone used as an embellishment to the tone it precedes.

Grand pas (Grand step) In ballet, a suite of individual dances within the story of the ballet. The suite serves as a showpiece for lead dancers and does not contribute to the storyline.

Gu shi In Chinese opera, the master drummer.

Habanera An Afro-Cuban dance with a distinguishing rhythmic ostinato, which is also used as the basis of numerous Western art music compositions to denote exoticism or ethnicity.

Hakamma bards Women of the Baggara people of Sudan who sing about social justice.

Half step (semitone) The smallest pitch interval commonly used in Western music (example F to F sharp).

Harmonic singing (or chanting) A vocal technique whereby a singer simultaneously produces a fundamental pitch and its overtones; also called overtone singing.

Harmonics Resonant tones (overtones) sympathetically produced above a fundamental tone.

Harmony The combination of simultaneously sounding tones that produce chords or chord progressions.

Head The precomposed part of a jazz piece.

Heterophony Musical texture in which slightly different versions of a melody are performed simultaneously by two or more performers. Heterophony is used more commonly in

Asian, Middle Eastern, and Native American traditions than in Western music.

Homophony A chordal texture; melody plus chordal accompaniment.

Hymn A religious song, usually sung by the congregation during worship services.

Idiophones Instruments that produce sound by shaking or striking the body of the instrument. Examples include cymbals, woodblocks, and sleigh bells.

Impressionism A late nineteenth-century French movement in painting concerned with shifting light and color. It also refers to some of the music of Debussy and Ravel, whose instrumental timbres are said to resemble the shimmering color palettes of their counterparts in the visual arts.

Improvisation The act of creating or performing music spontaneously.

Jali (or griot) A bard of the Mandinka ethnic group of West Africa (plural: jalolu).

Janya raga In Karnatic music, a raga derived from the Melakarta ragas.

Jews harp (or jaw harp) A small musical instrument of ancient origin that is held against the teeth or lips and plucked with the fingers.

Jīngjù see Beijing opera.

Juke joint (barrel house) An African American informal social establishment that featured music, dancing, drinking, and gambling.

Kabuki Japanese dramatic genre using stylized songs and gestures.

Kanun Turkish zither.

Karnatic (or Carnatic) music The classical music of South India.

Kemençe Turkish three-stringed bowed fiddle.

Klezmer An instrumental musical tradition of the Ashkenazic Jews of Eastern Europe.

Kol Nidre Aramaic for "all vows"; a prayer sung on the Day of Atonement service on the eve of Yom Kippur.

Komibuki Pulsing breath. A shakuhachi breathing technique used to focus the mind.

Kora A plucked 21-stringed harp-lute from West Africa.

Kotekan Interlocking rhythmic parts that form the foundation of the Balinese rhythmic system.

Kriti In Karnatic music, a musical form that consists of three sections: pallavi, anupallavi, and charanam.

Kumbengo A repetitive melodic style played on the kora.

Kundüm Paired kettle drums used by the Mevlevi Order of Sufism.

Lament A song that expresses grief at a person's death.

Leitmotive A recurrent musical theme that represents people, places, things, ideas, or emotions.

Libretto The text of an opera.

Lied German term meaning "art song." Lieder (pl.) were especially popular in the nineteenth century.

Lining out A way of performing hymns or psalms whereby a leader sings each line of the hymn slightly ahead of the congregation to cue the melody and lyrics.

Liturgy A fixed set of texts, prayers, and music that forms the basis for worship services.

Lute A pear-shaped, plucked stringed instrument popular in the Renaissance and Baroque periods.

Madrigal An Italian Renaissance vocal composition, usually written for several voices and often polyphonic.

Major scale A collection of stepwise pitches, ascending and descending, that comprise the syllables do, re, mi, fa, sol, la, ti (do).

Makam The melodic system used in Turkish classical music.

Mandala A work of visual art that symbolically represents the universe.

Mariachi A folk music tradition of Mexico. Mariachi bands usually consist of violins, trumpets, guitar, and guitarrón (a large acoustic bass guitar).

Mass The daily Catholic church service that features Holy Communion. It can also refer to a composition that sets to music the Ordinary sections of the Mass (see Mass Ordinary).

Mass Ordinary Sections of the Catholic Mass where the texts remain the same from day to day, including the Kyrie, Gloria, Credo, Sanctus, and Agnus Dei.

Mass Proper Sections of the Catholic Mass where the texts are different from day to day.

Measure A unit of rhythmic time in Western music that contains a designated number of beats. (It is also called a "bar.")

Melakarta In Karnatic music, the 72 parent ragas from which all other ragas are derived.

Melismatic singing Situation when multiple pitches are sung to one syllable of text.

Melody Distinct pitches sounding one after another through time; the "tune" of a piece of music.

Membranophones Instruments whose sound is produced through vibrating membranes. Examples include most drums.

Meter The number and accentuation pattern of beats in a measure.

Mevlevi Order A suborder of Sufism, the mystical sect of Islam. In the West, the Mevlevi are commonly known as the Whirling Dervishes.

Minimalism A style of music originating in the 1960s associated with composers Steve Reich, Philip Glass, and others. Distinctive features include repetitive but slowly developing melodies, harmonies, and rhythms.

Minstrel show Musical comedies popular in the nineteenth century in which white performers wore blackface and satirized African American culture.

Modal Music that is based on a melodic system of modes (see Church modes) rather than major or minor keys.

Modes see Church modes.

Monophony A musical texture in which a unison, single melody is sounded, no matter the number of performers.

Mora In Karnatic music, a thrice-repeated rhythmic cadential formula.

Motet A sacred, polyphonic composition, usually for voices alone. It is one of the main genres of the Medieval and Renaissance periods.

Movement In music, a self-contained portion of a larger work. (A symphony, for example, generally contains four movements.)

Mridangam A double-headed drum used in Karnatic music.

Nationalism A mid- to late nineteenth-century compositional trend that used musical ideas identified with particular nations, regions, or ethnicities.

Natural trumpet A valveless trumpet.

Ney A Middle Eastern end-blown flute.

Ngoni A West African five-stringed lute.

Noh A Japanese drama that uses masks, dance, and song.

Nondiegetic music Film music that does not exist in the world of the on-screen characters; also called the underscore.

Octave The relationship between one pitch and another with exactly twice the vibration speed. The consonance of the octave is recognized in all world cultures.

Opera A staged and sung dramatic work with instrumental accompaniment.

Operetta A short, lighthearted opera that includes spoken dialogue and song.

Oral tradition The passing of music from one generation to another by speech or song, without written notation.

Orchestration The way that instruments are used in a piece of music, or the practice of arranging a composition for multiple instruments.

Ordinary see Mass Ordinary.

Oríkì Praise poems from the Yoruba tradition.

Òrìṣà Sacred entities of the Yoruba religion.

Ornamentation Melodic embellishment.

Ostinato A repetitive melodic or rhythmic phrase.

Pants role An operatic role in which a woman plays a male character, generally an adolescent or young man. It is also called a "breeches role" or "trouser role."

Pas de deux A ballet duet, usually performed by female and male leads.

Pastiche An artistic work that makes use of pieces taken from a variety of sources.

Pentatonic scale A five-tone scale.

Percussion A classification of instruments that generate sound by being struck. This classification includes most membranophones and idiophones.

Peşrev An instrumental precomposed piece with roots in the Ottoman court.

Phrase A group of pitches that form a conceptual unit.

Pickup A beat that occurs immediately before the beginning of a measure; also called an upbeat.

Pirouette In ballet, a spinning turn on one leg.

Pitch The highness or lowness of a sound; also called a "note" or "tone."

Pitch bending The modification of a tone by slightly raising or lowering its pitch.

Pizzicato The technique of plucking bowed string instruments.

Plié A dance position with knees bent outward while the back remains straight.

Pointalistic style In twentieth-century music, when sounds appear as many separate, even disconnected, events.

Polyphony A musical texture in which multiple independent melodic lines sound simultaneously.

Power chords Loud, often electronically distorted chords that use the first and fifth degrees of the chord, which are a feature of many rock genres.

Pow wow A gathering that celebrates Native American culture. Music and dance play a prominent role.

Primitivism An artistic and literary movement that celebrated nature, instinct, and non-Western "native" or "tribal" subjects.

Program music Music based on written or nonmusical artistic works.

Proper see Mass Proper.

Qur'an The sacred book of Islam.

Raga In Indian music, a collection of pitches with characteristic intervals and embellishments used as the basis for melodic content. In Karnatic music there are 72 Melakarta (parent) ragas and hundreds of janya (derived) ragas.

Range The distance between highest and lowest pitches in a melody.

Recapitulation The final section of a sonata form in which the musical themes from the exposition are heard again, this time in the tonic (home) key.

Recitative Speechlike vocal style used in opera or oratorio that uses regular speech rhythms to carry the dialogue and forward the plot line.

Reclamation history The restoration of minority and women's contributions to the historical narrative.

Refrain A repeated line or section of a composition. In popular song, a refrain is sometimes called the chorus.

Requiem Mass A funeral mass. Its liturgy is slightly different from a daily mass, most notably in the addition of the *Dies Irae* (Day of Wrath) chant.

Rhythm The systematic arrangement of musical beats, accents, and durations.

Riff In popular music, a short repeated phrase or harmonic progression.

Ritornello A recurring instrumental refrain.

Rondo form A musical form with a recurring refrain that alternates with new material (e.g., ABACA or ABACADA).

Rounded binary form A musical form consisting of two main sections (ABa) where the beginning material returns briefly at the end.

Sabha A South Indian music society that holds and promotes concerts.

Samā' A multisectioned and highly formalized Mevlevi worship ceremony that calls the practitioners' attention to God.

Santería A religion that combines tenets of the Catholic and Yoruba religions.

Sataro A speechlike verse that includes praise, proverbs, and other commentary sung by the jalolu bards of West Africa.

Scale   The collection of tones (usually arranged in ascending or descending order) that forms the melodic basis of a composition.

Second Wave Feminism   A period of feminist activity from the early 1960s to ca. 1980.

Shakuhachi   Japanese end-blown bamboo flute.

Shape notes   Refers to a system of musical notation that uses note heads in specific shapes. Shape notes were designed to facilitate music reading in eighteenth- and nineteenth-century America.

Shofar   A ram's horn trumpet used in the synagogue for Rosh Hashanah and Yom Kippur.

Shruti box   A small wooden bellows-driven harmonium that provides the drone in Indian classical music.

Sonata form   A compositional form which developed in Europe in the eighteenth century and consists of three main sections: exposition, development, and recapitulation.

Song   A vocal genre performed with or without instrumental accompaniment. "Song" is not a generic word for all pieces of music.

Spotting process   The process in which a film's director and composer make initial decisions about where and what type of music should be used. Each such musical insertion is called a "cue."

Staff   A set of five parallel lines and the spaces in between on which notes are written in order to transcribe pitch.

Story ballet   Ballet genre with developed plot lines, often based on legends or fairy tales.

Strings   A classification of instruments whereby sound is generated by vibrations of a string or strings. Examples are violin, viola, cello, bass, guitar, and lute.

Strophic   A song form in which successive stanzas are set to the same music.

Subdominant   The fourth tone (or the chord built on the fourth tone) of a major or minor key.

Sufism   The mystical branch of Islam.

Suite   A collection of dances meant for listening.

Svara   One of seven syllables used to designate tones in the South Indian melodic system: sa-ri-ga-ma-pa-dha-ni-(sa).

Syllabic   A singing style in which each syllable of text is assigned a separate pitch.

Symphonic poem   An orchestral work that depicts a story or theme.

Symphony   A large-scale composition for orchestra usually in four movements, the first of which is often in sonata form.

Syncopation   The rhythmic displacement of accents or sounds to unexpected positions.

Taiko   A large Japanese double-headed drum; also refers to a Japanese drumming style and ensemble.

Tailpiece   The part of the violin that connects the base of the violin to the strings.

Taksim   A nonmetric instrumental improvisation in classical Turkish music.

Tala   The rhythmic system of Indian music.

Tambura   A long-necked plucked lute used to provide drone pitches in Indian music.

Tanbur   A Turkish long-necked lute.

Tango   A sensuous couples dance that originated in Argentina.

Tembang Sunda   A classical Sundanese (Indonesia) vocal genre that developed in the mid-nineteenth century.

Tempo   The speed at which a piece or passage of music is performed.

Ternary form   A musical form in three parts, designated as ABA.

Tetrachord   A scale of four tones.

Texture   The ways in which different musical lines or sonorities fit together.

Timbre   The character or quality of a sound; sometimes referred to as tone color.

Tin Pan Alley   The area in New York City where the popular song industry was based.

Tone   A musical sound; especially a particular pitch or note. It can also refer to the quality of sound a musician produces, as in "the flutist has a shimmering tone."

Tonic   The first pitch (or the chord built on the first pitch) of a major or minor key, which is considered to be the "home" tone.

Triad   A three-note chord built on alternating scale tones.

Trill   The rapid alternation of adjacent tones.

Troubadours   Composers and poets, usually of noble birth, in medieval southern France, who are associated with *fin amours*.

Trouvéres   Composers and poets, usually of noble birth, in medieval northern France, who are associated with *fin amours*.

Ud (or oud)   A Middle Eastern pear-shaped lute.

Usul   Cyclic patterns, usually from two to ten beats, that govern the rhythmic system of Turkish classical music.

Vaudeville   A theatrical entertainment popular in the United States and Canada from the late nineteenth through the early twentieth centuries. Acts included musicians, dancers, comedians, magicians, and trained animals.

Veena (vīnā)   In Karnatic music, a plucked long-necked lute with resonators on both ends.

Venu   In Karnatic music, a bamboo transverse flute.

Virtuoso   A highly skilled musical performer.

Vocable   Syllables with no textual meaning that serve as musical refrains or markers.

Whole-tone scale   A scale that consists entirely of whole steps.

Woodwinds   A classification of windblown instruments. Examples include the flute, oboe, clarinet, bassoon, recorder, and shakuhachi.

Yang Ban Xi   "Eight model plays." These works were promoted by the Chinese government during the Cultural Revolution (1966–1976).

Yoruba   Large and influential ethnic group that resides in the eastern and coastal areas of Nigeria.

PHOTO CREDITS

CHAPTER 9

138   KPA Honorar & Belege/United Archives GmbH/Alamy
139   JTB Photo Communications, Inc./Alamy
144   Jozef Sedmak/Shutterstock
146   Library of Congress Prints and Photographs Division [LC-USZ62-62687]
149   BenCar Archives
150   Dorling Kindersley, Ltd.
154   KPA Honorar & Belege/United Archives GmbH/Alamy

CHAPTER 10

156   Andrey Bayda/Shutterstock
160   Hodgson, 111 Fleet Street & Turner & Fisher/ Library of Congress Prints and Photographs Division [LC-USZ62-13935]
161   (bottom left) Al Aumuller/Library of Congress Prints and Photographs Division [LC-DIG-ppmsca-05806]
161   (bottom right) The Library of Congress Prints and Photographs Division [LC-USZ62-122087]
163   Gordon Parks/The Library of Congress Prints and Photographs Division [LC-USF34-013362-C]
167   (top) Mat of the Mint Drury Lane/Library of Congress Prints and Photographs Division [LC-USZC4-6255]
167   (bottom) Willaim P. Gottlieb/Library of Congress Prints and Photographs Division [LC-GLB13-0066 DLC]
170   Angus Oborn/Dorling Kindersley, Ltd.

CHAPTER 11

173   Dave Abram/Dorling Kindersley, Ltd.
177   Warner Brothers/Album/Newscom
180   M.G.M./Album/Newscom
182   Z1022 Patrick Pleul Deutsch Presse Agentur/Newscom
186   Dave Abram/Dorling Kindersley, Ltd.
188   RKO/Album/Newscom

CHAPTER 12

190   Ian Aitken/Rough Guides/Dorling Kindersley, Ltd.
192   Demetrio Carrasco/Dorling Kindersley, Ltd.
193   Guido Schiefer/Alamy
194   Ian Aitken/Rough Guides/Dorling Kindersley, Ltd.
195   Andy Crawford/Dorling Kindersley, Ltd.
199   Arbeau, Thoinot, Orchesographie, Lengres, Imprimé par Iehan des Preyz, 1589/ Library of Congress Prints and Photographs Division [0169]
201   (bottom left) Library of Congress Prints and Photographs Division [LC-USZ62-128254]
201   (bottom right) Bain News Service/Library of Congress Prints and Photographs Division [LC-DIG-ggbain-23062]
203   Bain News Service/Library of Congress Prints and Photographs Division [LC-B2- 5464-2]
204   (top) Arnold Genthe/Library of Congress Prints and Photographs Division [LC-G389-0958-C]
204   (bottom) Marion PostWolcott/Library of Congress Prints and Photographs Division [LC-USF34-052590-D]

CHAPTER 13

210   Universal Images Group/SuperStock
211   Library of Congress Prints and Photographs Division [LC-DIG-ppmsc-00433]
215   Detroit Publishing Co./Library of Congress Prints and Photographs Division [LC-DIG-det-4a27870]
216   Library of Congress Prints and Photographs Division [LC-USZ62-43354]
219   Dave King/Dorling Kindersley, Ltd.
222   William P. Gottlieb/Library of Congress Prints and Photographs Division [LC-GLB23-0685 DLC]

COVER

AF archive/Alamy